Popular Mechanics Complete Manual of Home Repair and Improvement

By Richard E. Nunn

Book Division, The Hearst Corporation, New York, N.Y. 10019

Printed in The United States of America

ISBN 0–910990–50–6

foreword

THIS IS NOT a bedtime book; it does not have a novel story to tell; it will not be made into a movie.

This book is a *work* book—a *reference piece* for the homeowner and some apartment dwellers who annually have to clean out gutters, paint a room, patch a concrete sidewalk, change a fuse in an emergency.

This book shows you how to do these jobs—and hundreds more—just as quickly and easily as possible with a minimum investment in tools and equipment. For example, if the job can be done with a putty knife instead of a super special air-operated chisel outfit, you'll find the putty knife technique every time. If you have a super special air-operated chisel outfit, you probably don't need this book.

If you're looking for a sense of accomplishment —the pride of doing the job yourself—this book will help you obtain it.

If you're looking for a quick way to get the gutters fixed and out on the golf course, this book will help you here, too.

If you're looking for ideas to improve your home or add more space to it in the attic, basement, or via a room addition, this book will deliver the goods.

In assembling material in this book, we've *simplified how-to techniques* for the homeowner who is not especially handy. After becoming involved in a specific job, this homeowner, or apartment dweller, will find shortcuts of his own, because involvement leads to innovation. The more experienced homeowner also will find a gold mine of how-to information to help him speed the jobs at hand.

We've also called attention to jobs that might be especially dangerous or costly to do yourself. Always know your do-it-yourself limitations, stay within them, and think the project through. You will not, therefore, clip an electric wire with the current turned on or unscrew a water faucet with the water turned on or rip into an expensive appliance without basic knowledge of that equipment.

how to use this manual

THIS BOOK has been designed to help you solve home maintenance and improvement projects easily and quickly. It has *two kinds of information* to accomplish this: the text and the photographs. In some cases, you will find problem-solving techniques in the *text only*. Here, the problem is one that is better explained in words than photography. Or you may find the how-to techniques *self-contained in step-by-step photographs*. An example is how to patch holes in gypsumboard. This is a problem that about 90 percent of all home-owners have; the photo solution is illustrated from the hole to the finished patch. And, you'll find a *combination* text/photograph presentation where both techniques will be of value.

The book also has been carefully indexed to help you find specific information under any heading. The Index starts on page 471.

You'll also find three more helps:

1. *The section headings.* These are located at the upper corner of almost every right-hand page. They include "exterior," "interior repairs," "lawn & garden," etc. At the start of each of these sections, you will find a large title that has been printed in color as a thumb-indexing help. Look at the edge of the book, when it is closed, and you will see these colored reference marks.

2. *Subject headings.* These are directly beneath the section heads, as explained above. The subject headings are specific references to the material you will find on that page. At a glance, this will help you sort out the material you need quickly and easily.

3. *Cross references.* These are numbers running down the margins. They represent page numbers of information elsewhere in the book that may be of interest in relation to the subject matter. *Example:* In the "Room Addition" section you'll find cross-reference numbers referring you to the "Foundation" section, since a new foundation usually is required for a room addition.

You'll also find that your book lends itself to *browsing.* An example here would be the section on remodeling, which contains a potpourri of

SMALL R
made the sa
line breaks
putty knife
For wide
way into the
required. He
1. With a
move all the l
to solid, firm p
2. With a ch
in an inverted
plaster patch fir
3. When the
cleaned, check t
alert to any moi
moist areas, trad
further. Some pl
roof, bad gutters,
or bathtub on the
that runs up the wa
If you find the l
the leak, call in a p
your entire home if
4. The break is a
patch. You can use S
ing plaster. If the ho
does a good job. If the
to use patching plaster
you add to water. *Mix*
plaster with powdered
color, but it's difficult
only small batches of pl
in an hour or so; then y
5. Moisten the area i
applied. You can use a so
old sponge. The area sho
dry plaster will absorb t
plaster patch, weakening it
6. If the hole is smaller
in diameter, you can fill it w
of Spackling or patching p
larger than this, you will ha
two or more layers. The first
the hole. You can use a scra
this. Then score the patch to g
next layer. You can do this wi

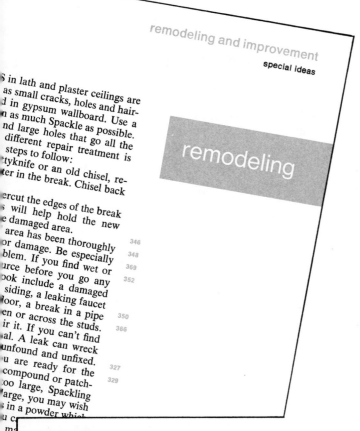

"idea" photographs, featuring special innovations you may wish to incorporate into your present home—whether you're planning a full-blown remodeling job or not. And, throughout the book, we've left little blocks of white space so you may jot down notes relating to your home. For instance, in the "Heating and Cooling" section, you may wish to list the sizes of your furnace and air-conditioning filters, fan belts, special lubricating oil, etc. In the "Electrical" section, you may want to note fuse sizes, location of different fuses, the number of wire you used for a specific outlet hook-up. These figures can become very valuable for replacements or in the event of an emergency.

Finally, we've included a unique listing of manufacturer and trade names, compiled from industry sources. If you don't find what you're looking for in your manual, you can contact these sources for special help. Almost without exception, these manufacturers will furnish you with brochures and other data that you may find helpful in selecting special products and in using them.

contents

special acknowledgments

Our sincere thanks goes to the following persons, companies, and associations for making this work possible:

Art Director: Ralph Leroy

Researchers: William J. Austin; Robert E. Tews; Beverly J. Keleher; Victor G. Morris; Ned Artman; William D. McGuire; Judy Krajewski; Bernie Slowinski.

Manufacturers, retailers, associations: Montgomery Ward; Sears, Roebuck and Company; General Electric; Bilco Door Company; Kwikset Locksets; Georgia-Pacific Corporation; Azrock Floor Products; Masonite Corporation; United States Gypsum Company; Marlite Division, Masonite Corporation; United States Plywood/Champion Papers; Western Wood Products Association; Portland Cement Association; Formica Corporation; Sherwin-Williams Paint; American Plywood Association; Gee Lumber Company (Chicago); Armstrong Cork Company; Toro Manufacturing Company, Lawnmower Division; Pittsburgh Plate Glass; Zenith Radio Corporation.

Consultants: Richard L. Bullock, Executive Director, National Association of Building Manufacturers; Jack Parshall, Editor, *Building Supply News* Magazine of Cahners Publishing Company.

The Shopping and Trade Names Section of this book was compiled from literature furnished by manufacturers, and multiple building industry source lists. We assume no responsibility for omission of manufacturers from the lists, incorrect addresses due to company relocation or merger, or duplication or similarity of trade or brand names.

8

PUT YOUR HOME on an annual inspection schedule, and you'll soon find that those big, costly repairs will shrink into small maintenance projects.

Late fall, when the weather is cool, is the best time for the inspection of the roof, chimney, gutters and the other structural components that make up your home. Make any necessary repairs as you find trouble, since winter weather can quickly wreck a roof, cause ice dams to form in leaf-filled gutters, and puff cold air into the house through cracks around doors, windows and in the siding.

With the right kind of preventive maintenance, as outlined in this section, your home will give you a lifetime of shelter with modest upkeep. And by doing most of the small maintenance jobs yourself, you will save the big money it can cost to hire a pro to fix damages that started out as little cracks.

Moisture is probably the biggest enemy of your home—a drop of water can wreck a roof, rot siding, and cause foundations to crumble. The best home maintenance is preventative maintenance: repairing small cracks and breaks in the home's structure as they occur. Put the exterior of your home on an annual inspection checklist. Spotting trouble early can save you hundreds of dollars in replacement materials and labor

roofs & chimneys

OF ALL COMPONENTS that make up a house —siding, doors, windows, foundation, floors—the roof probably takes the worst beating of all from the elements. Its temperature can rise to 140 degrees in the summer, then drop to minus 40 degrees in the winter. More damage is done by hail, wind, rain, sleet, snow and settling of the house structure. Yet, with a few maintenance procedures, a good roof will last at least 20 years—sometimes longer—before it has to be replaced or recovered. Tile and slate roofs last indefinitely.

Since chimneys and stacks are generally confined to the roof area, this chapter includes them along with roofs. As long as you're inspecting the roof, you might as well take the time to inspect the chimneys and stacks, too.

How you maintain or repair your roof depends upon the condition of the roof itself. There are many jobs you can do; there are many jobs that you should leave to a professional roofer. Those that you, the homeowner, can do are outlined here. But before you set up a ladder, there are several points of *caution* that you should consider:

• Do not attempt to make repairs on a highly pitched roof, unless you have the proper equipment to do so.

• Always wear rubber-soled shoes when working on a roof. "Sneakers" provide a non-slip surface.

• Never work on a roof in extremely hot weather. Composition and built-up roofing becomes very pliable and it can be easily damaged by walking on it.

• Do not attempt to replace tile or slate on a highly pitched roof. Call in a professional. On low-pitched tile and slate roofs, try to step on two or more tiles or slates at a time. This will distribute your weight more evenly. Both tile and slate are fairly easy to break with too much weight. They also tend to slide slightly, so be careful.

There are *six different types of roofing materials commonly used:* Wooden shingles, wooden shakes, asphalt, composition roofing, slate, and tile. These materials are usually laid over asphalt building paper, which in turn covers the sheathing. The

15

14
20
124
125
264

12
24
82
262
264

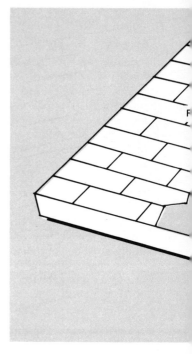

Cutaway of roof shows its component parts. Here, shingles can be wooden, or shakes, or composition. Under normal conditions, roofs last about 20 years before they have to be replaced or recovered

After you find a leak in the roof in the attic or crawlspace, push a wire through the hole so you can spot it on top of the roof

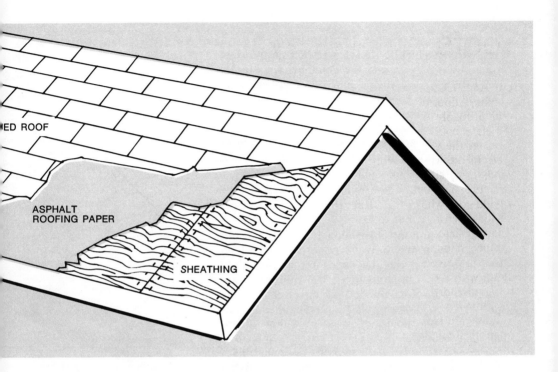

ED ROOF

ASPHALT
ROOFING PAPER

SHEATHING

sheathing consists of boards, plywood or extra-thick composition board—often used for roof decks.

SPOTTING A ROOF LEAK is like finding the proverbial needle in the haystack. First, the leak usually has to be found in the attic or crawlspace (or in a room below, if it is a built-up roof). You can be almost certain that the water you find on the attic subfloor or top of the ceiling is *not* directly below the leak. Water has a way of running down rafters before it drops off; the run can be 12 feet or more to the source.

The best time to search for the leak is on a sunny day at about noon when the roof is bathed in sunlight. Darken the attic so you can spot any sunlight filtering through. Anywhere you see a hole, push a piece of wire through the opening so you can spot it on top of the roof.

Another way to track down a leak is to trace water spots or markings on rafters or sheathing. If it is raining and the leak is at a flashing point, which it frequently is, you can measure from the side walls to the leak and transfer this measurement to the top of the roof. It won't be precise, but it will give you a good clue.

16
18
20

11

THE SEARCH FOR ROOF LEAKS should start at metal flashing around the chimney, soil stacks, roof ventilators, skylights and other appendages. The chances are good the flashing has pulled away from the brick or sheathing. The normal settling of a house can cause this.

Another key area to search is the ridge line of the roof and along the valleys—also layered with metal flashing. The ridge of the roof takes a severe pounding from the weather, while roofing in the valleys tends to pull apart when the house settles.

The last spot for inspection is the roof itself. Here, a shingle may have been loosened by a high wind, curled up due to exposure, or split. On built-up roofs, the laminations can pull apart letting water in. Or, the gravel covering can be washed away, exposing flashing or nailheads. For inspection and repair, it's best to follow a systematic procedure.

Wooden shingles and shakes. Loosened nailheads and split shingles are the leak problems on this type roof. If the roof is very old, you'll probably find rotted shingles, which let in the rain. Here the roof should be replaced; in some cases it can be recovered, but this is a job for a professional roofer.

Loose nails can be driven down, and it is a good idea to cover the head of the nail with a dab of asphalt roofing compound. For split shingles, you can insert a piece of aluminum or galvanized sheet under the course of shingles as a repair. Make sure the metal is wide enough to go completely under the damaged shingles.

Composition shingles are plagued with many of the same problems as wooden ones. Loose nails can cause leaks, and these should be hammered back down into the sheathing. Also cover the nail heads with asphalt roofing compound for a weather seal.

Wooden shingles are overlapped about a third or quarter of their length. The length is 16, 18, and 24-inches. The shingles are staggered in overlapping courses so the joints fit together over a shingle below. The shingles are laid on sheathing. Or, you may find that a new roof has been laid over an old one. In either case, walk carefully to prevent damage to the shingles

If the shingles are broken, you can replace them with new strips; how to do this is described below. Shingles curled by the wind are easy to stick back down with a walnut-size dab of roofing cement.

Built-up roofs consist of several layers of asphalt building paper or felt, then a top coat of tar and gravel. The problem with this type roof is that

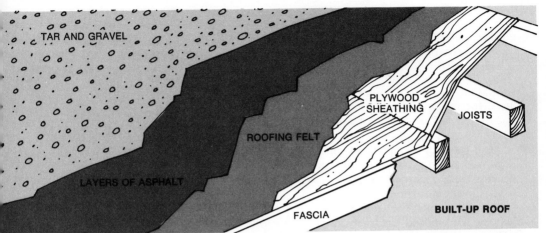

TAR AND GRAVEL

PLYWOOD
SHEATHING

JOISTS

ROOFING FELT

LAYERS OF ASPHALT

FASCIA

BUILT-UP ROOF

it tends to dry out over a long period of time, and humps and blisters appear, then break, and let in water. If the blister is fairly small, you can cut it open with a sharp knife (razor knife works best) and reseal it by forcing roofing compound under the layers of roofing.

Nail down both sides of the cut with flat-head roofing nails. Then cover the entire cut with a patch of asphalt roofing felt stuck down with roofing compound. A rim of roofing nails, also sealed with roofing compound, completes the patch.

If the area is a large one, you will have to cut out a square or rectangular piece of the roofing material, and replace it with new. Use a razor knife for this and match the patch perfectly with the defective roofing area you removed.

Cover the entire area with roofing compound, forming a bed of the material, and lay in the patch. Nail the patch down and cover the nailheads with roofing compound. Then cut a slightly larger patch and place it over the first one—again in a bed of roofing compound. Nail the top patch down and cover the exposed nailheads with roofing compound.

Tile and slate roofs. Leaks here are most often caused by broken tile or slate. Tile roofs have a base and cap row arrangement and they are fastened with nails and wire. Slate or flat tile roofs have hooks that fit over strips nailed to the roof. They are simply fitted into place.

Ridge line tiles probably are cemented into place. This is done to hold them securely to beat the wind.

Drawing shows cut-away of a built-up roof. It goes over plywood or composition sheathing or decking. A layer of roofing felt goes over this, with additional asphalt layers over the first one. These are stuck together with hot tar. Tar and gravel, usually referred to as T&G, provides the topping. Most problems with built-up roofs result from the asphalt drying out, forming blisters and bubbles. Or the felt layers may delaminate

13

ROOFING MATERIALS also include mineral-surfaced and smooth roll roofings, asbestos-cement shingles, and metal roofing such as galvanized steel, trene (tin), aluminum, copper, monel metal and zinc. The metal materials are not commonly used for residential building, although your home may have one of these types topping it in certain areas.

Roll roofings are quick to repair by finding the leak and sealing it with roofing compound. Large leaks usually occur at the seams, which run horizontal to the sheathing.

After you find the leak, split open the roofing with a hook-nosed linoleum knife. Then insert a new piece of material up under the old. The new roofing should extend about 8 inches past the edges of the break, while the lower edge of the patch should be flush with the horizontal edge that has been left exposed. Before you insert the strip, coat the part that will slip under the old roofing with roofing compound; then press it firmly in place and nail it with flathead roofing nails. The nails should be spaced about two inches apart and one inch from the edge of the patch. Cover the heads with roofing cement and wipe the cement into the horizontal seam. Renail this patch, and cover the nailheads with cement.

Smooth roll roofing does not have mineral granules, and it is generally used as a temporary roof or as an underlayment for other roofing materials. It is most often found on utility buildings, and provides satisfactory service if it is recoated with bituminous roof coating about every year or so. Leaks can be patched with roofing compound.

Asbestos-cement shingles—often used for siding—require little maintenance. The biggest problem is broken shingles, and they can be replaced this way:

Remove the shingle with a shingle ripper, or cut the nails with a hacksaw blade. Insert the new shingle and fasten it by nailing through the vertical joint between the shingles in the course that overlays it. Drive the nails in predrilled pilot holes about two inches below the butt end of the shingle in the second course above. To hold the new shingle rigid, insert a piece of aluminum sheet over the nailhead and under the shingle course above. As with tile and slate roofs, distribute your weight

For high-pitched roofs, a ladder makes an excellent support. It distributes your weight evenly over the roofing surface and provides safe footing. Tie a rope to the top of it, throw the rope over the ridge of the roof and tie it to a tree

Ladder support works like this. Keep the work right or left of side rail; move the ladder from left to right as you go across roof

Roof configurations are shown at right. Roofing materials include cedar shingles and shakes; asphalt materials, which make up about 90 percent of the roofs applied today; asbestos-cement shingles; metals; tile and slate

TYPES OF ROOFS

GABLE ROOF

HIP ROOF

SHED ROOF

FLAT ROOF

LAMINATED BEAM ROOF

over asbestos-cement shingles when you are working on them.

Metal roofs are probably the easiest of all to repair if leaks occur. You can work on them without danger of damaging the roof, too. Little maintenance is required, except with galvanized steel, which usually has to be painted at regular intervals —generally every four to six years.

To repair a small leak, you simply fill the hole with a drop of solder. If the leak is a big one, you will have to cover the area with a patch. The metal you use for the patch must be the same kind of metal as the roof.

Clean the area to be patched so it is bright and shiny. Steel wool or emery paper does a good job, or you can use a wire brush and abrasive wheel locked in the chuck of an electric drill.

Apply an acid flux to both the roof and the patch, and tin-coat both with a thin coating of solder. Then solder the patch on, making sure edges of the patch are "welded" to the roof.

If the leak occurs at the seam of a metal joint, the problem is most often due to improper nailing at the joint, or expansion and contraction of the metal at the joint that is faulty.

Try renailing or replacing all or part of the sheet, if the leak is really bad. If this doesn't work, the expansion joint material probably will have to be replaced. Here, you should call in a professional roofer, since special equipment is necessary to do the job correctly.

If the seam is flat and is the cause of a leak, you can resolder it without replacing any metal. The metal should be thoroughly cleaned first. Apply acid flux, then the solder. Use a big-tip iron.

To paint galvanized steel, you first have to clean off any old peeling paint and remove debris. A scraper and wire brush does the fastest job. Rust spots should be primed with a metal primer before you brush or roll on the top coats of paint.

You can paint wooden shingles with an oil-base aluminum paint formulated for this purpose. The paint is available in a variety of colors. Buy paint with a high linseed oil or alkyd content. Don't use varnish or asphalt-base paints. The roof should be clean and dry before application with a brush or roller. Or you can use a spray gun on a *calm* day.

Shapes of asphalt shingles are shown in this chart, along with the weight of the material, coverage, etc. Shingles are sold by the "square"—or 100 sq. ft. to a "bundle." Many building supply stores have broken bundles of all types of roofing so you don't have to invest in a bundle to obtain just one or two shingles

Small leaks or big ones—there are tricks to patching any of them

ASPHALT SHINGLES	WEIGHT PER SQUARE	UNIT SIZE	NAILS PER SQUARE	COVERAGE		
				PER BUNDLE	X-RAY VIEW	PERCENT
3-TAB SQUARE	210 LBS.	12" x 36"	1.9 LB., 1" OR 3.2 LB., 1¾"	33 SQ. FT. (⅓ SQUARE)		1 PLY— 2% 2 PLY—59% 3 PLY—39% 100%
ALIGNMENT LUG 2-TAB HEX	167 LBS.	11⅓" x 36"	1.3 LB., 1" OR 2.3 LB., 1¾"	50 SQ. FT. (½ SQUARE)		1 PLY—22% 2 PLY—63% 3 PLY—15% 100%
3-TAB HEX	167 LBS.	11⅓" x 36"	1.3 LB., 1" OR 2.3 LB., 1¾"	50 SQ. FT. (½ SQUARE)		1 PLY—22% 2 PLY—63% 3 PLY—15% 100%
CLIP DUTCH LAP	162 LBS.	12" x 16"	0.9 LB., 1" OR 1.5 LB., 1¾"	50 SQ. FT. (½ SQUARE)		1 PLY—61% 2 PLY—29% 3 PLY—10% 100%
THATCH	172 LBS.	10" x 36"	1.2 LB., 1" OR 2 LB., 1¾"	50 SQ. FT. (½ SQUARE)		1 PLY—14% 2 PLY—72% 3 PLY—14% 100%
INTERLOCK	138 LBS.	16" x 16"	0.6 LB., 1" OR 1.1 LB., 1¾"	50 SQ. FT. (½ SQUARE)		1 PLY—60% 2 PLY—31% 3 PLY— 9% 100%

PATCHING MATERIALS for most roof and flashing repairs include asphalt roofing compound, butyl caulking, aluminized sealer and caulking compound, and clear butyl sealer or caulking compound. All are available at building supply stores.

Asphalt roofing compound is applied cold to the roofing material with a putty knife. The consistency is like a plastic material; you also can apply it with an old paint brush.

Butyl caulking can be applied with a caulking gun to small cracks and splits. For big repair areas, you can trowel in this material with a putty knife. It also can be used for flashing repair.

Aluminized compound is generally used on metal materials—roofing and flashing, gutters and downspouts. It is sticky and tough enough to bond two pieces of metal together. Clear butyl is the same as its aluminized counterpart—only clear. It will bond to wood, glass, or concrete as well as metal.

MOST ROOF LEAKS can be found at flashings
—at the chimney, stacks, around skylights, in
valleys.

Flashings are made of metal (or plastic) and
the compound that seals the edges may dry out
so the flashing pops up or pulls away and lets in
water. Sometimes the metal will rust or corrode,
which causes leaks.

At chimneys, the flashing is fastened to the roof
sheathing and is bent up around the chimney. A
double layer of flashing is generally used for this.
Over a period of time, the roofing compound that
seals the joint between the flashing and the chimney may dry out. The flashing then pops away
from the chimney and water runs in.

To repair it, pry the flashing *slightly* away from
the chimney, and force in new roofing compound.
Use plenty of compound. Then push the flashing
tight against the chimney. You may have to brace

The joint between the chimney
cap and the flue liner should be
sealed to prevent water damage
to the chimney and chimney cap.
Inspect this annually, since expansion and contraction in the
joint usually separates the caulking. If the chimney cap is broken,
it can be repaired with a cement
patch. Clean out the broken area
and chisel the sound concrete
edges back in an inverted V
shape. Wet the area and trowel in
the patch, smoothing it to match
the surrounding surface

11
12
16
20
26
77

Tuckpoint crumbling mortar joints in brick chimneys when you spot them. Clean out old mortar with a chisel, as shown

Push in new patch of mortar mix. Tamp the cavity full. Then smooth joint with tuckpointing trowel. It is made to fit the joint

Loosened flashing at chimney base has to be resealed with roofing compound or caulk. Coat inside of flashing; brace it

Roofing compound can dry out over period of time, causing leaks. With putty knife, reseal flashing at chimney base

it with a wooden prop until the roofing compound has an opportunity to stick and dry.

Roof valleys can leak two different ways: The metal itself can rust and corrode, letting in the water. Or water can seep back under the flashing and the edge of the roofing material.

If the metal is rusted, you can either solder in a new patch or cover the leak with a patch of asphalt building paper or roofing compound. The compound works only if the hole is a small one. If you use metal, make sure it is the same type as the valley material. Don't mix metals.

Water seepage under the flashing at the edge of the roofing can be repaired with a seal of asphalt roofing cement. Use an old paint brush to work it under the shingles between the shingles and valley. The valley extends about 10 inches under both sides of the shingles.

Both types of repair described above are temporary. The proper repair is to have the roofing stripped back along the valley and new valley material installed. This is a job for a professional roofer, since the shingles have to be rematched perfectly after the valley has been replaced.

Skylights can leak at three places: around the flashing; at the dome seal; in the dome or glass.

Two types of flashing are used for skylights. One type unit has its own flashing—little flanges that fit between the unit and the sheathing. Another type utilizes the same flashing system as generally used for chimneys and some stacks.

To repair leaks in separated flashing, trowel in asphalt roofing compound the same way you would for chimney flashing. If the leak is no more than a large pinhole in size, you can solder it shut with a rosin-flux type solder. Or you can cover the hole with a dab of aluminized caulking.

Leaks in the dome seal can be fixed by replacing the seal with a new one. It is generally held in place with an adhesive. A chisel or screwdriver can be used to pry out the old seal.

Thoroughly clean the channel before you insert the new sealing strip. It should, of course, fit the channel and be installed with adhesive recommended by the seal manufacturer.

Leaks in the dome can be patched, although it usually is best to replace the dome with a new one.

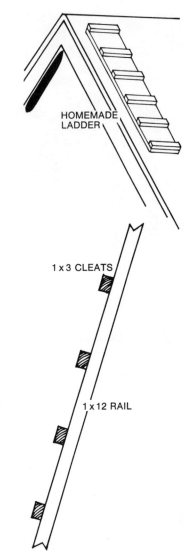

HOMEMADE LADDER

1 x 3 CLEATS

1 x 12 RAIL

"Chicken" ladder for roof repairs is quick to make from a strip of 1 × 12 wood with cleats of 1 × 3s or 1 × 4s. Space the cleats about 12 inches apart. The nails should go completely through both pieces of wood and be clinched over on the bottom side

To replace an asphalt shingle, remove the damaged one by prying out the nails, which are one course above the damaged one. A flat garden spade can be used as a pry bar, as shown. Or you can buy a shingle ripper for this. Work very carefully to avoid damaging the adjoining shingles

If the skylight involves panes of glass—similar to a horizontal window—you can reglaze the glass to stop a leak. If the glass is "fixed" in the mullions, caulk around the mullions, allowing the caulk to extend about ½-inch over the glass area.

Make a narrow, chisel-like tool out of a piece of soft wood. Dip this in water and smooth out the caulking around the glass—feathering it along the glass surface.

Most skylight domes are made from plexiglass or similar plastic material. If you don't want to replace the dome, you can patch the crack or hole in it with a clear butyl caulking. Patch the spot from both sides if you can reach it underneath. Skylights on pitched roofs involve a plywood shaft to funnel the light into the room below. This makes it almost impossible to patch underneath. In this situation, it's best if you replace the dome.

2 Nail locations will be similar to these on the course of shingles above so you know where to insert flat spade or shingle ripper

3 Piece of aluminum or galvanized steel sandwiched between courses of shingles can stop leaks. Let it protrude 2 inches

6 Blisters in built-up roofs should be sliced open, if they leak, and roofing compound forced underneath. Work on warm days

7 Cement patch over leak area, after it is nailed, feathering out roofing compound at edges. Press the patch into compound

4 New wooden shingle can replace a damaged one. Remove damaged one, tap in new, using wedge to hammer against. Seal nailheads

5 Patches in metal roofs can be made with roofing compound. Seal tiny leaks with drop of solder

8 Sprinkle new gravel or marble chips over repair area. Then press them into compound with flat board. Use very light pressure

9 Bare spots at ridge lines are common on built-up roofs. Replace gravel or marble chips; spread on heavy layer of roof compound first

23

Stick down curled or flappy shingles with a walnut-size dab of roofing compound. Press the shingle into the cement and hold it for a minute or two until it seals tightly

SOIL STACKS AND VENTILATORS also are good sources for leaks. Both involve flashing that can separate from the sheathing when the roofing compound dries out or the house settles.

Repair is similar to chimney and skylight flashing, utilizing roofing cement around the exposed area. Even if there are no leaks, it's a good idea to coat the flashing about every year or so with roofing compound as preventive maintenance.

CHIMNEY REPAIRS YOU CAN MAKE

Most chimneys have a chimney cap and tile flue liner. Some are single, some are double tiles. In either case, the joint between the chimney cap and flue liner should be caulked to prevent water leakage in the chimney below. Water can enter at this point, crack the chimney cap and damage the mortar joints in the chimney itself. Use an exterior type caulking compound. Clean the crack thoroughly before you run a new bead of caulking into the joint. Inspect this area for damage annually, since expansion and contraction are great from furnace heat and exterior cold.

Exposed nail heads can cause leaks. They should be covered with a dab of roofing compound to seal out the weather. Exposed nails usually are found next to flashing and roof appendages such as this exhaust ventilator

Ridge ventilators are often prone to leak since the ridge of the roof receives terrific wear from weather. Coat the area every year with roofing compound

Water seeping down the flue liner or past the chimney cap can cause mortar joints in the chimney to crumble and fall out. Inspection of the joints should be on your maintenance checklist annually.

To repair loose and crumbling mortar, clean out the joint with a narrow brick chisel or an old screwdriver. Probe and pry carefully; you shouldn't dislodge any of the bricks by hitting the chisel hard with a hammer. With a small brush, dust out all loose mortar left in the joint; if it is possible, clean out the joint with a garden hose with a moderate amount of water pressure.

Check the bricks around the joint you have just cleaned. Sometimes the mortar holding these in place also is loose—especially in older chimneys.

You can buy premixed mortar in small bags for this repair job. Just add water according to the manufacturer's directions and stir. If you want to mix your own mortar, use one part cement to 4½ parts of clean, fine sand and ½ part dehydrated lime. Stir this combination until it is blended well, then add just enough water to make the mortar into a plastic-like consistency. It's mixed properly when it slides easily off a small, triangular trowel or the blade of a scraper, which makes a good mixing tool.

Wet the joint with water and tamp in the mortar. A small trowel works best for this, although you can use a putty knife or a tuckpointing trowel that's just wide enough to fit the joint. The joint must be firm and fully packed, however, or the new mortar will crack and fall out when it hardens. The butt end of a split shingle also makes a good tamper for this kind of job.

When the joint is full, strike it smooth with a joint striking tool or the flat of your tuckpointing trowel. If the weather is especially warm when you make this repair, keep the new mortar wet for several hours, if at all possible.

Chimney caps also are subject to weather damage. Water seeps up under them and breaks the cap through expansion and contraction. Repairs are simple, however: Clean out the old concrete and chisel the sides of the break so it forms an inverted V shape. This helps prevent the new concrete from cracking out when it hardens and from winter/summer expansion and contraction.

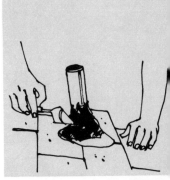

Soil stacks are rigid and won't settle with the house. To prevent leaks, reseal the gaps at the base of the stack

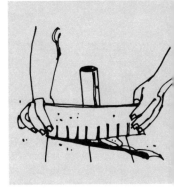

With tinsnips, make a series of cuts along one edge of roofing or flashing and draw it around stack base. Seat it in compound

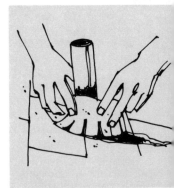

Pull the strip tight, and press the tabs into compound. Finish job with a heavy top coating of compound to waterproof joint

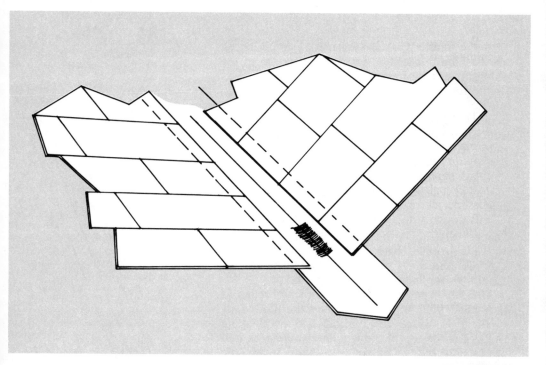

Wet the area with water and, using the same con-crete formula given above, mix the new patch.

Trowel it into the opening and smooth the top and exposed edge to match the old cap around it.

SPECIAL ROOFING PROBLEMS YOU CAN SOLVE

Attached porches and garages can present leak problems at the point where one roof joins another roof, or where a roof meets the side of a house.

As a rule, this joint is flashed with metal, but the settling of the house, porch or garage can pull the joint open, letting in moisture. The result often is rotted sheathing, siding, rafters, and other wooden components. Or the water can seep into the side-walls of either the garage or house and cause structural damage all the way down to the floor and foundation.

If roofing overlaps the joint, inspection is diffi-cult. You have to look closely for separated shingles, or, if possible, check the sheathing or decking underneath, if it is exposed. Water leaves marks and you can trace leaks from this point.

Small leaks in metal valleys can be stopped with a drop of solder. Or you can put in a metal patch, embedding it in roofing com-pound. Metal patch you use should be the same type as the metal valley. If the leak is up under the shingles at the valley, coat them with the roofing com-pound

88

If the joint is flashed with metal, simply check the flashing to see if it has pulled away from the siding. It usually breaks at this point, rather than at the roof. To repair this, renail the flashing to the siding of the house after you "butter" the inside edge of the flashing with roofing compound. Take your time here to avoid smearing the compound onto the siding. Along the top edge of the flashing, seal the joint with a thin line of roofing cement or exterior caulking compound. The latter is the easiest to do since you can use a caulking gun for this.

At the same time, check to see if the rafter or "nailer" that holds the attached roof to the sidewall has worked loose. If it has, simply renail it carefully and make any necessary patches in the flashing or roofing where it joins the house.

Mansard type roofs present another problem, if they have windows inserted along the flat. Many of them do. Here, the flashing and overlapping shingles at the top of the windows sometimes pull away, allowing water to seep back under the header into the sidewalls. In some cases, the water even flows down the inside of the windows.

Roofing compound, caulking, and/or renailing the flashing generally stops the leak. The material is applied in much the same way as described for other roofing repairs in this chapter.

Carport additions manufactured from metal are usually hooked onto the sidewall of the house via lag bolts and a strip of 2 x 4 or 2 x 6. This joint can cause leakage problems. To repair it, fill the joint with butyl caulk if the roof is metal. If the roof is shingled, flashing probably was used, and it should be repaired the same way as flashing on a regular roof. Also check and make sure the roof hasn't pulled away from the wooden member to which it is attached. If so, you can tighten the fasteners or run several more in to pull the joint tight again. Also check the slab for settlement.

Utility buildings such as the ones used for storing lawn and garden equipment, bikes, etc., generally come with metal roofs or plywood decks, over which wooden or composition shingles have been installed. Although leaks are not as bothersome as on house and garage roofs, they should be repaired when noticed to protect the sidewalls of

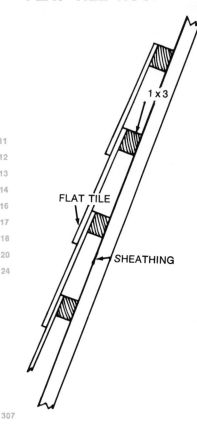

Flat tiles or slate are hung or fastened over 1 × 3 strips that run along the sheathing, as this drawing shows. One tile overlaps the other. Tiles are usually cemented at ridge lines and at valleys. To replace broken ones, you have to dig out the mortar first. Also, be careful walking on tile or slate. Try to distribute your weight evenly to prevent damage

the building from rust and corrosion and, of course, to protect the equipment housed inside.

Repairs to these roofs are exactly the same as those used on similar materials on houses, although you probably won't have to worry about flashing since the roofs are 1-piece components and flashing generally isn't used in installation.

REROOFING YOUR HOME

Most roofs will last 20 years—even longer when properly maintained. However, the time comes when the roof should be replaced. Otherwise, water will cause serious damage to the sheathing beneath the shingles and to the house structure itself. Unless you are especially skilled at it, reroofing is a job for a professional. Most often, the new roof can be laid right over the old shingles. In fact, a double layer is an advantage in protecting your home.

New wooden shingles or shakes are applied over old ones like a blanket, providing double insulation against heat loss, a stronger roof, and less chance for leakage.

If your roof is asphalt, manufacturers say it is best to strip off the old roofing before the new shingles are applied. Asphalt shingles, however, *can* be applied over an old roof. But, the deck and framing must be strong enough to hold up under the combined weight of the old roof, the new roof, and snow loads. A professional roofer or building supply dealer will have load tables for various types of asphalt shingles. From these, you can determine if your substructure is strong enough for overlayment.

A new built-up roof certainly is a job for a professional. Special equipment such as hot tar barrels, mops, gravel or marble hoists, etc., are required for this application. The cost of equipment to do-it-yourself is prohibitive.

EMERGENCY REPAIRS

If your roof is seriously leaking, you can make a quick and easy emergency repair by covering the leaking area on top of the roof with a sheet of heavy plastic film or waterproof canvas. Spread the material over the area and tack down the edges using wooden lath or 1 x 2s as tacking strips.

CURVED TILE ROOF

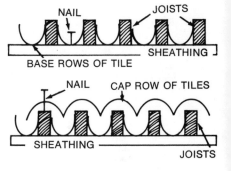

Curved tile roofs alternate in what's called "base" and "cap" rows. The base rows are fastened directly to the sheathing with nails. The cap rows are fastened over furring strips. Holes for both are predrilled for nails. When you replace a broken tile, check to make sure the underlayment is intact

drainage systems

OF ALL THE ELEMENTS—sun, wind, rain—the one that really wrecks your home in drips and drops is water. Whether it's in the form of liquid, ice or humidity, water is the cause of most damage, direct or indirect, from peeling paint to falling plaster.

To help solve the exterior water problem, most homes are equipped with gutters and downspouts (or "leaders" as downspouts are sometimes called). Some houses with very wide overhangs do not have drainage systems other than splash tracks around the perimeter of the house.

There are five common types of drainage systems: wood, galvanized steel, aluminum, copper and vinyl. Each has its own set of special maintenance problems.

Wooden gutters, in most cases, have been replaced in the last 20 years or so with metal or vinyl types, but there are still wooden installations made occasionally, and there are still plenty of them on older homes. Wooden gutters, frankly, are a headache as far as maintenance is concerned. They have to be inspected regularly and cared for, or they rot. When rot starts, it's usually best to replace the entire span of gutter than to patch in a new piece of wood.

If this is impractical, you will have to saw out the damaged or rotting section, and replace it with new wood the same thickness as the old. Cypress or redwood is usually the best and least expensive patch for this; both are fairly resistant to moisture.

Caulk the joints at both ends of the patch and overlap them with a piece of aluminum or galvanized steel. Then apply a couple of coats of trim paint to cover the new wood and metal.

If your home has *new wooden gutters,* you can use two techniques of preventive maintenance: line them with fiberglass or give them three heavy coats of linseed oil.

You can buy narrow rolls of fiberglass in many boating stores, along with the proper resin to bond it to the inside of the gutter. First, clean the gutter thoroughly, wire brush it, and clean it again. Vacuum it, if you can. Line the gutter with the

31
32
34
36
37
40
42

Coat inside of metal gutters with roofing compound or gutter paint. Do this about every 2 to 3 years, or when inspection shows it's needed. Gutters should be hosed and brushed clean before the coating is applied

Gutter components, and where they fit, are shown at right. 1. Downspout and bracket assembly. 2. Drop outlet. 3. Double elbow brings downspout toward wall. 4. Eaves-trough (gutter). 5. Slip joint connector. 6. Inside corner. 7. Outside corner. 8. End cap. 9. Right or left elbow. 10. Hangers

38
39

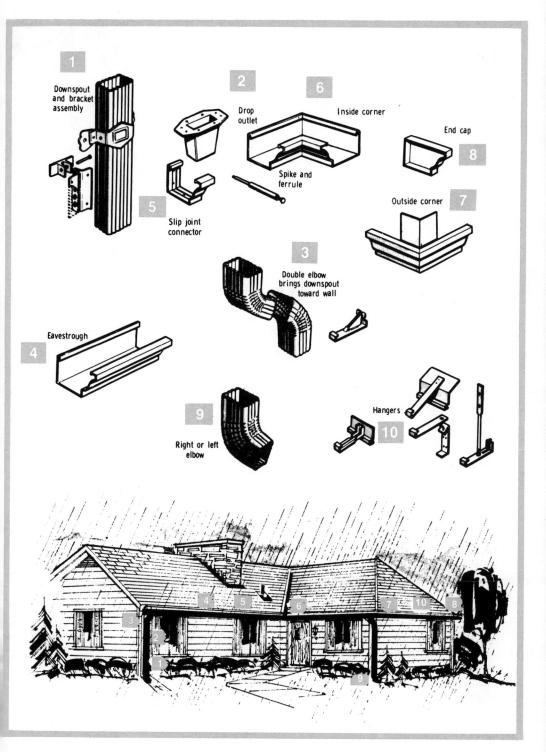

1
Downspout and bracket assembly

2
Drop outlet

5
Slip joint connector

6
Inside corner

Spike and ferrule

8
End cap

7
Outside corner

3
Double elbow brings downspout toward wall

4
Eavestrough

9
Right or left elbow

Hangers
10

fiberglass cloth after you apply the first coating of resin. When this is dry, apply a second, and final, coat of resin.

The linseed oil treatment is less expensive than fiberglass; it should be used on new, uncoated wood only. New linseed oil applications must be made annually. If the gutters have been painted, you will have to continue to repaint them—usually every year. The fall months are the best time.

Galvanized steel gutters are probably the most popular metal drainage systems. Rust is the big problem here; when a thin zinc coating on the metal wears off, the steel starts rusting.

You can buy metal primers to deter this, however, and at the first sign of paint pops or rust, the gutter should be cleaned, reprimed, and painted.

Small rusty spots are a warning signal. Chances are good that other gutter areas are starting to rust out. Check the rest of the gutter when you reprime and paint the obvious rust spots; you may find more areas that need your immediate attention.

Galvanized steel gutters should be coated inside with roofing compound or metal paint about every two to three years—or when close inspection shows that they need maintenance. Before you apply the coating, remove all debris from the gutter and hose and brush it clean. Make sure all roof granules are out. These can impede the flow of water. A small brush or a ball-shaped dishwashing mop makes a good applicator.

Aluminum gutters are more expensive than galvanized steel counterparts, but they have several advantages: they won't rust and corrode, and they don't require a protective coating, although you probably will want to paint them to match siding and other architectural elements.

You should not paint aluminum gutters—or galvanized gutters—when they are new. Both have to oxidize before the paint will stick properly. This usually takes about six months.

If you reside in an area where the air is filled with salt or chemicals, the oxidation time element is reduced by several months. When the time is right, don't delay sealing the metal surfaces. Rust and deterioration set in fast. If you are installing new gutters, consider buying prefinished ones. They cost more money, but a special plastic coat-

A garden hose is the best way to clean dirty gutters after you have removed leaves, twigs, and other debris. Start hosing from the center of the gutter and work toward the downspouts

Plugged downspouts are quickly opened by flushing them out with full water pressure from a garden hose. If you hit an obstruction, the hose also serves as a "plumbers' snake" to rod it out. If the downspout is really clogged, you may have to disassemble it to clean out the obstruction

ing makes the metal more impervious to rust, and to corrosion from air pollution.

Copper gutters are difficult to maintain, if you want to keep them shiny. The key is lots of steel wool for polishing and spar varnish for a protective coating. Otherwise, oxidation will turn the copper a dark green color, and after several years it is almost impossible to shine it again. However, copper takes on a pleasant patina that is desired by some homeowners. Since copper doesn't rust, about the only maintenance involved is cleanout of leaves and other debris twice a year—spring and late fall—so water flows properly.

Vinyl drainage systems are fairly recent newcomers on the residential scene. The only metal

involved is brackets and hangers, which have to be painted every couple of years to prevent rust. In some cases it is easier to replace the brackets and hangers than to paint them.

Since vinyl drainage systems won't chip, dent, warp, sag, etc., about the only maintenance required is a twice-yearly cleanout and inspection where the vinyl meets the fascia. Check this for wood rot. Generally, rot starts at the downspout openings. This is caused by overflowing. If you detect rot, saw out the section and replace with new wood, properly primed and finished with house paint.

GUTTER MAINTENANCE

The gutters on your home should be cleaned twice yearly—in the spring and in the fall after all the leaves are off nearby trees. If your lot has many trees on it, you may have to clean the gutters more often—especially during the fall months.

Leaves and twigs, when wet, become extremely heavy. This weight can break the gutter hangers —or pull them loose from the house structure. It's much easier to clean out the channels than to re-pitch the hangers or replace them.

However, there is no easy way to *clean gutters.* The best way is to start at one end with a putty

Downspout hangers are molded to fit the downspout—round or square. For masonry, as shown, the hanger has a point that is driven into the mortar joint. On wood, the hangers are nailed into the siding

Silicone patching cement can be used to fill leaky joints and connections in aluminum gutter. You squirt it into the joint and let it dry. This forms a water-tight "weld"

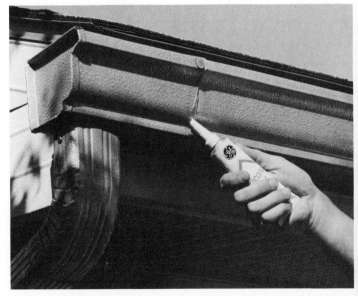

knife and a brush. An old, short-bristled paint brush makes a good tool for this; or use a narrow, stiff-bristled scrub brush. Go the full length of the gutter. With the putty knife, scrape out mud and roof granules that have stuck to the bottom of the gutter. Sweep as much of this debris out as you can.

With a garden hose, start at the center of the gutter and work toward the downspout ends. If there is only one downspout, work toward it from the other end. Watered-down debris flows smoother on a clean gutter, making the job go faster.

When the gutters are clean, check them for rust. They should be coated inside—especially galvanized steel gutters—with asphalt roofing compound or a special gutter paint. As pointed out before, inspection will show you how often to recoat them.

Gutter pitch is important for proper drainage. The pitch should be about $\frac{1}{16}$ inch per running foot of gutter. Since this is difficult to determine accurately, the best way is to pour a bucket of water into the gutter and watch the flow. If the water runs freely, don't worry about the pitch. If the water makes a puddle in one spot, adjust the nearest hanger *upward* to this spot. On most gutter installations, you can bend the hangers with pliers. Hangers are located about every three feet along the gutter span. If bending a hanger at the puddle spot doesn't work, you may have to add hangers to correct the sag.

Strap-type hangers are easy to adjust with pliers to obtain the right pitch. Nail type hangers also can be twisted slightly to correct the gutter pitch. If this technique doesn't work for proper water flow, try adding a hanger or hangers to correct the sag

44
45

THERE ARE SEVERAL TYPES of gutter hangers, as illustrated in this section, and there are several methods of installing them properly. Basically, however, there are only two types of hangers: those that nail into the fascia board and ends of the rafters, and those that are nailed to the edge of the roof, either through the shingles to the sheathing, or under the shingles to the sheathing or roof boards.

Hangers that have a *vertical rod* with a flattened end are bent to conform to the pitch of the roof. You then fasten this rod under the shingles.

Nail hangers go through the lip of the gutter, through the back of it, then into the fascia board. These hangers usually have a metal tube through which the nail is threaded. The metal tube actually is a spacer, the same size as the gutter trough.

Wooden gutters cannot be adjusted with metal hangers, of course. They are fastened directly to the fascia board through spacer blocks. If the pitch has to be corrected, you have to hammer the gutter loose and renail it to the fascia board. You must replace the spacer blocks at this time. If you don't, water can go up under the first course of shingles and drain down inside the exterior wall structure. Or, water can seep between the gutter and the fascia, producing mildew and rot.

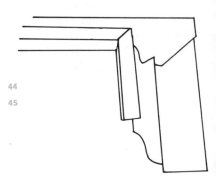

Gutter hangers are preformed so they match the outline of the gutter. Strap-type hangers simply snap around the body of the gutter. The hanger then is bent to fit under the first course of shingles on the roof. Nail the hanger to the sheathing and cover the nail head with a daub of roofing compound

GUTTER GUARDS REDUCE WORK

You can buy screen-type gutter guards that will keep leaves and twigs out of the channels. There are two types, both inexpensive: flexible and rigid. Installation is fairly easy: the screening goes under the first course of shingles and hooks to the lip of the gutter. The rigid screening usually has rows of tiny louvers. Here, the tabs on the outer edge of the section clip to the lip of the gutter.

Use *only* aluminum guards on aluminum gutter and galvanized steel guards on galvanized steel gutter. *Do not mix the metals.* If you do, a chemical reaction takes place and one metal destroys the other.

If gutter guards are impractical, you can install a downspout strainer to prevent the downspout from becoming clogged. It looks like a birdcage and is simply inserted into the top of the downspout.

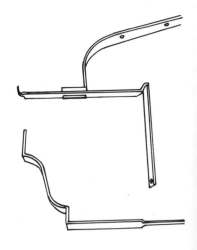

REPAIRING A LEAKY GUTTER or down-spout isn't a difficult task, and the repair can last several months before you have to replace either unit.

For gutters, the patch technique involves a strip of asphalt impregnated building paper or metal. If you use metal, make sure it is the same kind as the gutter: aluminum to aluminum; galvanized steel to galvanized steel, etc.

Thoroughly clean the gutter where you will make the patch. It should be down to bare metal, if possible. If rust is involved, be sure the rusty edges are stripped back to the good metal. Nipper pliers do a good job. Or use a wire brush attachment chucked into a portable electric drill to clean the rust back to sound metal.

Coat the area around the hole with asphalt roofing cement. Use plenty, and spread it out evenly. Have the building-paper patch pre-cut so you can slide it into the bed of roofing compound. Then cover the entire patch area with the compound. Feather the edges so the water will flow smoothly over the patch.

The same technique applies for *metal patches:* a bed of roofing cement; the patch; the second or top layer of roofing cement.

Patches in downspouts can be made with heavy-duty, self-adhesive aluminum foil. First, clean the patch area down to the bare metal. Use a wire brush and steel wool for this, or a wire brush attachment in a portable electric drill. Measure the amount of tape you need, cut it, and press it over the hole in the downspout.

For both gutters and downspouts, you can buy plastic repair kits. The kits have fiberglass cloth which you saturate in a special mixture of resin. The patch is then pressed into place after the area has been cleaned according to the manufacturers' directions. The kits cost about $2. You can apply fiberglass patches to wood or any kind of metal.

Gutter spikes go through the lip of the gutter, the back of it, and then into the fascia board or end of a rafter. Drive the nail through the metal before you slip on the metal tube, which goes across the top of the gutter

HOW TO REPLACE OLD GUTTERS/DOWNSPOUTS

Since water is so damaging to the structure of a house, it is less expensive to replace a faulty drainage system than to patch it. The repairs we have described are *temporary* and for *emergencies.*

For patch, clean gutter, trim it to sound metal. Apply roofing compound around hole. Use plenty and spread it out evenly

There are two standard shapes of metal and vinyl drainage systems: half-round (round) and box. The box shape is often called "K" or "OG." It is available in two basic sizes—four and five inches. If you reside in an area where rainfall is plentiful, you should use the larger size to prevent overflow and provide adequate drainage.

Galvanized steel gutters generally are less costly than their counterparts: aluminum, vinyl, and copper.

Gutters and downspouts are not difficult for a handy homeowner to install. Simple hand tools are all you need—a hammer, screwdriver, pliers, level.

Layout of your roof plan is the first step in installing a new drainage system. Make a rough drawing of the roof area, and determine the number of feet of gutter you will need. For every 40 running feet of gutter, you'll need a downspout. Also figure the number of corner pieces, connectors, downspout connections, hangers, gutter ends, etc., you will need for your job. The drawing at the start of this section will help you determine this.

Although more expensive, aluminum and vinyl gutters are probably the easiest for a less-skilled do-it-yourselfer to install, since connectors can be used for the joints. On other metals, the joints

Gutter guards slip under shingles and hook onto lip of gutter. For downspouts, you can buy cage type strainers to keep out debris

Prefit and cut asphalt building
paper patch or metal one. Press
it firmly in bed of roofing compound so it is properly seated

Cover patch with roofing compound, spreading material over
patch as evenly as possible.
Feather out edges

usually have to be soldered or sweated.

All connections should be made on the ground. One entire span of gutter should be assembled before you attempt to hang it. If the gutter is aluminum, an aluminum caulk is applied to the connectors before they are slipped into position. Downspout corners and regular corners also are attached to the gutter while it is still on the ground.

Whether you use gutter spikes or hangers, the *gutters have to slope* for drainage—about $\frac{1}{16}$ of an inch per running foot of gutter length. If the gutter run is a long one, make it high in the center so it slopes both ways to a downspout at each end. The outside edge of each gutter should be below the edge of the roof level. This is easy to determine by laying a board on the roof, then positioning the gutter so the outside edge of it doesn't touch the bottom edge of the board at its highest point in the run.

You can easily handle about 10-foot runs by yourself. Longer runs require a helper. Or, you can make a wooden prop to hold up one end while you work toward it from the other end.

124
125
126

SPECIAL DRAINAGE PROBLEMS

In heavy snow areas, drainage problems exist in the form of ice dams and avalanches. Both are caused by the snow melting, then freezing, causing dams to form at the gutter level or heavy melting snow to slide down the roof and damage gutters—and roofs—as it tumbles off the edge.

There are two ways to stop this: electric cable installed in a zig-zag line along the edge of the roof and/or metal snow guards. The electric cable is an insulated wire that is enclosed in a lead wrapper. It comes in various lengths, and it is fairly easy to install yourself along the roof line. To operate it, you simply plug it into a grounded outdoor outlet. The electric cable method is usually best for melting snow on roofs that are not highly pitched.

Metal snow guards have hooks that go around shingle nails. If the roof is metal, lugs are manufactured for this installation; they are usually soldered in place. The more pitch the roof has, the more guards you'll need. For installation, it is best to check the manufacturer's recommendations since the roof will determine how many guards are needed and how they should be spaced.

GROUND LEVEL DRAINAGE

Good water drainage doesn't stop at the gutter level. The water has to be channeled away from the house. The system is simple: Gutters carry the water from the roof to the downspouts, and the downspouts discharge it at foundation level. Maintenance problems exist here, too, especially if your home has a basement where water can seep in by drops or flow in like a river.

Ideally, the downspouts should carry the water away from the foundation and empty onto a driveway, walk, or patio surface. In many cases you can do this by simply adding a length of downspout to the bottom of existing downspouts. The length, of course, is determined by the distance away you want the water discharged.

If the distance is too great, you can add an elbow to the downspout (if there isn't one on the downspout already), a length of downspout to

Fill low spots in the ground next to the foundation to keep water out of the basement. The grade level should slope away from the foundation. Keep dirt about 6 inches from the bottom of the siding

346
347
351

44
45

the elbow, and channel the water around where you want it (see photo, this page).

Still another technique, and a simple one, is the use of splashblocks. You can buy these premolded at building supply stores, or you can make your own with premixed concrete. Dig a rectangular hole beneath the downspout about four inches deep. Simply pour in the cement mixture and trowel it so it is slightly lower in a path running down the center. You also can make splashblocks from bricks laid on a sand-and-gravel base.

Other aids include plastic splashpans and hoses that fit onto the end of the downspout. The hoses remain rolled until it rains. Then they uncoil and water is discharged like a lawn soaker. When the rain stops, they roll up again.

Don't overlook the *grade level* at the foundation. The ground should slope away from the foundation so water flows away. Keep earth about 6 inches from the siding to prevent mildew and rot.

Adding extra lengths of down-spouting channels unwanted water away from the foundation. Water should discharge onto a driveway, walk, patio, or splash-block to prevent the earth from eroding

44

If water is really a problem, the best way to solve it is with drain tile or a dry well. Drain tile are positioned around and away from the foundation—underground—and empty into a common or storm sewer, or private drainage system. Excess water also can be funneled via drainage tile into a drainage ditch or culvert, if local codes permit this in your community.

Another technique is a dry well, shown on the opposite page. Here, water from gutters goes down the downspouts in the usual way. The main downspout is connected to underground drain tile that empty into the dry well.

Dry wells are easy to make. Dig a hole that's deep enough to sink a 55-gallon steel drum. The top of the drum should be at least 12 inches below the surface of the ground. Drill holes at random in the drum. Then fill it with chunks of old masonry blocks, rocks, stones, etc.

The underground pipe feeds into the drum, so you have to cut a hole to fit it. Use a cold chisel, or take the drum to a welding shop. Connect the system and then cover the drum, which should *not* have a lid, with a couple of heavy wooden planks or a sheet of ¾-inch plywood (exterior). Pack the earth tightly around the drum and on top of it. Use a 2 x 4 as a tamper to compact the earth.

Locate the dry well about 10 feet from the foundation of the house to prevent backflow of water. As a rule, four dry wells are necessary to take care of abundant water. They should be positioned at the four corners of your house, or you can install them in the center of each wall span, if the main downspout is located in that area.

For really serious drainage problems, you may want to consider a very large dry-well system. This is constructed similar to a septic system. Since it involves fields of drainage tile, a large earth excavation, and masonry walls, this is a job best left to a professional.

If your home is *built on a slab,* chances are that downspout extensions and splashblocks are all that are necessary to funnel away excess water. However, slab houses should have adequate drainage systems or the water will settle at the corners of the concrete and eventually erode it away. Too, the siding generally covers the top of the slab and any excess water can soon cause the siding, sheathing, and sills to rot or decay.

Adjust splashblocks annually so they channel water away from the foundation, porches. You can buy premolded splashblocks or make your own from concrete or bricks

Downspout elbows often loosen over a period of time. Tighten them by crimping the edges slightly with pliers. For best results, do this in new installations

97
98
99

Connect downspouts to elbows, elbows to gutters with a single metal screw. This prevents them from slipping apart

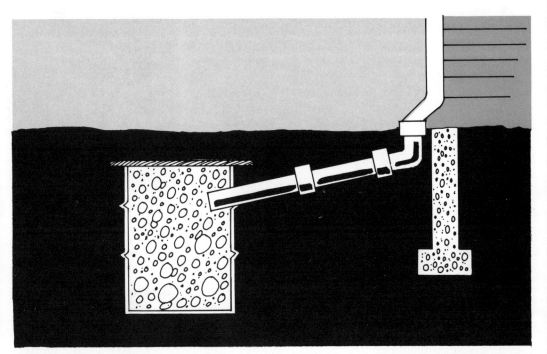

If you have a really serious drainage problem, a dry well may be your best answer. Basically, it is a 55-gal. steel drum filled with gravel and buried at least 10 ft. from the foundation.

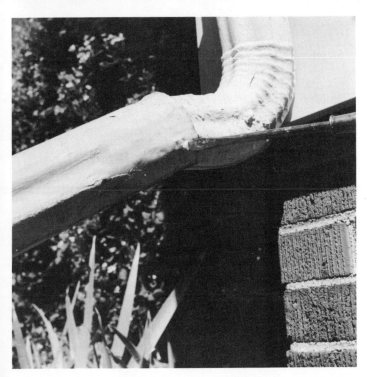

HOW TO HANG NEW GUTTERS

Metal gutters and downspouts are quite easy to install in new construction or remodeling. The first step is to determine the materials you will need for the job. Here is a checklist to help you:

Downspouts. Count the number of 10-ft. sections necessary. *Gutter.* Also count the number of 10-ft. sections needed. *Mastic. Left end caps.* One cap is needed for each left-hand section. The same count applies to *right end caps. Drop outlets.* Use an outlet where downspouts are located. *Slip connectors.* Use one for each length of gutter, corner, and drop outlet. *Inside corners. Outside corners. Hangers.* Use either a spike-and-ferrule set; strap-through-a-hanger method; or fascia bracket hangers. *Regular elbows.* These are used to bring the downspout against the wall—two elbows per downspout. *Pipe straps.* Use two of these for every 10 ft. section of downspout. *Funnels* join two downspouts into a single pipe. *Strainers* fit into downspout openings.

For the proper gutter slope, fasten a chalkline to the top edge of the fascia board. The gutter should slope about 1 in. in every 16 to 20 ft. Make all measurements needed, transfer them to the gutter sections, and assemble the entire gutter on the ground.

Start the gutter installation opposite the downspout. With fascia bracket hangers, first nail the bracket to the fascia board, and space the brackets about 30 in. apart. Line the top edge of the bracket with the chalkline. Slip the gutter into the bracket, and insert the hanger strap under the front lip of the gutter.

For strap hangers, align the bracket with the chalkline. Nail the gutter to the fascia with one 6d nail about every 30 in. Then hook the gutters into the underside of the front bead of the gutter and nail it to the roof sheathing. Use common nails.

For spikes and ferrules, align the gutter with the chalkline and nail it to the fascia board in several spots for temporary support. Drive the spike through the lip of the gutter, installing the ferrule. The spikes should be spaced at the first and every other rafter.

To join gutter sections, first fill the slip connectors with mastic. Assemble. Then bend the forward edge of the connector down against the gutter with pliers.

To drain water away from foundation, you may install plastic sleeves that are kept rolled up

End caps are inserted over gutter with mastic (simulated here). You can buy galvanized gutter pre-primed

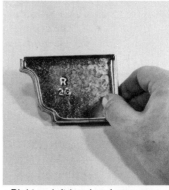

Right or left-hand end caps are marked "R" and "L." Make sure you buy enough of each. Wear gloves when handling guttering

Slip connectors join gutter runs; use mastic on each end of the connector. Lip of connector is bent over gutter

Downspout is forced onto drop outlet, then fastened with a metal screw. Support inside and outside corners with 6d common nails

Locate drop outlets so the downspout may be installed adjacent to a corner of the structure. Join the drop outlet to the gutter with slip connectors and mastic. If the structure has an overhang, install the end piece of the downspout and add a short section of gutter to complete the gutter run. Cap the end of the run.

Inside and outside corners also are attached to the gutter run with slip connectors. Support the corners with two 6d common nails driven through the back of the corners into the fascia board.

Downspouts and elbows have one end smaller than the other for a slip fit. You join the two by simply forcing them together. Secure the joint by driving a sheet-metal screw into both pipes. You'll have to drill or punch a pilot hole first to accept the screw.

It may be necessary, on wide overhangs, to use two lengths of elbow pipe to position the downspout against the siding. You can buy different angles for this.

Fasten the downspout against the wall with pipe straps. Use two of them for each 10-ft. section.

If the gutters are galvanized, let them weather for about six months before you paint them.

doors & windows

DOOR MAINTENANCE and repair problems fall into just three general classifications: the door won't work; the hardware won't work; the door doesn't fit properly into its frame. Diagnosis of why a door sticks or binds should start first with a careful inspection of how the door fits into the jamb—or opening. Then, follow this with an inspection of the hardware.

There are three basic types of doors: hinged, sliding and folding.

Most homes have three types of door construction: *solid-core doors* for exterior openings, *hollow-core doors* for interior passages, *panel doors* for both exterior and interior use. A *solid-core door* is laminated from strips of hardwood over which plywood or hardboard panels of the same dimension have been fastened. It's solid all the way through. A *hollow-core door* is a framework of hardwood strips covered with a skin of plywood or hardboard. A *panel door* has insets of glass; or it is made with a piece of wood that gives it a "raised panel" appearance.

There are variations of these types: some have plastic thermal barriers; others are encased in metal, stone, fake veneer, and so on.

Yet all operate on the same principal, making it fairly easy to get down to the reason for a problem and correct it without much difficulty.

Sticking and binding. If this is the problem, stand back from the door and check the crack between the door and jamb. The door, of course, should be closed. The crack should be about even around the frame. You can check this with a wooden shingle. Since the shingle is beveled, you can sandwich it into the crack, and locate the binding point by noting the point where the shingle won't penetrate the crack, or penetrate very little.

If you find a gap at one side and a hairline crack on the other, the problem can be: 1. A faulty hinge; 2. Swelling of the wood from dampness, or; 3. The house has settled slightly throwing the frame off kilter.

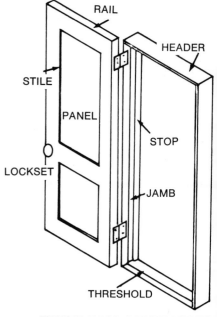

TYPICAL DOOR CONSTRUCTION

Typical door construction shown here applies to exterior and most interior doors. Door can be solid core or hollow core frame with skin of plywood, hardboard, metal, plastic or other material. Hinges are mortised into the edge of the door and the jamb; lockset can be counterbored into the stile or mortised. Most modern doors have counterbored locksets

LOCK AND DOOR PROBLEMS, AND HOW TO SOLVE THEM

Problem	Why	Solution	Maintenance
Frozen lock	Moisture, usually	Warm key with match. Try alcohol on key	Spray with graphite powder
Balky bolt; you turn key, but bolt in latch won't turn	Door alignment off	See cure, this chapter	Annually inspect alignment as described here
Key seems to bind in lock; bolt sticks	Improper mounting of lock. Bad duplicate key	Remove lock; use original key for test	Follow instructions for installing new lock
Key breaks off inside lock	Key not in all the way before it was turned	Try paperclip hook or hat pin to remove. Or you can buy a tool for this	Keep lock lubricated
Latch won't fit strike	Strike out of position—low or high in mortise	File slot lower or higher; recut mortise up/down	Check for latch fit in fall/winter
Hinge pin stuck in channels	Binding on paint; rusty	Try penetrating oil; tap pin out with cold chisel	Remove and lubricate with graphite
Door binds	Misaligned hinges; humidity has swollen wood	Correct hinges; Lightly sand or plane door	Keep hinges and doors on regular maintenance schedule
Door rattles in door frame	Door stops misaligned; door too small for opening	Move stops; use weatherstrip to tighten; new door	Doors stick in humid weather; don't plane too much
Door warped in frame	Moisture, probably	Need new door; see text, this section	Keep doors sealed with paint, stain, varnish to block moisture
Door has delaminated	Moisture, probably	Glue, renail. Or replace door	Keep doors sealed with finish, as with warped doors

SWELLING WOOD usually occurs in the spring and summer months when the humidity outside is high. In the late fall, winter, and early spring months, the humidity is low and the door will tend to shrink in the frame, causing rattling. If the rattling problem isn't too great, you can stop this with weatherstripping, as discussed elsewhere in this chapter. If swelling is the problem and humidity doesn't seem to be the cause, make sure the door isn't being subjected to water damage caused by poor roof drainage.

Hinges. Most doors are held with either two or three butt-type hinges. One leaf of each hinge is mortised into the frame; the other into the edge of the door. Generally, to make hinge repairs, you have to remove the door. Close the door, and tap up the hinge pins. Do the bottom pin first. A hardwood wedge makes a good pin remover since you can hammer against it without damaging the metal. If the pin is stubborn, you may have to use an old screwdriver to pry it out. If this fails, you can open the door, block up the bottom edge of the latch side, and unscrew the hinges on either the jamb or door side. The door should be held up in position to prevent the screws from being ripped out due to sagging.

Loose screws. If the sticking and binding problem is caused by loose screws, you can correct this by simply tightening the screws—without removing the door. However, the problem is usually caused by the holes becoming too large for the screws, so the screws can't be tightened. Remove the screws and stick a wooden match or a couple of toothpicks into the hole. reinsert the screw and try tightening it. Still loose? Try a longer screw. If this doesn't work, fill the screw holes with plastic wood putty, let it dry, and reset the screws. Or you can fashion a wooden peg from a piece of soft wood, dip it in glue, and pound it into the screwhole. If none of these techniques work, you'll have to reset the hinges.

Shimming hinges. If the sticking problem is not one caused by the screws in the hinges, but is on the hinge side of the door, you may be able to solve it by shimming the hinges with cardboard. Remove the hinge leaf from the jamb, cut the cardboard to fit the leaf, and reinstall the hinge with the cardboard beneath. Lay the cardboard

Locks need lubrication at least once annually. Puff graphite powder into the keyhole, insert the key, and turn it several times. Do not use liquid type oils for this job; as dirt accumulates they will gum and foul the lockset

Latches need graphite powder lubrication annually, too. Turn the latch in and puff graphite into the narrow opening between the "channel" and the latch. You can buy graphite at most hardware and building-supply stores

Remove a broken key from a lock by bending over tip of paperclip for use as a probe. Hairpin sometimes works, or you can buy tool for this job

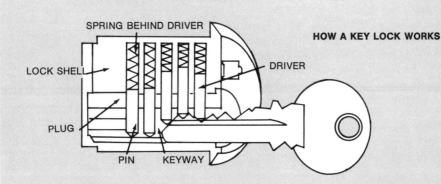

SPRING BEHIND DRIVER

HOW A KEY LOCK WORKS

LOCK SHELL

DRIVER

PLUG

PIN   KEYWAY

Here's how lock works: Ridges in key push pins and drivers inside the lock. Pins, drivers are spring-loaded. The right key triggers the correct pins and drivers to open the lock

in loose; don't glue it in position.

On heavy doors, sagging usually occurs at the bottom edge of the latch side. To raise the door, you can deepen the mortise of the upper hinge, which will pull the door up. Use a sharp chisel and shave slowly, testing as you go. A tiny bit of wood removed from the mortise may be all that's needed.

Sometimes inserting a piece of cardboard under the lower hinge leaf, as described previously, will pull the door back into position. Try this before you cut very deeply into the mortise on the top hinge leaf.

Also, on heavy doors there may not be enough "hinge power." By adding a third hinge between the top and bottom ones, you can prevent wobbling, rattling, and binding. This helps hold the door square, too.

Binding. If the hinge treatment doesn't correct the sticking and binding problem, you'll have to locate the binding point, remove the door, and plane down the spot. But, a word of caution: don't be too quick to start planing the wood. Often, light sanding, using a fairly course grit sandpaper on a sanding block, will do the job. Keep the block square to the wood; don't rock it at the edges.

Always start sanding or planing on the *hinge* side of the door. The latch side is slightly beveled so it fits tightly against the jamb.

Binding spots usually occur at the top or bottom edge opposite the hinges. If the area on the bottom or top edge that is binding is fairly large, remove the door and plane or sandpaper that area. When you are planing across the grain of the wood at the top or bottom of the door, run the plane from the edges toward the center of the door. This will help prevent splitting the edges.

If the door is binding on either edge, remove it and plane or sandpaper just the hinge side. For this, you will have to remove the hinges. You can plane over the edge of the door since you will be going with the grain of the wood. Be sure to use a plane with the longest sole possible. The blade should be wider than the edge or thickness of the door. Set the blade of the plane very shallow and keep the weight on the handle—not front end.

Settling of your house, although normal, may throw the door jamb out of square so the door

Strikeplate is used as template for scribing cardboard shim. Use sharp pencil, good scissors. Do not glue shim into position

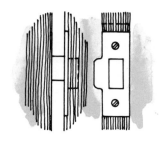

Raise strike plate by remortising it in door jamb, if door latch does not meet plate evenly

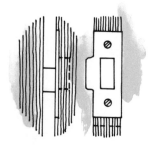

Or lower strike plate by also re-mortising it in jamb. If latch doesn't fit, door will not stay closed, or it will bind in jamb

Cardboard shim treatment works also for doors that bind. Use thin cardboard for this and punch in holes for screws with an awl

If hinge screws are loose, plug hole with toothpicks or matchstick. If this doesn't work, you can try longer screws

Keep hinge pins lubricated with stick type grease or graphite. Do not use household oil; it will become dusty and gummy

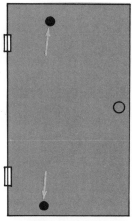

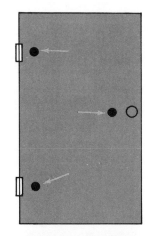

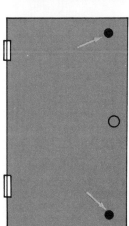

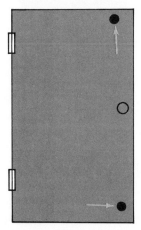

Binding points at door are shown on this drawing. Look for them where arrows point. Most common binding spot is bottom edge of latch side

doesn't fit properly. If the settling isn't too serious, and it generally isn't, you can often square the door in the jamb by adjusting the hinges with shims or planing the edges or ends of the door to fit the jamb. It is usually easier to shim and plane the door than to attempt to spring the jamb back into square.

If settling is very serious, you should call in a carpenter to check for structural damage to the house. The problem can be in the foundation or sidewalls, and this is a job for a pro.

Warped doors. The problem here can stem from three causes: moisture, improper hinging, or latching. These can throw the door into a bind that will cause it to warp over a period of time.

If the door is severely warped, it is usually best to replace it. There are tricks you can use to try to straighten it (wetting it and letting it dry in the sun with weights on the warp, for example), but these usually fail. Buying a new door is the easiest and most satisfactory answer.

A slight warp can sometimes be corrected by shimming both hinges on the pin side of the hinge leaf. The partial shim often will change the angle of the door slightly, bringing it back into alignment so it will latch.

If the door will close, but you have to slam it or lean heavily against it for the latch to catch, you can correct such a warp by resetting the door stop. This problem is usually caused by the door hitting the stop before it latches.

With a wide chisel, remove the door stop. You may have to score the paint along the edge of it with a razor knife first. Carefully pry the stop off, working the entire length so it comes off evenly. Tap out the old nails, close the door, and position the stop against the face of the door so there is about $\frac{1}{16}$ of an inch gap between the door face and the edge of the stop. Small pieces of cardboard make excellent gap gauges.

When the stop is aligned, renail it to the jamb, and remove the cardboard shims. Since the door has been moved slightly outward, you may have to readjust the hinges slightly with partial cardboard shims to compensate for the new angle at which the door strikes the stop.

Strike plates, where the tongue of the latch meets them, can become out of alignment. Here, the door won't latch at all, or it partially latches

1 Button or slot in knob handle releases the knob from its spindle. You depress the slot with tip of a small screwdriver blade

47
50
54
175
176
179
180

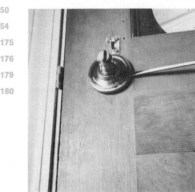

2 Rose simply slips from rose liner. You may need prying help from a screwdriver. Work carefully to avoid damaging the door surface

67

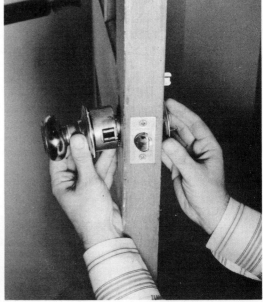

3 Remove metal plate holding spindle assembly in door. Two screws generally hold plate in position. It then slips off spindle

4 Entire lock assembly now slips out from the exterior—on an exterior door. Latch is removed by unscrewing the latch bolt plate

HOW TO INSTALL A CYLINDRICAL LOCKSET

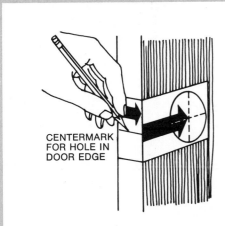

CENTERMARK FOR HOLE IN DOOR EDGE

For new doors, mark door 36-in. from floor. Apply template to high edge of door bevel and mark the center of the door edge

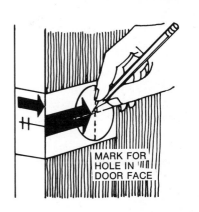

MARK FOR HOLE IN DOOR FACE

Mark center hole on door face through guide on template. A template is generally furnished with new locksets for this job

5 MARKING THE DOOR

only to open when a gust of wind hits the door or somebody pushes it gently from the outside.

Examine the strike plate to see if the latch is hitting it high or low. You can either file the hole in the plate to meet the latch, or unscrew the plate and cut the mortise higher or lower. If the latch tongue doesn't extend far enough to reach the strike plate, you can correct this by shimming out the strike plate with cardboard—as explained for hinges.

HOW TO REPLACE A DOOR

MOST DOOR OPENINGS are standard in size, making replacement doors easy to fit in the openings.

Here are the steps to follow in replacing a door:

First, remove the old door and the hinge hardware. Then measure the opening from top to bottom and side to side. Measure it at several points. There may be enough variation that you will have to compensate in fitting the new door to the opening.

Buy a new door that comes as close as possible to fitting the opening. If it is an exterior door, you will have no problem rough trimming it to fit, since exterior doors are generally solid-core types. If the door is hollow core, you only have about a half-inch trim margin.

To trim the door to fit, hold it tightly against the top of the jamb. At this point, the door should be square in the opening. If it isn't, you must align the latch side to the jamb, carefully mark the areas along the top that don't fit, then plane (or sand) the edges until the door fits the top of the jamb.

Very carefully measure the distance from the top of the door to the bottom of it at the sill. Do this at both the hinge and latch sides. If it is an interior door, subtract about ¾-in. from this measurement. This is so any rug or carpeting on the back side of the door will clear the bottom, and the door swings freely.

Locating the hinges and lockset is the next procedure, after the door fits properly in the opening. You can use the old hinge placements for the new door; here, it's a matter of marking the location,

Drill hole through door face as marked for lockset. To prevent splitting, drill from both sides of the door

For latch, drill a hole in the center of the door edge. The marks you made with furnished template show you where to drill

6 HOW TO DRILL HOLES FOR A LOCKSET

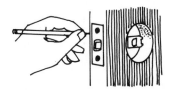

Push latch in the hole. Keep it parallel to the face of the door. Now, mark its outline with a pencil and remove the latch

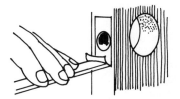

With a sharp, narrow chisel, cut a mortise for the latch. It should be about ⅛ in. deep. Cut it evenly and slowly, testing it

Insert the latch and tighten the screws. Locksets like this one can be used to modernize your present doors

For round-face latches, you must drill the hole the same size as the latch so it fits snugly. Press in the latch until it is flush

7 INSTALL LATCH

mortising in the new hinges (or one side of the old set if you don't buy new ones).

The door is now ready to hang. After it is in position, you probably will have to hand-fit it by sanding and planing. The final step is installing the lockset and latch, which is illustrated on these pages.

As you hang the new door, put in the top hinge pin first, then the bottom pin. Go slowly; don't force the pins through the guides. If they won't go, find out where the door is binding and shave it down with a plane or sandpaper.

The key to hanging any door is patience. It has to be fitted equally around the opening, and this takes careful planing and sanding, with frequent trials, until the door works smoothly.

SLIDING DOORS

WHETHER USED as an entrance to a patio or closet, sliding doors operate on tracks—with or without wheels or rollers to guide them. This is also true of sliding screen doors used at patio entrances.

Doors used for patios are considered medium-weight units, and generally ride on a bottom rail. Sliding doors in garages and closets ride along a top rail. In some closet installations, small metal or plastic guides are used along the floor to keep the door in alignment and operating smoothly.

If a sliding door is difficult to open or close, chances are there is dirt on the track or the wheels are misaligned. A dirty track is most often the cause of binding with patio doors, since the tracks are subject to foot traffic which can imbed mud and foreign material in the small grooves. To remove the debris, simply scrub it out with a mild detergent solution, using a stiff brush. If the debris is loose, you can vacuum it out.

If the tracks are clean and the door still is difficult to open and close, try tightening any loose screws in the frame of the unit or in the track. On some units, you can tighten the screws that hold the wheels. However, most are permanently fastened into the frame and they are made of self-lubricating nylon. Therefore, don't use oil in an effort to make the door glide more smoothly.

If the door jumps off the track, the problem is usually an obstruction on the track. If there isn't,

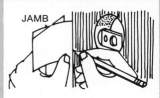

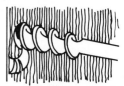

Template also is used to mark the latch position. Put it against latch and jamb, close door, and mark proper latch position on jamb

Drill hole for latch in door jamb according to template marks. Hole should be drilled a full ½ in. deep, or according to directions

On the center line of the jamb, match the screw holes on the strike plate. Outline the plate, mortise it to match thickness

Slip in the strike plate and run in the screws. You can adjust tang on strike plate to fit it between the door and door stop

8 INSTALLING
THE STRIKE PLATE

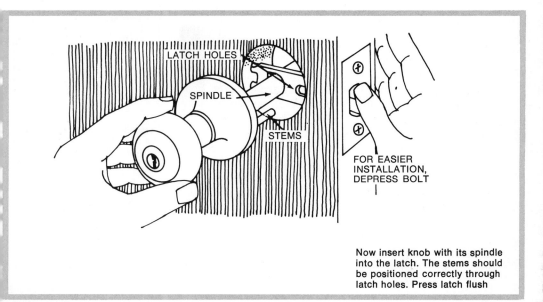

LATCH HOLES

SPINDLE

STEMS

FOR EASIER
INSTALLATION,
DEPRESS BOLT

Now insert knob with its spindle
into the latch. The stems should
be positioned correctly through
latch holes. Press latch flush

9 INSTALLING THE EXTERIOR KNOB

STEMS

SCREW GUIDES

SCREW HOLES

Install interior knob and rose.
Push this flush and insert screws.
Technique is similar, but opposite,
of removal photos in this chapter

10 INSTALLING THE INTERIOR KNOB

a wheel may be out of alignment. You can readjust the wheel by loosening a setscrew and relocking it so the wheel is straight.

Removing a sliding door for maintenance and repair is not difficult. If the door is supported at the bottom, you simply pick it up and pull it off the track. There is enough leeway at the top of the track to give clearance for this.

For doors that are supported at the top, one of three techniques can be used for removal. You can lift the door up and off the track; remove a metal shield that holds the rollers onto the track; or move the door to a key opening where it will lift up and out.

Patio sliding doors are usually made of aluminum; interior sliding doors can be stamped metal, a soft plastic material, or wood. Many are made from ¾-in. plywood, and these may tend to warp over a period of time. If warping is your problem, it's best to replace the door with a new one, since realignment of wheels and track is difficult.

GARAGE DOORS

OVERHEAD GARAGE DOORS can be considered sliding doors since they operate on a track and, usually, with a wheel device of some type. There are two basic types of overhead garage doors: one-piece units and sectional units. The one-piece door pivots up, helped by a heavy coil spring; the sectional door runs up on a track. It also is helped by a spring.

Maintenance of both types is easy: keep the tracks, wheels, and hinges lubricated. Cup grease works best on the tracks themselves; graphite or light household oil is satisfactory for wheels and hinges. Locksets should be lubricated with graphite powder.

Balky doors are usually caused by misaligned tracks. You can correct this situation by tightening the lag screws that hold the tracks to the garage structure.

Coil spring problems are jobs for a professional. Special equipment is used to tighten them, so don't attempt to do it yourself since the springs are under dangerous tension.

Locks and latches on overhead garage doors are usually spring-loaded, and have two steel

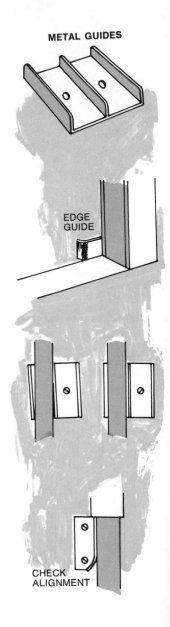

METAL GUIDES

EDGE GUIDE

CHECK ALIGNMENT

Door guides may be metal or plastic; either can be screwed or glued to the floor. If door is binding, it's probably misaligned in the guide

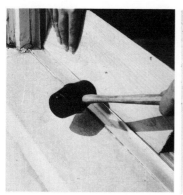

Straighten bent metal tracks by sandwiching wooden strip in the track slot and rebending it with a rubber mallet, as pictured

Keep tracks clean of debris, mud. Vacuum cleaner does good job. Or use a stiff brush with water and mild detergent. Rinse and dry

Cotton swab removes dirt from tiny grooves in tracks that can't be picked up by vacuum or brush. Don't oil the rollers

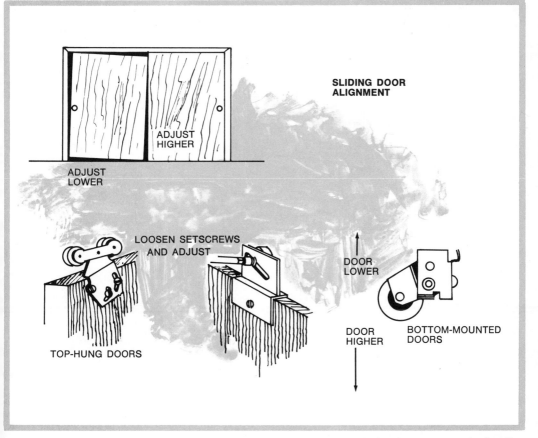

SLIDING DOOR ALIGNMENT

ADJUST HIGHER

ADJUST LOWER

LOOSEN SETSCREWS AND ADJUST

TOP-HUNG DOORS

DOOR LOWER

DOOR HIGHER

BOTTOM-MOUNTED DOORS

If door is up at one end adjust it lower; adjust higher at other end. Screw slots let you do this on top tracks or door-bottom rollers

bars or tapes that connect the latches to the side jambs or track.

If the latch doesn't catch, the problem is probably dirty bar or tape bands, the latch assembly in the middle of the door has become clogged with grease or dirt, or the bands are out of adjustment. First, try cleaning the latch and bands. If this doesn't work, you can make an adjustment to the bands at the point where they hook onto the lock.

If you have a one-piece overhead door, don't leave it in the "up" position constantly. The door will tend to warp and sag in the middle since it is wide and doesn't usually have special reinforcement across the center.

If your home has "barn" type garage doors (those that swing out like a house door), the big problem is sagging. You can often correct this by adding hinges to the door, or by using a wire turnbuckle stretched diagonally from the top hinge side to the bottom rail side.

Plywood overhead garage doors sometimes delaminate through moisture. You can correct this by regluing the delaminated veneer with exterior-type wood adhesive and clamping it until the glue sets. Also drive in several small nails to hold the laminations together.

34

STORM DOORS

STORM DOORS take the worst beating of all, since they are exposed to extreme temperatures and just plain wear and tear. Whether wood or metal, they are by design lighter and less rugged in construction than their entrance-door counterparts.

47
50
51
52

Damage is usually focused at the hinge points; a gust of wind can rip a storm door right off the hinges if the door isn't latched properly.

Several times a year check the hinges to make sure that the screws holding them are tight. If the door is wooden and the hinges are loose, you can tighten them with plugs, as described previously. If the door is metal, you can replace the screws with stove bolts after you drill holes completely through the door. Use washers on both sides for added strength.

If a wooden door cracks, it usually is at the stile at the hinged side. You can fix this with a flat

422

Flexible weatherstripping for garage door is nailed directly to bottom edge of the door. You can buy it in rolls—with nails—in widths to fit any door. Prime the bottom of the door with paint first to deter moisture

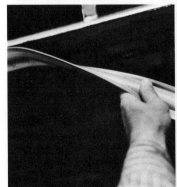

Graphite penetrating oil should be
used to oil locking mechanisms
on garage doors. Use graphite
powder for oiling locks operated
by keys

Locking rods or bands can be
lubricated with grease sticks.
Rods or bands should be lubricated yearly after you clean them

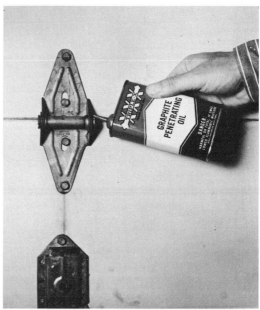

Use graphite oil or powder on
hinges of sectional garage doors.
You can put small amount of cup
grease on roller tracks

metal mending plate screwed across the break.

Another technique is drilling down through the edge of the door and inserting glued dowels into the holes. Spread plenty of glue in the break, and clamp the job until the adhesive has dried, An alternative technique is to screw the parts together if the distance you have to drive the screws isn't too great.

Storm door closers need annual inspection and lubrication. Oil the closer rod with stick-type grease or powdered graphite. If the tension on the closer has weakened, you can tighten it by turning down a screw or nut at the end of the closer housing. If the closer rod is bent, it's best to buy a new closer to protect the door.

WEATHERSTRIPPING

Weatherstripping on exterior doors and windows can quite literally save you thousands of dollars in fuel bills over a period of years—especially in older homes where doors and jambs tend to separate. The open cracks invite cold drafts.

There are many different types of weatherstripping available; you can find the type that serves your purpose best at most building-supply outlets.

The most common type probably is interlocking jamb weatherstrip. Metal strips are fastened to the door and to the door jamb; they simply interlock.

Easy for the handyman to install are spring-type metal strips. They are shaped to provide an air-tight cushion either with a V-shaped fold or a slight crimp.

Other types include pliable and rigid strip gaskets made from felt or vinyl. They are nailed to the door frame—or according to the manufacturer's directions that are included.

The bottoms of doors should also be weatherstripped to eliminate drafts. There are many products available for this. Some are fastened along the bottom edge of the door and form a seal of plastic, rubber or felt. Others involve a threshold/weatherstrip combination. A half-round piece of plastic is centered in a metal threshold and presses against the bottom edge of the door when it is closed. You usually have to trim about ½-inch off the bottom of the door for gasket type strips.

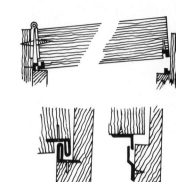

INTERLOCK

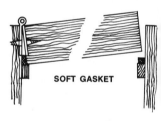

SOFT GASKET

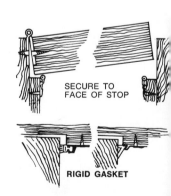

SECURE TO FACE OF STOP

RIGID GASKET

To cut mortise (simulated here for illustrative purposes), outline leaf of hinge with sharp pencil. Or use an awl to mark jamb or door

Outline mortise cut with tip of a sharp chisel. Tap blade into wood about same thickness as hinge leaf. Overlap the cuts slightly

Make small cross cuts the length of mortise outline. Space these about ¼ in. apart, to the depth of the mortise

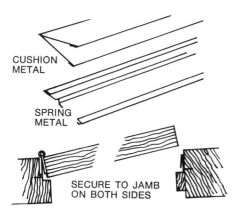

CUSHION METAL

SPRING METAL

SECURE TO JAMB ON BOTH SIDES

METAL

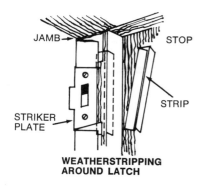

JAMB

STOP

STRIP

STRIKER PLATE

WEATHERSTRIPPING AROUND LATCH

Remove wood with "planing" action of chisel. Keep chisel fairly flat and shave wood out instead of chipping it away from mortise

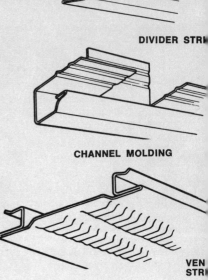

DIVIDER STRI

ROOF OVERHANGS help protect windows and doors from the weather. The panel that runs under the overhang is called a soffit. It can be made of metal, plywood, hardboard or dimension lumber.

The big problems with soffits are peeling paint and delamination of wood fiber. You often can stop peeling paint by installing aluminum ventilators along the soffit run—or by unplugging the ventilators, if they already are installed. If delamination is the problem, check for moisture along the gutters. If rot has taken over, you'll have to replace the soffits. The drawings here show how.

CHANNEL MOLDING

**VEN
STRI**

ALUMINUM ROOF EDGING

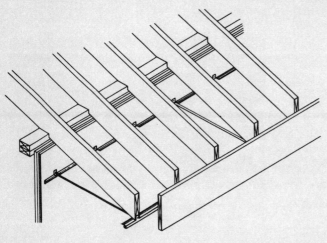

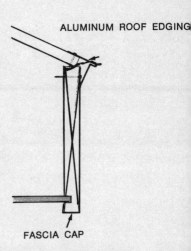

FASCIA CAP

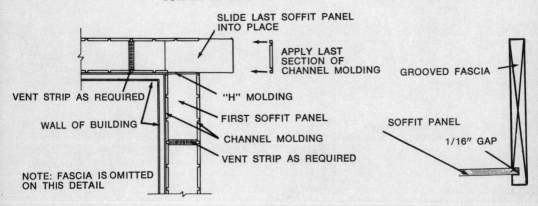

CORNER DETAIL

SLIDE LAST SOFFIT PANEL
INTO PLACE

APPLY LAST
SECTION OF
CHANNEL MOLDING

GROOVED FASCIA

VENT STRIP AS REQUIRED

WALL OF BUILDING

"H" MOLDING

FIRST SOFFIT PANEL

CHANNEL MOLDING

VENT STRIP AS REQUIRED

SOFFIT PANEL

1/16" GAP

NOTE: FASCIA IS OMITTED
ON THIS DETAIL

THE MAJORITY of modern windows are manufactured from wood, aluminum and/or steel. Many wooden windows have been specially treated with chemicals to help prevent decay; some are encased in plastic to reduce maintenance. Other than a few maintenance chores, and occasional replacement of a broken pane of glass, windows are relatively trouble-free. Any problems usually involve sticking or binding, a broken sash cord on older window units, and peeling paint.

Metal windows. Aluminum windows won't rust,

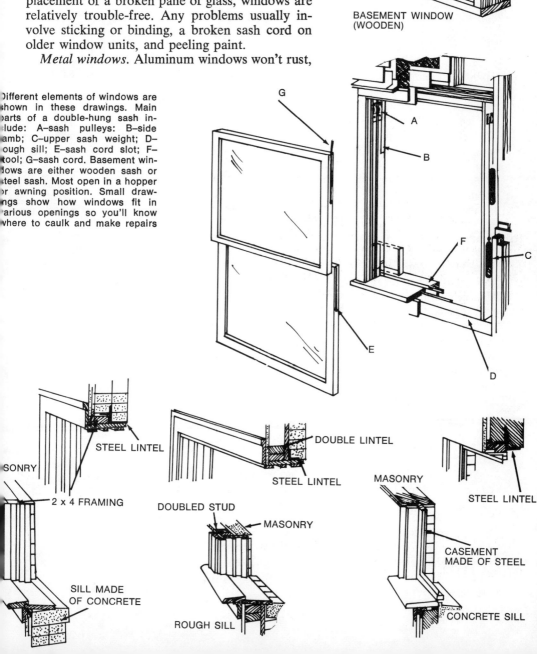

BASEMENT WINDOW
(WOODEN)

Different elements of windows are shown in these drawings. Main parts of a double-hung sash include: A—sash pulleys: B—side jamb; C—upper sash weight; D—rough sill; E—sash cord slot; F—stool; G—sash cord. Basement windows are either wooden sash or steel sash. Most open in a hopper or awning position. Small drawings show how windows fit in various openings so you'll know where to caulk and make repairs

G

A

B

F

C

E

D

STEEL LINTEL

DOUBLE LINTEL

STEEL LINTEL

MASONRY

STEEL LINTEL

MASONRY

2 x 4 FRAMING

DOUBLED STUD

MASONRY

CASEMENT
MADE OF STEEL

SILL MADE
OF CONCRETE

ROUGH SILL

CONCRETE SILL

but they do corrode from the elements. To keep them shiny, touch them up with fine steel wool every year or so. But you don't have to do this if dullish gray finish doesn't bother you.

Steel windows, unless they are specially treated with plastic, need painting to prevent rust.

Both steel and aluminum windows are subjected to condensation in the winter months. Ice forms on the inside of the frames and, when it melts, may cause damage to the painted or papered wall surface below the window. Although you probably won't open the windows in the winter months, a word of caution if you do: Forcing the window open with ice blockage can bend the frame so badly that you can't spring it back into position. If you have to open the window, you'll have to melt the ice first. Even then, don't force it.

Aluminum windows run in tracks. The tracks can become clogged or dirty, which will make the window bind and stick when you try to open, then close, it. Keep the tracks clean by vacuuming them.

Steel casement windows operate with a crank or a rod assembly that is threaded through a pivot channel. If the rod tends to stick, wipe it clean with a detergent in water and lightly coat it with paraffin or a grease stick. If your casements are the crank type, the crank housing can be disassembled and the gears cleaned and oiled: or you can replace the entire unit without too much work.

Wooden sash. These can be double-hung or casement types. If your home is fairly new (built in the last 20 years or so), you probably won't have much problem with the units. But you should include them in an annual maintenance schedule. Open and close the windows, if double hung, to make sure they glide smoothly. Casement types also should be opened and closed, and cranks and rods lubricated as explained for metal casement sash.

Sliding wooden windows and doors operate, generally, on top and bottom tracks. Pins or guides are in the upper track; rollers are used on the bottom track.

The tracks should be kept clean by vacuuming; if you have to remove the window for repairs, move the window along until the top guides slip into small channels or recesses, lift up, and slip the bottom out.

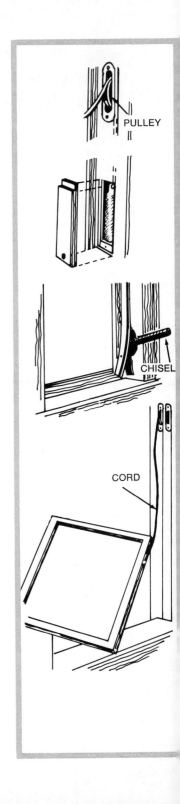

PULLEY

CHISEL

CORD

Break paint seal with putty knife, razor knife to loosen sash. If this doesn't work, you'll have to remove stop and reposition it

Grease-stick lubricant keeps sash working smoothly—especially if sash operates on metal tracks. Do not use household liquid oil

Moving parts of casement hardware should be lubricated with graphite powder. Do this at least twice annually—spring and fall

Pivot slots in basement casement or regular metal sash should be lightly oiled with graphite

STUCK AND JAMMED WINDOWS get that way through paint seals, or the wood swelling or warping.

28
184
178
182

If the sash is sealed by paint, you must break this seal. You can use a sharp knife for this, a spatula (if it's sturdy enough) or a thin-bladed putty knife. Break the paint seal along the entire run of stop molding, along the bottom and top of the window and at the parting strip where the two sashes meet (if the window is double-hung).

If this doesn't work, the window may be slightly warped in the frame or against the track. To correct this, you will have to readjust the stop moldings.

Pry the moldings off with a wide chisel or putty knife, working the molding off evenly up and down its entire run on both sides of the window unit. Remove the nails and place a thin cardboard shim between the window unit and the window stop. (But first, make sure you can open and close the window. If you can't, try tapping the frame lightly with a rubber hammer, using a block of wood as a buffer block. Don't hit it hard— just tap.) The thin cardboard shim (a cardboard from a shirt laundry makes a good gap gauge) will provide enough clearance for the window to glide properly. When it does, simply renail the stops back to the frame.

Swollen windows swell because of moisture. 40 First make sure that your rain-carrying system is working and runoff isn't draining into the window.

To free the window, take off the stop and remove the window. Then with sandpaper on a block, lightly sand the edges of the window.

Rattling windows fit too loosely in the frame. One way of tightening them is to move the stop moldings slightly. You can pry off the moldings and reset and renail them. But before you do this, try tapping the edge of the molding with a hammer and wooden block used as a buffer. Sometimes this trick pushes the stops just enough to stop the rattling.

Sagging hinges on windows get the same repair 48 treatment as sagging hinges on doors. You can use similar plugging and tightening techniques as described earlier in this chapter.

Replacing sash cords, sometimes necessary on older windows, can be quite a time-consuming job, but it isn't too difficult. Here's the technique:

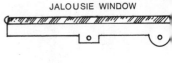

JALOUSIE WINDOW

SLIDING GLASS DOOR
WINDOW LOCK

Jalousie window slats are held by metal spring clips. You remove the clip and slide out the slat to replace it. Locking pins on metal sliding glass windows and doors sometimes become bent. You can realign them with pliers; some can be replaced, but take the part with you to store since many are similar but not identical

To repair screens with wooden frames, block up both ends of the screen and clamp the center, bowing the frame slightly, as shown here. When you release clamps, bow takes up screening, making it tight on frame

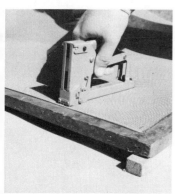

Automatic screen stapler does fast job; space staples about every 2 in. Stapler is good investment; it has other maintenance uses

For screen patch, unravel wire around patch as shown. Keep the tiny wires as straight as possible; unravel about ½-inch

Match patch with mesh in screen around rip. Poke wires completely through and bend them over on the other side.

Corner braces keep old screen frames square so they fit windows better. Predrill pilot holes for screws to prevent splitting

Metal screen frames have spline that holds screening tightly. Use wooden buffer block to replace spline, or special spline tool

Aluminum doors, windows, screens can be kept shiny by an annual rub-down with fine steel wool. Frames don't rust, but corrode

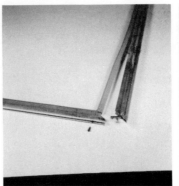

Metal storm windows are mounted in rubber or vinyl gasket, which is wedged in frames. Little screws open frame for glass replacement

Make sure mitered corners of metal storms go together tightly. If they tend to bind, check gasket to see if it is in frame

SWEATING WINDOWS

1. Remove the window stop on the same side of the window as the broken cord. You use the same method as described for jammed windows.

2. Take the sash out of the frame. You'll see a little pocket that seats the knot in the cord.

3. Remove all the broken rope and, at the same time, remove the other rope so the sash comes out. If it is the upper sash you're repairing, you'll have to pull the wooden separator strips out. You can do this with pliers. Now, you can lift the upper sash out of the frame.

4. Remove the strip of wood that covers the weight. This probably will be stuck tight with paint, so tap the strip with a hammer until you see where the joint is located. If you can't get it out by prying, use a keyhole saw to open it.

5. The weight will now be exposed. Instead of using new rope to fix the weights, we suggest that you buy metal chain for this purpose. It's a bit more costly, but it will last a long time. You also can buy sash balance to replace cords.

6. Replace the sash—just the opposite of taking it out—and test it to make sure it balances properly. The weight should not strike the pulley when the sash is opened. The weight should not clunk against the weight pocket when the window is closed. This is adjusted at the time you replace the cord.

Jalousie windows operate, usually, on a crank or lever system. It's easy to replace a broken glass panel by removing a spring clip.

If the mechanical unit is shot, you will have to

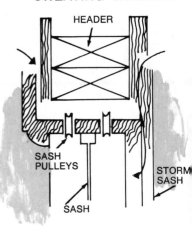

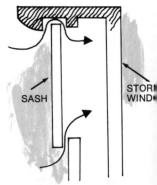

Moisture comes in window this way, causing the window to sweat. You can block this air passage with weatherstripping. Make sure glazing is tight so air is trapped

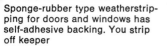

Sponge-rubber type weatherstripping for doors and windows has self-adhesive backing. You strip off keeper

Metal/vinyl weatherstripping also is available for windows. You nail it into position with tiny brads that are furnished in special kit

Metal gasket weatherstripping works well for doorways. Tension keeps it against the edges of the door. It is nailed into position

replace it. One side of the unit is fixed; the other side has a movable unit. The piece that moves is fastened to an off-center point on each of the carriers; the crank or lever moves it. To remove the unit, you first have to remove all the glass slats. Then pry or unscrew the mechanical unit from the window frame. The new one simply is fastened back into position. Use a level so you know the little carriers are in alignment.

Basement sash, other than those windows that are used in finished basements, usually are made of metal and operate on a "hopper" or "awning" principal: The sash is hooked at the top and opens out at the bottom, or it's hooked at the bottom and opens out at the top.

Since the windows are generally metal, the big problem is rust. They should be inspected yearly for rust, and primed and painted accordingly. If the windows stick, you can free them with penetrating oil applied to the slotted brackets in which the windows run. Many are not hinged to the frame, but merely are held into the framework by the slotted brackets and a lever-type latch. They are easy to remove by simply sliding them out to the keyway in the bracket and lifting them out of the frame.

Fixed windows are usually insulating glass. They are mounted in structural framework such as 2x4s in the case of large picture windows. The maintenance problem here is painting, since moisture often accumulates at and along the edges of the framing members.

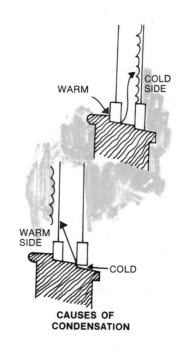

CAUSES OF CONDENSATION

Block cold air at bottom of windows with weatherstripping. Be sure the sash is tightly seated at window sill to stop air flow

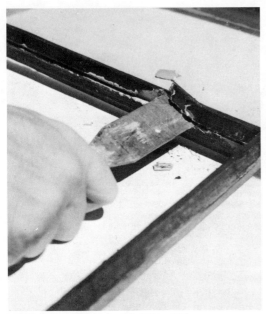

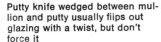

1. Putty knife wedged between mullion and putty usually flips out glazing with a twist, but don't force it

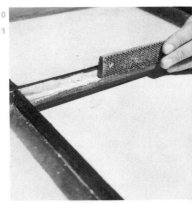

2. Old glazing snaps out with chisel blade, if putty knife doesn't work. Strip with flat edge out, as shown

IF A PANE OF GLASS in your home is broken, remove the sash and lay it on a table to make repairs.

Wear gloves to pry out the broken glass. You generally can do this without removing the glazing. If you can't get the broken glass out, you'll have to remove the glazing, however, to avoid breaking or splintering the wooden mullions.

If the glass you will replace is in a small multipaned window, you can use single thickness glass. If it is a large area, consider using *tempered* glass for replacement. Although tempered glass is somewhat more expensive, it is a lot tougher and has a high safety factor since it won't splinter if it's ever broken again.

The replacement glass should be about ⅛-inch smaller than the opening in which it goes. The smaller dimension allows for slight irregularities along the edge of the glass when it is cut. Buy glass cut to size; don't attempt to cut and snap it yourself unless you've had considerable experience in cutting glass.

3. Glazing you can't remove with putty knife or chisel can be "filed away with rasp. Keep it square to wood

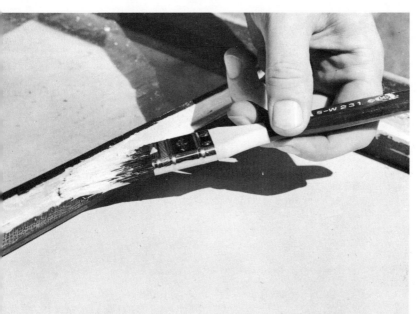

4
Prime wood with linseed oil or paint when old glazing is out. Let primer completely dry for best seal

METAL WINDOWS, used in basements, are easy to remove by lifting them up and out of the slotted metal brackets in which they run. *Casement* windows are hinged, and it is difficult to remove them for replacing broken glass. For both types of windows, however:

Remove the broken glass the same way as with wooden sash; you don't have to worry about damage to the mullions. Under the old glazing, you'll probably find metal clips that hold the glass in position. You either press down on the clips to remove them, or pry up on them. If there are no clips, no problem. Some manufacturers use only glazing to hold the glass in position.

If you have an *emergency,* polyethylene film or plastic food wrap can make a substitute for a broken window until you can replace it. Tack the plastic to the frame if it is wooden; strip it in with masking tape if it is metal. Double the tacking edges for more strength. Tack the top first, then the sides, then the bottom so there are no gaps. Cardboard or a piece of ⅛-in. hardboard cut to pane size also makes a quick emergency replacement until you get to the glass store. For large windows, you can brace or batten sheets of plywood over the opening to keep out most of the weather.

184

73

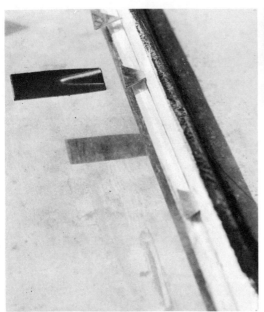

5 | Slip glass in opening and hold it in wooden sash with triangular glazier's points. Metal sash has clips

6 | Glazing compound is pressed at an angle to glass and mullion. Knead and "ball" it ahead of the knife

7 | Smooth glazing at angle with tip of putty knife, making about 60-degree slope. Remove excess

8 | Scour blade of putty knife in the ground so it produces a smoother finish on your final stroke

siding repairs/improvement

ALTHOUGH CONSTANTLY EXPOSED to the
elements, siding is remarkably durable and, if
properly maintained with paint or other finishes, it
will last indefinitely. Damage most often occurs
from peeling paint, dry rot, warping and/or splitting. When this happens the siding material sometimes becomes so bad that it's necessary to replace
or cover it.

BRICK, BLOCK, AND STONE

These are really "wall" materials although they
could be called types of siding since they serve this
purpose as well as a structural one. Some installations utilize a brick veneer—a layer of brick over
sheathing. Block walls are generally concrete; and
stone is used for architectural accent.

There are two maintenance problems with brick,
block or stone: crumbling mortar joints, or peeling
paint (if the material has been painted). You solve
the first problem by chipping out the old mortar
and filling the joints with new, as shown in this
chapter. Peeling paint is a common problem which
is generally caused by moisture and lime salts that
penetrate the paint film, causing it to flake and
peel. Repainting every two to four years with
special masonry paint is about the only cure for
this problem, although masonry paint may also
peel under certain conditions.

WOOD SIDING

Wood siding is the most commonly used type.
Most wood siding has a shadow pattern built into
it through the way it is cut. The common types are
drop (or rabbeted) and bevel siding. Rabbeted
drop siding has a groove cut along one edge. The
lap of each board over the next lower one is determined by the depth of the groove. This material is
usually ¾-in. thick and 6 in. wide.

On new installations, rabbeted siding—and
bevel siding—should be installed over sheathing.
On side walls that are too long for coverage by
one board, the butt joints between the boards
should be made at random. This prevents joint
"stacking."

BEVEL SIDING has one edge thicker than the other edge. The board in cross section looks like a wedge. The thin edge is usually 3/16-in. thick; the other edge varies from ½ to ¾-in. The boards are available in 4-, 6-, 8-, 10-, and 12-in. widths.

If you are doing residing or maintenance, galvanized or aluminum nails should be used in siding. Drive them flush with the surface. At corners, the ends of the boards must be butted against a corner board or mitered for the best appearance. Water tends to creep into mitered joints more easily than into tightly butted ones. Metal corners are available; they are preformed to fit over the siding and are fastened with nails.

Lay out your siding job so the bottom of one board will occur at the bottom of the window sill and the bottom of another board will run right over the top of the window frame. This eliminates extra cutting and makes a neater job.

General maintenance. Peeling paint, splits, cracks, warps, and rot are the most common ailments of wooden siding. Peeling paint can be caused by several things: Moisture is the most common. It gets behind the wood and pushes the paint film away. Painting over wet wood will cause peeling, as explained in the chapter on painting.

Venting the siding is one way to stop the paint from peeling, if it is really bad. One technique is to use aluminum louvered vents. You bore holes in the siding and insert them. Another method is to use tiny aluminum wedges that are driven up under the laps on lap siding. This releases the moisture. Still another system is to use tiny plastic louvers that are inserted into the butt of the siding between the studs.

Warped or split siding often can be repaired without replacing it. First, try renailing it into position, using threaded or ring nails driven into the studs. If the warp is too great, you can saw out small sections; then renail them with threaded nails. You must fill the saw kerfs with caulking compound, smooth it, and refinish the siding. Split siding often can be repaired with threaded nails and caulking compound.

PLYWOOD SIDING

Beauty, strength, high insulation value, economy and durability are the features of plywood siding. You can buy it in many grades and surface textures

Brick and block siding that has been painted frequently has a peeling problem due to lime salts and moisture. For this material, always use a masonry paint. And before repainting, be sure to scrape and wire-brush away any old flaking and peeling paint

Cracks in masonry joints are
quickly repaired by tuckpointing
with new mortar. Clean out the
old joint with a brick chisel

Moisten a broken joint with
water before you tuckpoint it
with new mortar. An old paintbrush makes a good tool

Mix mortar on a make-do plywood or hardboard "hawk."
You can push fresh mortar into
the joint with a tuckpointing trowel

Strike new mortar joints with a
special striking tool. Or use the
"bend" in a tire-changing iron.
Keep joint moist

including reverse board and batten (with deep, wide grooves cut into brushed, rough-sawn, coarse-sanded, or natural textured surfaces); rough-sawn and kerfed; circular-sawn; brushed; fine-line with fine grooves cut into the surface; striated; medium density overlaid; medium density overlaid reverse board and batten; and medium density overlaid horizontal lapped.

As thin as 5/16-inch, plywood siding can be applied over plywood and other wall sheathing with studs on either 16- or 24-in. centers. "Sturdi-wall" construction, where the plywood is applied directly to the studs, is accepted by the Federal Housing Administration and most local building codes. This technique of application can save you as much as 20 percent over a conventional two-layer wall.

General maintenance. Plywood siding is relatively maintenance-free, but like wood siding, it can split and crack. If moisture is especially bad, plywood can delaminate, since it is built up in layers held together with adhesive.

Threaded nails and caulking compound are the remedy for splits and cracks. Warps can be corrected by renailing; if the warps are especially bad, use screws instead of nails and countersink them below the surface. Then fill the hole with caulking or wood putty and refinish the panel.

Delamination is usually caused by moisture. It most frequently occurs at the corners of the panel where water can soak in. To repair this, the plywood has to be absolutely dry. Then apply a good adhesive between the layers. Nail the delaminations together with threaded nails; they serve as clamps until the glue dries. In most cases, you can leave the nails in place.

If moisture caused the delamination problem, find out where it is coming from—leaking gutters, inadequate drainage, siding too close to the grade level—and correct it.

Splits are seldom a problem in plywood. If you do have a split, however, try nailing it shut and filling the crack with wood putty or caulking compound. If this doesn't work, you'll have to replace the panel, which isn't too tough a job. For small breaks, you can drill out the damage with a hole saw or fly cutter and plug the hole with new plywood. Caulk the joint and smooth the caulking. Then refinish the panel.

New Sears vent system for drop siding helps reduce paint peeling. Plastic vents are installed, as shown, after holes are drilled

HARDBOARD SIDING

This material is manufactured in lap siding and in panels. The lap variety ranges in width from 6 to 12 in. and up to 16 ft. in length. You can apply it over sheathed or unsheathed walls with stud spacing not more than 16 in. on center. Most hardboard siding is preprimed at the factory. It must be painted within 60 days after it is installed. After that, you can reprime it with a quality exterior-grade oil-base primer.

Hardboard panel siding comes in 4-in. widths up to 16 ft. in length. The same application recommendations for lap siding apply. For batten strips at vertical joints, you may use either wood slats or strips of the siding cut to the desired width.

Intermediate batten strips can be used for design purposes. Some factory prefinished siding comes with matching plastic or metal snap-on batten strips. The sizes available are 4 x 7 ft.; 4 x 8 ft.; 4 x 9 ft.; and 4 x 10 ft. Thicknesses are 1/4, 3/16 and 1/8 in. The panel sizes listed above are for 1/4-in. thickness. Your building-supply dealer will be able to help you with other thicknesses and special installation problems.

General maintenance. Hardboard is actually wood that has been ground into a pastelike mixture and compressed under great heat. Therefore, it is actually wood, and has many of the same characteristics. Hardboard does not have grain, however. You must nail or screw through the material into another material such as a stud or sheathing.

There is little maintenance to hardboard other than painting it regularly. It sometimes splits or checks from moisture. The splits and checks can be renailed with threaded nails at the breaks and filled with caulking compound similar to plywood.

If the panel is badly damaged, it should be replaced immediately. You can patch hardboard by cutting out the damaged area and inserting new hardboard into the hole. The joint should be sealed with caulking and the panel refinished. If it is vertical siding, which it usually is, you probably can cover the joint with a batten strip after the patch has been made. Holes can be patched similar to those in gypsumboard, as discussed in the section on walls.

Special drill and jig is designed for plastic vents (shown on opposite page). Jig holds drill at proper angle

Hole goes through bottom of siding, as shown here, and up through it into the space between the studs

This siding ventilator utilizes a nail inserted in a metal sleeve. You drive nail into siding and pull out nail

106
107

131
136
to
145

First step for new siding (here hardboard) is to level first strip. Chalkline is snapped to mark level line for special starter strip

First strip of siding is leveled and nailed to starter strip, which is fastened to sill. Key to installing siding is to get first strip level

CEDAR SHAKES AND SHINGLES

Cedar shingles and shakes are a popular siding material. For siding, three types are generally used: rebutted-rejoined shingles, machine-grooved shakes, and handsplit shakes. Rebutted-rejoined shingles are precision-trimmed for sidewall use, both single-coursed and double-coursed. The edges have been worked to close tolerances, and the butts are trimmed at right angles to the edges. The shingles often are face-sanded to provide a smooth surface for finishing. The shingles are sold in cartons, with 56 courses of 18-in. shingles per carton, or 66 courses of 16-in. shingles.

Machine-grooved shakes are also called "processed" shakes. They have a striated or grooved face with parallel edges and squared butts. You can apply them double-coursed on exterior walls, with an underlay of low-grade shingles or insulation-board sheathing. Two sizes are available—16 and 18 in. They have a weather exposure of 12 and 14 in. They are packaged in a carton that provides 100 sq. ft. of coverage to these exposures.

Handsplit shakes are made in three different types: handsplit and resawn, tapersplit and

10
12
101
455

Additional siding strips are
stacked on first ones—like
blocks. Laps can be 11-in.
exposure on 12-in. material

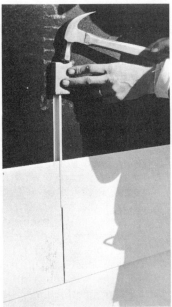

Special joint locking strip is
used for this product. Siding is
nailed through both courses
where it is overlapped

straight-split. Usually, the length for all three is
24 in. However, 18 and 32-in. lengths are sometimes referred to as "standard" sizes. You can buy
them in 4-bundle, 5-bundle, and 6-bundle squares,
depending on whether they are packaged in 20-in.
or 18-in. "frames." For maintenance replacement
purposes, many building supply dealers will break
a bundle for you, if you only need one or two
shingles or shakes.

When you are buying cedar in quantity, keep in
mind that it is sold by the "square," which, in
roofing terms, means an amount that will cover
100 sq. ft. when applied as recommended. Since
the sidewall exposure will usually be greater than
a roof, a square will cover more than 100 sq. ft.

General maintenance. Splits, cracks, and breaks
are the usual maintenance problems with cedar
shakes and shingles. Since they have been applied
individually, they are easy to replace. You simply
pry out the nails holding them to the course above,
insert the new shingle, and renail it. If you can, use
a shingle from the rear side of your home if the replacement will show. You can then use the new
shingle to make *this* replacement. If the shingle is

Outside corners are metal; inside
corners are wooden strips,
sealed with caulking compound.
Wooden corner boards can be used

just split or cracked, try renailing it with threaded nails along the damaged area. Then fill the joint with caulking compound and spot-paint.

To paint grooved shingles and shakes, you should use a short, stubby brush. It works the paint into the grooves better than a long-bristled brush.

HORIZONTAL/VERTICAL ALUMINUM SIDING

Aluminum siding is prefinished in a wide variety of colors, textures and designs. And because it is metal, it probably will outlast the structural members of the house. It is manufactured in Double-Four (two 4-in. panels on one 8-in. siding piece); Double-Five (two 5-in. exposures on one 10-in. siding piece); Dutch-Lap with special contours that produce a Dutch Colonial effect; vertical, which is 8 in. flat with no bends or contours, except for interlocking grooves; vertical 10-in. board and batten or V-groove effect; and vertical 12-in. board and batten or V-groove effect.

Textures include rough, horizontal wood grains, vertical wood grains, stucco effects, embossed and basketweave effects. The lengths of the "boards" run from 10 to 15 ft.

General maintenance. Since this type of siding is basically maintenance free, about the only problem you may encounter is denting of the aluminum. If the material has been backed properly, dents shouldn't be very obvious. If it hasn't, about the only way to repair it is to remove the piece of siding, straighten out the dent, and replace it. Since the aluminum is factory finished, it doesn't need painting, although a good washing with detergent and water is in order about every two years. You *can* paint the siding if you want to change color (although it's not advisable). Ask your paint dealer for the proper type of paint.

ASBESTOS-CEMENT SIDING

Asbestos-cement siding and shingles are durable, attractive, and can be applied over any type of sidewall surface. Because of their physical properties, they lend themselves to areas where the atmosphere is loaded with chemical fumes, smoke, smog, and other contaminants. The size most frequently used measures 5/32-in. thick by 12 in. wide by 24 in. long.

For asbestos cement shingles, break rest of broken shingle with a hammer or sledge and remove the pieces

For stubborn nails, drill through the nail head

Sandwich a hacksaw blade flat under the shingle to cut the nail

With old chisel, tap off the nail head, as alternate method of removing the shingle

Here's how you can remove an asbestos and wooden shingle that has been damaged. If you can, use replacement from back side of house for match

The shingles are applied with a 1½-in. lap, require no undercourse, and have an exposure of 10½-in. An asbestos-cement 4 x 8-ft. panel also is available, along with clapboard or wide siding board. In design, they are made in a straight vertical pattern—similar to striated plywood—in a wood-grain pattern and smooth. Various colors are available, and they go all the way through the material.

General maintenance. Broken shingles or boards 105 are the only problem. You solve it simply by replacing the damaged area. You can repaint asbestos-cement; a better answer is simply to scrub it down with detergent and water when it becomes dirty with soot and grime.

CORRUGATED METAL SIDING

Steel and aluminum corrugated siding are manufactured in two styles: 1¼-in. pitch and 2½-in. pitch. Both have a mill finish or a stucco-embossed finish. All styles, widths, and thicknesses are available in lengths of 6 through 12-ft. in 1-ft. increments.

Damaged drop or lap siding is repaired this way. Wedges (thick shakes often work) go under damaged siding so you have room to operate saw. Use a hacksaw to cut nails, if you can't pull them with hammer claws. When new material is in position and fastened, caulk joints, prime, and give surface a coat of finish paint

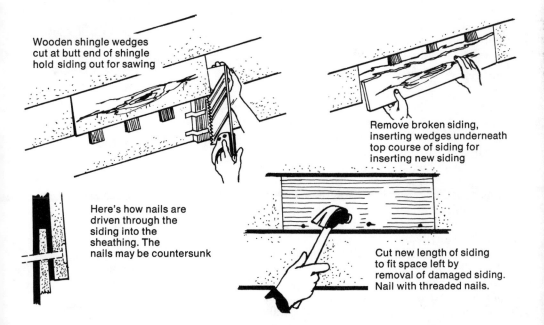

Wooden shingle wedges cut at butt end of shingle hold siding out for sawing

Remove broken siding, inserting wedges underneath top course of siding for inserting new siding

Here's how nails are driven through the siding into the sheathing. The nails may be countersunk

Cut new length of siding to fit space left by removal of damaged siding. Nail with threaded nails.

VINYL SIDING

Vinyl siding is a newcomer to the residential construction market. Vinyl also is being used to coat wood and metal sidings to increase their durability and decrease maintenance problems such as painting. Vinyl siding is manufactured from a plastic called polyvinyl chloride (PVC). Its big advantages are an end to maintenance and painting.

The colors go completely through the material, and only an occasional washing with a mild detergent and water keeps it looking new. Also, it won't dent or scar, corrode, stain or scratch.

Vinyl siding is manufactured in regular double 4 and 6-in. clapboard designs and single 6 and 8-in. sizes. A vertical 8-in. board is also made; it resembles regular tongue-and-groove siding after it has been applied to the house.

Installation of the material is nearly identical to putting on aluminum siding. However, a 3/16-in. gap should be left at the end of each "board" that butts against a stop, such as a corner or window. This allows for expansion and contraction.

The panel also should "hang" on the nails. The nails should never be driven in too snugly, since the material will expand and contract. This is also true of aluminum. No special tools are required to install vinyl siding.

FIBERGLASS STONE AND BRICK

This is another fairly recent development in the siding field. The material comes in sheet form—usually 2 x 4-ft. pieces—and it can be nailed directly to sheathing, or to furring strips on existing homes. Also, the material is ideal for interior use as an architectural accent.

The material is basically made from fiberglass—plus additives—so it is resistant to the weather and to chemical attack. Only an occasional hosing down with water is required to keep it looking new.

On one brand, the edges are lapped and nailed. After the panels are up, a special caulking compound is provided so the joints can be "tuckpointed" just like real stone or brick joints. This operation is done with a standard caulking gun. The "mortar" is then smoothed with a tapered piece of scrap wood. A similar item in the same line is "premortared" so the caulking operation

Concorde shingles (U.S. Gypsum) look like hand-split shakes. To install, courses are leveled and chalkline is snapped to maintain level

Short starter course is cut to match corresponding shadow line on joining wall

Material can be cut with portable electric or hand saw. Second and succeeding courses of shingles are self-aligning

L cut is made in siding to go around windows and doorways, as shown here. Inside and outside corners are caulked to block weather elements

Siding is cut to match other courses when short drop is encountered, as shown under a window. Material comes in eight colors with acrylic finish

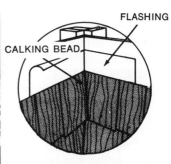

FLASHING

CALKING BEAD

WOVEN CORNER

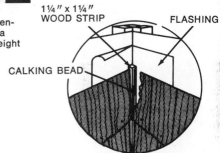

1¼″ x 1¼″ WOOD STRIP

FLASHING

CALKING BEAD

JOINTED CORNER

TREATMENT OF CANT STRIP, BACKER STRIPS, CHALK-LINE MARKINGS, CORNERS AND WINDOWS

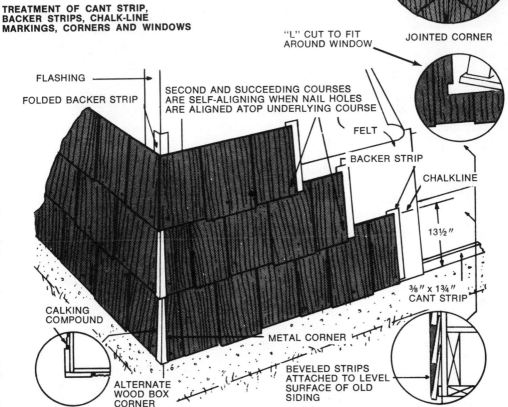

FLASHING

FOLDED BACKER STRIP

SECOND AND SUCCEEDING COURSES ARE SELF-ALIGNING WHEN NAIL HOLES ARE ALIGNED ATOP UNDERLYING COURSE

"L" CUT TO FIT AROUND WINDOW

FELT

BACKER STRIP

CHALKLINE

13½″

⅜″ x 1¾″ CANT STRIP

CALKING COMPOUND

METAL CORNER

ALTERNATE WOOD BOX CORNER

BEVELED STRIPS ATTACHED TO LEVEL SURFACE OF OLD SIDING

isn't necessary. Other siding includes simulated brick and fieldstone. It, too, is easy to install over sheathing or existing siding with furring strips.

Fiberglass panels are available in sheet form for both flat and corrugated siding jobs such as patio enclosures and windscreens. Many colors are available to match the decor of your home. Since the material is fiberglass, about the only maintenance problem is keeping it clean with a mild detergent and water from a garden hose.

A CONTRACTOR?

"Re-siding" has become a shady word because of the so-called suede-shoe contractors involved. Unless you are an especially skilled handyman, it is best to call in a contractor to re-side your home. However, it is understandable that you may be reluctant.

As in any other business, there are "good" guys and the "bad" guys in the re-siding business. The bad guys spoil it for everyone else.

If you contact a responsible siding company, you should have absolutely no problem with a re-siding job. These contractors, for the most part, are bonded. If you have any doubts, call the Better Business Bureau or Chamber of Commerce in your area. These organizations will run a free check for you so you can make your own decision whether to hire or not.

Beware, however, of siding contractors who:

1. Call from door-to-door and attempt to get you to sign up for a siding job before they leave.

2. Siding contractors who want to "make your home a model home in the neighborhood" at a reduced price, with construction starting the next morning at 6:30.

3. Contractors who "sell" you the job, arrive at your home early the next morning, put on three or four strips of siding, and leave for who knows how long. This is called "spiking" the job; according to law, they have you boxed in and you can't do anything about it.

Some states have a waiting-period agreement by law. The law states, generally, that the contract is not effective until three days after you sign. If your state has no such law, "enact" one for your personal use: *Wait a day or so after you make up your mind, before you sign anything.*

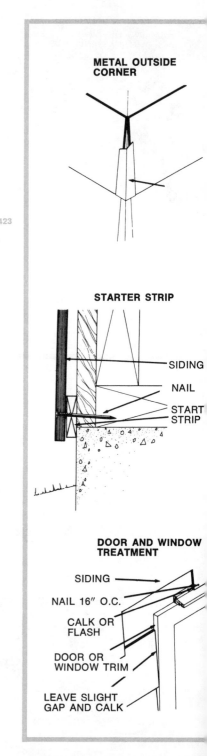

METAL OUTSIDE CORNER

STARTER STRIP

SIDING

NAIL

START STRIP

DOOR AND WINDOW TREATMENT

SIDING

NAIL 16″ O.C.

CALK OR FLASH

DOOR OR WINDOW TRIM

LEAVE SLIGHT GAP AND CALK

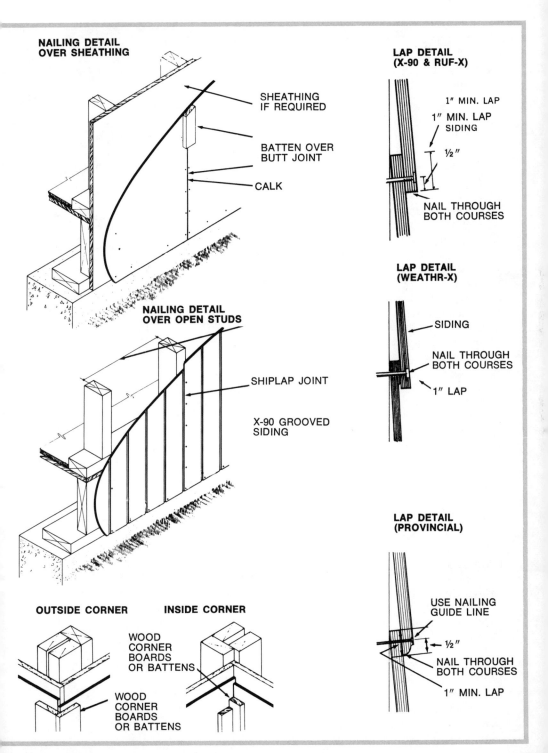

NAILING DETAIL OVER SHEATHING

SHEATHING IF REQUIRED

BATTEN OVER BUTT JOINT

CALK

NAILING DETAIL OVER OPEN STUDS

SHIPLAP JOINT

X-90 GROOVED SIDING

LAP DETAIL (X-90 & RUF-X)

1" MIN. LAP

1" MIN. LAP SIDING

½"

NAIL THROUGH BOTH COURSES

LAP DETAIL (WEATHR-X)

SIDING

NAIL THROUGH BOTH COURSES

1" LAP

LAP DETAIL (PROVINCIAL)

USE NAILING GUIDE LINE

½"

NAIL THROUGH BOTH COURSES

1" MIN. LAP

OUTSIDE CORNER   **INSIDE CORNER**

WOOD CORNER BOARDS OR BATTENS

WOOD CORNER BOARDS OR BATTENS

87

driveways/walks/ porches

THIS SECTION, basically, describes how to work with materials such as cement, brick, stone, sand, water, asphalt and the other components that make up driveways, walks and porches.

For small patchwork that involves maintenance, manufacturers produce premixed products to eliminate some of the heavy work: You can buy bags of premixed concrete and asphalt. Also many building-material outlets have prebagged sand and sell loose brick and block so you can buy small amounts for specific projects.

Working with concrete. If the patch is small, you can buy fast-drying latex, vinyl or epoxy-based cement that is easy to handle and extremely strong. *Latex cement* has two parts: cement and a latex liquid binder. You mix the two to a batter consistency. *Vinyl cement* is premixed; you merely add water. *Epoxy,* although costly, has three parts: dry cement, an emulsion, and a hardener. You mix the emulsion and hardener, and then stir in the cement to the right consistency.

If the patch is fairly large but still a patch, you should consider buying bags of premixed concrete. The sand (or gravel) and cement are in the bag; you simply add water and stir. If you have a lot of volume to fill, your best bet is to prepare the forms and buy concrete from a ready-mix company.

Crack repairs in concrete involve cleaning out the crack with a cold or brick chisel. Undercut the crack slightly, so it forms an inverted V-shape. This will help hold the new concrete. With a garden hose, clean the area, trowel in the new concrete, and smooth the surface. For this type repair, latex, vinyl and epoxy patch are all practical.

Broken concrete. Remove the old pieces, and undercut the edges of the break with a chisel. You probably will need a sledge hammer and crowbar for removal. Clean the area. If the patch requires formwork, use a piece of ¼-in. plywood or tempered hardboard for the form.

If the patch is quite a large one, you'll have to

With cold or brick chisel, remove broken debris back to sound material. Use this technique for all types of concrete repairs

Smooth patch with trowel; rectangular type works best for large areas, but you can use pointing trowel for small ones. Feather the edges into surrounding area and score joints with edging tool. If you don't have one, you can make-do with point of trowel

Latex-based concrete mixture does inexpensive patching job on small areas. Its sticking power hugs shallow breaks and chips without falling out. You can wipe in the patch with a putty knife or trowel

Form patch area, if necessary. A thin piece of plywood or hardboard makes excellent form. Hold it in place with stakes, bricks

Cut old concrete back with chisel to form an inverted V shape. This helps prevent the new patch from breaking away when it dries

Cover patch area with "neat" cement—cement right out of the bag. But tamp or impact fill first; sprinkle it with water

use 2x4s or 2x6s for forms; the stakes are nailed to the forms to hold them into position.

Asphalt driveways need a new coat of topping every several years—or when they start looking dull, rough-textured, and checkered with small pits and cracks. You can buy a coating and sealer for this. You also can buy premixed patching compound for any holes and large cracks in the surface.

If cracks are ½ in. or wider, force the patch into the cracks, filling them to the surrounding surface. Tamp the mix tight. Fill narrower cracks with driveway crack filler, but first clean the cracks with water, moisten the entire area, and sweep out any puddles. Fill the cracks to about ⅛ in. below the surrounding surface. The top coating brings the cracks to the surface level.

Asphalt driveway preparation tips. Remove all debris—mud, tar, etc.—with a trowel or flat spade. Then scrub the driveway with detergent and water to remove oily spots. Rinse thoroughly. Do not use an oil solvent for cleaning; it softens asphalt.

Pour ribbons of the coating and sealer, covering about 20–40 sq. ft. at a time. With a squeegee spread the ribbons in smooth, light strokes. The coating should fill the voids, but don't use too much. The first coat must be dry to the touch before you apply the second coat. You can drive your car on the surface in about 24 hours.

Brick and patio block are often laid on a sand base, and they tend to sink or tilt. You can raise them back to level by removing the bricks or block around the distressed area and spreading sand in the hole, then replacing the brick or block. If the brick or block are deeply sunken, you should tamp gravel in the hole first to form a base. Then use sand as a leveler.

Tamp sand under each unit as you lay it. After a brick or block is in position and fairly level, tap it with a hammer, using a wooden buffer to protect the block from chipping or breaking. When the repair has been made, sweep sand in the joints and sprinkle it with a garden hose. Then add more sand and repeat the washing until the joints are completely filled.

You can lay bricks and blocks on concrete. The slab should be 2 in. thick and poured over a 2-in. sand base. The bricks are laid in a thin mortar bed.

92

88
92

268
272
274

Vinyl cement is mixed with water and troweled into the shallow break. Wet the area first before you put in the patch, and feather the edges

Holes in asphalt driveways should be thoroughly cleaned out. Remove crumbling material with a brick or cold chisel

Pour in patching material; you can buy it in bags. Patch doesn't have to be heated, although it should be pliable for best workability

Tamp patch tight in hole. A square butt end of a 2x4 makes a good tamping tool. Make sure patch is level with surrounding area

Expansion joints go between sections of concrete to prevent breaking and cracking due to expansion. Different widths are available

YARDS OF CONCRETE IN SLABS						
AREA IN SQ. FT. (LENGTH × WIDTH)	THICKNESS OF SLAB IN INCHES					
	4"	5"	6"	8"	12"	
25	.31	.39	.47	.60	.95	CU. YD.
50	.62	.77	.93	1.2	1.9	CU. YD.
100	1.2	1.5	1.9	2.5	3.7	CU. YD.
200	2.5	3.1	3.7	4.9	7.4	CU. YD.
300	3.7	4.7	5.6	7.4	11.1	CU. YD.
400	4.9	6.2	7.4	9.8	14.8	CU. YD.
500	6.2	7.2	9.3	12.4	18.6	CU. YD.

How cracks are formed in asphalt toppings

Remove debris from asphalt driveway surfaces with trowel or flat shovel. Wash oily surface with water and a detergent.

PORCH FLOORS—especially those that are laid tight—are subject to rot through moisture. You can replace these areas fairly easily, if they are relatively small.

First, determine where the joists are located in relationship to the flooring. Then, at the four corners of the damaged area, drill holes so a keyhole saw may be inserted. The holes should be inside the joists, so you should make a couple of test borings to see if you're in alignment. Drill these holes, of course, within the damaged area.

Starting at the four points, saw out the damaged area. Make the cuts as square as you possibly can, since new wood will be butting against the ends of the old flooring. With the damaged area removed, nail cleats to the exposed joists. Use 2x3s for this, if possible. Predrill pilot holes for the nails to make the job go faster and easier.

Cut the new flooring to fit the patch. If it is tongue-and-groove lumber, you may have to plane off the tongues so the boards fit evenly. Nail in the new flooring and finish the job with a primer and a top coat of floor and deck enamel.

Deck boards are usually spaced about ½-inch apart for water drainage. Sometimes they rot or are damaged and need replacing. Here it is a simple job of prying up the old deck boards and nailing in new boards. Use aluminum nails to prevent rust streaks.

Wooden garden walks are subject to moisture damage. When it occurs, it's best simply to replace them with new lumber. Use specially treated wood for this, or redwood or cypress.

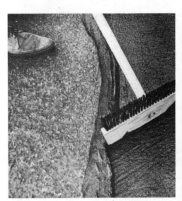

Pour asphalt coating/sealer in ribbons and use an applicator like this to spread it evenly. Use light and even strokes

If first coating/sealer doesn't fill all hairline cracks, give surface another coat. Wait until first coat is dry before applying second

94

95

Crumbling concrete in porch steps is caused by moisture. Clean patch with cold chisel, removing concrete back to sound material

Get more support for concrete patch by installing metal pins to hold it. Drill holes for pins with a masonry bit deep enough for them to hold

Stove or carriage bolt makes a good pin for this job. Insert it into the hole and tap it gently with a hammer to tighten

Trowel in concrete patch. One of the latex, vinyl or epoxy-cement mixes is best for this job. Fill cracks between treads and risers

PIER-TYPE PORCH COLUMNS, usually fabricated from brick or block, are subjected to dampness, causing the mortar in the joints to crumble. Inspect these columns every couple of years. Repairs take some effort, but they're not too difficult.

To repair the joints, you have to lift the porch. Use a jack for this, supporting it with wide, thick timbers at the bottom and along the top joists. Crank the jack up barely enough to get the weight off the pier so you can replace any broken brick or block, or tuckpoint the damaged mortar joints.

Wooden porch columns are subject to rot at the base from moisture. This takes the form of dry rot, usually, so you have to probe the base with a knife to make sure the wood is still solid. If not, there are several ways you can repair the damage, as illustrated on the opposite page. If the column is beyond any of these repair techniques, you'll have to replace it. Since a roof structure also is involved, it's best to have a professional replace it; the weight of the roof may be too much for support with equipment owned by a handyman.

At least once a year, inspect the joint between the wooden column and the base it sets on—wood, concrete, brick, etc. Generally, the caulking compound at this joint should be cleaned out and new caulking forced into the joint.

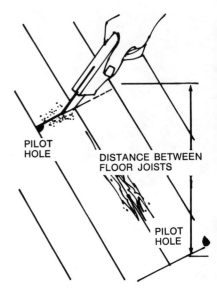

Drill four holes at corners of the damaged porch floor area—between supporting joists. Connect the holes with straight square lines. If you have a portable sabre saw, you can use it for this job

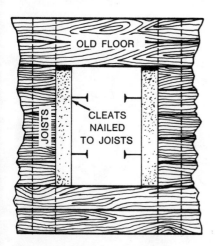

Use 2x3s for cleats to hold new flooring. Pre-drill pilot holes in the cleats to prevent splitting

New porch flooring is precut to slip into damaged area you removed. You may have to plane off tongue of flooring so it fits evenly

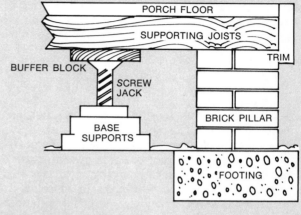

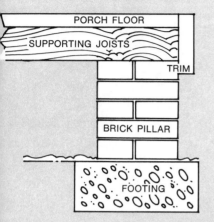

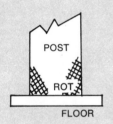

Porch column rot is at base (above) caused by moisture. To fix with cement, trim away unsound wood

Brick or block piers that hold up porches can be damaged by moisture. To repair, you have to jack up the porch slightly to replace the block units or tuckpoint the mortar joints. Use wide boards to even out the pressure on the ground, joists. Raise the porch evenly, slowly

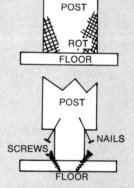

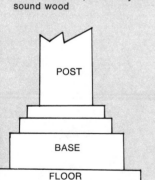

Another way: Trim off bottom of post and build new base. But support roof structure with jackpost or large timber while working

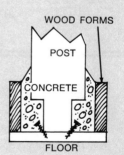

Concrete technique: Use nails and screws to hold in concrete; trim away rot; build forms around base, and fill forms with concrete

foundations

BASEMENT FOUNDATION problems fall into three basic classifications: dampness, periodic leaks, and active leaks. Do not overlook the possibility of a damaged roof-drainage system causing any of these problems. Check it first. 34

Dampness is the easiest problem to solve. It generally involves providing proper ventilation; covering sweating pipes with felt tape; and coating the basement or foundation walls with a quality concrete-based or alkyd-latex-based paint, manufactured specifically to deter dampness in basements and crawl spaces. 203 466

Note: Cement-based paints *usually* can't be applied over a wall that has been painted with a gloss paint. If the wall has been painted, first read the cement paint manufacturer's instructions to see if you can apply cement paint to the wall. If not, you will have to have the wall sandblasted before the coating can be applied. Sandblasting is a job for a professional. It can be expensive, so you may want to consider other alternatives discussed below. 12 151

If your basement leaks periodically, the reason 156

Window-well drains are connected to drainage system around foundation. If local codes permit, pipe can be plastic

Window-well drain from top looks like this. Grade fill comes to top of pipe; earth is covered with gravel to deter erosion

Concrete block wall rests on footing placed in trench below frost line. Waterproofing membrane goes over outside wall

Waterproofing membrane can be asphalt, plastic over asphalt, glass fiber. Covering must be continuous—no breaks

Joists are notched for sill bolts. Even if foundation wall is just for crawl space, it should be waterproofed

Support basement columns with footings before basement floor is placed. This helps distribute structural weight above

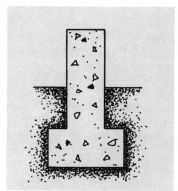

T foundation has trench footing. Concrete wall or concrete blocks are placed on it. Bottom width is usually 12 in.; top, 6 in.

probably is a high water table around your home. When rains are heavy or a lot of snow melts, the water level rises in the ground, causing hydrostatic pressure against the foundation. Any resulting leaks usually occur along the base of the foundation where the floor and wall meet. To seal a leak, first try hydraulic cement in this crack.

The technique is simple: Undercut the crack with a cold chisel and clean it. Carefully study the crack to see where the water seepage is the greatest. With hydraulic cement, work from the ends of the crack toward the point where the water pressure is the greatest. Press the cement into the crack with your fingers. Keep it wet for about 15 minutes, and then smooth the joint with a trowel. Don't mix too much cement at one time, since it sets rapidly. Also, mix it to a puttylike consistency —or according to manufacturer's recommendations.

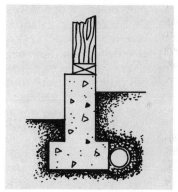

T footing with sill and studs. Drain tile can be clay, or concrete with gravel around it for good drainage

If the foundation or basement wall is actually gushing water, you can try the hydraulic compound treatment. Make a plug of the compound and stick it into the hole where the water pressure seems to be the greatest. Smooth the joint with a trowel after 15 minutes or so.

Hydraulic compound, however, may not work. The reasons why include these: There is structural damage to the foundation wall; the waterproofing on the exterior of the wall below grade is faulty; there is excess pressure from the earth against the wall from the outside.

You can repair all three of these troubles. First, dig a wide ditch or trench around the foundation.

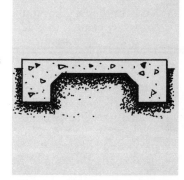

Slab foundation is placed directly on ground. Footings are around edges and at points where extra support is necessary

Clean the foundation thoroughly, installing drainage tile around the base, if there is none. Apply an asphaltic waterproofing membrane to the wall surface. Carefully replace the dirt and bring it back to grade level. This, obviously, is a lot of work, which you may prefer to turn over to a professional with digging equipment. If you have constant problems with foundation cracks, leakage, or bulging walls, you should consult a professional. The problems are usually structural.

NEW FOUNDATIONS

If you're adding a room to your home—or building a new home—the structure will have to be built on a foundation *approved by local codes*. The design of the foundation will depend on the structure you are building. You will find several foundation designs on these pages. They are typical.

96
97
99
251
256
257

For the average handyman, we recommend pouring a concrete foundation instead of laying concrete block. Unless you have had experience in setting block, you should not attempt to do so. That is why poured concrete is easier—although it can be more expensive.

A footing is poured in solid ground deep enough to reach below the frost line, and it distributes the weight of the structure. Reinforcing steel is usually placed in the footing to prevent the concrete from cracking and breaking.

To tie into an existing foundation for remodeling, use #5 reinforcing rod between the new foundation and the existing one. Drill holes for the rods in the existing foundation and place the rods in epoxy cement to hold them solid.

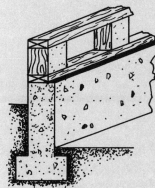

T footing with cripples raises the height of floor. Foundation does not have to be raised to match. Use 4 x 4s for the cripples

If the new addition will include a basement, you will have to open a doorway in the new and existing foundation wall. Support this with steel headers and tie both walls together with rod or special ties designed for this. Because of codes, additions usually require a building permit which, in turn, requires an architect's or engineer's drawing of the proposed construction. Thus, details of foundation tie-ins and the type of foundation will be required if you plan to do the work yourself.

Cripples, usually 4 x 4s spaced at very close intervals, are used to raise the floor level if a higher foundation wall is not used.

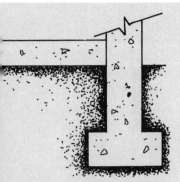

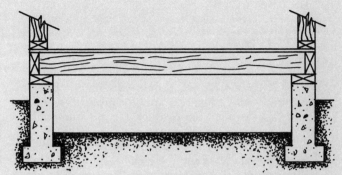

On-grade slab with T footing. Base of footing is usually 12 in., with 6-in. height. Basement? Excavate before you place the footings

Above grade, foundation plan takes this design with T footings. Plate, sills, joists or girders rest on top of foundation wall

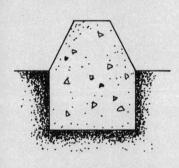

Pier foundation usually measures 12 in. at base and 16 in. high. Half of height is below grade. Joists rest on sills

Below-grade slab with T footings. Slab foundations must be waterproofed with membrane between slab and ground

Special forms are used for foundation walls. They are tied together with steel rods, left in place when forms are stripped

Sill bolts are positioned in foundation after top has been troweled. This wall is for crawl-space construction

Basement wall looks like this after forms are stripped. It sets on T footings. Metal pieces are ties for brick facing

painting

SWINGING A BRUSH, running a roller, or pulling a spray gun trigger to apply a protective and bright new finish to the exterior of your home all require special techniques. Learn them and you get the job done easier, faster, better, cheaper. This section shows you those techniques.

Preparation of the surface is the single most important effort you can make in painting or repainting your house. The more time you spend making sure the surface is properly prepared, the better the final result will be.

Next in importance to preparation is the quality of paint you use. You don't save money with

104

Get ready to paint by assembling the necessary preparation tools: scrapers, wire brushes, calking.

How much paint do you need? After preparation you can better tell the "soak-in" factor.

Application techniques can be with brush, roller, or spray—frequently a combination of all three.

cheap paint; the extra cost for good paint is little, and it saves you hours of work and gives extra years of protection. Don't ever hesitate to spend additional money for quality paint.

Paint has three basic ingredients: the *pigment* gives it color and body; the *vehicle,* such as oil, suspends the pigment; and the *thinner* gives both the pigment and the vehicle the right consistency for application. Exterior paints are basically of two types: one is for the *structure* of your home; the other is for *trim* and *metal*.

188

BASIC EXTERIOR PAINTS FOR YOUR HOME

Type of Paint	Type of Finish	Some Advantages	Some Disadvantages
Latex	Flat	Moisture resistant; easy to apply with brush or roller; easy tool clean-up; quick drying; can use it most times during the day.	Don't use over oil-based painted surface unless primer is used first; has a tendency to permit chalking surface beneath to go into pores of the wood.
Standard House Paint (titanium)	Glossy	Has good color retention; durable; good hiding power; remains clean uniformly for life of finish (3/6 years).	Harder to apply than latex; tool clean-up difficult; can't use over moist surfaces; longer drying time.
White Lead Paint	Glossy	Very durable; can be tinted easily; has good color retention qualities.	Lower hiding power; collects dirt and retains it; discolors from airborne chemicals; slow drying; can't use over moisture.
Cedar Shake Paint	Flat	Will stop bleeding action of cedar, redwood, other natural colored woods. Durable; some fading.	Use on natural wood only. It will produce very dull finish on other materials; harder than latex to clean brushes and drippings.
Trim Paint	Very glossy	Use for trim only.	
Metal Paint	Varies from flat to glossy	Use for metal only; primer or prime coat works best on rust surfaces; then apply top coating.	Do not use on wood.

HOW MUCH PAINT do you need? It boils down to how dry the surface is; how many coats you will apply; and, of course, how big your home is.

If the siding on your home has a heavily textured surface such as striated shingles, you'll need about 20 percent more paint than for smooth siding. Narrow lap siding utilizes about 10 percent more paint than wide lap siding, while masonry surfaces such as concrete block can require about 50 percent more paint. Here is a good rule of thumb: figure a gallon of paint for about every 500 square feet of normal surface. If you use trim paint, figure one gallon of trim for every five gallons of "structure" paint. (See chart, next page.)

How often you should paint your home depends on the the surface. As a general rule, your home needs a paint job about every five years when quality materials are used. Don't paint it too often since the build-up of paint film will crack and peel from thickness. The same holds true for not painting often enough; the paint becomes thin and starts to peel and flake.

Here's the quick way to estimate how much paint you'll need

Use house paint and stain for most wooden surfaces; metal paint for gutters, porch railings. Masonry? Check your dealer for paint for it; depends on whether it's block, brick, stucco or reinforced concrete.

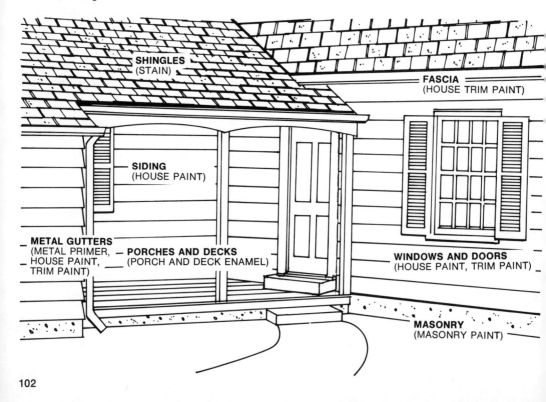

SHINGLES
(STAIN)

FASCIA
(HOUSE TRIM PAINT)

SIDING
(HOUSE PAINT)

METAL GUTTERS
(METAL PRIMER,
HOUSE PAINT,
TRIM PAINT)

PORCHES AND DECKS
(PORCH AND DECK ENAMEL)

WINDOWS AND DOORS
(HOUSE PAINT, TRIM PAINT)

MASONRY
(MASONRY PAINT)

ESTIMATING CHART FOR EXTERIOR PAINTING

1. FIND PERIMETER OF HOUSE AT TOP OF TABLE
2. MOVE DOWN COLUMN TO FIGURE OPPOSITE HEIGHT OF HOUSE — THAT'S THE NUMBER OF GALLONS YOU'LL NEED FOR ONE COAT

	100′	125′	150′	175′	200′	225′	250′	275′	300′	325′
24′	5½	6½	7½	8½	10	11½	12½	14	15½	17
22′	5	6	7	8	9	10½	12	13	14½	16
20′	4½	5½	6½	7½	8½	9½	11	12	13½	15
18′	4	5	6	6½	7½	9	10	11	12½	13½
16′	3½	4	4½	5½	6	7	8	9	10	11
14′	3½	4½	5	6	7	8	9	10	11	12
12′	3	3½	4	5	5½	6½	7	8	9	10
10′	2½	3	3½	4	5	5½	6½	7	8	9

PREPARATION

GETTING YOUR HOME READY to paint can be a dreary job—especially if there is a lot of scraping to do. However, it is the most important part of the painting process.

Wash your home first with clean water and, if necessary, a very mild detergent. A good tool for this is a long-handled brush often used for washing cars. Start at the bottom of the wall section and work up, rather than starting at the top and working down. This prevents streaking. Make sure the detergent is thoroughly rinsed off with clean water. Do not paint your home until it is thoroughly dry.

Assuming your home does need a new coat of paint, here are checkpoints to follow as you prepare the surface:

Chalking paint is a normal condition. It helps keep the house looking clean. But if it has occurred very soon after you applied the last coat of paint, you probably applied the paint too thin. Or wet weather affected the paint before it had an opportunity to dry properly. To clean this, scrub the surface with water and a mild detergent. Or use a stiff "dusting" brush to remove the chalk.

Checking paint is not serious, if it has not gotten to the flaking point. It is generally the result of applying the top coat of paint over a still wet undercoater. If the paint is flaking, scrape off all flakes that will come off and rub the surface with No. 1 sandpaper over a sanding block.

Alligatoring paint can start as small checks. It is caused by using incompatible paints (flat over enamel) or too much oil as a thinner. Too, it can be due to the build-up of paint on the surface. Before you repaint, the alligatored paint has to be removed with a sharp pull scraper or a heat-removing device, or the new coat will fail in a short period of time. This is not the paint's fault.

Blistering paint is another painting problem. It is simply caused by moisture pushing out in back of the paint film. To fix this, you have to find the source of the moisture. It can be a leak in the wall structure or gutters above; the lack of a vapor barrier in the wall's insulation; or paint applied over "green" wood or damp wood. After finding the source of the moisture and curing it, the blisters must be removed as described above.

Mildew manifests itself as patchy and darkened

Remove hardware; move potted plants, any decorations before you get ready to paint. Proper preparation will save you hours of work later

Remove outdoor lights, letter boxes, escutcheon plates. Cover lights you can't remove with plastic film held with masking tape or light twine

How to prepare the surface; it can make a tremendous difference

Fasten metal corners with galvanized or aluminum nails. If the
metal corners are badly rusted
or damaged, it is best to
replace them

Renail siding that is loose. Check
carefully at joints and corners.
New "threaded" rust-resistant
nails deter "pops" and rust
streaks later on

Screens and storm windows
should be removed; this is easier
than trying to remove paint splatters from them. Always mark
them for identification

Wash your home with clean water.
Use a long-handled car brush
to remove mud, grass, insect
webs. Let siding dry thoroughly
before you paint it

spots. It often is mistaken for "bleeding" or staining. To identify it, apply a tiny amount of household bleach to the wall. If the problem is mildew, the darkened patch will vanish. If it doesn't, the spot may be dirt or grease. You can buy a special liquid to get rid of mildew at paint stores. Also, when you repaint the mildewed area, buy a finish that contains mildewcide to discourage future mildew problems.

Running paint, or sagging paint as the pros call it, appears like a "curtain" on the surface. This is caused by applying paint over a glossy surface without first dulling the finish with sandpaper or steel wool. It sometimes is caused by applying too much paint to the surface, causing it to sag or run. Always brush out the finish, using long, straight strokes. To remedy sags before repainting, you will have to either sandpaper down the sagging area, or remove it with any number of paint-removing devices on the market. Sandpaper usually does a good job, cutting away enough old finish so the new paint hides the problem.

Non-drying paint, paint that remains "tacky" to the touch, is caused by too much or too thick paint; not enough drying agents in it; painting over an undercoater that hasn't hardened properly; or painting over a dirty surface such as grease.

Before you repaint this, you will have to remove the old paint. Many times, you can seal the surface with a coat of shellac or aluminum primer. There are special products available at paint stores for the problem of tacky paint.

Wrinkling paint is caused by the top film drying first. This leaves soft paint under the film. You can prevent this by avoiding the application of too much paint, and by making sure you apply new paint only to properly prepared surfaces.

Before repainting, try sanding the wrinkles out. If the ridges are really deep, the only other solution is removing the old paint film completely.

As a general rule, most paint-peeling problems stem from moisture. If the paint on the house was a quality product to start with, the chances are good that the paint isn't at fault. Other problems, such as running paint, wrinkling paint, and so on, are application problems, and, again, the paint can't be blamed for this.

Calk broken joints in siding, forcing the compound into the cracks until they are full. Also, fill any depressions and nail holes. Smooth the calking compound to match surface

A wide scraper is the best tool for removing loose paint to the under-coater or bare wood. Badly scaled finish can be removed with heat devices or often with just sandpaper

Heating device "melts" problem paint areas so they can be scraped away to bare wood with a scraper. Other removal equipment includes torches and liquid removers for small areas

Loose paint under lap siding can be scraped and wire-brushed away. Make sure all loose material is removed by going back over the area a second time just before you start painting

Blistering and peeling paint can go undetected, since it can pop away from the surface of the siding or trim, yet remain intact. To find it, you have to dig and probe with a scraper and wire brush.

Siding and casing joints around windows and doors, and points where dissimilar materials (brick and wood) meet, can hide loosened paint. The old finish should be scraped and wire-brushed away and a bead of calking compound should be forced into the joints.

Another spot to check is drip caps at the top of doors and windows. Make sure the cap hasn't rotted and the flashing is properly installed. The flashing should extend beyond the bottom of the drip cap; the ends also should be covered.

Other probe points include joints at the bottom of door and window casings, window sash, the wood's contact with concrete window sills, siding joints, the line where the siding meets the ground, joints between the roof and wall structure, porch columns, and points where gutters meet wooden trim pieces.

Special surfaces such as aluminum, cedar shakes and asbestos-cement shingles offer no real painting problems, although there are some rules to follow.

Aluminum doesn't need finish to protect it from the elements. It will take on a dull, grey appearance through natural oxidation, but it won't stain surfaces adjacent to it as copper will. You can paint aluminum for decorative purposes. First, wipe it down with a phosphoric acid mixture. Then prime it with zinc chromate primer and add the finish coat of your choice.

Asbestos-cement shingles—many of them now prefinished—actually don't require paint for protective purposes. However, you can "decorate" them with latex, special solvent-thinned paints, or oil-based masonry paints.

Wooden shingles and shakes are best finished with quality stains formulated with a penetrating type oil. Whether semi-transparent or solid color, the stain usually provides a flat—not glossy—finish which is generally preferred on this surface.

If you want a natural silvery grey appearance (like you see on sea coasts where the salt air blows freely) there are a number of weathering and

With sandpaper block, feather edges of small spots where paint has peeled. Then prime bare wood. Sandpaper often solves peeling problems fast

Wire-brush metal corners, even if paint film is tight. This provides a better sticking surface for new paint, and pops any peeling film

Attached metal surfaces, such as railings, should be cleaned with a wire brush or emery cloth. Spot-prime the rust

Calk joints between dissimilar
materials such as wood and brick
or concrete. A putty knife and
wire brush cleans out the joints
for new calk

Calk joints between wood and
concrete casings and sills—
especially where the joints fit
tightly. This helps discourage
decay, paint failure

bleaching compounds available which will speed
the natural and weathering process. You also can
use varnish or lacquer to preserve the natural color
and grain of the shingles and shakes, but you have
to follow a rigid maintenance finishing schedule,
since cracks in the film may turn the exposed wood
dark due to mildew penetration.

Paint also may be used, but pick an exterior
latex finish and make sure you don't have a moisture problem that will quickly blister and pop the
finish.

Copper won't rust, but it will leave stains on
the surfaces next to it. And, often, these stains
are next to impossible to remove. If you want to
paint it, first clean the metal with one pound of
copper sulphate to one gallon of water. Rinse the
surface thoroughly, making sure all of the mixture

is off. Then paint the metal with outside trim paint. If you want to maintain the copper appearance, clean it, according to the above instructions, polish it with a medium grade steel wool, and then apply exterior or spar varnish. You will have to maintain a rigid maintenance schedule.

Fir plywood can be stained or painted, but first use a prime coat of flat oil, alkyd paint, enamel undercoater, or a penetrating resin. Do not use a water-thinned paint. It will raise the grain. If you want to use latex-based paint, first use a clear resin sealer or flat white oil paint as a primer.

Galvanized metal, such as gutters, should be painted first with a metallic zinc paint for a primer. The finish coat can be most anything. Or you can let the metal weather for about six weeks. This removes the "slick" film on the metal applied during its manufacture.

Iron and steel surfaces, such as porch railings, need a primer of red lead or zinc chromate. Then finish coats of oil or alkyd base paints may be used. Always remove any rust spots before priming.

Masonry surfaces all have an alkali substance when the surface is new or becomes damp. Therefore, you need special paints for masonry. Some include Portland-cement paints and silicone finishes. Here is where your paint dealer and the manufacturer's label on the container can help you. Tell your dealer the type of masonry you are painting.

Tempered hardboard is used for many exterior surfaces, and much of it comes pre-primed—especially siding. If the factory-applied coat is damaged, you'll have to spot prime it. If you don't paint the surface for about 60 days, you also should pre-prime it again. Generally, just a good quality exterior house paint will provide the best service; use a primer recommended for this top finish.

If hardboard panels are installed on horizontal surfaces (such as roofs or decks) where water can stand in pockets around the edges of the sheets, a good grade of floor and deck enamel should be applied as the top coat. But use a primer, and make sure all joints are calked and edges are primed and painted.

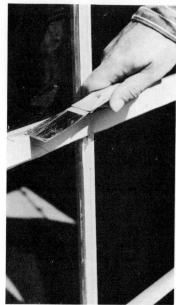

Check glazing in windows. Remove any loosened section with a putty knife. If the glazing is tight, you don't have to replace it

Prime the mullion, running paint onto the glass where the glazing will go—about 1/2-inch. Use a "chiseled" edge sash tool for this job; it helps you follow the glazing lines

Screen frames and screens may
need refinishing. A "screen
painter" pad brush does an even
job on the wire; use regular
brush for frames

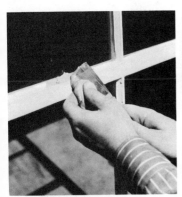

"Wipe" new glazing into the
mullion, after the primer has
dried. Press it in tightly so the
patch will be "full."

Smooth glazing with the flat of
the putty knife, using adjoining
glazing as a guide for height and
angle

Spot prime new glazing after it
has set for several days. Run the
primer onto the glass about 1/8-
inch for a weather-resistant seal

111

FOR EXTERIOR PAINTING, you'll need a variety of equipment—most of it fairly inexpensive and re-useable for future painting projects. Much of it can be used for interior painting, too. The key to buying painting equipment is to purchase quality items. This, of course, holds true for any tools. Cheap stuff results in a cheap-looking job. Too, it actually makes your work much harder, since you try to correct the errors the tool is making.

Your equipment checklist might include a strong extension ladder, step ladder, several metal or cardboard containers for mixing paint, wooden or metal paddles for stirring paint, and dropcloths. Dropcloths are made in canvas, plastic, and paper, and they can save you countless hours in clean-up, if you will take a few minutes' time to use them. They mold and hold better than newspapers to walks, driveways, exterior hardware (lights, railings, locks and latches) and other cover-up places such as bushes and flowers. It pays to buy good dropcloths and to use them properly.

You'll need several grades of sandpaper, a sanding block, emery paper for metal, steel wool, lots of calking cartridges, a calking gun shell, a dusting brush (a cheap, short-bristled 4-inch paintbrush makes a good duster), an *expensive* scraper and putty knife (don't skimp here) and a wire brush. Also handy to have is a solvent you can use to clean paint splatters from your skin.

Don't disregard safety before, during, and after your exterior painting project.

For example, always wear gloves when you work with liquid paint removers and some heat-type devices. When you're through using rags for wiping up drips and drops with solvent-based paints, either get rid of them or store them in a tightly-sealed metal container. Rags with turpentine on them can start fires through combustion—especially during hot summer months. Many materials you probably will work with are very combustible, so be careful with lighted cigarettes, blowtorches and heat devices that remove paint.

Also be careful around electric power supply lines that enter your home. Don't run into them with extension ladders—especially aluminum ones. Don't touch the lines with paintbrushes.

124
to
129

396

347
351

Before you start to paint, cover shrubs and flowers carefully. Over flowerbeds, use wooden stakes to hold dropcloths off plants—make a tent. Plastic dropcloths are light-weight, so they won't damage the foliage on most bushes and shrubs

Here's a checklist for the painting equipment you'll need

A shield of thin cardboard protects surfaces you don't want to paint such as brick next to staircasings. You don't have to tape it in place; simply move it along as the paintwork progresses

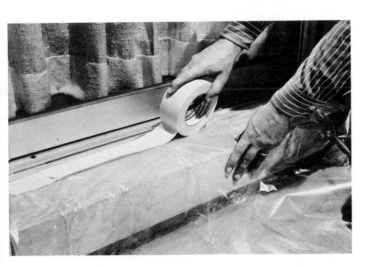

Cover concrete—steps, sills, walks. Paint splatters on concrete are extremely difficult to remove since concrete is porous, and drips and drops soak in. Plastic dropcloths are somewhat slippery on concrete and wooden surfaces; hold them in place with tack strips of masking tape. Wide strips work best

113

How to find quality paint brushes, rollers and other equipment

"Box" paint, after stirring up pigment, by pouring it from can-to-can. Always stir premixed paint before you use it—even if it has just been mixed at the paint store

 APPLICATION TECHNIQUES

CHEAP PAINTBRUSHES are definitely a no-no, if you want a professional-looking paint job. Cheap brushes become like wet floor mops or whiskbrooms when used for any length of time. So do cheap paint rollers and covers. Buy good application equipment, care for it properly, and it will last for years.

You can spot a good paintbrush by the bristles. They should not be coarse or fanned out at the end and they should be elastic—springy. If you are shopping for a hog-bristle brush, look for the number of split-ends at the tips of the bristles. These are called "flags." The more flags, the better the brush. Synthetic bristle brushes are also good tools, but you must buy quality. Look for the same qualifications as pure bristle brushes—without flags—with elastic qualities and trimmed ends.

Brushes and rollers should "fit" the job you will be doing. For large flat surfaces and most siding, buy a 4- to 6-inch brush. Trim and window glazing needs a 1- to 3-inch sash brush with a "chiseled" or angled edge. For trellises and sash frames, a sash brush works well, as does an oval one.

Roller covers are made for the type of finish you'll be using. Roller "shapes" are made for corners, and narrow and wide surfaces. Like brushes, pick the type that "fits" the job. Roller

"Strain" lumps from paint through a piece of screening. This usually isn't necessary on newly-opened buckets of paint, however

Fill the paint bucket about 1/3 full and dip the brush about 1/3 bristle length into the paint. Then gently "slap" the side of the brush on the side of the bucket. This removes excess paint and helps prevent it from running down the handle and your arm. If you do get paint on the handle, wipe it off immediately and continue to do so

Paint mixer locked in the chuck of your electric drill does a fast job, and mixes the paint into a smooth, consistent liquid ready for use

pans should be very sturdy for exterior work, since they will be hooked onto a ladder rung much of the time.

The application of paint by brush is a "swinging" or "slopping" proposition. The words describe results. You can paint like a pro, and the job will look pro, by following a few simple techniques shown here.

Always work from the top down, and work across the surface. Don't start at the top, brush across arm's length, and move down to the next arm's length and height. Work from left to right—*completely* across. The purpose of this is to avoid "lap" marks. These are caused by the paint drying before the next series of tie-in laps are completed. The result is that you get two coats of paint at the lap points.

Some paints boast that they are "lap" free: start and stop anytime, anyplace. This sometimes is true, but don't count on it.

Start right at the start. Dip the brush about 1/3 the length of the bristles in the bucket. "Slap" the sides of the brush against the bucket to remove excess paint. As work progresses, the bristles will fill up; this can't be avoided. However, at this point, wipe out the brush on the rim of the bucket and continue dipping the bristles 1/3 length. With a soft cloth, constantly wipe running paint off the handle of the brush.

Always attempt to follow the grain of the wood, or the texture, with the brush. This is especially true on new wood; it may be more difficult on painted surfaces. On lap siding, "tip" the brush into the corner areas, and move the brush downward to smooth out the paint. Then paint the underside of the lap with the tip end of the brush. Do several of these laps at one time. Complete the series by painting the flat surface. Work the paintbrush back and forth in long, even strokes. When the surface is properly covered, smooth out the brush marks with one long, flowing movement, using just the tips of the bristles. Work back from the unpainted surface to the newly painted surface. Never lay the brush down on wet paint and drag it through to the dry or unpainted surface. This will leave an ugly brush "track" when the material dries and weathers in a few months.

Paint from left to right. Point tip of brush into corners, making sure tiny cracks of joints are sealed tightly with the paint film

Bucket holder, when you're painting from a tall ladder, can be fabricated by bolting a 9-inch metal strap to an empty can and bending the end to form a hook. Bucket rests on rung below for adequate support

On raised panel doors, paint panels first, then the crossmembers. Always smooth the paint out in the same direction with the tip end of the bristles. Use a sweeping, fluid stroke; don't stop and start

Paint underneath lap siding, sealing joints. Do 3 to 4 laps at once, going the length of the entire span, or stop painting at a vertical joint

On bottom boards, tip the brush down to prevent bristles from smearing the paint onto foundations and walkways. Also, point brush away on verticals

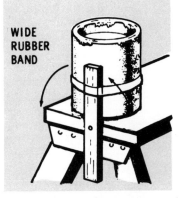

WIDE RUBBER BAND

On stepladders, use this simple swing-up holder to secure the paint container. Rubber band keeps the paint can from skidding off

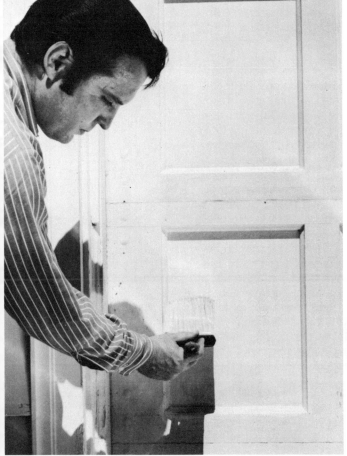

Rusty nail heads and small bare spots can be spot-primed with the tip of a finger, if you are applying one coat. This often works better than a brush

By brushing the surface this way, the brush breaks the surface tension of the paint. The paint then has a tendency to break the moisture film and the air in the surface cells of the material, which actually forces the paint into the surface. Wrinkling, running or sagging paint is eliminated through this proper brushing technique.

Paint with the edge of the brush on narrow edges; use the flat of the brush on wider surfaces. If you reverse this procedure, the bristles will soon bunch together in clumps, spraddle out at the ends, and become as difficult to use as an old, water-logged mop.

When you're working with enamel, the technique is almost the same as with other paints, except you use shorter brush strokes, and you brush the paint out thinner and more evenly. The big reason for this is that enamel (and varnish and lacquer) has a tendency to sag, even though it may first appear that it has been brushed out evenly. Go back over enamel and varnish jobs about 15 minutes after you have completed them to make sure there are no sags. If there are, brush them out by lightly stroking the tip of the bristles across the work. Have the brush in motion before you touch it to the painted surface. In short, sweep it lightly across the work. This will prevent brush tracks.

When using a roller, first wash the cover in warm water and mild detergent, then rinse it carefully. This removes lint. Make sure it is absolutely dry before putting it into oil-based paints. If you are using a water-based paint, the roller should be damp before you start the job.

You fill the cover from the roller pan by rolling it into the paint until it is uniformly covered. Roll it back and forth a couple of times to remove excess paint. Don't overfill the roller pan with paint. If you do, you will get too much paint on the cover; then running and dripping occurs.

Lift the roller from the pan onto the surface, rolling it very lightly back-and-forth. This distributes the paint evenly on the surface. On large panel surfaces, start the stroke upward and every new stroke away from the already painted surface. Roll toward the completed work—just like the brush technique.

Overnight roller and brush storage is possible with plastic wrap to block air passage. If stored for any length of time, wash out paint

Stray bristles are easy to remove by snapping them off with a putty knife or scraper. Press downward and lift against ferrule

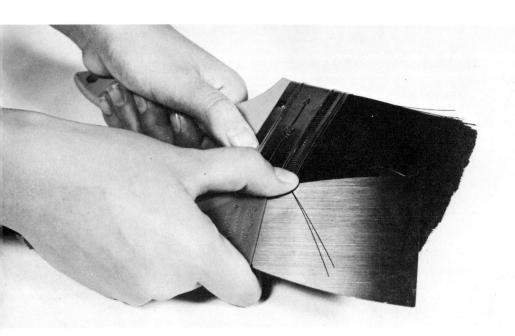

Overnight brush storage also is easy with aluminum foil. It's best not to leave excess paint in the brush since it tends to harden. However, you don't have to clean the brush or roller thoroughly

Brush storage for oil-based paints: Hang the brush in a can of thinner using a wire through a small hole drilled in the handle. Use a deep container so the bristles won't touch the bottom and splay out

The finish you get with a roller is a "stippled" effect.

When you paint with a roller, you have to use a measured amount of thinner. Paint right out of the container tends to wrinkle and crack. The solvent you use should, of course, match the type of paint you are using. Water-based paints tend to settle quickly in the roller pan, so you have to mix the paint frequently. Latex-based paints dry quickly, sometimes leaving little hard lumps on the roller and in the roller pan. The roller picks up these lumps and distributes them on the surface you're painting. You can solve this problem by thinning the paint slightly.

When should you paint—what time of year? The best time, usually, is in the late summer or early fall, since wood surfaces are generally dry. Heat is not a problem, drying the paint too quickly and making it difficult for you to spread, and insects are fewer at this time of year. A good rule of thumb is not to paint in extremely hot weather, when it's too cold, or when dampness will affect oil-based paints. Beat the sun around the house by starting on the west side in mid-morning, the south side in the early afternoon, and the north and east side in the afternoon.

A word about color: It can play an important role. Light colors reflect light, making surfaces appear larger, and making surrounding structures seem farther away. Dark colors absorb light; make surfaces appear smaller. Bright colors seem larger in area than they really are; they are used most often to draw attention away from an unattractive feature of your home. Warm colors come up to meet you; cool colors make surfaces retreat.

Angle shot with a spray gun coats lap siding properly; keep the nozzle about 8 inches away from the surface. Use smooth, even strokes

SPRAY GUN APPLICATION

About the toughest part of spray painting is cleaning the overspray off your windows, the next-door neighbor's windows, closely parked cars, and, sometimes, cars that have driven past your home while you were using the spray gun.

The ultimate words of caution are: *Don't spray in the wind and always keep the spray against a surface.* Don't shoot it around corners or out into

Pressurized spray can or "bomb" has a round spray pattern. It's tops for small paint jobs—such as inside gutters, railings, garbage cans, etc., but becomes too expensive for large structural areas. When using a "bomb," keep the can level since spray piles up at an angle. Overlap the first stroke by about a third

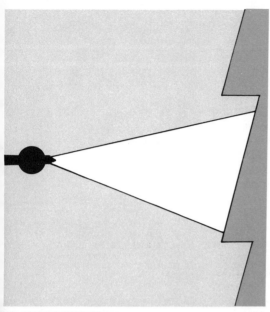

Finish spray stroke on siding
with a straight, even movement,
too. Paint will be thin on the
outer spray edges and thick in
center of pattern

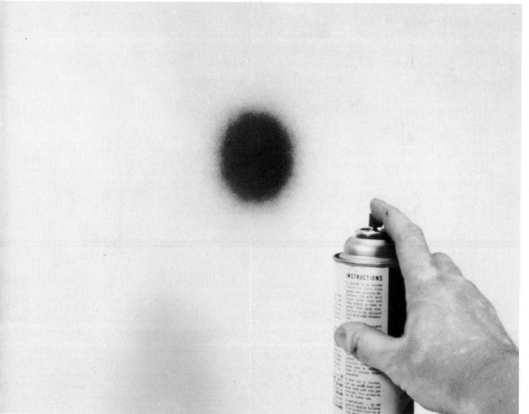

space. On your home, tightly cover anything you don't want painted—window glass, concrete, brick, metal, anything else.

SPRAY GUNS ARE IDEAL for textured surfaces and small, intricate surfaces such as lattice and picket fences. Coverage is fast and complete.

There are two main parts to a spray rig: the *compressor* and the *gun*. Simply, the compressor compresses air—much as a bike pump does—and the air goes through a hose to the spray gun. At this point, you pull the trigger and the air blows the paint from the gun in a fine mist onto the surface you're painting. Of course, compressors and spray guns come in different sizes, shapes and types for different jobs. The ones you'll be interested in for exterior work are those with a paint cup or a paint container that is separate from the spray gun. The containers generally hold about three gallons of paint so you don't have to refill them often; the cups hold a quart of paint.

There are several types of spray guns: external and internal mixing, pressure, gravity, and suction-feed types, and bleeder and non-bleeder types. Since this equipment is specialized, let a dealer help you pick the type that will suit your particular needs best—especially if you are considering buying it.

There are three "tricks of the trade" to follow when spraying paint outside:

- Cover anything you don't want painted.
- Get the right mixture of paint to be sprayed.
- Practice using the gun before you start.

After the usual surface preparation for paint, and application of the material with a spray gun, you *may* notice that little cracks in the wood are not properly covered. At this point, you should brush over the sprayed paint with a paintbrush. In effect, you'll rub in the paint. Since the surface is already coated and wet, you'll find the brush work an easy job. Just avoid brush marks.

And, one more time: Don't use a spray gun on a windy day.

Always spray against a surface. Don't blow the paint out over gutters, around corners, or through fences or lattice. Back the latter two up with sheets of cardboard to block the overspray.

The secret of spraying paint is really to deter-

Move spray bomb in a circular motion to mix the paint inside. As you do this, you will hear a tiny metal mixing ball rattling against the can

113
102
104

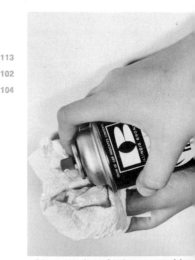

After spraying, tip the can upside down and push the button. This clears the paint passage. Then wipe the spray nozzle

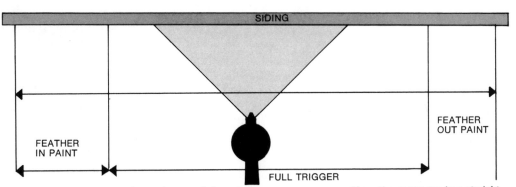

Move the spray gun in a straight line. Air projects first, then paint, when you pull the trigger on some models. Feather into laps

mine the proper paint mixture. Most failures start here.

Oil-based paint should be used in a pressure-fed gun only. Generally, oil paints are not thinned unless specified by the manufacturer. Some paints for exterior use are made for spraying; they are almost free from misting.

Rubber-based paints should be pressure-fed with an external-mix gun only. This paint tends to clog internal-mix spray guns and it is too heavy to spray with a suction-fed gun. A maximum fluid flow works best, and you'll find that the paint is fairly free from misting.

As a rule, all paints should be strained into the cup or container through a fine piece of material such as a nylon stocking. Most paint dealers have the right straining cloth for this use. This removes any lumps that will clog the paint passages of the spray-gun assembly.

Before you spray, *practice*. The gun should be held about 6 to 10 inches from the surface. It should be held at right angles to the surface during painting. Don't use an arcing motion with your wrist. Keep your wrist straight and parallel to the surface and to the ground.

Since paint from a gun is thick in the middle and thin at the edges, you have to overlap each stroke by about a third or fourth, depending on the gun. You determine the best overlap by practice.

When you have to spray at an angle, paint the part nearest to the nozzle first. When you spray inside corners, paint the adjoining walls first; the overspray will cover the corner. At outside corners, point the spray gun in; at gutters, have the gun above the gutter and point it downward. Otherwise, you'll paint the shingles.

Spray guns are great, but you have to know how to use them

LADDERS CAN BE DANGEROUS, but by following a few simple rules, you can be almost as safe on a ladder as on the ground.

Buy a quality ladder. Don't skimp with so-called "bargains." A good ladder won't cost you much more than a bargain one at the outset but it will be a safer platform from which to work, and it will give you years of service if you maintain it properly.

You can buy metal or wooden extension ladders and stepladders in a wide range of lengths. Metal ladders, made of aluminum or magnesium, have the advantage of being somewhat lighter than their wooden counterparts. This could be an important consideration if you have a two-story home and have to move the ladder frequently.

If you buy a wooden ladder, *don't paint it.* Paint hides defects in wood that may develop after you use the ladder for a number of years. Instead, give the surface a coat of linseed oil or clear penetrating wood sealer.

Legs and arms; not back. Since you can hurt yourself lifting, the first key to safety is knowing how to carry, raise, and set a ladder. To pick up an extension ladder or heavy stepladder, flex your knees and *lift it with your legs,* not your back. When the ladder is up against the house and you want to move it, pick it up so one of the side rails fits in the hollow of your shoulder. Balance the ladder with your shoulder, lifting it with one hand on a rung and the other hand steadying the weight on the other side rail. Again, bend your knees as you start to lift and let your legs do the lifting. The trick is balance. When you learn this technique, you'll find that you can lift a great amount of weight easily, and it will save you the time lost by lowering the ladder to the ground and "walking" it up the side of the house again.

Some extension ladders are equipped with a pulley and rope which you operate to raise or lower the top half of the extension. If your ladder doesn't have this feature, block one side rail with a foot, pull the ladder out with one hand, and raise the top half with your other hand. This, too, is a balance technique that you can quickly learn.

Safety settings. Most ladder accidents occur from improper setting of the ladder.

1. The ladder should slope about one-fourth of its length away from the house. If you set it closer,

Lift an extension ladder like this, using the hollow of your shoulder to balance it and your legs and arms to lift it. Don't lift with your back. Also, watch out for power lines when you carry a ladder like this. If you knock down a power line, have someone call the electric company for repairs

20
116
264
450

127
128

"Walk" a ladder into position, as shown. When it's up, pull the bottom of it out to about one-fourth of its total length

Keep your hips between the side rails of the ladder; do not over-reach. Always hold to a rung with your free hand

Ladders should always be level and on firm ground. You can level a leg by digging a slot for it with a puttyknife or scraper

the ladder may pitch over backwards. If you set it at too wide a slope, it can either break under your weight or slip out from under you.

2. The legs of the ladder should set on *level* and *firm* turf. If the ladder isn't level, you can correct this by digging a slot for the "long" leg with a puttyknife. After the ladder is setting level, climb onto the first rung and bounce your weight on it. If the ladder is going to tip, it usually will tip at this time. You'll then have to shore up one leg with a sturdy board—at least a 1 x 6. Test it again before you climb higher.

3. Never open up a stepladder when you can lean it against a sidewall with the legs level. If you have to open the ladder, make sure it is completely opened to its fullest extent and that the bucket tray in the front is down and locked.

4. If you're climbing onto the roof, the ladder should extend several feet above the edge of the roof. Don't climb over the gutter onto the roof from either an extension or stepladder. It may be easy going up and over; it is very difficult to climb over and down.

5. Don't over-reach on a ladder. Keep both feet on the rungs and work only to where you can comfortably reach; don't stretch. Instead, get down and move the ladder.

6. Unless you're especially skilled at ladder know-how, avoid scaffolding extended between ladders. If you do use scaffolding, make sure it is safe by checking the planking and the bolts.

QUICK SUMMARY: HOW TO BE SAFE ON A LADDER . . .

1. Spend more money and buy a good ladder. Don't skimp. Buy "enough" ladder. If your gutters, for example, are 12 ft. off the grade level, buy a 16- to 20-ft. ladder.

2. Set the ladder properly. If it is not level or solid on the ground, do not climb it.

3. Watch out for power lines when you move a ladder; do not set the rails or rungs against a power line or straddle it; work around it.

4. Slope a ladder away from a sidewall about a fourth of its total length. Also, lap an extension ladder by at least three rungs—more if you are a heavyweight.

5. Do not paint a wooden ladder.

6. Test the rungs of a ladder by laying the ladder flat on the ground and walking along the rungs. If a rung breaks and you can't replace it, throw the ladder away and buy a new one.

7. Do not use scaffolding on an extension ladder if you've had no experience.

8. If you are working at any great height, have a helper stand against the bottom rung of the ladder to prevent it from slipping.

7. Watch electric power lines when you move a ladder into position. If you happen to break a power line, stay away from it and call the electric company immediately. However *do not leave the line unattended;* call for help.

8. You can use a ladder for support on a high-pitched roof, but tie a rope to the top rung and the other end of the rope to a tree or sturdy fencepost on the other side of the house.

9. Do not extend an extension ladder too far. It should lap at least three rungs—more if you are heavy. Doublecheck the extension hardware where it hooks over the rungs of the lower section. If it's not properly locked, do not climb the ladder until it is in position.

Maintenance. Both wooden and metal ladders should be stored under cover in a reasonably dry space—your garage or basement, or in a crawl-space under a porch. Moisture can rot wooden ladders; improper storage can cause metal ladders to twist and warp—especially when something heavy is laid over them. Hang them up.

If you're using a ladder for painting, always wipe off the paint drips and drops with a rag and paint thinner when you're through for the day. Paint can build up on the rungs and rails, making them slippery and difficult to raise and lower.

HOW TO BUY A LADDER

WHETHER YOU ARE BUYING a wooden or metal ladder, shop for safety—not a bargain. Here's what to look for:

Extension ladders consist of a "base" or bottom section and a "fly." The sections should overlap at least 3 ft., which would give you a 21 ft. reach on a 24 ft. extension ladder. On "bargain" ladders this overlap may be more to increase the rigidity. Check the location of the pulley. It should be on the top or second rung of the base, not several rungs down.

As a rule, good ladders have a rung every foot of their nominal length. A 12-ft. section, for example, has 12 rungs. The lowest rung should be about 7 in. from the bottom; the top rung should be about 5 in. from the top. Bargain ladders may have only 11 rungs in a nominal 12-ft. section.

A good ladder should be about 15 in. wide—or more. A good industrial grade ladder may be 20 in. wide. The more width, the more stability and comfort for the user.

Check the rung construction. Wooden rungs should be about 1-¼ in. in diameter. The wood grain should be straight and clear, and the edge

Approximate specifications of well-made extension ladders are listed in the chart below. The height-in-place listing is less than the nominal height since ladders are used at a slight angle and the sections overlap

TYPICAL DIMENSIONS OF METAL EXTENSION LADDERS									
		Utility-household grade				Industrial-commercial grade			
NOMINAL HEIGHT	ACTUAL HEIGHT IN PLACE	WIDTH	CROSS SECTION OF RAIL	SIZE OF RUNG	WEIGHT	WIDTH	CROSS SECTION OF RAIL	SIZE OF RUNG	WEIGHT
16'	12'	15"	2½"x ¾"	1³⁄₁₆"	20 lbs	18-20"	3"x 1½"	1⁵⁄₁₆"	36 lbs
20'	16'	15"	2½"x ¾"	1³⁄₁₆"	25 lbs	18-20"	3"x 1½"	1⁵⁄₁₆"	44 lbs
24'	20'	15"	2½"x ¾"	1³⁄₁₆"	30 lbs	18-20"	3"x 1½"	1⁵⁄₁₆"	52 lbs
28'	24'	15"	2½"x ¾"	1³⁄₁₆"	35 lbs	18-20"	3"x 1½"	1⁵⁄₁₆"	59 lbs
32'	28'	15"	2½"x ¾"	1³⁄₁₆"	40 lbs	18-20"	3½"x 1½"	1⁵⁄₁₆"	73 lbs
36'	32'	Not recommended				18-20"	3½"x 1½"	1⁵⁄₁₆"	82 lbs
40'	34'	Not recommended				18-20"	3½"x 1½"	1⁵⁄₁₆"	90 lbs

grain should face the top of the ladder. Metal rungs should be closed. A rung that is less than 1-3/16 in. in diameter may be considered too light. Look for rungs 1-5/16 in. in diameter.

Side rails of a wooden ladder should be straight-grained fir, hemlock, pine or spruce. Spruce is best. The grain should fall on the edge of the rail.

The back rails of a stepladder, if it's metal, should be channel or angle-crimped. Open the ladder and flip down the shelf. It should be able to support 50 pounds without failing. The ladder also should be 1 ft. wide at the top, and each side should spread away from the vertical at the rate of an inch per foot. Example: a 6-ft. ladder will spread to about 24 in. at the base.

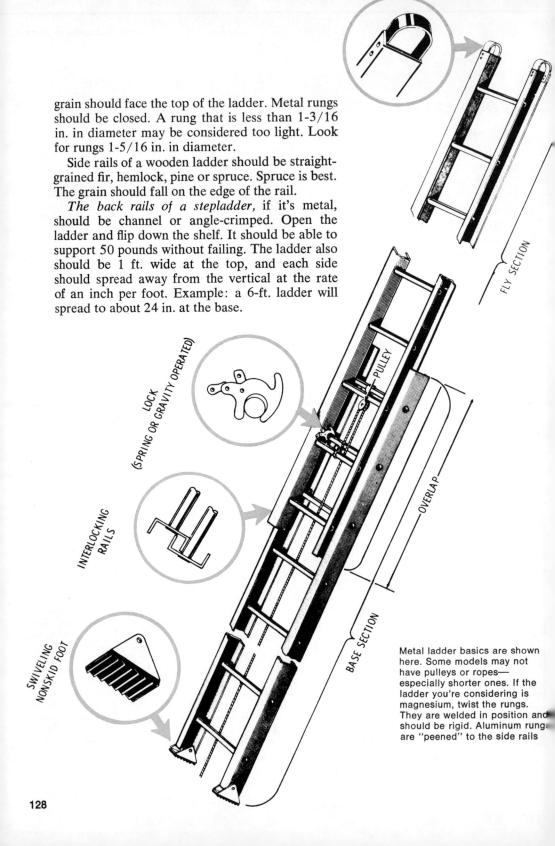

FLY SECTION

LOCK
(SPRING OR GRAVITY OPERATED)

INTERLOCKING RAILS

PULLEY

OVERLAP

BASE SECTION

SWIVELING NONSKID FOOT

Metal ladder basics are shown here. Some models may not have pulleys or ropes— especially shorter ones. If the ladder you're considering is magnesium, twist the rungs. They are welded in position and should be rigid. Aluminum rungs are "peened" to the side rails

Replacing or covering up
damaged interior materials can
also offer you the opportunity
to update your home. There are
many new building materials
that are not only functional but
also highly decorative

INTERIOR REPAIRS are generally easy to spot
without an annual inspection tour because you live
with the trouble on a daily basis. A sticking door,
a rattling window sash, unsightly holes or nail pops
in gypsumboard walls frequently *demand* attention.

In this section you will learn how to fix these
minor irritations quickly and easily with a minimum of cost. As a rule, interior maintenance and
repair jobs are not complicated—especially if you
tackle them in a step-by-step fashion as the photos
and text point out. The secret to satisfactory repairs is to first determine the problem, then assemble the tools and materials to solve it.

You should, of course, put the structural parts
of your home on an annual inspection tour. The
old saw, "a stitch in time," applies to minor interior problems that have a way of becoming major
crises if they are ignored.

ceilings—repairs and improvements

MOST CEILINGS are either gypsumboard (plasterboard) or plaster. The most common problems are holes and cracks. These, for the most part, are caused by the normal settling of the house on its foundation. Occasionally, a ceiling will sag. If it is gypsumboard, this can be caused by poor nailing of the panels. Or, the nails may have worked loose through settling of the house, causing the panels to pop at the joints and sag. Usually, you can remedy this by simply renailing the panels at the joints with threaded nails. If a troweled plaster ceiling sags, the problem can be water seepage from the roof, or from a room upstairs in a two-story home. You'll have to find the source of the water, correct it, then remove the damaged plaster and replace it with new.

Ceilings covered with acoustical tile can absorb as much as 60 percent of the sound that strikes them. Other features include decoration, some insulation value, and the ability to hide unsightly cracks, holes, and unevenness in plaster or gypsum wallboard

Suspended ceilings (dropped
ceilings) often have the features
of acoustical tile, but are installed in larger units. They
hang on metal channels that
are attached to the ceiling or
joists. Indirect lighting is very
easy to build into suspended ceilings since there is a void between the top of the panels and
the bottom of the ceiling itself

Gypsumboard repairs. Small holes can be filled
with Spackling compound, leveled, and sanded.
Larger holes must be undercut in an inverted V
shape, and then filled with Spackling compound or
patching plaster. If there are large breaks or holes
in the ceiling, they should be plugged, similar to
walls, filled with Spackling compound, sanded and
refinished. This technique is shown in the chapter
on wall repairs.

Popped gypsumboard nails are common, especially in newer homes that are still settling on their
foundations. You fix these by driving them in until
the heads leave a tiny dimple in the surface. Then
fill the dimple with Spackling compound. If this
seems to be a serious problem in your home, drive
in threaded nails, then pull out the old, loose ones.

Sometimes the joint tape on gypsumboard walls
pops loose. First try to reseat the tape in a thin bed
of joint compound. If this doesn't work, remove
the tape that is loose and retape the joint.

SMALL REPAIRS in lath and plaster ceilings are made the same way as small cracks, holes and hairline breaks are filled in gypsum wallboard. Use a putty knife to force in as much Spackle as possible.

For wide cracks and large holes that go all the way into the lath, a different repair treatment is required. Here are the steps to follow:

1. With a good puttyknife or an old chisel, remove all the loose plaster in the break. Chisel back to solid, firm plaster.

2. With a chisel, undercut the edges of the break in an inverted V. This will help hold the new plaster patch firmly in the damaged area.

3. When the damaged area has been thoroughly cleaned, check the lath for damage. Be especially alert to any moisture problem. If you find wet or moist areas, trace the source before you go any further. Some places to look include a damaged roof, bad gutters, damaged siding, a leaking faucet or bathtub on the second floor, a break in a pipe that runs up the wall between or across the studs.

If you find the leak, repair it. If you can't find the leak, call in a professional. A leak can wreck your entire home if it is left unfound and unfixed.

4. The break is clean; you are ready for the patch. You can use Spackling compound or patching plaster. If the hole isn't too large, Spackling does a good job. If the hole is large, you may wish to use patching plaster. It comes in a powder which you add to water. *Mix well.* You can tint patching plaster with powdered paint to match the ceiling color, but it's difficult to get a good match. Mix only small batches of plaster. The material sets up in an hour or so; then you can't work it.

5. Moisten the area in which the patch will be applied. You can use a squirt bottle for this, or an old sponge. The area should be moist, since the dry plaster will absorb the water from the wet plaster patch, weakening it after it sets.

6. If the hole is smaller than about five inches in diameter, you can fill it with just one application of Spackling or patching plaster. If the hole is larger than this, you will have to build it up with two or more layers. The first layer should half fill the hole. You can use a scraper or puttyknife for this. Then score the patch to give it "tooth" for the next layer. You can do this with the point of a nail

Damaged tile can be removed in "sections"; no need to rip out the entire job. Here, tile has been damaged by water from above

For direct ceiling applications, ceiling tile is "buttered" with walnut-sized daubs of adhesive on four corners; press in place

Level metal channel is first step to suspended ceiling. Measure down far enough to bypass hanging objects such as heating ducts, pipes. Snap a level chalkline around the entire room

Support channels hang on wires or brackets. Stretch a line between wall channels to determine how far down the supports should extend. Use eye hooks to hang wires; metal brackets are fastened with nails

Hook channels to ceiling wires. If joist spacing is off, you may have to span joists with a piece of bridging (shown at left). Make sure channels are secure on the wires even though panels are light

Cross channels interlock with others in snap joint. When you're finished, the system looks like a large metal grid

Ceiling panels drop into metal grids this way. They don't have to be fastened; gravity holds them in place

133

or ice pick. Let this patch dry for about four hours —longer if you can.

7. Trowel in the next coat of plaster after you have moistened the surface of the patch. This layer should just about fill the hole—about 7/8 ths full. Scratch this patch, too, for "tooth."

8. The final coat is applied after the second one has dried. Again moisten the patching area. You should use a trowel or concrete float to smooth the surface if it is large. If it is fairly small, you can use a wide scraper. For a glassy-smooth surface, wipe the patch with a wet sponge just before you finish troweling it. If you want a rougher surface, you can wipe the patch with the tip edges of a paintbrush. You also can "swirl" the patch to match surrounding area with a paintbrush. Many plaster walls have this light swirled effect.

9. After the patch is dry, seal it with a light coat of shellac, or use a good primer, then repaint the ceiling.

Damaged ceiling tile is fairly easy to replace. If the area is small, try cutting out separate tiles with a razor knife. Go between the joints with the blade, cutting through the overlapping edge or tongue. Be careful not to damage the good tiles surrounding the bad ones. If you hit a snag, it probably will be a metal staple. You may have to remove a series of tiles to get at the damaged ones. To replace single tiles, use adhesive, which should be spread evenly on the corners.

Sagging wallpaper, as a rule, has to be replaced, since gravity is working against you. It is very difficult to work any adhesive back under sagging paper to make it stick properly. This technique will work only on very small areas. On large areas, remove the wall covering completely; a paper-removing liquid will help speed the job—or rent a wallpaper steamer.

Moisture can be a cause of sagging wallpaper, so be sure to check the gypsum wallboard or plaster to make sure it shows no signs of moisture damage.

Peeling paint on ceilings is generally caused by moisture. However, this doesn't necessarily mean that there is a leak above. Sometimes plaster is painted before it has thoroughly dried, causing the paint to blister, flake or peel. Solving this problem is simple: Clean the area thoroughly and repaint it, using a primer coat and two top coats.

Some cures for damaged ceilings can be quick and easy

147
152
236

186
188
189

If damaged tile is fastened to furring strips, you'll probably have to remove a couple of rows, so new material will match joints

Add spacers (similar to bridging) for nailers. With this type installation, it's best to tack the new tiles to the strips

Tack tile on edges, as shown, using a staple gun for best result. Make sure joints are aligned with other tiles

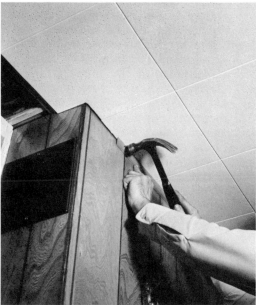

Molding or trim strips complete job; use finishing nails and countersink them. Then fill the holes and paint the trim

wall repairs & improvements

TWO MATERIALS—gypsumboard and plaster over lath—are the most common interior wall coverings. Over these, paneling, wallpaper, vinyl wallcoverings, ceramic tile, simulated brick and stone, high-pressure laminates, and a host of other decorative products are often installed. In basements, wall materials consist of poured reinforced concrete or concrete block. In some older homes, brick may have been used, and it is supported by special pillars and/or footings.

Basic wall problems fall into just two classifications: cracks and holes. Problems with *wall coverings* involve sagging wallpaper, rotting paneling, broken ceramic tile, peeling paint, and similar ills.

Small cracks are usually caused by the house settling on its foundation. The cracks appear at door and window headers, joints in gypsumboard, in corners where the wall and ceiling meet, in archways. Don't be alarmed. Such cracks usually occur —especially in new construction. Get upset only if the cracks open up an inch or two. This can be a sign of basic structural problems, and a professional should be consulted immediately.

The small cracks in plaster and gypsumboard are easy to repair with any of several patching materials. The most common of these is *Spackling compound* which you can buy in dry powder form and mix with water. Premixed Spackle also is available in a can ready-to-use. You pay more for this convenience.

If the patches you'll make are on "sand-finished" walls, you can add sand to Spackle to match the finish. You also can color Spackle with paint, substituting paint for water when you mix it. You usually have to apply a finish coat to the wall, but the paint trick eliminates the need for prime coats—especially where small cracks and holes are involved. If you get a good match (tone it about a shade darker than the finish on the wall), you may not have to refinish the wall.

For larger holes and cracks in plaster or gypsumboard, *patching plaster* can be used. Like Spackling compound, it can be colored with pow-

162
444
447
457
458

142
143
144
145

Typical gypsumboard puncture ▮ small. A gypsumboard patch is the best repair for this damage. For smaller holes you can use steel-wool plugs with patching plaster; for larger holes, you ca▮ replace a section of the wall

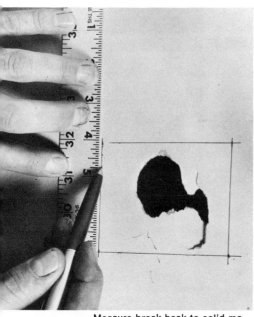

Measure break back to solid material and use guidelines for cutting paper. Use pencil; ballpoint pen ink bleeds through final finish

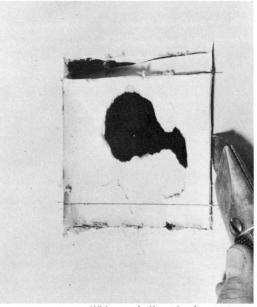

With razorknife or hook-nose linoleum knife that's ultrasharp, cut along lines at about 45-degree angle *into* patching area

When plug is removed, hole should look something like this. Clean up torn and ragged edges with the razorknife for smooth fit

Cut oversize gypsumboard patch, drill two holes, thread wire through holes, spread glue around edges, and put it into the hole

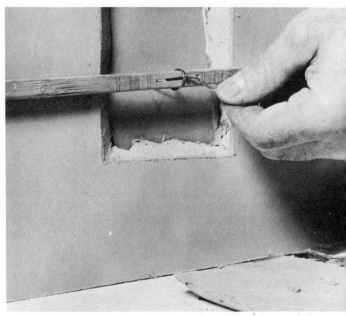

Cinch wires tight by twisting them with pliers around a piece of thin scrap wood. This serves to clamp the patch until the glue dries. Patch you use should be about 1 in. larger than the hole you've cut in the wall

dered paint, sharpened with sand for sand-finished walls, and troweled into the breaks with a putty knife, wall scraper, flat masonry trowel, or a regular plaster trowel.

For base coats, you may want to mix it stiff; for finish coats, it can be mixed thinner. Either way, the material sets up fast, so mix it in small amounts or it will harden before you can use it all. (The same holds true for Spackling compound.) Once patching plaster has set in the mixing container, throw it away and stir up another batch.

Specialty fillers include *lead putty, wood dough,* and *silicone calk* (or bathtub and lavatory calk). You shouldn't use any of these materials on gypsumboard or plaster. It is formulated, basically, for wood paneling and clay-based tile.

Lead putty is for small holes and cracks in wood; it is manufactured in a variety of colors to match various wood species. If you are going to paint over the patch, you can still use lead putty, which is usually wiped into the hole with a finger or a putty knife with a fairly flexible blade. Do not use it on plaster or gypsumboard. It contains oil which will stain plaster or gypsumboard.

188
189

Back of patch looks like this behind the wall. Let glue dry for
several hours before you move on
to the next step

Cut a gypsumboard patch to fit
the hole you have cut in the wall.
It should also have a 45-degree
angle on the edges

Remove the clamping brace and
thread the wires through predrilled holes in the patch. Then
twist the wires to tighten

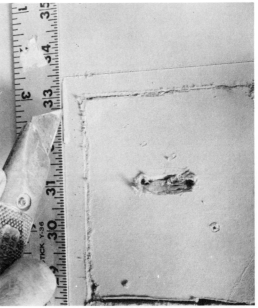

Cut the gypsumboard paper
around the patch with the razorknife, using a straightedge. Then
peel the paper layer

Wood dough or wood filler, lives up to its name: it looks like a dough, and is wiped into holes with a finger or putty knife. You also can use this material to patch cement, tile, and porcelain around sinks and bathtubs. It comes in colors to match various wood species. Since it generally has a lacquer base, you have to pinch out small portions of it, apply them quickly to the crack or hole, keeping the lid on the container while you do so. Otherwise the dough dries out and becomes useless.

Tub and sink calk is similar to the regular calking compound you use outside. It is available in a cartridge that slides into a gun unit, or you can buy

223

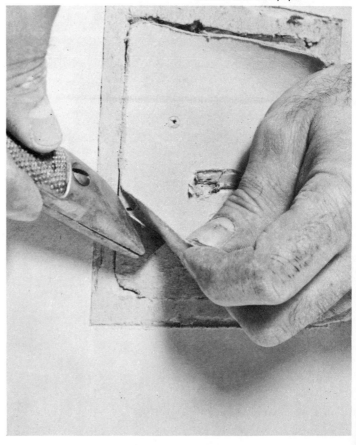

Peel off paper covering the patch. Work it off easily so it doesn't rip plaster loose as you go. This technique provides a slight "mortise" in and around the patch, making it easier to apply the Spackling or patching plaster in the next step. Torn paper? Smooth with sandpaper

Cover patch area with Spackle or patching plaster. First coat should cover "mortise" and indentation where wire is twisted

When first coat of patching material is dry, apply a second one over gypsumwall joint tape that has been embedded in the patch

With a trowel or wide wall scraper, coat the area with patching compound, smoothing it as much as possible. Use a thin mix

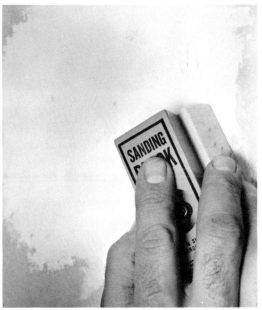

When patching compound is dry —at least an hour after it is applied—sand the area smooth with medium-grit sandpaper

141

The most common
problem with
gypsumboard is
popping nails; here's
how to cope with
that frustration

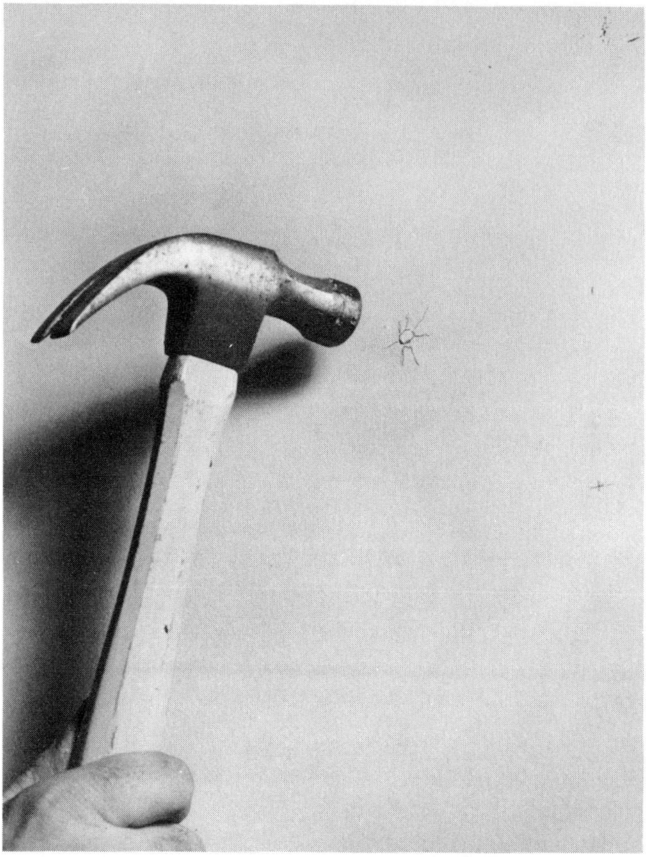

Nail pops can be fixed this way:
(1) Drive nail flush and hit it one
more time for "dimple"; (2) replace nail with "threaded" one

it in a tube. Use it on nearly any type of wall surface for small crack and hole repair. After it sets,
sand and paint it.

Joint cement is especially formulated to apply
joint tape to gypsumboard walls. It comes in powder form and is mixed with water. The cement
dries fairly fast and very hard, so mix it in small
batches. You can use joint cement to fill cracks
and holes in gypsumboard and plaster; it is more
expensive than regular patching plaster, but because of its hardness you may want to pay the
price.

Concrete patches, generally used on basement
walls and floors, consist of premixed dry mortar.
There also are new vinyl and latex-based cements.
The premixed mortar dries slowly—if this is a

270
271
444

88
97
150
443

Fill "dimple" with patching compound so the compound is slightly higher than the surface of the wall. This allows for shrinkage

Let patch harden—at least an hour or so. Then sand it very lightly with medium-grit sandpaper on a sanding block

consideration; the latex and vinyl types dry fast and hard.

HOW TO REPAIR GYPSUMBOARD

For small holes—those made by nails or screws —wipe in Spackle or patching plaster with a putty knife or your finger. Sand smooth, and finish.

For cracks, undercut the slot in an inverted V, remove any loose plaster, and fill the crack with Spackle or patching plaster. Use a wide scraper and wipe the filler across the crack, feathering the edges. Sand and finish.

For larger holes, there are several repair techniques. One method is pictured in this chapter. Here are two more:

136

To remove Molly bolts in walls, simply turn the screw down until head is below surface of the wall. Or, punch the bolt through

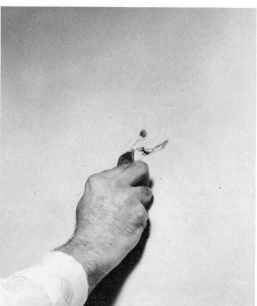

If gypsumboard or plaster cracks around anchor, you can trim away broken material and patch. For togglebolts, unscrew to remove

Stuff the hole with fairly coarse steel wool. The steel wool should go all the way behind the wallboard; then "hook" the steel wool onto the rough edges of the break after you trim the break back to sound material.

"Tack" the steel wool to the sides of the break with Spackle or patching plaster, and let it harden. Then, very carefully, apply another coat of patching compound to the steel wool. Don't push or force it. When this hardens, give the spot another coat of patching compound. This should bring the patch level with the surrounding surface. Let it dry, sand lightly with medium-grit sandpaper, and finish.

If the hole isn't too large, you can cover it with joint tape and cement. Tear off a piece of joint tape and trim the edges square. Mark the outline on the wall with a pencil. Then, with a sharp razorknife, cut away the paper that covers the gypsumboard. This will form a very shallow recess. If there are rough paper edges, smooth them with sandpaper.

With a thin mixture of joint cement, cover the recess completely and embed the tape. Then cover

Although patch may be fairly large, you usually don't need plug. Wipe in three layers of patching compound for build-up

144

the tape with joint cement. When dry, sand it smooth, and finish.

For very large damaged areas, you should re- 270 move the broken gypsumboard and install a new piece the same thickness. Some building-material dealers sell gypsumboard in half-sheets or broken sheets for this very purpose.

Since the patch is a large one, you will uncover wall studs or furring strips to which you can nail the board. For a really smooth job, you can "mortise" in joint tape by cutting away the paper that covers the gypsum. Then follow the same technique you would use to tape joints.

On the inside surface of exterior walls, when 162 making large patches, make sure that you don't damage the insulation. A break in the vapor barrier should be mended with tape, or with sheet plastic tacked over the break and into the wall studs.

If gypsumboard is badly damaged, you should replace entire sheet with new one. Nail it to studs

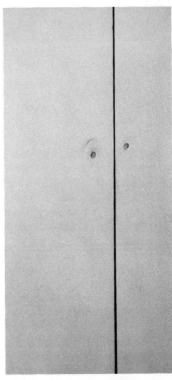

Edges of board are slightly tapered to accept joint cement and tape. Dimple each nail head

SMALL HOLES AND CRACKS in plaster walls are repaired exactly like gypsumboard walls. You can use the same materials and techniques.

Large holes—those that go down to the lath—are not difficult to fix either; in fact, they can be patched easier than large holes in gypsumboard since there is a solid base from which to work. Here are the steps to follow:

1. Clean out all crumbling plaster.
2. If the lath are loose, renail them to the studs.
3. If the lath are broken, you'll have to replace them. This necessitates enlarging the hole so you can get to the spot where they are nailed. Cut the new lath to fit and tack them to the studs. Maintain the same spacing as the old lath—usually about ½-in. between lath.

At this time you should check for any moisture problems that might have caused the plaster to disintegrate.

4. When the hole is properly prepared, trowel in the first coat of patching plaster or undercoater. When it is almost dry, score the surface with a tip of a nail or an old comb. This gives you a base for the next coat.
5. Apply the second coat of plaster to the patch, and leave it rough as you did the first coat.
6. When the second coat is dry, apply the thin finish coat of plaster, using a wide trowel and feathering out the edges. In large patches, the patch may tend to sag or bulge. You can correct this by overlapping the patch with a straightedge that projects onto the surrounding surfaces. Don't use it as a "screed"; rather, use it as a check to see if you have too much plaster in the hole. If you have, remove some and retrowel it. Work from the center out, feathering the edges as you go.

Another way: For large holes, you can cut out the crumbling plaster and fill the hole with a piece of gypsum wallboard. Nail this to the studs or lath, but go easy with the hammer so you don't break the lath.

Then apply a finish coat of plaster over the gypsum wallboard patch, sand it smooth, and apply a finish coat.

Bulges in plaster are common.

With a hammer, brick or cold chisel, knock out the bulging plaster and all loose plaster. Go right back to sound material. Then fill in the hole with

Plastic or fiber plugs work in plaster, gypsumboard, concrete walls. You drill hole to plug diameter and insert it.

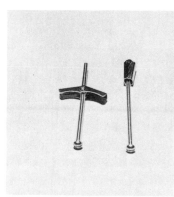

Toggle bolts are fitted into holes drilled in hollow wall construction. Fold the "butterfly," insert it in hole. It opens behind wall

Lead expansion anchors are generally used in concrete or brick to fasten heavy objects to a wall or floor. Bolt expands anchor

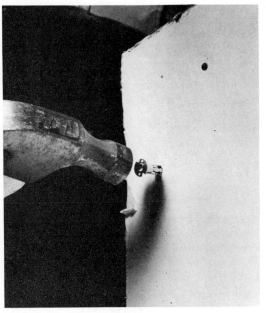

Molly bolt works this way: You
drill hole in hollow wall and tap
in anchor. Then you expand its
flanges by turning the screw

Molly "fans" out in back of wall
like this. You then can remove
the screw and hang the object.
Different sizes are available

any of the plastering repair techniques explained
above.

REPAIRING LOOSE WALLPAPER

Popped edges, bubbles, and loose areas in wallpaper are jobs for a sharp knife and regular wallpaper paste, which you can buy in small bags.

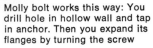

136
236
240

If the seams have popped, you can reglue them
by simply coating the wallpaper and the wall with
a very thin layer of paste. Then press the paper
down. If it is not an embossed paper, you can roll
the seam with a seam roller or even a rolling pin.
Go over it several times. Then wipe the seam with
a moist, soft sponge.

For bubbles or loosened wallpaper in the center
of a strip, you can slit the paper with a razorknife,
force adhesive behind it, then roll it flat again. A
thin kitchen knife makes an excellent paste
spreader for this project. Sometimes the paste
squirts right back out of the slit. If it does, sponge
it off immediately with a moist cloth. If left to dry

on the surface, adhesive can stain the wallpaper.

For small tears in regular wallpaper, you can sometimes follow the pattern of the tear with a razorknife and remove it. Cut a new patch to match the pattern from matching paper.

Wallpaper is cleaned with a doughlike cleaner. (If you have washable wallpaper, you can go over it with a sponge moistened with lukewarm water and a very mild soap.)

Wallpaper cleaner is formed into a wad and stroked over the paper. As the stroke is made, dirt is collected. Some of the dirty dough crumbles and drops to the floor. Therefore, you should cover the floor with a dropcloth to prevent damage to finishes and carpeting. The secret in using this material is to have the dough in motion before it meets the surface of the paper and as it leaves the surface. Do not set the dough on the paper and wipe it across. This can leave a permanent mark.

Stains on wallpaper—grease and ink—usually can be removed fairly easily. For *grease* stains, use a mixture of fuller's earth and cleaning fluid. You lightly brush this material over the stain, let it dry, then brush it off. You may need to apply fuller's earth several times before the stain is removed. Another trick is to use ordinary blotting paper. Place the blotter over the grease spot and warm it with an iron. The heat sucks the grease into the blotter. This technique, however, is a last-resort attempt.

For *ink stains* use ink eradicator you can buy at stationery stores. First try the eradicator on wallpaper that is hidden from view. (Eradicators can take the color out of some wallpapers.)

If you have to remove wallpaper, the easiest way (though still not easy) is to rent a wallpaper steamer. This is hot and heavy work, but the job goes fast. If you find more than one layer of paper, take off each layer separately. This is easier than trying to steam off several layers at once.

You also can buy commercial wallpaper removers. Most of them are liquids applied with a brush or squirting device, and the idea is to soak the paper loose from the wall or ceiling. The trick here is to use plenty of liquid and give it enough time to saturate the paper. You'll spend about two-thirds of your time squirting on the fluid and

There's a hanger for every type of wall and every hanging job

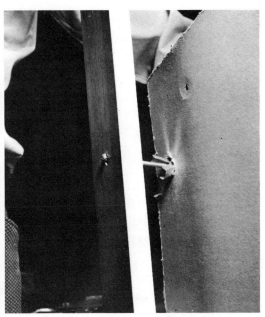

Toggle bolt assembly goes together like this. Fasteners are generally used for furring strips and very heavy objects

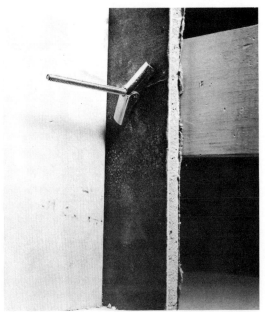

Behind wall, toggle bolt "wings" flip out; they're spring-loaded. By tightening screw on other side of wall, "wings" bite into board

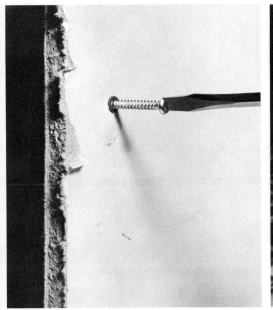

Hanging light objects such as pictures is a job for plastic or fiber anchors. You also can use them for light furring strips

Plastic anchors spread or bulge out when screw is inserted. Material grips sides of hole so it won't slip

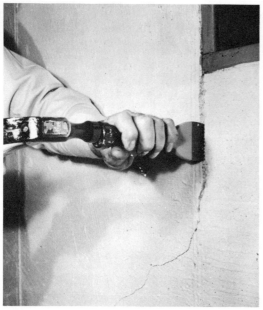

Clean cracks in concrete walls with a brick or cold chisel. Undercut crack enough so filler you use will stick

Water-mixed latex compound makes quick-drying patch for cracks in concrete. Mix it to whipped cream consistency

Cracks in concrete blocks in foundation walls are cleaned with brick or cold chisel. Remove all crumbling mortar

Trowel in latex compound with a putty knife or narrow scraper. The joint should be fully-packed or patch will shrink and fall out

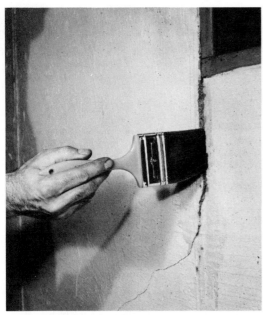

Wet joint in concrete wall with water, using old paintbrush or sponge. It should be thoroughly wet, not just damp

Don't skimp on patching concrete; completely fill the crack, feathering out the edges along the surface of the wall

Striking tool you can buy for under $2 matches patched mortar joint with others. Strike patch after it has set

Water pipes running through foundation sills are often a source for air leaks. Fill these with latex cement or insulation

151

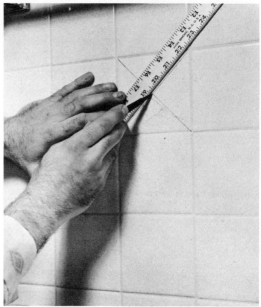

Broken ceramic tile is easy to replace by removing just the tile that is broken. Chip off small piece for match at tile store

the rest of the time scraping off the paper.

Removing wallpaper from gypsum wallboard is another problem, since the wallboard itself is covered with paper. Soak it too much and you can soak the paper right off the wallboard.

With straightedge, mark a cross in tile. Use a fiber-tipped pen or grease marking pencil for this. Go just to the grout lines

Go easy, wetting and scraping. When you are finished, let the wall dry for a week or so. Follow this by coating the wall with a varnish size, sand it lightly when it is dry, and refinish with new paper or paint.

Painting over wallpaper should only be attempted if the wallpaper is firmly attached to the wall. Also, the patterns and colors in the paper may bleed through, requiring several coats of paint.

185
186
187

PANELING

Paneling can be plywood, hardboard, decorated gypsumboard, plastic laminate, or simulated stone and brick.

136
156

Serious damage to wood paneling such as plywood usually calls for replacement of the panel or, at least, part of the panel. This can be a tough job since the fastening system can vary from installation over furring strips to adhesive to special clips.

158

Here's how to replace a damaged tile

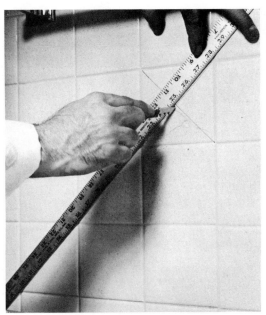

Score tile with a glass cutter
along the marked lines. Use a
straightedge to guide the cutter.
Cutter will be ruined

With a small cold chisel or punch,
lightly tap the scored lines where
they meet in the center of the tile.
This should break it loose

Clean away tile adhesive with an
old chisel or sharp putty knife. If
the ridges in the adhesive are
fairly smooth, you don't have to

Butter the back of the new tile
with tile cement, after you prefit
it in the patch area. Use a fairly
thin coating of tile adhesive

The first step is to determine how the paneling is fastened to the wall.

Studs. Since studs are usually located on 16-in. centers, you can pry off the base molding and see where the paneling has been nailed to the studs. If you find this situation, start tapping on the paneling with your knuckles. You'll hear a hollow sound between studs; a solid sound on the stud. Panels are usually butt-joined at the center of a stud—every 4 ft., or the width of each panel. After you spot the stud, check for nails or other fasteners to find out how the panels are attached.

Another technique is to measure out about 17 in. from a corner. A stud is usually positioned here and you can try tapping and listening until you find it. You also can buy stud locaters. These are small magnetic devices that zero in on nails in the studs.

If the panels are hung on studs and you want to remove a damaged one, remove the baseboard and the molding at the ceiling line. Then pry out the panel, being very careful not to damage the adjoining panels. Since the panels are usually butt-joined instead of lapped, they come out easily.

Furring strips usually run horizontally across the wall, and the panels are nailed to the strips. The strips are usually spaced on 16-in. centers. Again, you can use the tapping technique to determine this, or a magnetic stud finder to determine where and how the panels are nailed.

For panels with clips, start at a corner, which is usually trimmed but with a locking strip. Remove the strip, and the panels are easy to remove one by one across the room until you get to the one that needs replacement.

Adhesive-mounted panels over wallboard or plaster are fairly easy to spot since tapping produces a continuous solid sound. You have to pry the panel that is damaged away from the wall; this takes careful work since the adhesive is tough to break loose. Use a long, flat prybar for this, working from the floor up.

MOISTURE AND DAMPNESS ON WALLS

Beads of moisture appear on plaster walls because of excessive humidity within the house. Another possible cause is inadequate insulation of the wall. You can correct this by lowering the humidity, proper weatherstripping of windows

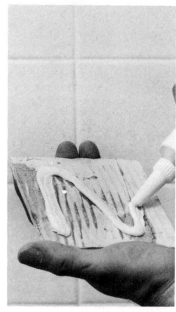

Silicone seal in a tube can be used as an adhesive for replacing ceramic tile. Squeeze it on in a zig-zag as shown

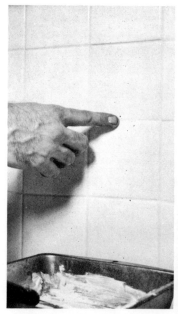

Wipe in ceramic tile grout with a finger to smooth it properly. Wet your finger first. This makes proper indentation in the grout

If you test buttered tile in hole and find it's not level with surrounding tiles, add adhesive to wall to build out the tile

Press new tile in place, making sure the joints between the tiles are the same. Then, with a putty knife, trowel in stiff grout mixture

Big source of leaks around tub is between bottom row of tiles and top rim of tub. Calk this shut with silicone sealer or grout

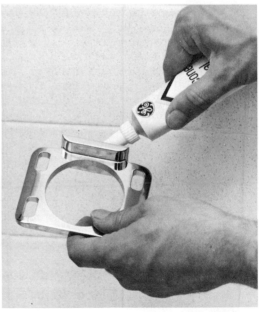

Reglue metal fixtures such as soap dishes, towel racks, glass holders with silicone sealer or standard tile cement

and doors, or by adding insulation.

If your house has not been insulated you can have loose-fill insulation blown between the studs. It is made of mineral wool or vermiculite. This usually stops any moisture problem above ground level.

Moisture on basement walls is usually the result of warm air hitting the cold masonry. You can minimize this by painting the wall with one of the cement-base waterproof compounds, or with alkyd/latex masonry paints. These are made for both interior and exterior application. Also, dehumidify the basement if practicable.

Still another way to overcome damp basement walls is to build a false wall out from the masonry, and insulate it. The new wall can be gypsum wallboard or almost any type of paneling.

Hydrostatic pressure is probably the most frequent and serious cause of wet-basement wall and floor problems. This is the result of a high water table around the house. Pressure forces the water through cracks and porous spots in the foundation.

Hydrostatic pressure varies with the weather. If your basement is dry most of the time and then there is a great surge of water, it is caused by the height of the water table.

If the water is running in and you can't stop it, your best bet for an emergency is to use a water plug. It is like putty in consistency. You mix it with water, roll it into a ball, and push it into the crack. Then smooth the surface. It is quick-drying —usually in five minutes or so.

But this is a stop-gap measure; you should have a professional install an exterior drainage system. Since there are various types of drainage systems, shop around. Check any installer through the Better Business Bureau, and his former customers. Insist on a guarantee. A leaking basement *can* be stopped, but it may cost several hundred dollars.

A FINAL SOLUTION FOR PROBLEM WALLS

Just as paint can hide many defects, paneling can hide problem walls that can't be patched, covered with wallpaper or wall coverings, or hidden behind closed doors. Paneling does for walls what ceiling tile does for similar ceiling problems.

Air bubbles in contact-adhesive wall coverings can be removed by pricking them with a pin and pressing down on the bubble. Use fingers, not a roller for this

Edges of contact paper that peel back can be stuck down by applying a layer of contact cement or rubber cement. Coat both edges, let dry for 15 minutes, then press down. Don't roll flocked papers

A paneled wall usually is applied over furring strips fastened to the damaged wall. These are fastened horizontally on 16-in. centers with anchor bolts and screws or expansion bolts. The key to the project is to get the furring strips plumb and level; otherwise, the paneling will be wavy and mismatched. This is done with shingle shims, as illustrated.

If the walls are so bad that you can't anchor furring to them, you'll have to build a false stud wall. This requires a top and bottom 2 x 4 plate and studs on 16- or 24-in. centers.

PANELING MATERIALS

Hardboard isn't a new paneling product, but many designs it offers are new. You can buy simulated wood grains, textures, and special effects such as fleeced, louvered, striated and embossed.

Hardboard paneling is inexpensive and is manufactured ¼ in. thick, 4-ft. wide and up to 12-ft. in length. A standard panel is 4 x 8 ft. Perforated hardboard sizes are ⅛ in. thick in 4 x 8 and 4 x 4-ft. panels and ¼ in. thick in 4 x 8-ft. sheets. Finishes you apply can include oil or water-emulsion paint, enamel, lacquer, shellac, stain, varnish, penetrating sealer and wax. Of course there are a good many types of panels prefinished by the manufacturer.

For bathrooms and kitchens (and perhaps some damp basement installations) you should consider hardboard panels with a baked-on plastic finish. They will resist moisture, grease, stains, heat and scuffs. You can buy solid colors; some panels are scored to simulate tiles. Ceiling blocks and tiles also are available with identical finishes.

Also available are metal and vinyl-clad, color-matched wood moldings and trim. These include outside and inside corner, shoe, stop, base, cove and casing.

Plywood paneling has so many different finishes that the problem becomes one of proper selection.

Hardwood-faced plywood, fir plywood, and the softwood plywoods (knotty pine) are manufactured in sheets and planks. Many are prefinished with a tough coating that resists almost any type of damage.

Softwood-faced plywood and hardwood-faced plywood panels—consist of a sandwich of several layers—or plies—of veneer. These plies are bonded with a tough adhesive. There are three types of cores: veneer, lumber, and particleboard. *Veneer-core* has a series of laminated wood veneers. They are alternated at right angles to each other. *Lumber-core* has veneer surfaces, but the core is solid wood. *Particleboard cores* have resincoated wood particles that are pressed together, and the veneer—or high pressure laminate —is glued to one or both sides of the core.

Hardwood-faced plywood and softwood plywood are graded differently. The hardwood type: No. 1 is custom grade. It is free of knots, patches, and plugs. No. 2 is good grade. It has tight veneer and the joints are evenly matched for grain pat-

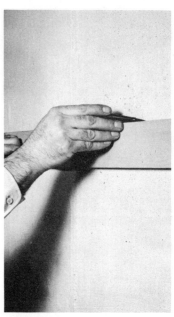

Extreme roughness and defects in concrete walls are easier to cover with wall material than attempting to patch them

After you mark furring strip, as pictured above, measure width of board, split difference. Use mark you made on wall for this

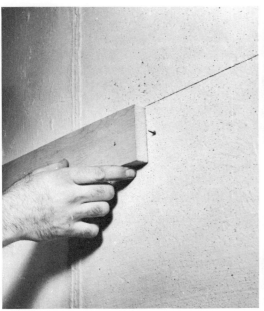

Example shows how center of furring strip looks after correct measurement has been made

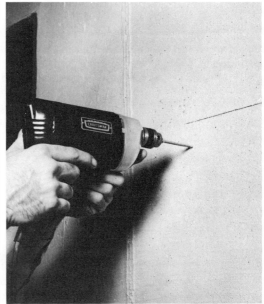

Drill holes with masonry bit. Or you can use a star drill for anchors that will hold furring tight to wall

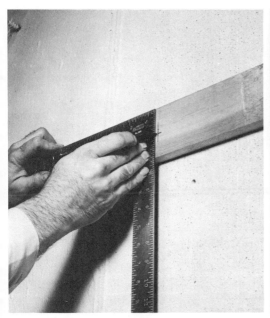

Another way to hang furring strips: Measure half width of strip and mark it at 2-ft. centers. Drill hole; use it for masonry bit guide

Using framing square after first anchor is in place and strip is attached, mark off 2-ft. centers along the entire strip

tern. No. 3 is sound grade; it is free of defects, but the veneer isn't matched and it can have mineral streaks and stains running through it. No. 4 is utility grade; it has discolorations. No. 5 is reject grade, with knotholes up to 2 in. in diameter. Three types of bonds are available in hardwood-faced plywood: waterproof for exterior; water-resistant where the panels won't be directly exposed to water or weather; and dry bond where panels won't be exposed to any water, dampness or even high humidity.

Softwood and fir plywood panels are graded by a letter system. Interior grades are A-A for cabinet doors, built-ins, and furniture—or where both sides of the panel will be seen. A-B has one very good side; the other side is solid and smooth. A-D is good one side for paneling; B-D is utility grade; it has one good side. C-D and B-B are used for underlayment, sheathing and concrete forms.

Hardwood-faced panels range in width from 16 to 48 in. and in lengths from 48 to 120 in. Softwood and fir panels run 30, 36, 42, and 48 in. wide and 5 to 12 ft. in length in increments of 1 ft. Special panel sizes are made for special jobs.

You can buy precut plywood squares of various hardwood-faced plywoods for a wall with a checkerboard effect. The squares should go over plywood sheathing. This type of installation will cost you a bit more than other applications.

Solid hardwood paneling is costly since it is solid wood all the way through. Because of the price, you may want to consider it only for an accent wall, installing plywood panels on the rest of the room. Solid woods readily available include pecky cypress, willow, maple, pine, cherry, ash, cottonwood, red oak and walnut. The panels or planks range in thickness from ½ in. to 1 in. (25/32 in. dressed). Widths vary from 4 to 8 in. in 1-in. increments. Lengths are random; some material is packaged, however, in specific lengths.

SPECIAL PANELING FINISHES

You can finish new wood paneling yourself. Many finishes come in a wide range of stains to alter the natural color of the paneling.

Before you make a final decision on what type stain you want, test the finish on several pieces of

Anchor screws must be counter-sunk in furring strips so wall covering will lay flat. Use any type of countersink bit for this

If concrete wall tends to become damp, you can insulate it with styrofoam boards before applying wall covering. Install with glue

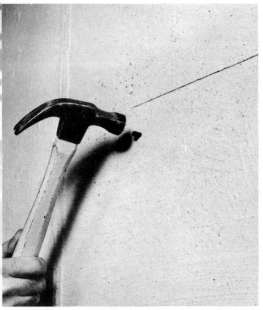

Heavy lead, fibre, or plastic plugs are best for hanging furring strips. Drill proper diameter holes just deep enough so plug is flush

Furring has to be plumb (vertically level) or the wall covering will be wavy. You can shim it plumb with wooden shingles

Wall covering, here gypsum wallboard, is nailed to the furring strips in vertical sections. Board is then taped at joints

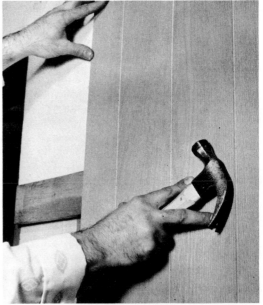

Paneling goes up just like gypsum wallboard and is edge-nailed to the furring strips. You can also nail it in false joints

scrap wood. Don't rely completely on samples in a dealer's showroom, since wood grains vary greatly.

If you want a *clear finish,* you'll need a penetrating sealer to give the paneling a waxed or oiled look. First, apply a coat of the sealer. Wipe off the excess with a soft cloth after the sealer has set for about 15 minutes. Let this dry for 24 hours. Then apply the second coat, rubbing it off. When this has dried to a hard surface, rub on paste wax and buff the wax to a high polish.

Varnished finishes can also be clear. You brush on the first coat of varnish—or lacquer or shellac. Use a clear sealer coat. Let the finish dry for 24 hours. Then sand it lightly, remove all debris with a tack rag, and apply the second coat. Follow the same process for the third coat.

Stained finishes require a resin sealer (clear) before you apply the stain to soft woods. Let the sealer dry. Brush on the stain and wipe it off in 15 minutes with a soft cloth. When the stain is dry, apply two coats of varnish. Or you can use a couple of coats of shellac.

Light-colored finishes involve a pigmented or pastel-colored stain. You also can use paint that has been thinned. Wipe this stain onto the wood, let it penetrate, then wipe off the excess. When the stain is dry, give the surface two coats of water-white, clear plastic, or satin-finish varnish. The first coat should be thoroughly dry before you apply the second one. Sand lightly between coats and use a tack rag to remove sanding debris.

SPECIALTY MATERIALS

Fiberglass brick and stone panels are another way to hide defective walls that you can't repair in any other way. These materials also make excellent accents for walls that are in good repair.

The panels are actually made of crushed stone bonded to a fiberglass mat. They are practically indestructible and need only an occasional washing with mild detergent and water to keep them looking new. In one type application, the panels are fastened to furring strips. They also can be fastened to stud construction and flat walls.

186
187
225
452

If paneling is badly damaged, it should be replaced by removing the entire panel. If insulation is involved, make sure it is in position

First panel in new construction or for repair job must be absolutely plumb, or additional panels or strips will not fit. Check plumb top, bottom

Use a vertical furring strip at corners for panel-type walls. Use horizontal furring on rest of wall. This makes strongest joints

Insulation must be fastened to studs in any installation—new construction or repairs—with the vapor barrier facing the inside of the room

Nail panel to bottom plate or furring strip first. Trim will hide nail. Then plumb other edge and tack it to top plate or furring so trim hides nail

A false accent wall of translucent plastic is another way to hide defects. In this application, you nail the panels over studding. As an added feature, you install lights behind the panels to provide a lighted wall. Fluorescent strip lighting provides an even, soft glow to bring out the design in the plastic.

Gypsum wallboard is now available with a finished surface in many different designs. You simply nail the panels to furring strips and/or studs like regular paneling. One advantage of this material is its low cost, making it ideal for basement wall installations where you want to hide unsightly concrete or block.

Still another new product is a dual-use wall covering in the form of decorated insulation. The insulation has a two-tone basket-weave pattern on the front (vapor barrier). You install the insulation with a stapler—just like regular insulation—between the studs in an attic or basement room. The insulation has a narrow flange on each side; it is tacked to the sides of the studs instead of the edges. The insulation also can be used to brighten walls in attached garages where insulation protection is needed. If it's applied with care, you don't have to cover the insulation with gypsum wallboard or paneling.

256
270

449

For a topnotch job use the right cutting, fitting and nailing techniques

Colored nails to match paneling
are driven at an angle in edge
joints of wood. They go into studs
or furring

You can drive colored nails in
the machined joints, simulated
in this photo. Countersink regular
nails and fill holes

To go around obstructions such
as heating ducts, it's usually
easier to trace pattern on paper,
transfer it to panel, and then cut

For wall switches and outlets,
mark panel, remove it, drill hole
from face, saw out pattern with
keyhole saw—also from the face

floor repairs and improvements

OAK, PINE, WALNUT, ASBESTOS-CEMENT, resilient tile, carpeting—there are dozens of different types of floors. Maintenance and repair problems, however, are fairly limited—usually confined to damaged floor tile, scratches in wood finishes, and squeaks.

Wood flooring. Scratches are the most common problem. To repair them, lightly buff the scratch with a ball of steel wool. This removes wax and finish. Then with a cotton swab, wipe on the same color stain or finish, feathering the edges. When this is dry, buff the area lightly with steel wool, apply varnish or shellac to the spot, let it dry, buff again with steel wool very lightly, and wax.

Resilient floors, including most types of tile, are easy to maintain with a periodic washing. Once a week is enough, as a rule. Dampmopping in between will keep the floor shiny and bright. When washing floors, use a mild detergent. Occasionally use a wax remover to clean off the old finish. Do not use strong cleaners such as gasoline, turpentine or naphtha. And *do not use oil-based cleaners on asphalt or rubber tile.*

If you have resilient flooring such as "Solarian," which is "nonporous," you should not wax or polish it. Simply damp-mop it to keep it looking new.

To replace damaged tiles in resilient floors, make sure the replacement is the same type—asphalt, vinyl, vinyl-asbestos, cork, rubber, linoleum or vinyl sheet. You also should use the proper adhesive for these materials. When you purchase replacement tile, take along a sample of your existing floor so the dealer will know for sure what type flooring it is. Also make a note of the subfloor: is it plywood over asphalt building paper, concrete, strip flooring? This can make a difference in the type of sealer or adhesive you use. You usually can remove the old flooring with heat—as shown in this chapter. Remove the adhesive with water, heat or solvent. Or peel it up with a wide chisel or scraper.

To remove tongue-and-groove flooring that is damaged, first mark outlines around the damaged areas. Let a joint serve as a starting base; then back off about ¼-in. from the cracks so saw won't hit nails

Adjust saw so you go through the flooring just to the top of the subfloor. This will be about ¾-in. If you have a piece of scrap, this will help you determine the depth. Sabre saw does a good job, too

Mark across cracks, making sure
that the cut is absolutely square.
Use a framing square for this
instead of improvising

Here's how nails are set in
the flooring, and why you have
to mark the patch area wider
to miss them with the saw blade

After you make the saw cuts,
use a fairly wide and thin
chisel to "split" out the flooring

Pry block gives you more
leverage to remove the
damaged strips

Make sure the cut you've made is square after you have removed the damaged section.

Carefully square the patching strips so they fit the damaged area perfectly. Countersink nails on adjoining strips

Prefit new strips first, making sure the edges are square. They should be a "squeeze" fit. Then nail in the strips

Countersink nailheads in strips. If strips are oak, it helps to predrill pilot holes for nails with a slightly undersize drill

Tap in last strip, using a hammering block to protect it. Then tap down the entire patch, using the same technique

Fill end joints with matching wood putty, forcing this material deeply into the cracks. When dry, sand the patch area

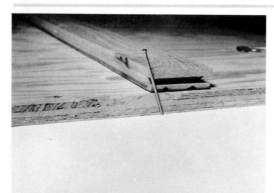

Nails in strip flooring should go in at about 60-degree angle, as illustrated here. When you buy strips for patches, avoid twists

You also can nail strip-flooring this way; predrill pilot holes for the nails, and countersink them. You also can use screws

SAGGING FLOORS, fortunately, occur most often on the first level. If you have a basement or crawlspace, you probably can make the repairs yourself. A sagging or vibrating floor is caused by lack of support from the joists under it. The joists sometimes shrink from dryness, or they may have rotted. Check to see if these conditions exist. If the joists have rotted, you will have to have a professional replace them.

92
94
257
272

If the sag is great, you can support it with jackposts that are adjustable. If you don't pour a new concrete footing under the jackposts, you're taking a chance on cracking your basement floor. Only you can make that decision. In any case, don't attempt to level the floor in one operation. Instead,

Squeaky floors can be silenced in several different ways, as pictured on this page. 1. Puff graphite powder into the floor crack at the squeak. Then "tromp" on the spot to work the powder down into the joint. 2. If you have basement access, drive a shingle wedge between the subfloor and joist where the squeak seems the loudest. 3. Brace the subfloor with a strip of 1 x 3. Press the edge of the strip firmly against the subfloor. 4. Bridging between joists can become loose, causing squeaks. Renail this, or add it if it isn't in place. 5. Rugged bridging of 2 x 8s not only helps a squeaky floor, but a sagging one, too. The bridging is end-nailed through the joists

give the jackposts about a quarter-turn once a week. Do this until the floor is level. You can determine this by stretching a line between two points in the room. If you attempt to level floors that are sagging badly in just one operation, you can damage the sidewalls and foundation of the house.

Jackposts, as indicated, need a solid base. In a crawlspace you can try sinking a block of solid concrete into the ground below the frost line.

In older homes, a steel girder or beam may be needed to span the joists above the jackposts. For this, span the joists at right angles at the midpoint of the run. If you use a beam instead of a steel girder, it should be a well-selected 4 x 4 timber.

If the second floor is sagging, you'll have to rip up the flooring to find out why. The reason usually is broken or cracked joists, caused by running pipes through them or notching them out for duct-work. Replacement is a job for a professional.

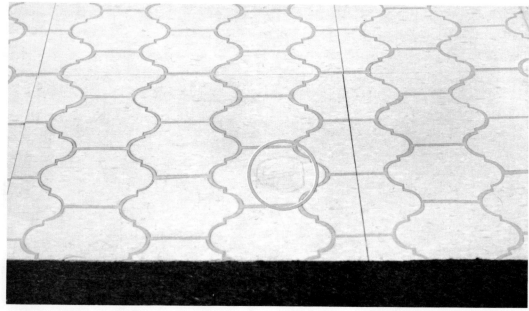

Breaks and dents in resilient tile often are caused by bad underlayment. Sharp heels can cause holes

To remove damaged tile, heat it with a light flame from a propane torch. Or use an iron covered with a towel

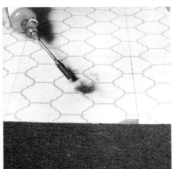

Go completely over the tile with the flame. Use asbestos board at joints to avoid damage to adjoining tiles

With an old chisel, break out damaged tile. Keep bevel of chisel down. You may have to reheat areas as you go

Clean subflooring and make any patches necessary. If floor is concrete, use latex cement for patch; it dries very quickly

Sand the subfloor smooth and level so there are no humps or holes. Use a wide sanding block .

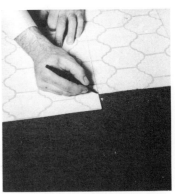

For partial tile repairs, mark edges, as shown, and connect the lines with a straightedge. This assures more accuracy

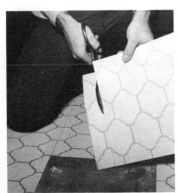

Cut new tile with tinsnips or on a bench saw. You can cut some types with ordinary scissors. Keep the cut edge square

"Butter" the back of the tile with tile cement. Spread it fairly thin—especially at the edges

Butt new tile against adjoining one and drop it into place. Then "slip" it until joints match

171

REFINISHING HARDWOOD FLOORS is a job 257 272 448 you can do yourself if the floors aren't in too bad shape. You can rent sanding equipment, but check it out on an open-end arrangement, so you won't have to turn it in when you're only half finished. Sanding can be very time-consuming. Here are the steps:

1. Remove the old finish. The fastest way is with the sander, but you can use paint and varnish remover, then sandpaper and a woodscraper. *Ventilate the room if you use a paint remover!*

2. Countersink nailheads before you use a sanding machine. If you don't, you'll rip the paper.

3. Use coarse sandpaper for the first cut, working across the grain of the floor. *Do not run the sander in a stationary position.* You will "groove" the floor. Always have the sander in motion when it is running. With an electric edger, finish the first cut around the wall areas; hand-sand in the corners.

4. Use a medium-grade paper for the second sanding. When this is completed, give the floor a final sanding with fine-grade paper.

5. Before you apply any finish to the floor—stain, shellac or varnish—make sure all the sawdust has been vacuumed away, and go over the floor with a tack rag. Sand lightly between coats of finish by hand, or use fine steel wool. Pick up the resulting dust with a tack rag.

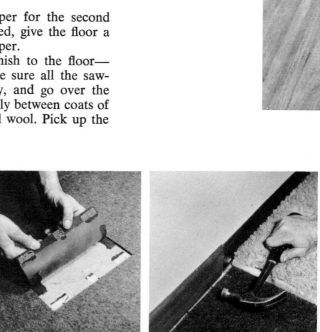

Reseal ceramic tile floors about every two to three years with a clear liquid sealer you can buy. This helps protect the grout

Carpet tiles can be replaced by simply prying them out and installing the new ones with double-faced tape

Joints in molding you pry off to replace flooring don't show as much if you miter them instead of butting them

Remove quarterround and/or base shoe around the room. An old chisel makes a good tool for this

You can cover old floors fast with peel-and-stick tile. First, clean the floor, removing all wax and dulling the finish with steel wool. If the floor is really wavy, you might have to sand it before installing the tile. You can rent sanding equipment for this project

Split the room into quarters and snap a chalkline at the half-way points. Be sure your measurements are accurate

Check spacing of last tile and wall. If it is over 8 in. or under 2 in., move the centerline over. The space between the wall and last tile should be about half the "leftover" width. This will give you even rows on opposite sides of the room

After measurements are correct and you test with dry tile, start peeling and sticking where centerlines cross. Be precise with first tile!

Butt tiles together; don't slide them into place, since adhesive will stick and you'll have to break tile to remove it. Press down

At edges, lay edge tile down (white for illustration) and cover it with another tile for marking edge. Then cut (white) tile to fit the space

FINISHES FOR WOOD FLOORS include shellac, a special sealer, varnish or a plastic-type finish.

Shellac dries fast, but it tends to be "soft," which may not meet your requirements. If you use shellac, buy three-pound cut (this means it's thinned) and give the floor three thin coats of it. If you use shellac as a varnish base, make sure the shellac is compatible with the varnish you will brush over it. Check the labels.

Varnish dries to a very hard finish. If you brush it over an oak floor, a filler has to be wiped on the floor first to fill the wood pores. You then sand the floor lightly, remove the debris with a tack rag, and apply three coats of varnish. Let the varnish dry at least 24 hours between coats. Lightly buff the finish with fine steel wool between coats.

Plastic floor finishes can be used on any wood floors except pine. You'll need three coats of the liquid plastic. Let the first coat dry for two hours. Apply the second coat and let it dry for about six hours. The third coat should dry at least 15 hours before you walk on the floor.

Sealers penetrate into the wood. You apply most of them with a brush, and then wipe off the excess with a soft, lint-free cloth. Then rub the surface with fine steel wool before the finish dries. Let this coat dry overnight. Apply the second coat, wipe and buff with steel wool. Let this dry 20 hours. Apply the final coat, buff with steel wool, let it dry, and apply wax.

doors and windows

INTERIOR DOORS and the inside surfaces of windows require about the same type maintenance and involve the same type repairs as their exterior counterparts.

Interior doors are usually hollow core. This means they consist of a wooden frame of thin slats covered with a skin of plywood veneer. You have your choice of different kinds of wood if the door is to be finished natural. These include birch, Philippine mahogany, gum and several others. If the door is to be painted, the type of wood, of course, doesn't really matter, but the quality of the door should be good to block sound and drafts.

Sticking and binding. Check the hinges first. The screws may be loose. Tighten them if you can. If you can't, replace with longer screws. If this still does not work, plug the holes with matchsticks or other wooden plugs, and reset the screws.

If the door is binding at the top or bottom edge, which is usually the case, you can shim out the hinges with a piece of thin cardboard. Rule of thumb: If the door binds at the top, shim out the bottom hinge; if the door binds at the bottom, shim out the top hinge.

Changing a passage door lockset is almost identical to changing an exterior door lockset. The lockset will either be bored or mortised into the door. Here are the steps in changing a mortised lockset:

1. Remove the knobs and plates. Since mortise locks were used on older homes, the knobs and plates are probably painted over. You can break the paint seal on screws with the tip of an ice pick. Clean out the screw slot with the pick; use a razorknife to cut the paint seal on the plate. The lock should slip out with a little prying encouragement from an old screwdriver.

2. Most lock conversion kits come with installation instructions, and you should follow these for special types of locksets. In general, however, the second step is to mark the center of the mortise on the door. Use a square to trace the line on the face

Passage door (interior) lockset is removed by first releasing tabs that hold on knob and plate. Screwdriver triggers the tabs, shown here on the plate. Tab on knob is on shank. New passage locksets are inexpensive; you can facelift older doors with new locksets for just a few dollars

of the door, using the edge for alignment. Then mark the spot vertically where the doorknob will go. At this point, you bore a hole in the door with a hole saw or fly-cutter bit.

3. Now mark the edge of the door—horizontally and vertically—where the latch will go. You may have to extend the mortise to accept the latch plate, and you may have to drill out a hole for the latch.

4. Slip in the latch and install the lockset.

5. Install the strike plate on the jamb. You may have to mortise out wood on the jamb for this, after you remove the old strike plate.

Locked doors. Small children sometimes lock doors from the inside, then don't know how to open them. With modern locksets, it's not difficult to open them from the outside. Look at the doorknob. It probably has a small hole or slot in the center. If it has a pin hole, stick a pin or piece of stiff wire in the hole. This will frequently trigger the lock.

If the lock has a slot instead of a hole, try any thin key. If this doesn't work, substitute the tip end of a thin screwdriver blade or penknife.

On old locks, the unlocking job may be harder. Try wedging a putty knife between the latch and the strike plate on the jamb, or slip a thin piece of sheetmetal or a plastic credit card between the latch and the jamb.

If none of the above tricks work, you'll have to remove the hinge pins, and then remove the door. Sometimes the hinge pins are on the other side of the door. If they are, try removing the lockset and pushing it through the other side of the door. Can't? Then you'll have to break down the door to get in.

Cabinet doors most often develop hinge problems so they won't close properly, or they won't meet friction catches. First, try tightening the hinge screws. If the wood has been pulled out or the threads are stripped in the screwholes, try running in longer screws. You also can try the plug treatment.

Bathroom medicine cabinet doors are usually hinged with a piano hinge or continuous hinge which is welded to the metal. If it sticks or binds, try silicone lubricant or graphite powder to make it turn smoothly again. Or use penetrating graphite oil. It is impossible, or impractical, to attempt to

Back out two screws, turn the plate, and the entire lock assembly can be removed from the other side of the door. If plate is stuck, tap it lightly

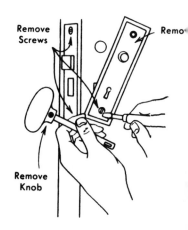

Remove Screws

Remo

Remove Knob

1 REMOVE OLD MORTISE LOCK

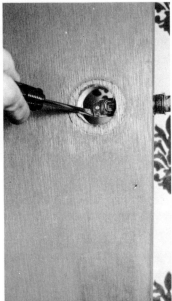
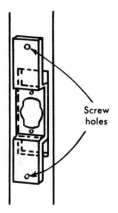

Screw holes

Latch is made in a single unit. It is simply pushed into the correct size hole bored into the edge of the door. Doorknob holds it in correct position

To remove the latch, pry it out with the tip of a screwdriver. Be careful as you pry so you don't damage the hole for the replacement

2 MARK DOOR

Remove Lock

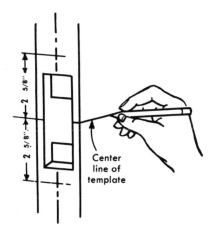

2 5/8" 2 5/8"

Center line of template

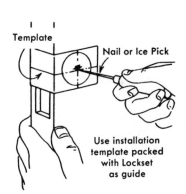

Template

Nail or Ice Pick

Use installation template packed with Lockset as guide

change a welded-on hinge. Instead, you'll have to replace the cabinet.

TROUBLESHOOTING WINDOW PROBLEMS

How to "unstick" windows, how to replace sash weights, how to replace broken glass, and other common problems are discussed in the exterior section on windows. Below you'll find a potpourri of general information on windows and their accessories.

Types of window glass. For most windows, you should buy plain sheet glass. This material is graded according to quality. The better the quality, the more it costs: AA is special-order glass; A is superior grade; B is standard. Standard is often used for regular windows and storm sash. You can also buy greenhouse grade.

Plate glass is usually ¼-in. thick and there may be some distortion in it. Heavy polished plate glass is at least ⅜-in. thick. It is used only for large windows.

65
72
73
74

3 BORE HOLE IN DOOR

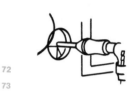

4 INSTALL LATCH

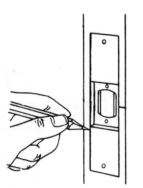

5 INSTALL LATCH PLATE

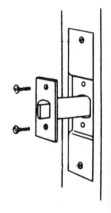

7 INSTALL STRIKE

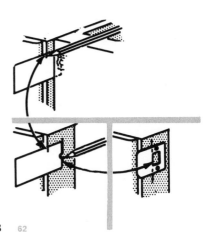

6 INSTALL LOCKSET

FOR INSTALLATION
OF LOCKSET, SEE
INSTRUCTION SHEET
PACKAGED WITH THAT
PARTICULAR LOCKSET

Insulating glass is simply two pieces of glass with an airspace between. The edges are sealed— usually in metal with some sort of gasket in the metal. Don't confuse this material with laminated glass, which is two pieces of clear glass sealed together with a piece of plastic sandwiched between. This glass is used in auto windshields. It won't fly into jagged pieces when broken.

Tempered glass is the best material for patio doors and windows, since it is rated up to five times stronger and impact-resistant than glass that has not been treated through a heating and cooling procedure.

You can buy tinted glass in several different colors. This might be beneficial to reduce airconditioning loads. Use it in stormwindows that go on the south and west side of your home; leave the storm windows up during both the heating and cooling season.

Wired glass is used in commercial buildings, but you may want to consider it for basement windows. It is glass that has wire mesh laminated into it. If the glass should break, the wire helps hold it together.

Fixing window shades. If a window roller shade does not operate smoothly, check to see if the brackets have pulled loose. The tiny nails that hold them often do. Replace the nails with screws. If the bracket is bent, you can straighten it with pliers. There should be about 1/16- to 1/8-in. between the bracket and the end cap of the roller.

If the spring tension in the shade is too tight:

Kids locked in bathroom?
Screwdriver or hat pin inserted
in hole in center of doorknob
triggers lock. If this won't work,
you'll have to remove hinge
pins to get the door open

179

If, after tightening hinges or shimming them out, door still sticks, plane edge at binding point. Take off just as little wood as possible and test door in opening as you go. When you have a good fit, refinish the edge

1. Roll up the shade completely. 2. Remove it from the brackets and unroll the shade about 6 to 8 in. Put the shade back on the brackets and work it up and down a couple of times. This balances the tension in the spring.

Shades that have a weakened spring can be repaired by removing the shade from the brackets and rolling it back up by hand. Put the shade back in the brackets and roll it up and down to get the proper tension.

Drapery rod repairs. Draperies that are difficult to pull shut or open can be caused by rods that are bent, loose on the wall, or unevenly adjusted.

Brackets attached to the wall with nails are quick to work loose through the push-pull of the cords. Before you look further, check the brackets and if they are loose, replace the nails with screws, toggle bolts or Molly anchors. Also check the screws on the bracket attachments. These sometimes work loose causing the rod to malfunction. The attachments should be set evenly.

A dirty track also can cause poor operation. Make sure it is clean. A vacuum cleaner does a fast job of removing frayed cord, dirt, dust and other debris. Some rods are very difficult to clean without opening a "gate" at the end of the rod.

Need simple storage cabinets? Try the easy construction shown at right

59

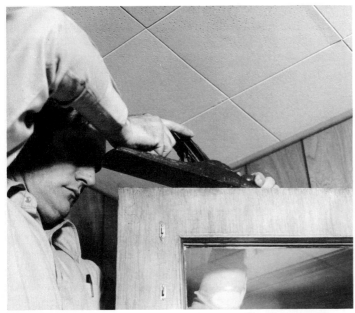

Plane top edge of doors from outside edge in toward the center. This prevents splitting the wood when the plane runs off edge. Doors swell in spring and summer from moisture; shrink in late fall and winter

"Invisible" type hinges are excellent to support heavy doors on cabinets; they are easy to install with a screwdriver. You need only insert them into a saw kerf. Predrill pilot holes for the screws

Top invisible hinge rides on top edge of door and is fastened to the framing members with screws. Three hinges are best to support long cabinet doors

Doors can be cut from a sheet of ¾-in. plywood with one (preferably two) smooth unblemished faces. Or fasten ¼-in. plywood to ½-in. backing

Shelving frame is simple 1 x 2 stock butted, glued, and finish-nailed to hide raw plywood shelf edges. Put in shelves first, then frame them

For special purposes, you can build your own windows, using thin slats to form channels for the frames to run in. Fairly thick glass doesn't have to be framed, although the edges should be beveled slightly—a job the dealer will do for you. Window pull shown here was simply glued to the glass. Boards for channels are redwood slats nailed to structural framing; trim is standard casing

Cords are subject to wear and because of this they can cause malfunctions in the rod. If the main carrier is sluggish, push it to the right as far as it will go. At the same time, you'll have to loosen the cord so it will travel to the left.

How to repair Venetian blinds. The problems here generally are worn tapes that hold the slats together, and dirt in the gear that operates the slant of the slats.

To replace the tapes, remove the little clamps that are on the bottom rail. Staples are sometimes used as fasteners; you can pry these out with the tip of a screwdriver. You now have access to the cords that raise and lower the slats. Here, you'll find knots that hold the cords in place. Untie the knots and pull out the cords, remove the slats, and unfasten the tapes from the tilting device. Install the new tapes in the same way you removed the old ones—but in reverse.

If the tilting device is lagging, try lubricating the pulley and the locking device with powdered graphite.

Shutter problems. Today's shutters are mainly for show, not service. Many are made with fixed slats, so problems that do exist are in hinges that are loose. Tighten them.

If the slats operate but are broken, chances are that the vertical rod that controls them is broken or the little wire pins that hook onto the slats and rod are pulled out. You can rehook the wires with pliers; try gluing a broken rod.

Plastic pressure latch keeps windows tight against frame so they don't rattle. Latch is flush-mounted with screws

To open the windows, you simply unlock the plastic latch. You need one for each sash—outer and inner sections

Plastic guides are inserted into the channels to make the windows run smoothly without binding

To install large patio windows, you have to cut studs to insert header. You can do this most easily with a circular saw

Patio window (pre-fabbed) simply sets in precut opening. Double the studs at the sides for additional support

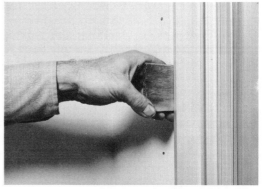

Level and plumb the patio window with shingle shims. Final job is to patch wallboard and refinish it

Wooden blinds. These are the roll type—very narrow slats laced with a cord that pulls the blind up in accordion-fashion. To replace the cord, you untie the knot that holds it, pull it out of the channels, and off the pulley above. Then, retrace the same procedures in reverse to thread in the new cord.

CONDENSATION ON WINDOWS

If condensation is a problem it usually is first noticed on windows, then on walls and ceilings. This *is not* a window or wall problem. Condensation is caused by "wet" air inside the house hitting a cold surface such, as a window or exterior wall. First, you must check to see if there is too much humidity inside the house. This can be caused by poor water drainage in bathtubs, sinks, and laundry tubs; an unvented clothes dryer; too much water from a humidifier.

Assuming these problems are corrected and the windows still steam over, you should make sure the storm windows are tightly sealed, which provides double insulation. Tape or caulk them shut, if needed, or use weatherstripping to block the outside air.

If moisture is collecting on the inside of the storm window, this means that the main window is leaking air. Weatherstrip it if necessary. And *do anything you can to reduce the humidity inside the house.*

Aluminum windows should be double-glazed to prevent ice from forming along the frames during the winter months. If you have aluminum windows, by all means invest in storm windows to cut fuel bills and prevent moisture damage to sills, walls and the structural members behind the walls.

If ice dams do build up along window frames, do *not* try to force the windows open to break the ice. You'll bend the frames or tracks. Instead, install storms and let the ice melt, wiping up the water.

Steel-framed basement windows are especially subjected to ice and air leakage during the winter months. If you don't have storms for these, you should buy them. As a stop-gap measure, you can cover basement windows with a sheet of polyvinyl film such as is used for painting dropcloths. Staple or tack the material to the frame if possible. Or tape it over the window. The material is translucent so light will filter in during daylight hours.

Basement windows drafty in winter? You can seal out the weather with sheets of polyvinyl film tacked to the frame of the window. It lets in light

Stubborn screens and sash on aluminum combination windows and doors slide easily after you coat them with silicone lubricant or graphite powder. This lubricant can be used for wood as well as most metals

painting shortcuts

A NEW PAINT JOB can hide a multitude of old 100
sins. And, best of all, you can perform such a
facelift easily and inexpensively. In just two or
three hours, you can paint an average-sized room;
and it's ready for guests an hour after the last
stroke of the roller.

There are two basic types of wall paints (you 101
use them for the ceilings, too): solvent-thinned
and water-thinned.

Solvent-thinned paints include modified-alkyd,
resin-based enamels (oil-based enamels), and
alkyd enamel. They are made, usually, with a synthetic resin as the film-forming material.

Water-thinned paints use latex particles emulsified in water as the film-forming resin. The three
common types are rubber, PVA or vinyl, and
acrylic. Other types include thixotropic or dripless
paint, epoxy, and urethane or polyurethane
finishes.

One of the newer types of paint is a *semigloss
latex enamel*. Using it in combination with flat wall
paint, you have the convenience of a total latex
paint system—flat finishes for walls and ceilings,
matching semigloss for woodwork, kitchens and
bathrooms. The coatings adhere like a politician's
bumper sticker to new and painted surfaces, and
to plaster, concrete, brick, cinder block, wood and
gypsumboard.

Here is a summary of what paint to use where
and why it is best suited for that surface. A quick
reference chart in this chapter will also help you
make a selection before you arrive at the paint
store:

Walls. If the walls are lath and plaster, you can 104
use nearly any paint on them. But the plaster has
to be aged and thoroughly dried for at least three
months; five months is best. Seal the surface first
if you use a flat *oil* paint. Manufacturers do not
recommend flat oil paints for kitchens or bathrooms. Instead, use an enamel or semigloss, rubber-base, or a quality emulsion paint. Gypsum
wallboard can be painted with the same paints you
would use on plaster. Most people prefer working
with rubber (latex) wall paints because lap marks
don't show and tools are easy to clean up.

Puzzled by all those
new and exotic
paints? Actually, there
are only two
basic types

185

Ceilings. Since they are light-reflecting surfaces, ceilings should have a dull surface paint that will reflect the light in a uniform way without bright highlights. For bathroom and kitchen ceilings, use semigloss finishes. They are easier to wash. You can coat plaster and gypsum wallboard with flat oil paint or paints of the semigloss, emulsion or rubber-base types. You also can use casein. If the ceiling hasn't been painted before, use a primer before you apply the paint.

Woodwork and trim. Use a semigloss, enamel or flat oil paint if the wood is new and you want an opaque finish. Flat oils are easy to finger-mark and are not the best surface for window sills. Here, use an emulsion or rubber-base paint.

All of these coatings can be used to refinish wood that has been painted or varnished. Make sure all wax has been removed before you repaint. Any surfaces that appear to be glossy should be sanded lightly with a fine grit sandpaper before they are painted. Paint creeps on glossy surfaces and doesn't cover well.

You'll probably need more than one coat of paint if you are changing from a deep color to a light one. If you use an enamel or semigloss, you should apply an undercoater first.

For a transparent coating, so you can see the grain underneath, use an interior varnish followed by a coat of wax. Open-grain woods such as oak need a wood filler. Stains are used to lend color to the wood. Run a couple of test strips before you actually use the stain. Stain has a way of changing color depending on the wood to which it is applied. Don't depend on the color chips in the dealer's showroom.

Metal surfaces. Steel windows need a metal primer first, then a top coat. Aluminum windows don't need a primer. You can coat both types with aluminum or rubberbase paint, enamel, semigloss or flat paint.

Heating ducts, radiators, pipes. Use a metal primer first. The finish coat can be the same type of paint used for steel windows.

Wood paneling. For a pigmented finish, use the same paint that you would for woodwork. Prepare the surface the same way. You can use flat paint, semigloss, emulsion or rubber-base paint. If you want a transparent or semitransparent coating, fill the wood first—if it has a porous grain. Then,

120

101

110
116

You can find out what type paint to use on various surfaces in your home by checking the reference chart at right

When you open a new can of paint, punch holes around the rim with a nail. This lets the paint in the lid channel drip back into bucket

WALL PAINT: WHAT TO USE WHERE	flat paint	semigloss	enamel	casein	interior varnish	shellac	wax	wax (emulsion)	stain	wood sealer	floor varnish	floor paint—enamel	aluminum paint	sealer-undercoater	metal primer	latex types
plaster walls & ceiling	X	X		√										√		√
wallboard	X	X		√										√		√
wood paneling	X	X			√	√	√		√	√						X
kitchen/bathroom walls		X	X													
wood trim	X	X			√	√	√		√							X
steel windows	X	X											√		√	X
aluminum windows	X	X											√		√	X
window sills					√											
heating ducts	X	X											√		√	X
radiators & pipes	X	X											√		√	X
old masonry	√	√		√									√	√		√
new masonry	X	X								\				√		√

X = a primer or sealer may be needed on this surface before you apply the finishing coat, unless it has been finished

Before you reseal a can of paint, wipe out the channel with the tip of your paintbrush. Also wipe away drips down side of can

Always stir paint with a paddle— even if it has just been shaken on a machine at the paint store. Pigment starts to separate immediately

To reseal paint container, cover top with old piece of cloth and hammer the lid in place. This prevents any splattering

apply shellac or varnish, then wax. For wood tone, apply a stain after the wood is filled. Apply varnish or shellac followed by a coat of paste wax.

MORE INTERIOR PAINTING SHORTCUTS

In selecting paints, don't forget light reflectance of colors. For example: white reflects 80 percent; ivory 71 percent; apricot-beige 66 percent; lemon-yellow 65 percent; light buff 56 percent; salmon 53 percent; pale green 51 percent; medium gray 43 percent; pale blue 41 percent; deep rose 12 percent; dark green 9 percent.

Don't work over the furniture in a room—work around it or without it. Take a couple of extra minutes to properly cover the floor with dropcloths and masking tape. It will save you hours of cleanup time and may save you the expense of having a rug or carpet cleaned.

Hardware in the way? Remove it if you can. Can't? Then cover it with masking tape. This is usually easier than trying to "cut" around it with a sash brush.

Grease and ballpoint pen marks on walls can "bleed" through paint. Wash off all grease with mild detergent and warm water. Seal pen marks with a daub of shellac or sealer. If your walls are fairly clean, you don't have to wash them. But you should dust them. If the existing coat is an enamel, sand the surface before you repaint. Use a fine grit sandpaper over a block for this. You don't have to wear out an elbow to be effective. You just want to "tooth" the surface.

Rollers are faster than brushes—unless the brush is a six-incher or so. But rollers emit a fine spray of paint as you run them over a wall or ceiling surface. This is why you should cover everything you don't want painted. When buying roller covers, *read the label* on the package. There are many different types of roller piles that will give you a variety of surface textures. Be sure you pick the texture you want, which is usually listed on the package.

Use this trick when you're painting a ceiling: Go across the width of the ceiling rather than the length. This gives you time to start a second lap before the preceding lap is dry.

Always work from a dry or unpainted surface to a wet one. Keep the edges wet throughout the

Fill holes and cracks in walls and ceilings with Spackling compound or patching plaster. When dry, sand the patch smooth

Spot-prime patch areas with same paint you'll use on the wall or ceiling surface. Feather out the edges

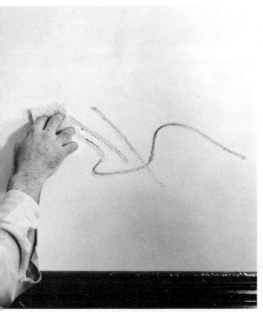

Wash off all dirty marks you can with a mild detergent and water. Use a flat sponge and scrub hard

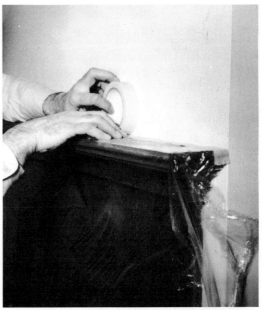

Cover everything you don't want splattered with paint. Plastic dropcloths are inexpensive; use masking tape to hold them

job—even if the paint may be advertised as "lapless."

In selecting colors, remember that lighter colors will make a small room look larger. Bright colors in large rooms can detract from furnishings and accent pieces. Use a bright color to accent one wall if you wish; go to a more neutral color for the rest of the walls.

Color should be harmonious; it should flow from room to room. Don't switch from bright to dull colors in rooms that adjoin each other and where doorways are left open. If you paint woodwork, use the same color as the wall.

Pipes and radiators should be painted the same color as the walls. If there is a hanging duct, paint it the same color as the ceiling.

EQUIPMENT KNOW-HOW

With a roller extension handle, you can paint ceilings while you stand on the floor. If you don't want to use an extension—or you are using a brush for the job—use a sturdy stepladder and

Mask windows so about ⅛-in. of paint will cover glass for a seal between the window frame and the glass

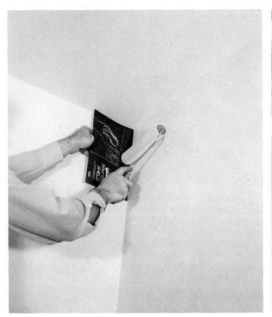

Paint shield of cardboard keeps
the spatters off ceilings and
walls you don't want painted.
This is often easier to use than
masking tape

Clean-up is easy with non-oil
paints. Roll out excess paint on
old newspapers, as shown. Remove as much paint as you can
before washing the roller

spread it out as far as it will go. Also, lock the
bucket holder in position. If you use an extension
plank between ladders, make sure the plank is
solid and don't stretch it to its full length. Take the
time to move the working platform; don't risk a
fall.

Bargain paintbrushes are a bargain, and they
are best suited for trim painting where you will fill
in the large areas with a roller. If you are going to
paint a large area with a brush, buy a good one.

Brushes used in oil-based paints (rollers too)
can be kept overnight by wrapping them in aluminum foil or plastic wrap, or inserting them in a
plastic bag. Always wash out brushes and rollers
used in water-based paints, even if you are going
to work with them the next day. These paints dry
fast; don't take a chance of trying to store them
overnight in paint that may harden just enough to
ruin them.

Wash roller under running faucet until the water is clean. A mild detergent may help. Be sure to clean off ends of roller

Clean brushes the same as rollers: Wipe out excess paint on newspapers. Then rinse brush under running faucet

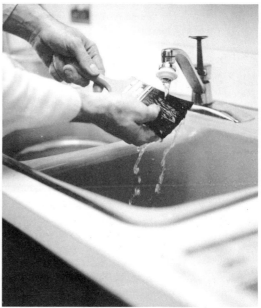

Wash paint from brush with liquid or bar soap. Work it into the bristles, and then rinse them until the bristles come clean

Fill brush with clean water and press out excess. Then form the bristles into their original shape. Wrap the brush in plastic

IN REMODELING AND HOME IMPROVE-
MENT, the big cost is labor—not the materials.
By doing the work yourself—or at least some of
the work yourself—you can save countless dollars,
which can be re-invested into bigger and better
projects. These improvements add to the value of
your home and tend to appreciate over the years
in your basic shelter investment.

This section on remodeling contains a potpourri
of ideas for your home: kitchens, bathrooms, attics, basements, room additions, general living
areas. You also will find how-to details to help
you do most of the improvement work yourself.
Some of the work, however, may involve profes-
sionals, since building codes restrict the work to a
pro. For example, we recommend that you hire a
professional for hooking up wiring circuits and
plumbing runs. You can, however, do a lot of the
rough-in work yourself—but conform to the codes
and the building permit that you are issued.

And, we suggest that you buy prefabricated 274
materials when large quantities are specified. Although you may pay a bit more for these materials,
the ease of handling will make your project easier
to complete with more professional-looking results.

kitchens

OF ALL HOME IMPROVEMENT projects, kitchen remodelings are the most frequent. If your kitchen is 10 years old or older, it probably needs some type of remodeling or improvement help, from new appliances to more efficient working space.

Your kitchen can be remodeled in stages, or you can do the entire project at one time. Generally, if you do most of the work yourself it is better to work in stages, since food preparation is a daily function, and part of the kitchen has to remain functional. You can block off sections in which to work; as one section becomes completed, move to another.

Planning is the key to kitchen remodeling. It also is the key to *all remodeling projects*. Start by gathering a batch of good published material on the subject. Consumer magazines are an excellent source for ideas. Building-supply dealers will gladly provide brochures from building-product manufacturers that will help you select products, dimensions and colors. Appliance dealers can furnish you with a host of material that well help

remodeling

Ceiling beams, paneling and new floor help tie this kitchen and dining area together. Island range also serves as counter

After you have made some primary decisions as to new appliances, cabinets and finishing materials such as floor, wall, and ceiling treatments, buy a pad of grid paper. *The grid paper will permit you to lay out your plan to scale.* For example, 1 square can equal 1 square foot. Or it can be a larger dimension. Just maintain the same scale throughout, for appliances, cabinets, and modular building materials.

200
242
456
201

Kitchen layouts should be designed around a *triangle*. The centerpoint of the triangle should be the sink. From this point, the distance to the refrigerator and to the range should not be less than 12 ft. nor more than 22 ft. If the distance is less than 12 ft. or more than 22 ft., the homemaker will be cramped for space or will have to take too many steps. On page 201, you can find more information on the triangular concept.

Kitchens along one wall are considered a *minimum* layout. Space becomes too cramped to work in comfortably, since appliances have to be jammed together. Avoid this type of plan if at all possible.

Island kitchens, at first glance, may appear to be a waste of space. This is not true if the island can be made into a base cabinet, incorporating a dishwasher or range. It also can become added counter space, if the island is large enough. In any case there should be about 3 ft. of walking area between the island and other countertop or working areas.

U-shaped kitchens have the range and refrigerator on or near opposite legs of a triangle, and the sink at the base of it. The biggest advantage to a U-shaped kitchen is little cross-traffic. It also provides you with a better plan for storage space.

Corridor kitchens are designed with cabinets down opposite walls. If this kitchen has both ends open, you may encounter a traffic problem. If possible, close one end, forming a long U-shaped unit. Cabinets in this type arrangement should have a minimum "walk-between" space of 5 ft.

L-shaped kitchens have cabinets on two right-angle legs. Unless you have plenty of space, the L-shape plan can also have poor traffic patterns.

A shortage of counter space is a prime problem in many kitchens. In planning, here are several rules of thumb adaptable to the triangle principle:

Beside the refrigerator, you should have at least

Before remodeling, this kitchen had adequate space, but poor planning. Space was wasted around range and along window wall

During remodeling, cabinets and appliances were completely removed, but in stages, so kitchen remained functional for food preparation

New kitchen including a utility room centers around work island placed near an appliance wall. A suspended luminous ceiling provides glare-free light

1½ ft. of counter space for loading and unloading foods. Plan this space on the latch side of the refrigerator door.

At the range, you should have about 2 ft. of counter space. It should have a wooden or ceramic inset in the working surface so you can set down hot pans and dishes.

At the kitchen sink, you should have about 3 ft. of space on either side of the sink. If you have a built-in dishwasher, it should be installed on the left side of the sink.

Other countertop areas should include space for mixing and preparing foods. This space should be at least 4 ft., if possible. *A serving area* also is desirable if space permits. The best spot for this is near the range or refrigerator. If the space is next to the range, install a heat-resistant panel in the countertop for serving hot foods.

COUNTERTOP WORK AREAS seldom stand alone or in a single-purpose unit. Therefore, countertop work space that is shared (most of it will be) should be as long as the longest countertop use required—plus one more foot.

As an example: A refrigerator and serving center countertop should be about 4½ ft. long. The serving center will utilize about 3½ ft., and the refrigerator counter 1½ ft. However you take the longest countertop—which is 3½ ft., and add one foot. This measurement is approximate. If the space available offers more countertop area, you should, of course, make use of it. The formula above is based on research studies of best kitchen working arrangements.

Countertop height should be 36 in. If the homemaker is exceptionally tall or short, the height can be altered. Here's how: Have the homemaker stand straight at a countertop. Have her bend her elbows. Measure the distance between the floor and her elbows. This measurement, less 6 to 9 in., is the right height.

Countertop surfaces are important. The most common material used is high-pressure laminate

Laundry incorporates homemaker's planning area and laundry folding center—on opposite side

Appliance wall consists of vegetable sink, refrigerator-freezer, dishwasher, garbage compactor, washer and drier

Fireplace wall before remodeling had useless opening, which was used for infrared food warmer (top). After fix-up, dining area was added

which, in kitchens, should be installed by a professional. A topnotch job requires the use of special equipment. Another possible surface material is ceramic tile with hardwood insets, although you may want to cover an entire countertop with either material for decorative purposes. You can buy hardwood inset kits.

Storage and base cabinets are the second biggest expense (second to appliances) in remodeling a kitchen. Relate them to the various centers you plan. For example, base and wall cabinets near the range should be designed to handle pots, pans and the utensils you use in the food-preparation process. Next to the sink, the cabinets should be designed to hold products related to washing dishes.

Cabinets for pantry supplies, for the most part, should be at eye level where you can read labels.

For convenience appliances such as coffee-makers, blenders, toasters and mixers, you should have cabinets with deep and widely-spaced shelves. If at all possible, don't store these appliances on countertops. They cheat you of valuable working space, and they add clutter.

New cabinet hardware, cabinets, and matching drawer fronts are an inexpensive way of updating a kitchen, as shown at right. New floor tile also was installed, and some equipment replaced

Homemaker's center includes handy desk, telephone, intercom system. Only 3 ft. of countertop space was utilized for center. Desk top is 32 in. high

TAKE A SYSTEMATIC APPROACH to re-modeling your kitchen, if you plan to do most of the work yourself.

1. Plan the new kitchen, using the triangular principle for sink, range and refrigerator placement.

2. Get a building permit, if needed. You will need a permit if the job involves changing the structure of your home; or running in new plumbing or electrical wiring.

3. Plan your work in stages so you have use of kitchen facilities as long as possible.

4. Unless you have lots of storage space—such as a carport or garage—schedule material deliveries.

Perforated hardboard panels are ideal for kitchen installation. You can buy metal hooks and brackets to hang almost any item you want

KITCHEN PRODUCTS

Since cabinets are prefabricated, and most are approved by a kitchen-cabinet manufacturers' association, it is easier for a do-it-yourselfer to hang the prefab units than to build them. You can buy base and wall cabinets in wood or metal. The widths vary from 9 to 48 in., usually in 3-in. modules. Wall-cabinet heights run from 12 to 33 in., in 4-in. modules. Depth runs about 12 in., although you can buy cabinets that vary from this depth. Base cabinets are 34½ in. high as a standard. The top increases this to 36 in. You also can buy special cabinets less than this measurement.

When installing cabinets, set the base cabinets first, then the wall cabinets.

Appliances naturally are a matter of choice, and the money you have to spend. There are so many types made in so many different combinations and colors that a choice is bewildering. However, you will want to consider ranges with self-cleaning ovens; dishwashers; microwave ovens; refrigerator-and-freezer combinations; garbage disposers; trash compactors; intercom systems; range hoods; and ventilating systems.

Ceiling treatments can include everything from painted plaster to tile suspended on metal channels. Indirect lighting can easily be built into suspended ceilings. 442 443

Floor treatments also vary. Vinyl tile and strip flooring is easy to install and maintain; indoor-outdoor carpeting and carpet tiles also can be used for kitchens. The floor should blend, in color and design, with your cabinets and appliances. 173 220 448 457

Kitchen cabinets are made in metal or wood. Here, the cabinet doors are particleboard with hardwood veneer faces. Pick good cabinet hardware. Nylon rollers, metal tracks, nylon drawer slides, and magnetic catches are recommended

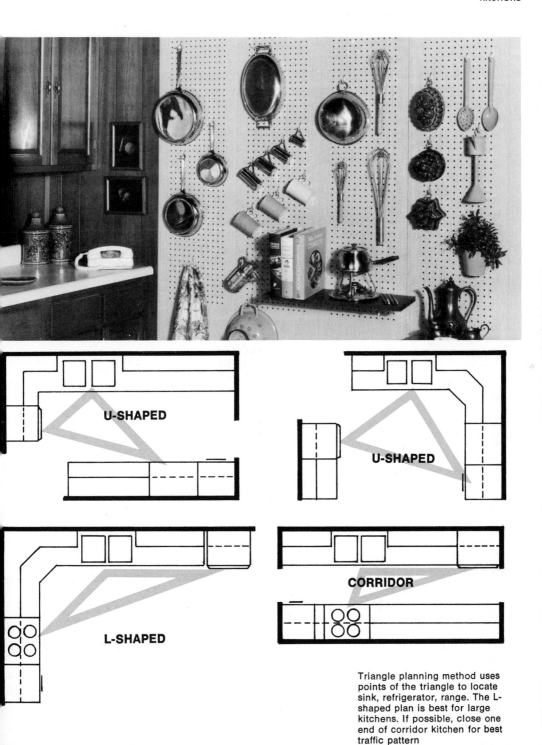

U-SHAPED

U-SHAPED

L-SHAPED

CORRIDOR

Triangle planning method uses points of the triangle to locate sink, refrigerator, range. The L-shaped plan is best for large kitchens. If possible, close one end of corridor kitchen for best traffic pattern

Walls should be painted with a gloss or semi-gloss paint for easy maintenance. Or you can cover them with easy-to-clean vinyl wallcoverings. Simulated stone or brick can be used as an accent, along with ceramic tile.

Electric power must be adequate in kitchens to run the various appliances. It is recommended that you add new outlets for countertop appliances, and that you have 240-volt, three-wire electrical service installed for electric ranges and other large appliances.

TIPS ON INSTALLING CABINETS

For proper support, wall and base cabinets should be fastened to studs with screws. Measure 84 in. up the wall from the floor. This is the top height of wall cabinets.

Base and wall cabinets have to be level and plumb. Shingle shims can be used to adjust this. Install the cabinets from one corner, and add cabinets to each side.

For installation holes, drill left front stile 6 in. down from top edge and 6 in. up from bottom. On 12-in. wall cabinets, drill only one hole. On base cabinets, drill 8 in. from top and bottom edge.

Fasten the cabinets to the wall with 2-in. wood screws. Shim with shingles, if needed. For corners, use a corner filler.

187 224 225 240 444 451 458 146 149 157 257

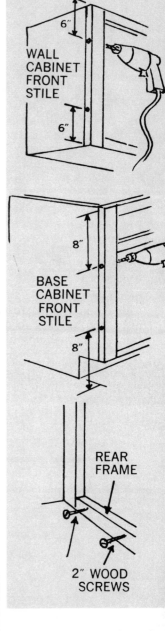

WALL CABINET FRONT STILE

6"

6"

BASE CABINET FRONT STILE

8"

8"

REAR FRAME

2" WOOD SCREWS

If kitchen is an open plan and it will adjoin a living area, it's best to tie both together with the same wall, floor and ceiling material. Here, the kitchen planning center also blends with the dining and family-room furnishings as a unit

basements

BASEMENT SPACE IS BONUS SPACE. Yet the basement usually winds up as a junk catch-all.

Space planning is the key to basement remodeling—as it is with other rooms. Since a basement follows the same outside wall line as the rooms upstairs, you can (if you wish) plan on the same type of room arrangement downstairs. Before you buy any materials, first plan how the basement space will be used: as additional living space in the form of living and sleeping areas, as a recreation room, as a hobby center, as a sewing room.

Dampness and the lack of light are probably the major problems in most basements. With materials now available, you can dampproof basement walls, vent moisture out of the entire area, and properly heat and cool the space. And you can widen windows to create more light, or fill them in with glass block to deter moisture. To prevent tracking through upstairs living areas, you can in-

96
446
458

Paneling is the easiest way to hide defects in walls in the basement. This arrangement uses several types for interest

If ceiling is high enough, you can add false beams and tie-in paneling to carry out decorating scheme.

stall an outside door and steps.

To dampproof basement walls from the interior, patch all cracks with cement and apply asphalt waterproofing along the joint at the base of the wall and the floor. If you have water problems from the outside, these troubles will have to be solved with drain tile and/or a waterproof membrane installed from the exterior. You may also need a sump pump, professionally installed, if the water problem is a severe one.

From the interior, brush a coating of waterproof paint on the wall. The wall should be thoroughly covered. Then install furring strips for either wallboard or paneling. The lowest strip or tip of furring on a basement wall should be about 1 in. above the floor. Fasten insulation with a thermal barrier between the furring strips—or over them. Use cypress or redwood for furring strips. Or use wood treated with a preservative to discourage moisture penetration into the wood.

Basement floors with a water-vapor problem can be treated with masonry paint. Or you can use poly sheet in a thin coating of waterproof adhesive.

154
159

75
76

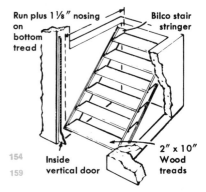

Areaway with stair stringers is framed this way. Before you buy door, determine the inside dimensions of the opening: height, width, length

For indirect lighting, cover window with valance. Set out from wall. Recessed lighting in ceiling goes between joists

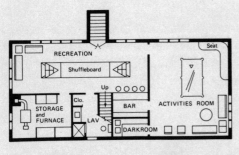

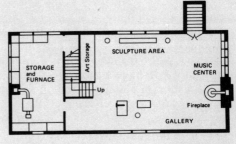

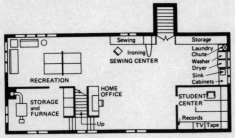

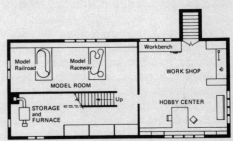

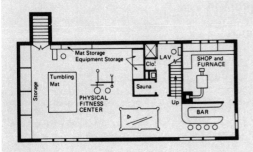

HOW TO FIGURE A ROOM

Perimeter	Number of 4 x 8 ft.
36′	9
40′	10
44′	11
48′	12
52′	13
56′	14
60′	15
64′	16
68′	17
72′	18
92′	23

Determine the perimeter. This is the total width of each wall in the room. Then use the chart above to figure the number of panels you need. Deduct ½ panel for a door (A); ¼ panel for a window (B); ½ panel for fireplace (C). These figures are for rooms with 8 ft. ceiling heights, or less. If your ceiling is higher, consult a dealer. If the perimeter falls between the figures, use the next highest number for panels you need.

The poly sheet should be 4 mils thick. Many times all that is necessary to deter dampness is a coat of masonry paint teamed with a dehumidifier. You can tell if you have a moisture problem this way: Place a sheet of aluminum foil on the floor. Weight it. After three days, check the foil. If it has moisture on it—tiny water droplets or beads—you have a moisture problem.

Resilient flooring is a broad term covering tile, linoleum and vinyl strip material. Since resilient flooring will tend to follow the contour of the floor, it is important that the basement floor be dry, smooth, and free of dust, grease, wax and other foreign material. Dusty concrete floors should be cleaned with a vacuum cleaner; remove any base trim before you start.

Do not use asphalt felt over concrete as a base for resilient flooring. You can, however, lay tile over old vinyl asbestos or asphalt-tile floors. The surface must be flat, tightly bonded, and free from wax, paint and other coatings.

Lighting is important in a basement, since the source of outside natural light is usually limited. If you want more natural light, you can excavate below grade, remove part of the foundation, and install windows or glass block. A much easier way is with artificial light installed between floor joists or behind valance boards.

Wall outlets and switches are easy to install, since most walls will be furred out for a finish treatment. The junction boxes are installed between the strips—or in partition walls.

166
173
220
238
272
457

448

266
347
348
351

For deep areaways, doors with door extensions are available. They are furnished in 6, 12, 18, and 24-in. sizes, and are easy to assemble

Bottom step is recommended in basements where distance from top of finished floor to top of foundation wall exceeds 7 ft. 7 in. (below left). This permits shorter areaway and provides 6 ft. 2 in. headroom

Vertical Door

Foundation Wall

Stair Stringer

Concrete Step

Stairwell Floor May Be Here

Finished Basement Floor

8¼″   Stairwell Floor

H

L

W

After wall has been properly prepared, paneling can be installed over furring strips. You can attach panels with glue

Adhesive fasteners go on furring strips like caulking compound. The strips are attached to masonry walls with lead anchors

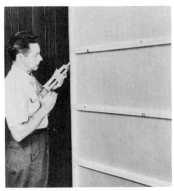

On some adhesive installations, you must run the adhesive bead completely along strips to hold the weight of the panel

To lay floor over concrete, clean the floor first. Then find center point of room. Snap a chalkline. Lines cross at center

Spread adhesive over one section of floor at a time. Spread it thinly. Make sure tile adhesive is for below-grade use

When adhesive is tacky, start laying tile in the first quarter-section. The first tile goes at the point where lines cross

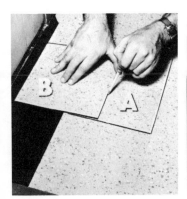

To trim tile to fit against wall, measure it this way. As you lay the tile, make sure the joints are butted tightly

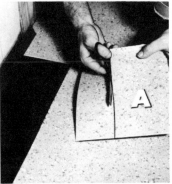

Cut tile with scissors after you scribe measurement. With some types of tile—asphalt, for example—you score it

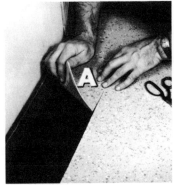

Insert trimmed tile. When you complete entire job, roll floor with 150-lb. roller. Or use a rolling pin. This assures a tight bond

WATER SOFTENERS are, in many areas, a necessity, and they are fairly easy for a homeowner to install with just a Phillips' and regular screwdriver, hacksaw, adjustable wrench, slip-joint pliers and a ruler.

266
448

You can locate the softener in the basement or a utility closet. The cold-water line to it should be ahead of your water heater and all cold-water outlets you want softened. For outside water lines, provide a separate hard-water line ahead of the softener.

Minimum water pressure at the softener inlet usually is 20 pounds per square inch. Your local water department will give you the pressure reading. The maximum pressure should not be over 120 pounds. A minimum flow rate of 2 gallons per minute is required for some softeners, while a 3-gallon-per-minute flow is required for others. You can check the water flow by filling a 1-gallon container from a fully-opened faucet nearest the

Water heater and softener connections are shown at right. Electric water heaters are hooked up very much the same as their gas counterparts

Hardboard teak paneling was used in this basement remodeling. Paneling also was used to cover support posts. Floor is covered with indoor-outdoor carpeting; ceiling is acoustical tile

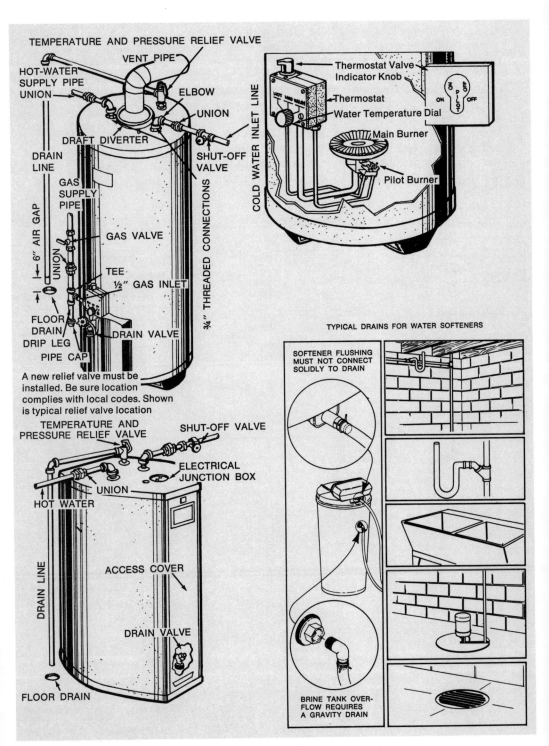

TEMPERATURE AND PRESSURE RELIEF VALVE

VENT PIPE

HOT-WATER
SUPPLY PIPE
UNION

ELBOW

UNION

DRAFT DIVERTER

COLD WATER INLET LINE

SHUT-OFF VALVE

DRAIN LINE

GAS SUPPLY PIPE

GAS VALVE

TEE
½" GAS INLET

¾" THREADED CONNECTIONS

6" AIR GAP

UNION

FLOOR DRAIN
DRIP LEG
PIPE CAP

DRAIN VALVE

Thermostat Valve
Indicator Knob

Thermostat
Water Temperature Dial

Main Burner

Pilot Burner

ON PILOT OFF

A new relief valve must be installed. Be sure location complies with local codes. Shown is typical relief valve location

TEMPERATURE AND PRESSURE RELIEF VALVE

SHUT-OFF VALVE

ELECTRICAL JUNCTION BOX

UNION

HOT WATER

DRAIN LINE

ACCESS COVER

DRAIN VALVE

FLOOR DRAIN

TYPICAL DRAINS FOR WATER SOFTENERS

SOFTENER FLUSHING MUST NOT CONNECT SOLIDLY TO DRAIN

BRINE TANK OVER-FLOW REQUIRES A GRAVITY DRAIN

softener. The container must be filled within 30 seconds to assure a flow rate of 2 gallons per minute, or within 20 seconds to assure a 3-gallon-per-minute flow rate.

Before you start working with the pipe, shut off the heat to your water heater and all water at the main valve. Open a couple of faucets to drain the water lines. You can buy flexible connectors, which can be used with galvanized pipe or copper tubing to compensate for any misalignment when you hook up the softener to the main plumbing lines.

When you complete installation and you're sure connections are tight, turn on the water.

334
335
339
340

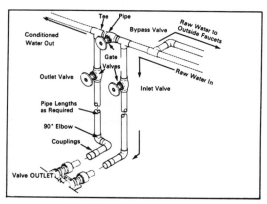

Copper-tubing installation of water softener uses three gate valves as the bypass system. Disassemble valves before sweating joints

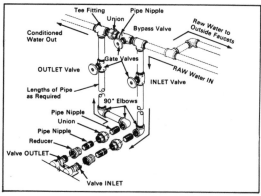

Galvanized-pipe installation also uses three gate valves. You'll need pipe wrenches and pipe-threading tools for this

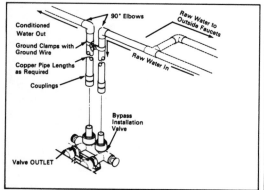

Bypass installation with copper tubing. For tubing you'll need a propane torch, solder and flux, file and reamer

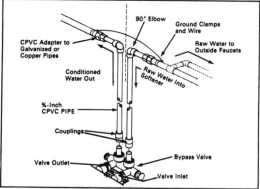

Galvanized or copper tubing with ¾ in. CPVC (plastic) pipe. Piping shown is ¾ in. If pipe is 1 in., use regular couplings

210

bathrooms

REMODELING AN EXISTING BATHROOM is easy, since the difficult parts—plumbing and electrical lines—already are completed. It boils down to switching fixtures and dressing up the room with a new wall, floor and ceiling.

Standard bathtubs, in white or colors, are made 5 ft. long by 30 in. wide. You can buy larger tubs, if you have the space available. Standard tub depth is from 12 to 14 in. Buy a tub that has an

438

218

acid-resistant finish. Colored tubs have this feature already built-in.

Installation of a tub is hard but not difficult 343 work. To remove the old tub, you have to disconnect the water and drain lines. If the tub butts against a stub wall, you may be able to disconnect the lines through an access panel in the bathroom, or on the opposite side of the stub wall. Look for a trapdoor that may be under tile or taped with gypsum wallboard on the stub wall. If you don't find either, you will have to open the wall to disconnect the water pipes.

Modern steel tubs, designed to rest on the floor, completely fill the area from wall to wall. When the space is just large enough for the tub, the wall covering may have to be removed from the three adjoining walls to fit the tub properly. If the space is longer than the tub, you can open the walls at one end and the side only. Then build the unopened end out to fill the additional space.

When the walls are open, nail 1 x 4s to the studs. Tops of these members should be level and at the height required to rest the tub flanges on them. Lower the tub into position with flanges resting on the 1 x 4s; anchor each end of the tub to the end boards with screws through the flange holes. Then refinish the walls. If you buy a cast iron tub, the 1 x 4s usually are not necessary.

The drain fitting for the new tub will be similar 268 to the one you removed. It should be accessible through the access panel in the tub. Simply connect the fixture drain to the branch drainpipe end in the floor behind the tub. The connection is usually made with a slip-joint nut, similar as those used for lavatories. Supply-line connections, which also can be reached through the access panel, are made like lavatory connections.

Toilets are manufactured both with the flush 455 tank and bowl as a single unit and with the flush tank and bowl as separate units. After you turn off the water, remove the old toilet.

To set the new bowl, install the floor flange (on 329 most models) that rests on the floor around the 330 drain line. The flange has spots for two bolts. If the bowl requires four bolts, locate the bowl on the floor, in position, and mark the spots for the two additional bolts. Then set these bolts.

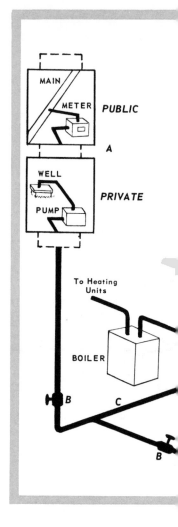

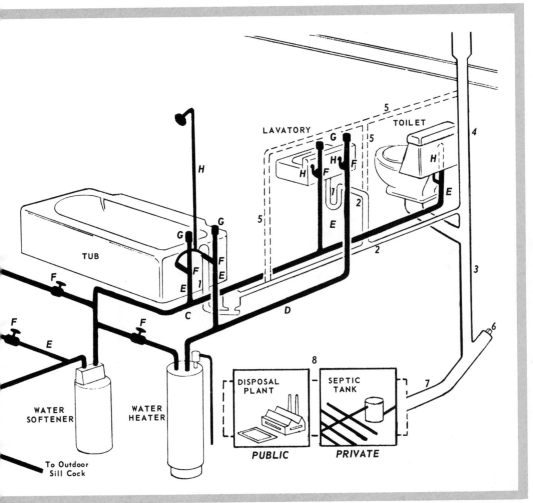

LAVATORY

TOILET

H

TUB

WATER SOFTENER

WATER HEATER

DISPOSAL PLANT

SEPTIC TANK

PUBLIC

PRIVATE

To Outdoor Sill Cock

Water-supply system parts. A: water source; B: stop and waste valve; C: cold water main line; D: hot water main line; E: branch line to fixture; F: shut-off valve; G: air chamber; H: fixture supply line

Drainage system parts. 1: fixture drain; 2: branch drain; 3: soil, main, and secondary stacks; 4: vent; 5: revent; 6: cleanout; 7: building drain; 8: final disposal. Systems shown are typical of many installations

ROUGH-IN MEASUREMENTS

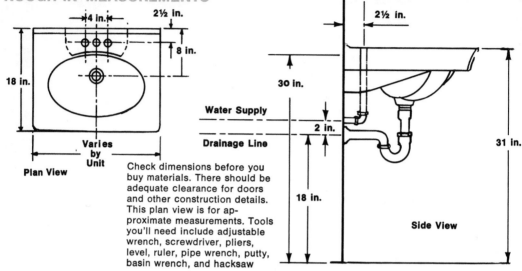

Plan View

Side View

Check dimensions before you buy materials. There should be adequate clearance for doors and other construction details. This plan view is for approximate measurements. Tools you'll need include adjustable wrench, screwdriver, pliers, level, ruler, pipe wrench, putty, basin wrench, and hacksaw

INSTALLING A CABINET-MOUNTED LAVATORY

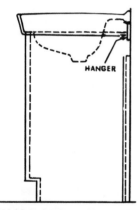

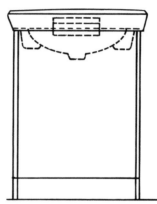

Locate and set cabinet. Scribe around baseboard and trim so cabinet sets flush on floor and against the back wall. Temporarily set the lavatory on the cabinet in installed position. If needed, use wooden shingle shims under base of the cabinet so the cabinet and lavatory are level. The installation instructions provided here are typical. Specific guides usually are available for any model lavatory you purchase

WALL-MOUNTED LAVATORY

Lavatory hangers

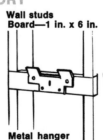

Wall studs
Board—1 in. x 6 in.

Metal hanger

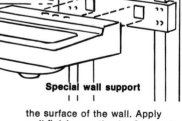

Special wall support

Hangers are furnished for wall-mounted lavatories. In some installations, you have to add proper support for hangers on the wall

Mortise 1 x 6 into wall studs to provide necessary support. Use wood screws to fasten the 1 x 6 to the studs; the board must be flush with

the surface of the wall. Apply wall finish over the 1 x 6; mount hanger with at least four screws. When fittings are on, hang lavatory

RECONNECTING SUPPLY LINES

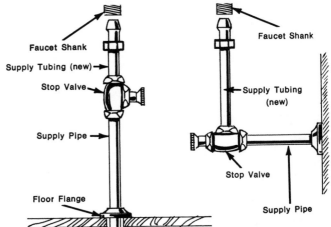

Typical floor and wall-pipe connections. For later servicing, put shut-off valve in both the hot and cold-water supply line. Carefully bend the supply tubing to fit, and tighten the coupling nut with an adjustable wrench. When completed, turn on the shut-off valve and the water. If there are any leaks, tighten the connections. If chrome-plated pipe is used, pad wrenches with adhesive bandages

INSTALLING A DRAIN

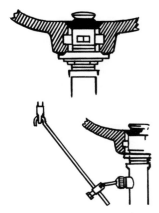

Remove stopper from drain. Then assemble rubber washer under drain-plug flange. Insert plug in lavatory and apply plumber's putty between lavatory and washer. Then attach other washers, locknut, pop-up assembly. Lift rod should point to rear of unit. Loosely assemble lift rod to pop-up rod. Try it to see if it works properly. Then tighten the set screw and sealing cap to hold up lift rod and knob

CONNECTING THE DRAIN LINE

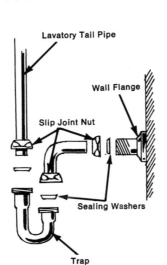

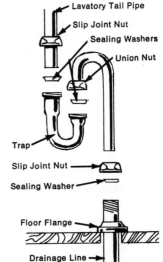

To block sewer gases from entering house, fixture drain line must have a trap. Replace the old trap during this job; a 1¼ in. size is needed. Slip trap over tailpiece and match it to fit drain line. If it is too short, add an extension. Tighten the assembly and check for any leaks

Trap connection can be made to a drain offset as much as 6 in. from the fixture drain center line, or as little as 2 in. from it. Slip the trap over the tail pipe and rotate it so it will match the drain. Tighten the connections to a snug fit; check carefully for any water leaks

If your floor is wood, you'll need bowl bolts that have wood threads on one end and machine threads on the other. *If your floor is concrete,* set the heads of the machine bolts in holes drilled in the concrete; fill holes with epoxy cement.

The bowl is ready to set in position at this point. Turn the bowl upside down and distribute putty completely around the rim of the bowl. Then distribute the putty completely around the discharge opening on the floor. The putty should be 1 in. high.

Arrange the putty on the rim so it will press inward when pressure is applied. The putty ring on the floor should be set so the putty will press outward. This prevents it from going into the drain and clogging it.

Set the bowl. Weight it by sitting down on the lid. Check the bowl for perfect level. If it isn't, you will have to wedge it level. Then tighten the bolts to a snug fit.

The flush tank sets on the rear end of the bowl, if it is not a part of the bowl unit. Two bolts usually hold the bowl in position. The water connection is sealed with a gasket. The fixture supply lines are fitted on flanges on the tank. The water supply can come through the floor or from the wall. In either case, you should install water shut-off valves for service.

NEW CONSTRUCTION PLANNING

If you are building a room addition with a bathroom in it, or adding a bathroom facility to your attic or basement, plan the space for an adequate water-supply and drainage system. You also should plan on how best to provide a new soil stack for the fixtures, when adding a new room or converting an existing room. In either case, it is often advisable to add a new stack, which can run through a closet or up an outside wall. The stacks should be located close to the toilet. You may run a branch drain from this stack to the existing sewer. It has to be reached in as straight a line as possible. Floor plans of the new bathroom may have to be altered slightly to accommodate the water supply, drainage system, and stack location. A close inspection of your present plumbing system will help you determine this planning factor. *A rule of thumb:* Put the bathroom as close to existing plumbing as possible in remodeling. In

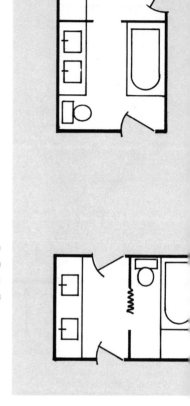

Typical bathroom floor plans include these, from top left: double lavatory with storage built-ins; single lavatory; large master-bedroom plan with access from a hallway door; separate lavatory, toilet, and tub facilities; adjoining bedroom facilities; separate lavatory, toilet, and tub facilities in a different door-arrangement

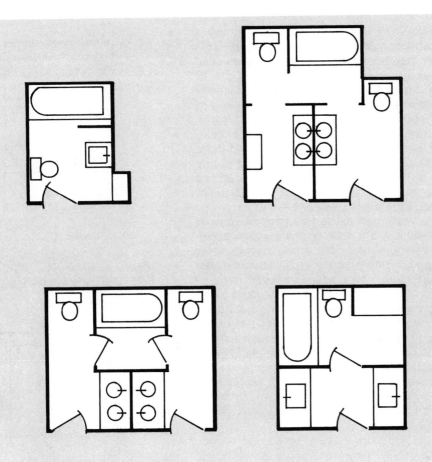

new additions, this may not be as critical.

Other planning tips include these:

• Lavatories, showers and bathtubs should be located away from window areas, since windows tend to create drafts. The fixtures also should be planned with traffic patterns in mind.

• If an inside bathroom is planned, you should vent it with a skylight or exhaust equipment. You may have to conform to building codes in your area. Check the codes at the outset.

• Heating and lighting will have to be provided. In existing bathrooms, this usually isn't a problem. In new construction, both will have to be installed according to codes. For some installations, you may be able to use an electric or gas wall heater. Either requires only a simple hook-up to the power source. *Do not use portable heaters in the bathroom.*

342
343
344
345

FOR NEW CONSTRUCTION, you can buy a prefabricated bathroom. It is manufactured like a huge shell, which is assembled on the job and can be lowered into position by a crane. Or it can be assembled in the space allotted for it. When completed, it has all the fixtures in place—tub, shower, toilet, lavatory.

You also can buy prefabricated bathroom components. These include a bathtub, walls and floor. A prefabbed shower unit has fixtures, walls and a floor. It is simply connected to the water and drain lines. Components often can be utilized for remodeling, as well as new construction.

Wall treatments in bathrooms include gloss or semigloss paint, vinyl wall coverings, wood paneling in lavatory (not bath) areas, high-pressure laminates, decorative hardboard, ceramic materials, and simulated brick and stone panels.

Around bath and shower areas, ceramic materials and high-pressure laminates are most often used since water can't penetrate them.

Storage in the bathroom should be considered in your plans. Even if the bathroom is small, there are several tricks you can use to add storage.

If the walls are gypsum wallboard, you can cut out the wallboard from between studs for shallow storage of cosmetics, medicines and other small bathroom items.

Don't overlook the space over the bathtub or toilet for a cabinet for towels and wash cloths. If you buy cabinets for this, make sure they are fabricated from waterproof materials.

Walls offer space for narrow shelves for additional towel and wash cloth storage, as well as cosmetics and sundry decorative jars and boxes.

Fixtures such as towel bars, soap dishes, toilet-tissue holders, and medicine cabinets are fastened to the wall or recessed into the wall surface.

Medicine cabinets and recessed soap and tissue holders are mounted between the studs; most cabinets project from 2 to 6 in. into the room, although you can buy shallow, flush-fit cabinets for between-the-studs installation. The cabinets are fastened in with screws. Holders are either screwed or cemented into the wall.

Floor treatments include ceramic tile, resilient floor materials, indoor-outdoor carpeting, or carpet tile. If you plan on using a fiber material to cover the bathroom floor, stick with one that is

274

136
157
160
187

256

444

451

457

448

220

445

457

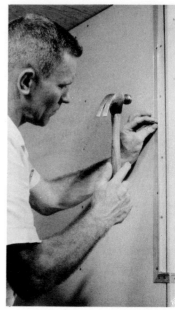

For high-pressure laminate bathroom installation, lay out job, nailing mouldings into studs. Technique is termed "Panel System 202"

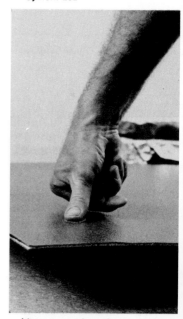

After you apply activator, let it dry until sticky. Test tackiness by pressing material with a finger. Then wait five minutes

Dry-fit sections to assure good fit. Use of paper templates reduces fitting time in aligning panels in tub or shower

After test fitting, apply activator to the perimeter of wall area. Then remove film from back of panel and apply coating to it

Use a J roller to assure uniform contact with cement. For corners, use a hammer and wooden block to tap the surface tight

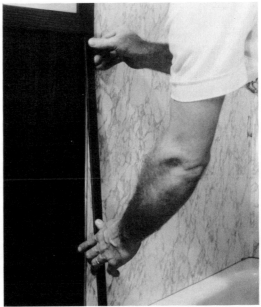

Mouldings are shaped to fit 18 panel-edge situations. All provide joint coverage and panel edge hold-down

water resistant. Otherwise, dampness may cause mildew or rot.

For indoor-outdoor carpeting installations, you can either lay the carpeting with a backing pad or it can be glued to the floor. *Carpet tiles* are already padded. You install them with adhesive or double-face adhesive tape. If you use tape, run two strips of it at right angles across the room. Apply the tiles to the strips. Then lay the rest of the tiles in place; friction holds most other tiles in position. You can also buy self-stick carpet tiles. To install these, peel off the protective film backing and lay them in place similar to resilient tile. In any carpet or tile installation, make sure the floor is free from wax, paint and dirt.

Sheet vinyl and linoleum can be used in bathroom floor installations. Both materials are generally laid over the same underlayment materials as their tile counterparts. Check your dealer for specific instructions.

Seamless floors go down like paint. After you clean the floor, apply the opaque base coat of plastic. Mix the colored flakes together, and then sprinkle them onto a wet coating of clear laminating plastic. When the entire floor is covered and dried, sand it lightly. Use a fine-grit abrasive to remove any projecting flakes. To complete the job, add several more coats of clear plastic.

Ceramic floor tile is usually sold and installed in 2-ft.-square sheets, with a paper covering on one side.

To install wall tile, find lowest spot. Snap vertical line. Determine tile height from lowest point; add half-tile for fitting

Mark tile for cutting where it will go around fixture or outlet. Trim will cover tile, hiding any measurement mistakes

Snap scored tile over a nail to break it. Nail should align with score mark; press firmly down on both sides of the tile

Cap strip completes field tile. Since it may be wider than field tile, the joints may not align. Level cap strip as it is installed

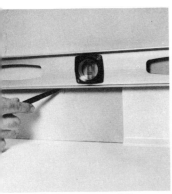

Level the bottom row of tiles and mark this line. The vertical chalkline mark and the horizontal level line should intersect

Using a tile for a template, mark the rows of tile up to the height you want the tile to go. Make this measurement accurate

With notched adhesive spreader, cover small section of wall with adhesive where first row of tiles will go up wall

To go around irregular shapes, mark shape on tile. Then score as well as possible with glass cutter. Nibble excess

Install cut tile this way, after adjoining tiles have been set in place. If there is a low spot "shim" it with extra adhesive

To cut tile, score it with a glass cutter, using another tile as a guiding edge. Press hard; score tile several times

When tiling is completed, clean the tile with a special cleaner. It will remove excess adhesive from the surface of the tile

Tile grout is mixed with water to a fairly stiff consistency. Let job set two days before grouting. Force grout into joints

When grouting is done, clean tiles again. Let job set another five days or so. Let grout dry and coat it with sealer

To install a ceramic-tile floor, first remove old flooring material. If there is underlayment, remove this so the subfloor is exposed. Carefully clean the floor, taking time to pull nail stubs and checking the subfloor for warping and rot. If you find damage, it should be repaired.

Remove any doors into the bathroom and the thresholds. Also take off baseboard or shoe moulding. The tiles will be butted against the wall. If you can remove any obstructions from the floor, such as heat registers or radiators (you can usually jack them up slightly), do so, since the tile should go under these obstructions. If you can't remove them, the tile will have to be cut to fit around.

Install waterproof paper over the subfloor. It should overlap about 3 in. at the joints. Turn edges up at the walls about ¾ in. Then tack down the paper to hold it in place. A stapler does a fast job.

Install fine-mesh metal lath you buy in sheets over the waterproof paper. It, too, must be tacked down at about 8-in. intervals over the entire span. You can cut metal lath with snips to go around obstructions and into corners.

Mix a batch of stiff concrete, using 1 part portland cement to 3 parts fine sand. The mixture must be stiff or the tiles will sink. Apply the mixture to the floor with a trowel to a ¾-in. depth. Screed this level, working in small patches at one time. You can use divider strips ¾ in. wide for the screed to ride on; remove the strips as you place each section of tile into the cement.

To place the tiles, lay the sheet down on the cement with the paper side up. Lay adjoining sheets the same way, making sure the joint lines between each sheet are the same. Fit around objects as you go. You can score and break tiles to fit, or nibble them with pliers to go around irregular objects.

After the tiles are in position, take a short length of 2 x 4, lay it face-side down over the tiles, and tap *very gently* with a hammer. Level the tiles as you go; you'll have to tap harder in some spots than in others.

Remove the paper backing with water. Then grout the joints in the same way you would grout wall-tile joints. Remove the excess grout, let the job stand for several days, and then seal the joints with grout sealer. You can mix your own grout: 1:3 concrete-and-sand mixture.

To install shower door, level bottom track on edge of tub. Ends are joined in vertical track; joints are sealed with adhesive

Doors roll on top track; bottom track helps guide them and keeps doors from slipping out. Thread doors on top track

Plumb vertical track on wall.
Bottom of track slips into both
bottom and top door track.
You don't have to remove tile

Fasten track to walls with
screws and/or masonry anchors.
You will have to drill pilot holes
through tile and wall

Door bumpers in end tracks keep
doors from slamming against
metal track and breaking. They
screw in position

With doors in place on track,
lift entire unit into place and set
it on vertical track members.
You may need a helper

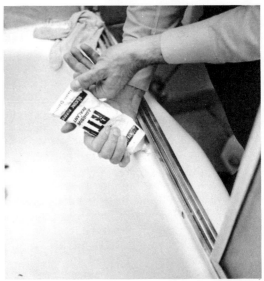

Bottoms of doors slip easily into
the track. Fill the joints with a
sealer-adhesive, pushing it
forward along joint lines

specialty materials and how-to tips

BUILDING MATERIALS can be classified into two categories: structural and decorative. Structural materials include rafters, joists, studs, sheathing, underlayment, etc. Decorative materials include wall coverings, window treatments, paneling, paint, etc. Many materials are, of course, both structural and decorative. In this chapter, you will find some of the more popular materials available, and how to install them.

Wall and ceiling beams used to be hand-hewn, and helped hold up the house. Today many are made from plastic materials that look more like real beams than real beams! Polyurethane-foam beams are sold in kits. You can buy a ceiling-beam kit or full beams with wall braces. *To install them,* snap a chalkline across the ceiling—or down the wall—for a straight guideline. Spacing can be any dimension, but about 4 ft. is best. Adhesive is applied to the beams with a caulking gun; the beams are then pressed into position. Most beam materials are U-shaped, so the hollow space permits a channel for concealing wiring for lighting, stereo, etc. For cutting the beams, use a fine-toothed hand saw; for small cuts, use a razorknife.

Real wood beams feature natural chisel marks. They are three-dimensional, and the three sections are attached with cloth strips. To install them, nail 1 x 6-in. strips to the wall or ceiling at about 4 ft. intervals. Unfold the beam material and nail it to the edges of the 1 x 6s. Countersink the nails, fill the holes, and finish.

Simulated brick and stone are generally used for accent walls in any room in the house. They are manufactured in panels and individual units.

Panels can be nailed directly to the studs in new construction. In remodeling, the panels go over 1 x 3-in. furring strips fastened to the studs with nails or to hollow-wall construction with toggle bolts or Molly anchors. You nail the panels to the furring and grout the joints with a special adhesive that is applied with a caulking gun. Some panels are pregrouted.

Individual units are installed with a mastic.

Typical closet can become catch-all since it is not organized (top). Rods, shelves, boxes, and drawer units make same space more functional

First, determine the pattern you want: basket weave, herring-bone weave, or running bond. Then coat the clean, dry wall surface with mastic. Press each brick or stone in the mastic with a slight twisting motion. This provides a mortar line between facings. Work three to four rows at once.

Curtains and draperies. Fabrics you can use are almost limitless—from bamboo through cloth to plastic. The rods and rollers to hang curtains and draperies are fairly standard in dimensions, but parts may not be interchangeable.

Before you buy any material, first determine what you want it to do. *Some rules of thumb:* If the window frames a pleasant view, choose drapery or curtain material that is sheer to filter the light during the daylight hours, with an over-drapery for privacy at night.

If the windows are in a corner, the curtains usually should draw away from the corner. You can buy right or left traverse tracks.

There are four basic types of shades: pull-down, pull-up, Austrian shades and Roman shades. The

Wall accents, such as paneling, can create a "new" room in a matter of hours—and at low cost. Other materials include specialty wallpapers, simulated brick and stone

latter two are not on a roller; both are adjusted with cords, rings and pulleys. Austrian shades are used in somewhat formal areas, while Roman shades have deep pleats in them when they are raised. The Roman shade is usually chosen to go with contemporary or country furnishings, with or without matching draperies.

To measure for shades, find the *exact* distance between brackets. If the shade will be an "outside" hang, the brackets should overlap the casing or trim pieces by 1½ to 2 in. *The length of the shade* should be the length of the window, plus 1 ft. *Always measure each window.* Windows may look alike, but there may be slight variations.

Prefabricated fireplaces can be decorative or functional. There are several types: free-standing,

197
236
447

Ready-to-finish cabinet was used here to form base for closet built-ins. Upright supports are 1 x 10s with shelving butt-jointed

Scraps from a paneling job were mounted flat to accent a wall here. Decorative columns hook to joists to support seats

Open-end plywood boxes offer
excellent storage for kids' toys.
Boxes are butt-jointed, glued and
nailed

Home entertainment center
utilizes screw-on shelf brackets,
spotlight lighting, and a table
with a 2 x 4 frame covered with
plywood

Window treatment has sheer
curtain for daytime use; roller
shade for night. Valance is cut
from tempered hardboard

False beams carry out decorative
theme of the paneled wall. Beams
are hollow, and conceal the
wiring for the lighting

227

wall hung, and ceiling hung. Some burn wood; others provide electric heat. Still others are for show, not glow.

Electric heater fireplaces are usually installed with brackets that are screwed to the ceiling joists, wall studs, or floor. Heaters are 110/120-volts, and are simply plugged into an outlet. There are 220-240-volt models, which require a 220-volt outlet. Heat is fan-forced and controlled by an automatic thermostat.

Log-burning fireplaces have to be chimney vented. Flat-roof installations are the easiest, since the insulated chimney goes through a hole cut in the built-up roofing material. The fireplaces also can be vented through attics and installed on pitched roofs. For two-story houses, venting becomes more of a problem. The stack can run into the furnace flue system or be installed in a closet space.

BASIC STORAGE IDEAS
Through prefabrication, you can buy a wide range of case-type furniture pieces to form the base for

Girl's room has bed centered on wall with storage closets at each end and above. Alcove plan is excellent for small rooms where storage is a problem

Plywood paneling forms boxed beams in a family room. Hidden adjustable brackets are used for the shelves. Framing is 2 x 4s

Oak cubes stained chocolate form bedroom study area. Base is 12-drawer case piece; doors are plastic-coated hardboard

High-pressure laminate was used on countertop, then run up wall to tie Dutch bar into an attractive alcove unit

Beams are polyurethane, stove is backed by brick tile. Shutters carry out family-room theme in Early American

many storage units. Some case pieces are unfinished so they can be stained or painted to your taste.

Basic storage consists of shelving, drawers, rods and cabinet units. Typical shelving is 8 to 10 in. wide, with approximately 10 in. space between shelf units. For ¾-in. shelving, the maximum dimension between supports is 30 in.

For closet rods, pole height is 66 in. for men's clothing, 62 in. for women, and 72 in. for evening clothes and garment bags. Closet rods should be about 12 in. from the back wall of the closet.

Storage space is where you find it; here are often overlooked spots: dead corners; over bathtubs; over lavatories; under stairsteps; across solid end walls; under windows; sides of windows; over a hallway or entrance; room dividers between entrance doors and living and family rooms, and between dining, kitchen and living areas. You also can build shallow storage between studs on walls; and between joists in open basement ceilings.

181
456
226
230
264

Cabinet for circular saw is framed with 1 x 4s and skinned with ¼-in. tempered hardboard. Shelf is held by 1 x 3s

Utility closet is framed with 2 x 2s, with ¼-in. perforated hardboard on one side, regular hardboard on other

Perforated hardboard panels also make garden storage easier. Panels are nailed to furring strips or directly to studs

Garage can be turned into informal entertaining space by adding paneling to the walls and grease-resistant tile to the floor

For woodworker, walls of perforated hardboard offer needed tool-panel space. Note excellent lighting over workbench

ANY ENCLOSED STORAGE SPACE takes the basic form of a box. Think of it this way, and you suddenly will see many storage possibilities in your home.

For storage units without framing, you can use ¾-in. plywood with an A-B, A-C, or A-D face. Joining can be with simple butt joints with nails or screws and glue; single rabbet joints; or miter joints. The miter joint is the weakest and most difficult, but also the neatest. You need a power saw to cut it.

For storage units with framing, use 1 x 4, 2 x 4, and 2 x 2 framing members, butt or dado-joined. Use nails or screws and glue for fastening. The skin over the framing members can be ⅛- or ¼-in. hardboard, plywood, or particleboard.

You can buy prefabbed drawers, or build them yourself with plywood fronts and backs, solid wood sides, and hardboard or plywood bottoms. Drawer bottoms can be dadoed into the sides and end, or simply glued and nailed in place. Metal drawer glides and channels are available.

412
413

418
419

Framing for closets is shown in these drawings. Horizontal framing members are end nailed to the verticals. Or they can be cross-cleated. Use glue. Sliding doors operate on metal track with rollers. Guides are fastened to the floor after doors are hung. Top members form a soffit. With shelving, you can utilize this space for out-of-season clothes storage. Interior of closet can be covered with hardboard or plywood; unit can be sectioned with shelving and unfinished chests of drawers

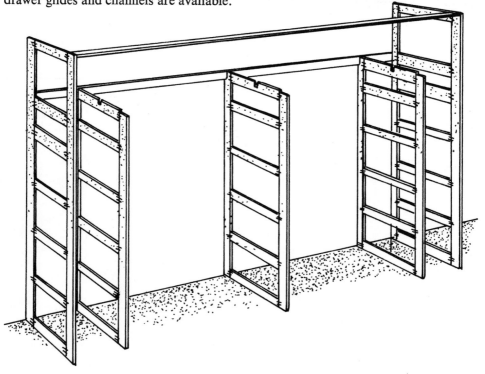

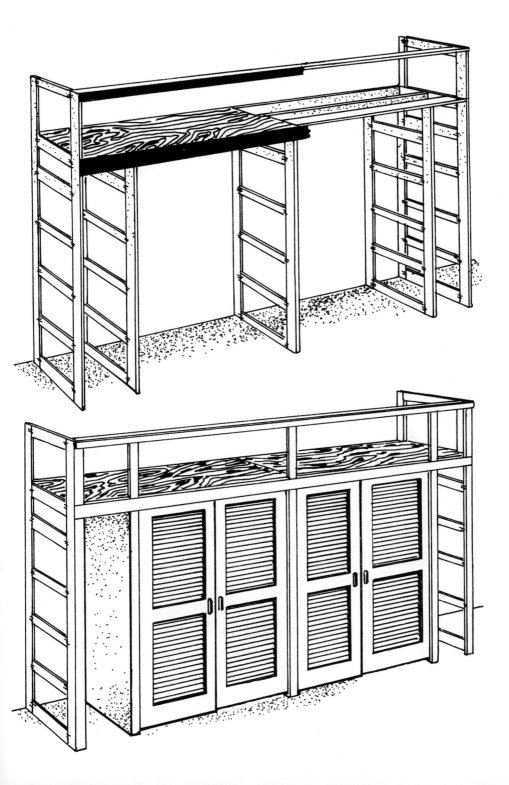

YOU CAN BUILD CABINET DOORS with regular hand tools, although for many applications you should buy them unfinished or prefinished.

For short spans, cabinet doors are best made of plywood or hardboard. Sliding doors are simple, since you can buy metal tracks and install them easily. Swinging doors, in short dimensions, can be hinged with regular butt hinges, invisible hinges, pivot hinges or H-hinges. For larger doors with considerable weight, use continuous hinges.

For large spans, doors should be framed with 1 x 4 lumber that is butt-joined or rabbeted at the corners and fastened with glue and screws or nails. The framework is then covered with a sheet material, such as plywood or hardboard, which in turn may be covered with a decorative plastic. Heavy doors should be hung on a track. The track is fastened to the top horizontal member of the cabinet and hidden from view with a trim piece. Bottoms of heavy doors can run in metal track, or you can install rollers in the bottom edge. They are mortised into the wood. A simple way is to cut a dado in the edge to accept the track.

176
178
46
54
56
274
446
449

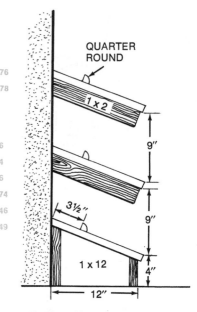

Section of built-in shoe rack. The cleats for the heels can also be ½ in. battens. Assemble with glue and screws or nails

Sturdy workshop bench can be made by laminating a series of 2 x 4s together with glue and screws

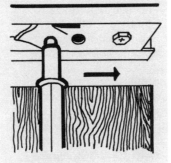

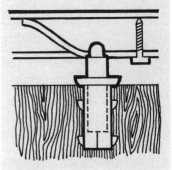

Bottom of louver door fits in metal bracket installed in the floor. Pin is set in bottom edge of the door

Top bracket for folding door is fastened to the header. Pin slips into the hole as it slides across the bracket

Pins are inserted into the door this way. You simply drill a hole in the edge of the door for the pin assembly

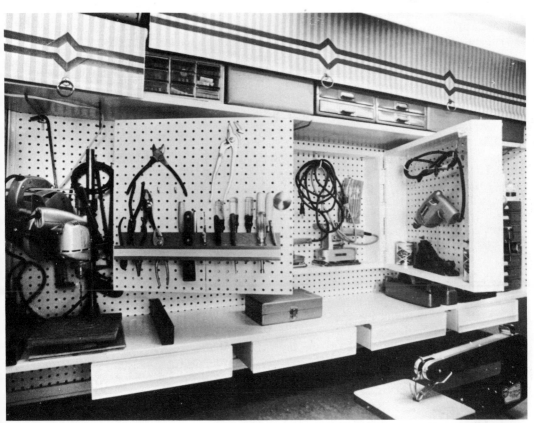

Over-the-workbench-storage has wide door framing, which accepts small portable electric tools. Soffit above stores small hardware

235

HANGING REGULAR OR VINYL WALL-COVERINGS involves six basic steps, which are easy to master. Tools you'll need for the job are scissors and razor-knife for cutting; paste brush and paste bucket; a scraper and window squeegee (or wide brush); the recommended adhesive; and a plumb bob.

1. Prepare the wall. If the old wall covering is tightly bonded, you can cover over it. However, remove any loose pieces of paper and feather the edges of the spot with sandpaper. Patch all holes and cracks with Spackling compound, and smooth with sandpaper. You must sand the walls lightly before hanging metallic or flocked wallcoverings.

2. For new construction, the walls should be sized with a coat of shellac. All walls should be coated with quality glue or gelatin wall size.

3. Drop a plumb line in an inconspicuous corner—one with a door or window, if possible. Measure out from the corner ½ in. less than the width of the wall covering and drop the plumb line. This is your starting point.

Then measure the height from the ceiling to the baseboard at several points around the room. Pick the maximum height you find and add 4 in. to it. This will allow for shrinkage, and usually for pattern match.

4. Mix the adhesive. It should be smooth; no lumps. Strain it through nylon pantyhose if necessary to remove any lumps.

5. Cut one strip of wallcovering at a time, according to your measurements. You can tie two card tables together for a pasting board. Work the paste into the paper so it is even. Pay particular attention to the edges.

Fold one wet end of the paper toward the center; do the same with the other; pick up the strip, and carry it to the starting point.

Hang the first strip to the plumb line mark. It should overlap onto the ceiling, onto the baseboard, and into the corner.

6. Brush or squeegee the paper onto the wall, avoiding air pockets by brushing them out toward the nearest edge. Continue hanging the paper around the room, butting the edges and matching the design along the edges of adjoining strips.

After you hang the second strip, check the pattern to see if it runs true at the ceiling. It may be necessary to mismatch the vertical edges line to hold the ceiling line.

Electric heat fireplace here utilizes flexible piping from hearth area to distribute heat into the room. False wall holds the pipe

To hang wallcoverings, drop plumb bob in corner. If possible, pick a corner with a window or door nearby. Snap the chalkline

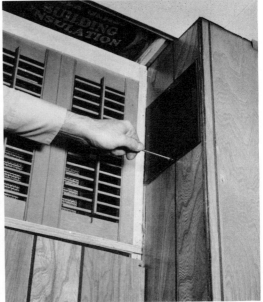

Fan at bottom of fireplace wall, recirculates air back through hearth and up to register. Plywood is used for ductwork

Plywood panel strip and register hide the recirculating heat system, which is installed on both sides of the fireplace unit

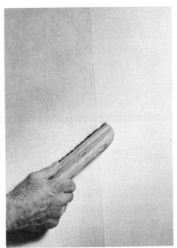

Measure up all walls at several points in the room you will paper. Cut the paper to the longest measurement you find, plus 4 in.

Smooth paper with sweeping stroke using wide brush or squeegee. Work out air bubbles toward edge; check often for matching

Make sure edges of paper are thoroughly bonded with adhesive. Edges are often skipped in applying paste. Edges must fit tightly to wall

After three strips are hung, trim the excess at the top and bottom. Don't bypass doors and windows; hang the paper continuously. After each strip is up, go back and wash off any excess adhesive with clean water and a sponge. Don't rub hard; keep the water clean. When you compare paper while matching, test wet paper to wet paper and dry paper to dry paper.

Other hanging tips include these:

• If shading appears at seams when you're hanging plain colors or non-match textures, reverse every other strip from top to bottom. This will make the finished wall appear more uniform.

• If you have to overlap the paper at corners, the ceiling, or at archways, apply adhesive to both the paper and the wall.

• When you hang a strip of paper to, and above, a door or window frame, match the strip to the previous strip and press firmly to the wall. In order to set the strip over the protruding corner of the door or window, cut the strip diagonally toward the corner as far as necessary to fit it.

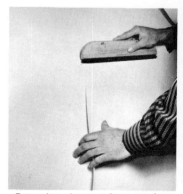

Butt edge of new strip to previous strip and brush. If it does not match at first, pull it up and out and then reseat it again

Wood floor tiles are laid the same as their resilient cousins. Some wood tile, however, has tongue-and-groove joints

Roll the seams of the paper with a wooden roller. Do not roll the seams of flocked or metallic papers

After you hang three strips of paper, stop and trim them at ceiling and baseboard. A sharp razorknife does the best trimming

To go around an electrical outlet, paper right over it, then go back and cut an "X" across the outlet. Fold the paper back and trim it

Mark tile with a felt pen to fit around obstructions. You can cut wooden tile with a handsaw— or use a saber saw

For piece work, cover back of tile with adhesive. Otherwise, use a notched spreader for adhesive distribution across large areas

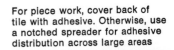

Special wallcoverings include cork, mirrors, snap-in color slats for accent walls, and mood finishes.

To install cork blocks, walls have to be clean and flat. Patch all holes and cracks with Spackling compound and sand the patches smooth.

Measure the wall at its halfway point from the ceiling and the floor, and snap a level horizontal line. Measure the wall in several places, since it may not be square.

With a notched spreader, distribute floor tile adhesive in about a 2-ft.-wide patch across the wall at the horizontal line. Set the tiles along this line, starting at one end of the wall and working toward the other.

The next course of tile should butt the first; do one row at a time, top and bottom. For trimming, use a razorknife. If edges are exposed, cover them with a strip of ½-in. moulding. Moulding keeps the edges from crumbling.

To install mirror squares, the wall surface must be level and clean. If it is not level, you should install shimmed furring strips and cover the surface with sheets of tempered hardboard.

If the mirrors are patterned, lay out the squares on the floor to establish the design you want.

With a level, chalkline and plumb bob, draw a line horizontally across the wall to establish the lowest edge of the installation. At the left of this line, snap a vertical line perpendicular to the horizontal line.

Since most mirror tiles are self-sticking, remove the backing from a tile and place it at the lower left corner of the pattern. The first tile goes inside the base and vertical lines. Stick the squares along the base line until the bottom row is complete. Then stick on the remaining rows.

Snap-in color slats are actually an aluminum paneling system. The slats are formed in an angle, and they are snapped in a horizontal channel system fastened to the wall or ceiling like furring strips. To install the slats, you pinch the angle lightly and slip it into small catches on the strips.

Mood finishes are created with paint and an applicator that has soft fins protruding from it. You paint the wall with a semi-gloss. When it dries, apply a different color with a roller, and spread the paint thin. Then jab the applicator in the fresh

458 148 152

Dimmer switches can help set the mood in any room. They're excellent for dining rooms to lower the lights during special occasions. To install a dimmer switch, remove the switch cover and the old switch after you turn off the power. Then attach the power wires to the switch poles—just like any other switch

Add beautiful accents to any room with one or more of the specialty wall coverings

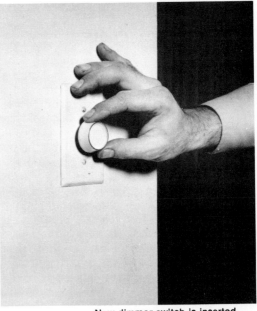

New dimmer switch is inserted into the junction box and screwed into position. The knob to raise and lower lights is a push-fit on the switch stem. The replacement of the switch plate and installation of the knob completes job. Dimmer switches range in price from about $2 to about $6

187

188

paint. The result is a stipple-like finish with a dimensional appearance.

Color and texture can change the proportion of a room. That's why it is important to plan the types of material you'll use in a specific room. This applies to paint as well as regular and vinyl wallcoverings. It also applies to paneling, simulated brick and stone, plastic laminates, cork, mirrors.

Pale colors will have a receding value. Walls will look farther away; ceilings higher.

Heavy or dark colors work the opposite of pale ones.

Contrasting colors are used for centers of interest. They should be used basically for accents.

Glossy surfaces appear to be larger than they are, due to light reflectance; dull-surface finish absorbs light and makes rooms seem smaller.

Patterns also can affect the size of the room. Vertical patterns can make a wall seem to be higher than it is. If the vertical pattern is only on certain walls, it will make the room look narrow as well as high. Horizontal patterns widen a room.

Furnishings also play a big role in the proportions of a room. Traditional furniture is best for big, square rooms with high ceilings. Contemporary furniture, with long, low lines, goes best in medium-sized rooms with fairly low ceilings.

LIGHTING TECHNIQUES

Light from fixtures can change the color, texture and mood of a room just as readily as paint, wallpaper and furnishings. With light, you can dramatize an accent wall, make a ceiling look higher, or create a soft golden mood in the living or dining room.

204
206
217
448
458

Lighting fixtures are available in so many designs and types it would be impossible even to categorize them here. Broad classifications you may want to consider during remodeling include general over-all lighting, accent lighting, and localized lighting. Most rooms should have a combination of all three. *Some rules of thumb:*

Kitchens should have general lighting of 200 watts for every 150 sq. ft. of area. Localized lighting should be included in special work areas such as over the sink, in serving areas, over the range.

Bathrooms also should have general lighting, plus localized lighting for grooming purposes.

General living areas should have lighting that is evenly balanced. To create moods or highlights, you can use valance lighting or spotlights. *Table lamps* should have a height of about 42 in. if they are to be used for reading. Light should be about 20 in. from the top of a desk.

To install valance lighting, use a single-tube fixture. It should be installed a minimum of 72 in. from the floor line, and at least 5 in. from the ceiling. Block the fixture out from the wall with a strip of 1 x 3 or 1 x 4. The valance board should be approximately 7 in. out from the wall; you can install the valance with metal angle brackets. The valance should be at least 7 in. wide. Paint the inside of the valance white for light reflectance. The outside can be finished to match the room decor.

Outdoor lighting is generally confined to spotlighting entrances, outdoor living areas, walks and driveways. It can also be used to highlight trees, plantings, shrubs, fences, retaining walls, and reflective pools, and to illuminate game areas. The use of colored lighting has become popular. *Colors* that are best are off-white, light blues and reds, and dense yellows. Do not overdo outdoor lighting. A little light goes a long way. Also, *always use outdoor-approved fixtures.*

To install garage-door opener, find center of door and determine clearance you'll need between top of door and opener track

Brackets are attached to joists in ceiling to hold drive unit. The brackets can be easily bent to conform with joist spacing

Manual knob operates drive to adjust for height of door opening. It should open far enough so door bottom is even with header of door frame

Attach forward track bracket to wall above door. Then attach track. Track slips into notches in bracket and is held with fastener

Support the opener on a step-ladder, if you don't have a helper. Brackets that hold opener have to provide clearance for pulley

Bracket that supports opening arm is attached to top of door. Bolts go completely through door with nuts inside

Opener arm is hooked to drive unit and door bracket with a pin held by a cotterkey. Operate drive unit to find right angle

Clutch regulates pressure it takes to trip reverse if door accidentally is operated when there's a child beneath

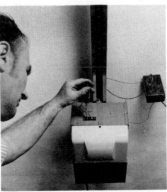

Radio controls are connected to drive unit to complete installation. You simply push a button in your car to open the door

attics

ATTICS ORIGINALLY WERE designed to insulate the rooms below against heat and cold. The air space between the roof and ceiling offered a fine insulation barrier.

With today's insulation and ventilation products, the attic is a prime source for expansion. If the roof is high enough, finishing doesn't even involve structural changes.

Measure the floor area of the attic and then the headroom at the ridge line. Transfer these measurements to graph paper. If there isn't at least 7½ ft. of headroom *from a point 4 ft. out from each sidewall,* you can obtain it by building a dormer. Otherwise, floor space will be limited.

Construction sequence starts with a subfloor.

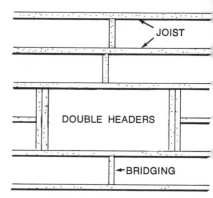

Typical ceiling detail for stair steps into attic area. Stairs can go through closet or hallway. Use double 2 x 4s for headers

412
413

Attic finishing profile follows the roof line. Construction involves wall framing; wall, ceiling and floor finishing. Attic walls and ceiling should be insulated; windows or other ventilation must be provided

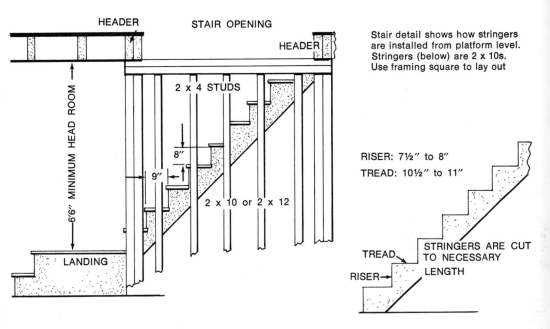

HEADER   STAIR OPENING

HEADER

6'6" MINIMUM HEAD ROOM

2 x 4 STUDS

8"

9"

2 x 10 or 2 x 12

LANDING

Stair detail shows how stringers are installed from platform level. Stringers (below) are 2 x 10s. Use framing square to lay out

RISER: 7½" to 8"
TREAD: 10½" to 11"

TREAD
RISER

STRINGERS ARE CUT TO NECESSARY LENGTH

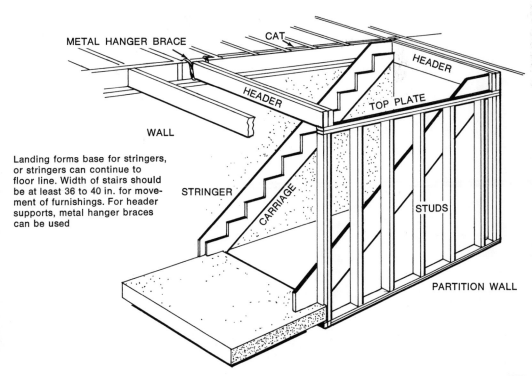

METAL HANGER BRACE   CAT

HEADER

HEADER   TOP PLATE

WALL

Landing forms base for stringers, or stringers can continue to floor line. Width of stairs should be at least 36 to 40 in. for movement of furnishings. For header supports, metal hanger braces can be used

STRINGER

CARRIAGE

STUDS

PARTITION WALL

Use ¾ x 4 x 8-ft. plywood sheathing for this. Do not finish the floor. If you build a dormer, do it at this stage of construction.

To construct a dormer, lay out the position of it. Trim back the roofing and roofing felt. From inside, double the rafters that will frame the opening. The new rafters should extend 4 ft. beyond the top and bottom of the opening for strength. Saw out the roof boards along the inside of the doubled framing and above and below the top and bottom of the framing.

Erect the side walls of the dormer over the doubled rafters on sole plates nailed through the roof sheathing and into the rafters. Use 20d nails. Build the front frame first, nail it in position, and brace it. Then cut the rafter plates by measuring

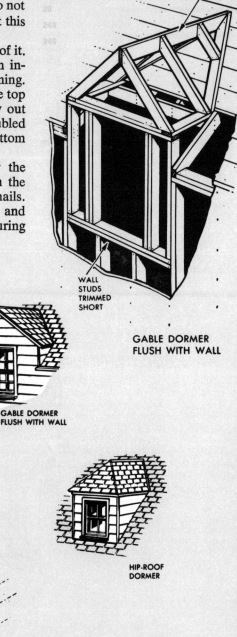

RIDGE BOARD

WALL
STUDS
TRIMMED
SHORT

GABLE DORMER
FLUSH WITH WALL

VALLEY JACK GABLE DORMER
SET BACK ON ROOF

GABLE DORMER
FLUSH WITH WALL

HIP RAFTER

HIP JACK

HIP-ROOF
DORMER

HIP-ROOF
DORMER

DOUBLED RAFTER

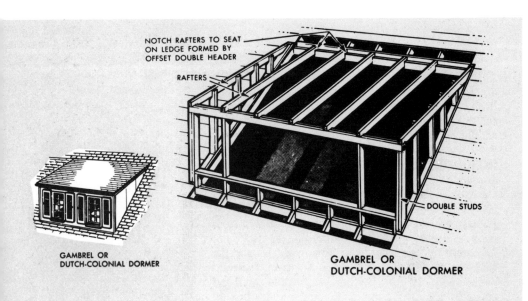

NOTCH RAFTERS TO SEAT ON LEDGE FORMED BY OFFSET DOUBLE HEADER

RAFTERS

DOUBLE STUDS

GAMBREL OR DUTCH-COLONIAL DORMER

GAMBREL OR DUTCH-COLONIAL DORMER

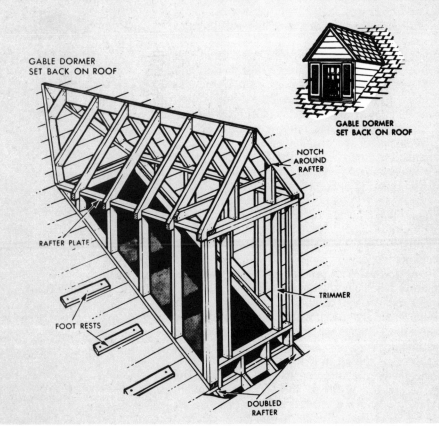

GABLE DORMER SET BACK ON ROOF

GABLE DORMER SET BACK ON ROOF

NOTCH AROUND RAFTER

RAFTER PLATE

TRIMMER

FOOT RESTS

DOUBLED RAFTER

back to the roof line.

The rafters are fastened in place with 10d nails. Start from the outer end and trim the ridge board flush with the outer rafters. On shed dormers, ridge-board fitting is eliminated. A shed dormer should be used where head room is necessary.

INTERIOR FINISHING

About the only framing needed for the interior of the attic is studs for knee walls and collar beams across the ceiling rafters. The collar beams (or joists) provide a flat ceiling surface. Use 2 x 4s to frame the knee walls. They should be positioned at least 4 ft. out into the room. Face-nail them to the rafters and toenail them to a 2 x 4 plate fastened to the subfloor. For finishing, you should put 2 x 4 spacer blocks at the top of the studs. Space behind the knee walls can be utilized for storage.

Collar beams are also 2 x 4s or 2 x 6s. Level them across the peak of the roof and nail them to the joists.

Framing for windows in gable ends should be next in the construction sequence. Use double 2 x 4s or 2 x 6s for headers, and double the framing at the jambs and sills. You can buy prefabricated window units to fit the space; dimensions will have to be planned around the units you purchase.

Partition walls are installed next, according to your plan. They can be partially prefabbed on the attic subfloor and raised into position. Then install insulation, heating ducts, plumbing runs, and wiring.

When this is buckled up, you can start finishing the ceiling and side walls with the materials you have chosen—gypsum wallboard, paneling, acoustical ceiling tile, etc.

Ceiling and sidewall insulation can be fiberglass or mineral wool batts. The thickness of the batts may depend on the climate in your area. Your building-materials dealer will know the answer to this question. Staple the batts to the rafters and studs, making sure that *the moisture barrier faces the interior of the attic*. If the floor of the attic is not sheathed, you should insulate between the studs before the plywood sheathing is installed. For this, you can use insulation batts or loose fill insulation such as vermiculite or loose mineral

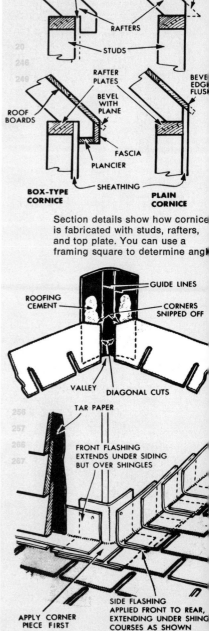

Section details show how cornice is fabricated with studs, rafters, and top plate. You can use a framing square to determine angle

Use copper or aluminum flashing to weatherproof the joint between the dormer walls and the roof line. Coat joint with asphalt

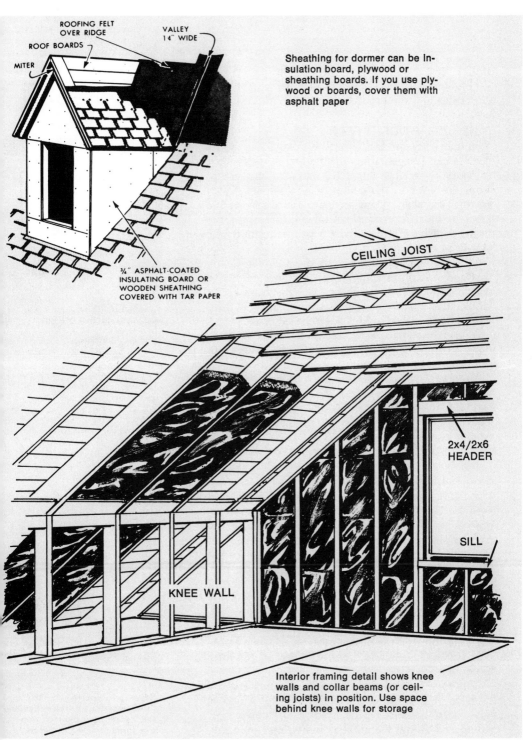

ROOFING FELT OVER RIDGE

VALLEY 14" WIDE

ROOF BOARDS

MITER

¾" ASPHALT-COATED INSULATING BOARD OR WOODEN SHEATHING COVERED WITH TAR PAPER

Sheathing for dormer can be insulation board, plywood or sheathing boards. If you use plywood or boards, cover them with asphalt paper

CEILING JOIST

2x4/2x6 HEADER

SILL

KNEE WALL

Interior framing detail shows knee walls and collar beams (or ceiling joists) in position. Use space behind knee walls for storage

wool. This material is packaged in bags. You simply spread it between the joists so it is at least 2 in. thick.

BUILDING STAIR STEPS

You can buy prefabricated stairways, or some dealers can furnish you with the precut parts for a stairway. You first have to measure the height from the floor to the ceiling where the stairs will go into the attic. Then measure the width of the joists in the attic. Armed with this information, the dealer will be able to advise you of the materials you will need.

204
206
244
322
441
457

To assemble the stair, nail the stringer to the carriage. Two carriages will support standard width stairs; if your project calls for a 48-in. or wider stair installation, you should have a third carriage spaced evenly between the other two.

The risers, then treads, are nailed with finishing nails to the carriages after they are fastened in position.

Most stair installations require a *partition wall* to fasten one carriage onto. Build it with 2 x 4s— top and bottom plate and studs placed on 16-in. centers. You fasten the top and bottom plate to the ceiling joists and the floor.

At the ceiling, you will have to cut out space for the stair opening. Tie off the joists with double headers and double the joists on the sides.

Landings or platforms are usually fabricated with 2 x 8s, butt-joined and nailed. If a step is required, you can use outriggers of 2 x 8s, supporting the platform framing with 2 x 4 legs nailed in all four corners of the square or rectangular frame. The framing should be covered with ¾ in. plywood sheathing.

At the top of the stairs, you can create a hallway by erecting standard partition walls. If you prefer, you can simply use a railing to form a landing into the attic rooms. It is best, however, to use a partition system to provide doors to close off the attic area.

The final step of the remodeling is finishing the exterior of the house where dormers or windows have been installed. This involves patchwork of siding and shingles, caulking joints, and painting.

Standard partition-wall construction is used for new attic walls. Use trim pieces around doors, windows, and at top, bottom of paneling

Knee walls are framed like this for storage doors. Finish material can be fastened directly to the studs, top, and bottom plate

room additions

IF YOU CAN'T MOVE UP into the attic, or move down into the basement for extra living space, then move out with a room addition. If you take time to plan the addition with the help of an architect or designer, you'll find that construction goes fast without complications.

Determine the type of addition that best suits your present and future needs: a family room, new kitchen, bedroom wing. *Then check local zoning and building-code ordinances.* Either can alter the type of addition you may want to build. Also take into consideration the amount of work that will have to be done to change plumbing, heating and wiring. Structural changes, if any, to your present home may alter your design.

The foundation is the starting point. If the foundation will be a slab, you can make a form with 2 x 6s, usually, after excavation has been made for the footings. The footings have to go

Add-on living space can be attached to your present home in many different ways. Here are three of the most popular types of room additions. Since design is so important, it is recommended that an architect be consulted—even though you may do most of the construction work yourself. You must also obtain a building permit

below the frost line in your area. Your architect or local city building department can furnish you with this data.

An integral slab or a T-footing is probably the easiest type of foundation for you to construct, since the forming details are fairly simple. With a T-footing, you can have a crawlspace under the addition. If you prefer a basement, it is best to have this type foundation constructed by a professional, since it involves special forms and equipment that are too expensive for one project.

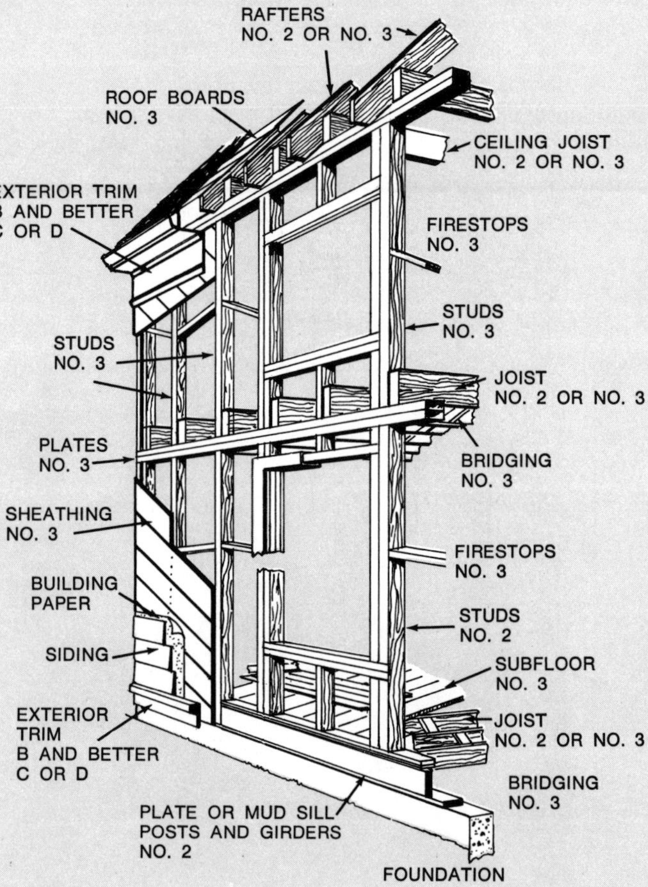

Here are the recommended grades of lumber for the average one-story house or addition. Detail also shows how the various framing components go together. Take your plan to a lumber dealer. He will determine the materials needed

RAFTERS
NO. 2 OR NO. 3

ROOF BOARDS
NO. 3

CEILING JOIST
NO. 2 OR NO. 3

EXTERIOR TRIM
B AND BETTER
C OR D

FIRESTOPS
NO. 3

STUDS
NO. 3

STUDS
NO. 3

JOIST
NO. 2 OR NO. 3

PLATES
NO. 3

BRIDGING
NO. 3

SHEATHING
NO. 3

FIRESTOPS
NO. 3

BUILDING
PAPER

STUDS
NO. 2

SIDING

SUBFLOOR
NO. 3

EXTERIOR
TRIM
B AND BETTER
C OR D

JOIST
NO. 2 OR NO. 3

BRIDGING
NO. 3

PLATE OR MUD SILL
POSTS AND GIRDERS
NO. 2

FOUNDATION

The site will have to be excavated for a basement —also a job for a contractor with equipment.

Subgrade preparation for slab construction generally requires these steps:

1. Remove all organic matter such as grass, roots, etc., from the site. If there are soft spots, they should be filled with sand, gravel, crushed stone, and/or slag; the materials must be compacted thoroughly.

2. Granular fills of sand, gravel, crushed stone, and/or slag are recommended for bringing the ground to uniform bearing and final grade.

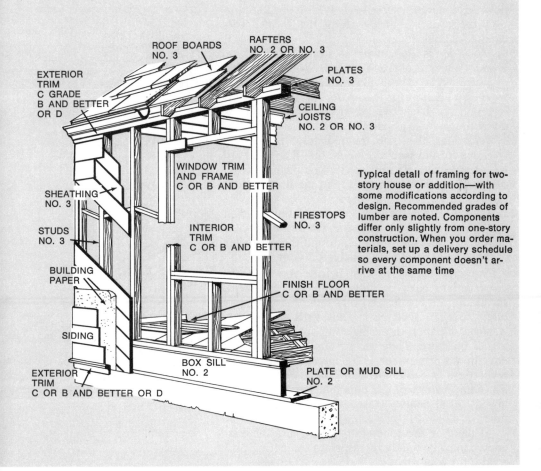

ROOF BOARDS
NO. 3

RAFTERS
NO. 2 OR NO. 3

PLATES
NO. 3

EXTERIOR
TRIM
C GRADE
B AND BETTER
OR D

CEILING
JOISTS
NO. 2 OR NO. 3

WINDOW TRIM
AND FRAME
C OR B AND BETTER

SHEATHING
NO. 3

FIRESTOPS
NO. 3

STUDS
NO. 3

INTERIOR
TRIM
C OR B AND BETTER

BUILDING
PAPER

FINISH FLOOR
C OR B AND BETTER

SIDING

BOX SILL
NO. 2

EXTERIOR
TRIM
C OR B AND BETTER OR D

PLATE OR MUD SILL
NO. 2

Typical detail of framing for two-story house or addition—with some modifications according to design. Recommended grades of lumber are noted. Components differ only slightly from one-story construction. When you order materials, set up a delivery schedule so every component doesn't arrive at the same time

3. The type of concrete depends on the design of the addition. Number 5 reinforcing rod is used in footings, with wire-reinforcing mesh used in the slab. The rods are tied into the foundation of the house. Holes are drilled for the rods; the rods are held in position with epoxy cement. Foundation levels have to be maintained, unless the design calls for a step up or down into the addition from the existing house structure.

After the formwork has been set and the grade is properly prepared for drainage and compacted, the concrete is ready to be poured.

Place the concrete as uniformly as possible to the full depth of the forms. Work from a corner with the ready-mix concrete truck; don't drag or flow the concrete excessively. With a spade, compact the concrete firmly along the forms. This eliminates honeycombs.

Screeding is done with a straightedge strike. Usually a length of 2 x 4 is used. Work the screed in a back-and-forth sawlike motion. You probably will need a helper for this. After the slab is rough-screeded, go back over it again to work out as many rough spots as possible.

Bull float the slab immediately after it is screeded for the second time. A bull float is a very wide trowel with a handle on it. You push it across the fresh concrete with the toe of the float slightly raised so it won't dig into the surface.

After floating, the surface should be troweled and, for a smooth job, edged at the forms only. At this time, insert the sill bolts around the perimeter of the slab, according to spacing on your plan.

The concrete must cure before you continue construction. Keep it moist with wet coverings, sprinkling, or ponding to offset the loss of moisture. You can seal the surface with poly-sheets, waterproof paper, or curing compounds to prevent loss of moisture. *The concrete should cure for five days* in warm weather (70 degrees or higher) or seven days in cooler weather (50 to 70 degrees). The temperature of the concrete must not be allowed to fall below 50 degrees during the curing time.

At the time the concrete is placed, ask the concrete company to advise you as to the curing procedure for your area.

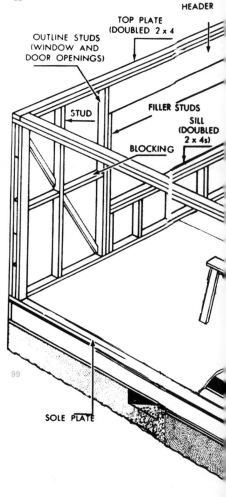

BRACING

SUBFLOOR

CORNER-POST
ASSEMBLY

JOIST HEADER

FLOOR JOISTS

MUD SILL

WHEN THE FOUNDATION HAS PROPERLY CURED, you're ready to start construction above it. The mud sill goes down first and is attached to the foundation via the sill bolts. Lay the sill over the bolts, align it perfectly, tap it lightly with a hammer. The tops of the bolts will make small impressions in the sill, showing you where to drill the holes for the bolts. The bolts should be countersunk below the face of the sill. If construction is over a crawl space or basement, the same procedure applies.

A joist header (box sill) is fastened to the foundation plate (mud sill) in crawl space or basement construction. No. 2 stock is usually used for

Outside walls are framed this way. Sequence of erection is shown, along with the nails that should be used in specific framing locations

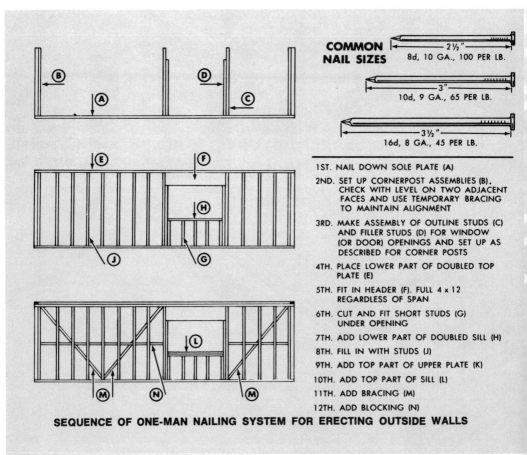

COMMON NAIL SIZES

2½"
8d, 10 GA., 100 PER LB.

3"
10d, 9 GA., 65 PER LB.

3½"
16d, 8 GA., 45 PER LB.

1ST. NAIL DOWN SOLE PLATE (A)

2ND. SET UP CORNERPOST ASSEMBLIES (B). CHECK WITH LEVEL ON TWO ADJACENT FACES AND USE TEMPORARY BRACING TO MAINTAIN ALIGNMENT

3RD. MAKE ASSEMBLY OF OUTLINE STUDS (C) AND FILLER STUDS (D) FOR WINDOW (OR DOOR) OPENINGS AND SET UP AS DESCRIBED FOR CORNER POSTS

4TH. PLACE LOWER PART OF DOUBLED TOP PLATE (E)

5TH. FIT IN HEADER (F). FULL 4 x 12 REGARDLESS OF SPAN

6TH. CUT AND FIT SHORT STUDS (G) UNDER OPENING

7TH. ADD LOWER PART OF DOUBLED SILL (H)

8TH. FILL IN WITH STUDS (J)

9TH. ADD TOP PART OF UPPER PLATE (K)

10TH. ADD TOP PART OF SILL (L)

11TH. ADD BRACING (M)

12TH. ADD BLOCKING (N)

SEQUENCE OF ONE-MAN NAILING SYSTEM FOR ERECTING OUTSIDE WALLS

the header; it should be as straight as possible and nailed into the sill every 16 in.

Joists, spaced 16 in. on center, are nailed in next. The ends of the joists fit over the mud sill and are fastened to the joist header or box sill. At this time, you can install the joist bridging or blocking. If you will be able to gain access to the joists in the crawl space or basement, fasten the bridging in loosely; nail it permanently later.

In slab foundation construction, the outside walls are usually erected next. Another sill may be nailed onto the mud sill, and these may be insulated. Again, this construction detail depends largely on design.

166
272
318
448

MEMBER	NAIL SIZE	HOW MANY	NAILING METHOD
Joist Header to Floor Joists	20d	3	Into end joist
		2	Into other joists
	10d		Toenail into sill every 16″
Plywood Sub-floor	8d		Along all edges, space 6″; 12″ along joists
Soleplate	16d		Into joist header and joists, space and stagger 16″; space 16″ along border joists
Posts	10d	3	Through basic studs into each filler block
		1	Through remaining stud (or studs) into each filler block
		about 8	Into basic studs, space and stagger about 12″
Studs	8d	4	Toenail twice on each wide surface
Bottom Part of Top Plate	16d	2	Through plate into each stud
Top Part of Top Plate	10d		Space and stagger 16″ apart—two at each end
Diagonal Let-in Bracing	10d	2	At each stud crossing
		3	At each end
Header	10d	4-6	Through outline stud into header
Window Filler Stud	10d		Nail to outline stud, space and stagger 16″
Lower Part of Sill	10d	2	Into each stud under it
Upper Part of Sill	10d		Into lower part of sill, space 8″
Door-Opening Filler Stud	10d		To outline stud, space 16″
		2	At bottom into soleplate

Foundation, mud sill, joist header, joist, and sheathing detail are shown here. Joist at right supports porch. Sheathing for floor is ¾-in. plywood

FRAMING DETAILS are fairly standard, although they may vary slightly according to local codes. Outside walls and partition walls are 2 x 4s spaced 16 in. on center. They are nailed into the top and bottom plates, which are doubled on outside walls. Much of this work can be prefabricated on the subfloor—or concrete slab—of your addition, with the studs edge-nailed to the plates.

Bracing at corners of outside walls can be let into the studs after the wall has been erected. To erect the wall, you should have a couple of helpers, since the assembly usually is very heavy for one man to lift by himself. After the wall is in position, you can brace it with diagonal bracing pieces (2 x 4s) nailed to the plate or joist headers. Use doubleheaded nails, which are easy to remove.

As you frame in the walls, check your measurements carefully. It's easy to make a mistake. For example in some construction, when cutting a header to length, you may forget the filler studs. The opening is between the faces of the filler studs, but the header must pass across the top of them. Length is the distance between outline studs.

If you don't use standard framing techniques, you may run afoul of your local building code

Foundation wall with outside walls in position. Shingle shims are used to level plate. Note waterproofing membrane

If steel I-beams are used to support the flooring above basement, joists are positioned this way. They are face-nailed together

Corner detail shows how bracing is mortised into studs. Scribe lines on studs, saw them, chisel out mortise

Framing detail under window uses double 2 x 4s at jambs and sills. Cripple studs are toenailed to sill and bottom plate

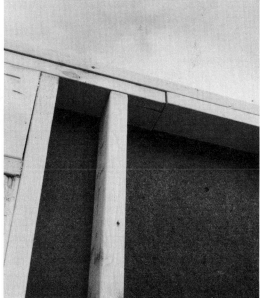

A 2 x 10 header (double) is used on window with a 2 x 4 beneath it because of large span of the window. Note double plate

For extra support, additional stud is used at joint of top plate where it overlaps window. Insulation board sheathing was used

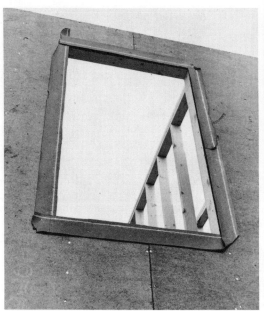

Framing detail at window shows
asphalt paper around window to
insulate the prefab unit. Paper is
fastened on with stapler

Keep framing square. Check it
often, and if you have made a
mistake, correct it immediately.
Shingle shims can be used for
plumbing and leveling

IF YOUR ROOM ADDITION calls for a pitched
roof, consider the use of prefabricated roof trusses.
The trusses are manufactured stronger than any
you can build; they will save you many hours.

The roof goes on next. If it is a flat roof, you
probably will use post-and-beam construction with
extra-thick roof decking to support the layers of
asphalt, building paper, tar and gravel. You can
install the decking yourself. It is advisable, however, to have a professional apply the asphalt
roofing. This involves hot-mopping, a crane for
tar buckets, and other special equipment. Most
rental shops do not carry this type of equipment.

If you install a pitched roof, rafters are notched
to accept the top plate and the ridge board. One
end of the rafters has to be mitered to accept the
ridge board; the other end cut at an angle for the
plate. You can determine the correct angle with
a framing square. Until you get started, the rafters
have to be braced. The braces are then removed
as the roof sheathing is nailed on. The sheathing
can be standard roof boards or plywood sheathing.
Install rafters on 16-in. centers, unless design spec-
ifies otherwise.

Completed window framing detail. Note extra stud support. Bracing at right and left holds walls plumb until roof goes on

From top down: wall sheathing, roof sheathing, rafters, and wall studs. This detail is for an adjoining double garage

Corner post detail (simulated) showing how 2 x 4s are nailed together to form strong corner. Filler block is cut from a 2 x 4

Corner detail utilizing three pieces of 2 x 4 for strength. Center block can be partial filler strip; assembly is face-nailed

SIDEWALLS AND ROOFING MEMBERS are attached to the existing structure this way: *Siding* has to be removed from the house so the framing can be attached to the sheathing of the house. You don't have to remove all the siding on the house; just take off that part that is necessary to expose the sheathing to the sidewall framing members.

Roofing members extend into the existing roof, where angle cuts are made on the ends of the members to fit the pitch of the existing roof. They can be nailed through the roofing into the sheathing and existing framing members below. Codes and design will determine how best to do this.

After the new roof is sheathed, it has to be covered with asphalt building felt (assuming it is a pitched roof). Composition or wooden shingles are then installed over the felt (or tile or slate may be installed). It is recommended that you do not apply wooden shingles, tile or slate yourself. This is a job best left to a professional with the proper equipment. You can, however, apply composition roofing yourself, provided the roof isn't steeply pitched and you're not nervous.

The key to installing composition roofing is getting the starter strip nailed correctly. Here is the procedure:

1. The starter course is regular shingles turned upside down. It projects about 1 in. over the edge of the eave and about ⅝ in. over the gables. Use rust-resistant nails; drive them in straight—not at an angle.

2. With a chalkline, snap a mark down the center of the roof. The edge of a starter strip should match the edge of this line. Work from the starter line out toward the gables with the starter strip. Cut the last shingles to fit.

3. The first course of shingles lays over the starter strip. Adjust the shingles so the vertical joints do not match the vertical joints of the shingles below.

4. Nail on the second course of shingles so they overlap the first course and the starter course under the first course. The amount of exposure (shingle left exposed to the elements) depends on the type of roofing that you use and pitch of the roof. Follow the manufacturer's recommendations. Shingles are nailed four nails to a shingle—unless otherwise specified. Many manufacturers

Studs are toenailed into top and bottom plates at an angle—two nails to one side and one nail centered on the other side. If possible in prefabrication, end-nail the studs, too

Roof overhang is supported by top plate of outside wall and studs; rafters and studs align for the most strength

Corner detail with inside support. All members are face-nailed and toenailed to the top and bottom plate. One spacer was used here

Cutout for heating duct in floor can be made with a keyhole saw or saber saw. This is done after room is enclosed

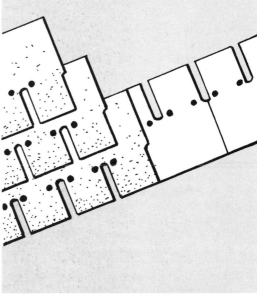

Composition roofing goes on like this: starter strip; first strip over starter; remaining. Most shingles have 5-in. exposure

263

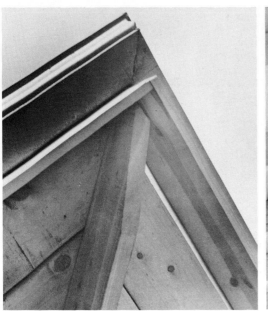

Corner detail shows how rafter
is beveled to match trim boards.
Gutters are installed after roofing
is on and trim completed

Rafters are notched to fit top
plate and beveled at one end for
facia trim. Soffit will be installed
over rafters to complete overhang

mark shingles to show the precise nailing points.

Before you start shingling, install flashing in
roof valleys and around chimneys and stacks. Use
copper or aluminum flashing. For valleys, the
flashing should be in one piece; don't overlap it.
If you use aluminum flashing, use aluminum nails.
Do not mix metals since this will cause corrosion.

All metal should be coated with asphalt roofing
compound where it is nailed to the sheathing and
where it overlaps chimneys and stacks.

For ridges, use ridge shingles as recommended
by the roofing manufacturer. Otherwise, you have
to cut the tabs off regular shingles and carefully fit
them to the ridge areas.

Do not apply composition shingles on cold days
when the shingles are brittle. Also, don't apply
shingles in the rain, if there is snow on the roof,
or if you are not wearing laced, rubber-soled shoes.
Use a safety line or "chicken ladder" when applying shingles on steeply pitched roofs. Better yet,
hire a professional roofer for steep roofs, if you
have had no experience.

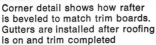

Pocket door is framed this way.
Horizontal supports help guide
the door and offer a nailing surface for finishing materials

Rafter detail shows how members are joined. Overhang rafters in corners are mitered to main rafter for support

On extra wide picture window openings, double 2 x 10s support the span with 2 x 4 cripples spaced 16 in. on center

WHEN THE ADDITION IS ENCLOSED, the next step is to install heating and ventilation ducts, plumbing and wiring. If the addition is a large one, you may have to install a separate heating plant. However, in most additions, an area heating system usually is adequate if your present heating unit will not handle the extra capacity. The separate unit can be gas, hooked onto your present system and piped into the room. Or you can use electric heating, which may prove to be practical in a small addition. Your local utility will be able to quote you special heating rates.

Plumbing usually can be inserted into your present system. If the addition is on a slab foundation, the plumbing runs must be installed in the slab, so it's a matter of hook-up at outlets and drains.

For electricity, an additional circuit breaker can be installed in the existing house and current wired to the addition. If the addition will have kitchen facilities, a three-wire electrical system probably will have to be installed. This is a job for a professional, due to building codes. You may, however, be able to run conduit to outlet boxes, etc.

313
315
318
319
321
324

212
213
452

346

Soffit for kitchen cabinets is framed like this. Material is 2 x 4s, face-nailed to accept finishing material. Gypsum wallboard was used in this construction project

Where codes permit, you can use plastic pipe for plumbing runs. Pipe is prefitted; then it is connected with special adhesive

Holes are cut through framing members to accept plumbing. Where holes are large, double framing is used

Detail of sliding door. The
vertical members are aluminum;
the horizontal members are wood.
Unit is prefabbed, ready to install

Framing members are notched to
accept conduit running to junction boxes. Note detail of plastic-
pipe plumbing lines

Plumbing detail of bathroom
hook-up, showing copper tubing
used for water lines and plastic
pipe for drainage lines

Toilet drain and plumbing line,
with both copper tubing and
plastic pipe. After floor drains
are installed, cover them

AFTER MECHANICAL WORK is completed, the next step is to install insulation between the joists and studs. If you have used insulation-board sheathing, insulation may not be necessary, since this material furnishes adequate insulation values to meet some code requirements. If you apply batt insulation with a staple gun, *make sure that the vapor barrier faces the inside of the room* and that there are no large rips in it.

Cover the walls and ceilings with gypsum wallboard, paneling or other sheet materials. If you prefer lath-and-plaster walls, you should call in a professional contractor to do this work.

Exterior finishing can be scheduled during good weather; work inside during bad weather.

There are many different types of siding materials. As a general rule, you should stick with the same kind of siding that is already applied to your home. If you use a different type of siding, it can spoil the architectural lines of the house. If you do use a different siding treatment, make sure it complements the existing siding.

Unless you're experienced, *laying up brick siding* is another job for a professional. Here are the basic steps in applying brick:

There are three standard types of brick—common, face, and firebrick. *Common brick* measures 8 in. long, 3¾ in. wide, and 2¼ in. thick. It can be utilized on nearly any type of construction except the inside of a fireplace.

Face brick is more attractive, and is the type most used for exterior applications. It is manufactured in many different sizes, shapes and colors.

Firebrick is manufactured for use in fireplaces and other applications which are subject to heat.

Brick mortar for exterior and below-grade use is a mixture of 1 part portland cement to 3 parts clean sand. Mix it to a puttylike consistency. For bricks used elsewhere, mix the mortar with 1 part portland cement to 3 parts sand, and with about 10 percent of the portland cement replaced with hydrated lime. Lime makes the mortar work easier.

To lay bricks, you will need a brick trowel, brick chisel, a chalkline, level, and a tape measure. You'll also need a mortar platform, made of exterior plywood, to hold small amounts of mortar. Do not mix large batches of mortar at one time.

160
179
248
449
450

86
456

Bathtub is connected in this fashion to drain line in floor. Copper pipes run to hot and cold water fixtures and run up to junction for shower-head above the tub

Drain line has to be connected to overflow drain as well as the drain in the bottom of the tub. Note how stud is notched to accept plumbing

Junction boxes for switches and outlets are screwed to framing members. All wiring should be inside conduit

Four lines run in and out of this junction box in the ceiling of an attached garage. Cross blocking is used between joists

Metal masonry ties lock bricks to sheathing. They are nailed to the studs and are sandwiched in the mortar lines of the brick

Mortar lines in brick can be smoothed with strike, as shown; left flush with face of brick; or "squeezed" joints

269

HORIZONTAL LAYERS OF BRICK are called *courses*. If bricks are laid in length, they are called *stretchers*. Bricks laid at right angles to a wall are *headers*.

In most construction, the minimum thickness for a brick wall is 8 in. If the brick is laid in stretchers in two rows, the wall will be 8 in. thick. This includes the mortar between the rows. If the bricks are laid at right angles to the wall, or as headers, the wall will also be 8 in. thick.

To lay bricks, soak them first in water. The mortar joints should be about ⅜ in. to ½ in. thick. The joint can be made flush by swiping off the mortar with the edge of the trowel. Or the joint can be smoothed with a strike. Some like the unusual effect of a squeezed mortar joint where

The secret of a good gypsumboard job is taping the joints properly

Gypsum wallboard edges have slight taper to accept the joint compound and tape. Butter the joint first with joint compound	Joint tape is embedded in compound with blade of scraper. Apply plenty of pressure so the tape adheres	Second coat of joint compound is spread over taped joint. Use plenty, but even it out over the tape, feathering the edges

Simple inside corner joint with gypsum wallboard is formed like this. Material is nailed to the studs with special nails	Instead of taping corner wallboard joint, you can trim it with cove moulding. Same treatment can be used at ceiling line	Base shoe also can be used as inside corner treatment for gypsum wallboard. Moulding should be painted wall color

Corner moulding hides raw edges of paneling on outside corners where the paneling butts. Moulding is stained to match paneling

This moulding butts against edge of panel and overlaps other edge. It is nailed into corner of wallboard backing or the studs

When joint compound dries, sand the joint smooth. Use fine sandpaper on a sanding block to avoid digging into the tape

Metal mouldings are made especially to fit corners of plywood panels. Moulding is embossed to match the wood grain

Vertical joints of paneling can be joined this way. Mouldings are aluminum; joint is slip fit, after panels are nailed to furring, studs

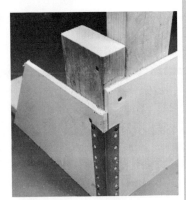

Outside gypsum wallboard corners have special metal bead that is nailed to the material. Edge is then taped

Backer strips of same paneling material provide interest for vertical joints. Edges of paneling have to be leveled and stained

If edges of paneling are square, you can bevel them to make V-joint treatment. Stain the joint to hide raw edges of the plywood

the mortar oozes out and over the face of the brick.

The trick to laying brick is keeping the courses level. You can use a chalkline stretched the entire run to help determine level; then move the line up a notch as the course is finished. You also should have a fairly long level so you can check the position of several bricks at a time as you lay them. By tapping the bricks here and there, you can level them.

FINISH FLOORING

Installing the flooring in a new addition should be the final step after all finishing work is done, including painting.

For hardwood flooring over a concrete slab, you will have to install short pieces of 2 x 4s in rows about 12 in. apart across the room. The 2 x 4s are lapped from 4 to 6 in. Before you install them, brush a coat of waterproof mastic on the floor. This will block any moisture from penetrating.

The hardwood flooring strips are laid at right angles to the 2 x 4s, and the strips are nailed to them. Around the perimeter of the room, install a 2 x 4 as a nailing base to support the flooring.

If the subfloor is sheathing, cover it with asphalt building paper. Lap the joints about 3 in. and staple the building paper here and there.

With a chalkline, snap a straight line down one edge of the room. Use this mark to align the first strip of hardwood. It should be out from the wall about ¼ to ⅞ in. Moulding will cover the gap. Nail the strip to the floor with the groove facing the sidewall. The end of the strip also will have a tongue on one end and a groove on the other. Put the groove end against the end wall.

Move on across the room, toenailing each strip just above the tongue. Use 7d finishing or flooring nails. Space the nails every 12 in. and countersink them. Do not nail down through the face of the hardwood. You will have to face-nail the last strip of wood, however, since you won't have room to swing the hammer for toenailing.

Before you finish the floor, you will have to sand it. Rent a sander for this, and go across the floor first with No. 2 grit sandpaper, and then No. ½. You can rent an edge sander to get into corners and next to the walls. *Keep the sanders moving to prevent damage to the floor.*

Trim treatment at floor level can utilize baseboard and quarter-round mouldings. You can stain the mouldings to match the paneling. Or you can paint them, if the wall surface is gypsum wallboard or another sheet material. Single strip of baseshoe moulding is used at far right

Baseboard moulding can be used alone to form attractive trim piece. Or you can use a ½ x ½-in. batten. At ceiling line (right) inverted baseshoe hides joint between paneling and ceiling tile. Use 3d finishing nails. Countersink them and fill the holes with wood putty

Picture mouldings make good ceiling trim pieces, especially if there are gaps between wall and ceiling surfaces. Cove mouldings are dressy (right) and tend to form a smooth joint that is difficult to see after it has been properly finished with either stain or paint

A REAL BOON TO CONSTRUCTION—including remodeling—has been manufactured house parts. You can buy many components that are ready to be put in place and finished. Some are even prefinished, saving you this trouble.

Included in the list are prehung doors, windows, soffit systems, wall panels, roof trusses, floor panels, chimney surrounds, cabinets, countertops, shower stalls, and entire bathroom units. Most of these components are available to the homeowner/handyman through building-supply outlets. Whenever you can, buy the component. It will save you more time and trouble than the extra cost.

In remodeling and additions, for example, you can frame in a door opening with 2 x 4s and slide in a prehung door, nailing it into position. The jambs, header, trim, and door are ready to go. The same holds true of trusses, soffits, and some of the other manufactured parts mentioned in this chapter and throughout the book. As engineering has progressed and building standards tightened, there is no longer any stigma attached to prefabrication. Exactly the opposite!

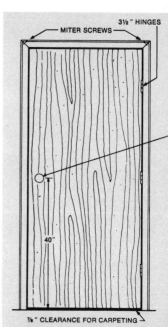

Prehung interior door is for right or left opening; mortise for lock is predrilled, and hinges are already installed

Pieces for laminated beams include decorative plywood; dimension lumber; plywood core; decorative lumber

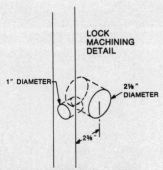

LOCK MACHINING DETAIL

1" DIAMETER

2⅛" DIAMETER

2⅜"

Standard locksets fit mortise. Hardware includes jamb and casing nails, screw casing and jamb heads, and matching hinge screws

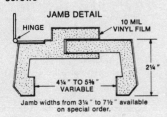

JAMB DETAIL

HINGE

10 MIL VINYL FILM

2¼"

4¼" TO 5⅜" VARIABLE

Jamb widths from 3¼" to 7½" available on special order.

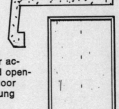

ACCESSORY MOLDINGS, CASED OPENINGS, BIFOLD AND SLIDING DOOR JAMBS ALSO AVAILABLE.

Some manufacturers offer accessory mouldings, cased openings, bifold, and sliding door jambs. You can buy prehung doors in standard sizes

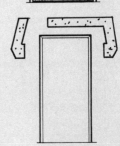

Rough door opening should be 2 in. wider and 2 in. higher from finished floor than door size on this prehung unit. Four woodgrains are available

Two 2 x 12s are sandwiched with ⅝-in. plywood to provide inexpensive beam to add substantial support to ceiling

Prefinished mouldings in a variety of patterns are available to harmonize with paneling. Polyfilm protects surface until applied

275

landscape and gardening basics

LIKE ALMOST ANY PROJECT, planning is the key to gardening and landscaping. Start with a pencil and paper and draw a sketch of your lot. Use a ¼-in. scale: ¼ in. equals 1 ft. Put everything on your lot on the graph—even the telephone poles and fence lines. This way, you can use tracing paper over this master drawing. It's easier to move shrubs and trees on paper than with a shovel!

Your planning should include outdoor living 298 and entertaining areas, playgrounds, grass areas, 306 tree and shrub placement, fences, reflective pools, 307 walls, walkways, flower beds, and tool sheds. 308

LOW-UPKEEP IDEAS
1. Plan every landscaping move on paper.
2. Avoid large areas of lawn where grass is not needed.
3. Avoid small, angled, broken-up areas of grass.
4. Edging strips help contain grass.
5. Ground cover is better than grass for steep slopes.
6. Ground cover is also good for shaded areas.
7. Use gravel instead of grass around tree bases.
8. Apply crabgrass killer in March or April.
9. Cut grass high to discourage crabgrass and weeds.
10. Keep luxuriant-growth shrubs away from the house.
11. Plant outside the overhang, so rain can reach plants.
12. Select hardy varieties suitable for your area.
13. Mass flowers, shrubs and plants in containers.
14. Rely on flowering shrubs, perennials and bulbs.
15. Concrete and asphalt require less maintenance than gravel.
16. Buy weatherproof, uncushioned lawn furniture.
17. Do not place an outdoor cooking unit over grass.
18. Use mulch to keep down weeds and to avoid cultivating.
19. To avoid pruning chores, allow shrubs ample space.
20. Avoid formal hedges that require frequent and precise pruning.
21. Define flower beds with bricks or retaining walls.
22. Utilize materials that do not have to be painted.
23. Use perforated hose for deep soaking.
24. Buy good, appropriate tools, and keep them in top condition.

ZONE 1 BELOW −50° F

ZONE 2 −50° TO −40°

ZONE 3 −40° TO −30°

ZONE 4 −30° TO −20°

ZONE 5 −20° TO −10°

ZONE 6 −10° TO 0°

ZONE 7 0° TO 10°

ZONE 8 10° TO 20°

ZONE 9 20° TO 30°

ZONE 10 30° TO 40°

APPROXIMATE RANGE OF
AVERAGE ANNUAL MINIMUM
TEMPERATURE FOR EACH ZONE

lawn and garden

Landscaping starts with the selection of trees. Choose trees for shade and decorative value. Generally, shapes of trees are columnar, oval, pyramidal, round, spreading, horizontal, and vase-shaped.

Don't buy trees which are subject to disease such as the American elm, or trees with shallow, wide-spreading root systems such as cottonwoods. Spreading root systems can rob your lawn of nutrients.

A selection of shrubs is the next landscaping step. Plan your choice: hedges with screening effect; evergreens for entrances, along with yews, junipers, Mugho pine, and Globe arborvitae. For fall color, berry-producing shrubs are the answer: barberries, Rugosa roses, viburnums, dogwood, and callicarpa. As a rule of thumb, shrubs planted in masses are better than single plantings. For example, a bank of lilacs makes a big show in the spring; a single lilac doesn't.

Flowers should be selected next. They can be used to fill areas under and around shrubs. If you keep them in containers, you can move them about where and when color is needed. Again, use masses for effect; lots of mums, for example, are more dramatic than one plant.

280
281

279
288

290

MORE ABOUT TREES AND SHRUBS

For shade trees, you have to first consider the climate in which you live. The second consideration should be trees for cooling shade, warming windbreaks, flowers, fruit and colorful berries.

Shade tree recommendations by region, include these: *High Plains:* thornless honey locust, green ash, Norway maple, hackberry, littleleaf linden. *Midwest:* sugar maple, Norway maple, green ash, Crimean linden, white oak. *Southeast:* evergreen, live oak, or willow oak, American holly, Magnolia grandiflora, dogwood, loquat. *North Central/East:* Norway maple, sugar maple, red maple, littleleaf linden, pin oak. *Desert Areas:* Arizona ash, pecan, thornless honey locust, fruitless mulberry, Aleppo pine. *Southern California:* fruitless mulberry, fern pine, Magnolia grandiflora, Koelreuteria integrifoliola, Brazilian pepper.

Flowering trees usually are small, but they pop with blooms in season. They're also functional for light shade. A selection includes redbud, crab apple, English hawthorn, European mountain-ash, flowering cherry, peach, plum, dogwood, red horse-chestnut, silver-bell, tree lilac, and Washington hawthorn.

For shade all year, evergreens are the answer. The kinds that mature at 30 ft. or more include American arborvitae and holly, Austrian pine, Black Hills spruce, Cedar of Lebanon, Colorado spruce, Douglas-fir, Eastern hemlock, Norway spruce, Scotch pine, and white pine.

Hedges can frame a garden, screen a bad view, add privacy, block the wind or direct it. Hedges may include evergreen, deciduous, clipped, unclipped, flowering, or with berries. They grow from a few inches high to 15 ft.

Shrubs provide the material for hedges. A slow-growing hedge makes for little maintenance; it needs infrequent clipping. *Flowering shrubs*—forsythia, lilac, and weigela used as a hedge—should never be clipped into formal shapes.

Pick shrubs for spring to fall flowering. In order are doublefile viburnum; abelia; pyracantha; Andorra juniper; lilac; callicarpa; tamarix; buddleia; forsythia; crape-myrtle; smoke tree; Blue Mist spiraea; potentilla; mockorange; hypericum; pussy willow; Japanese holly; red spiraea; red-twig dogwood; deutzia.

Aphids are tiny green, pink, yellow, or black insects. Control them with rotenone, pyrethrum, nicotine sulfate, or malathion. Ladybugs are harmless. In fact, they like to eat aphids, which spread plant viruses

Bagworms make bags of silk on leaves and twigs; this is how you can spot them. The worms feed on leaves. Pick off the bags and burn them. Spray the worms with diazinon, dylox, malathion, or lead arsenate

Borers are larvae of certain insects. You'll find them in rose canes and stems, berry vines, and fruit trees. Spray before the eggs hatch with carbaryl, diazinon, or dichloride. Prune and burn infested canes

Holly leaf miners are tiny yellow larvae of flies. They make serpentine blotches in leaves of American and, sometimes, English holly. As new leaves appear, spray with rotenone, malathion, or diazinon

298

HEDGE	CLIPPED OR INFORMAL	HEIGHT (in ft.)	HARDINESS ZONE	EVERGREEN OR DECIDUOUS
Barberry, Japanese	Unclipped	1½-3	3	D
Korean boxwood	Clipped	2	5	E
True dwarf boxwood	Either	3	6	E
Russian olive	Either	15	3	D
Bigleaf wintercreeper	Either	4	6	E
Japanese holly	Either	3	6	E
Canaert juniper	Clipped	5	3	E
Amur River privet	Clipped	1½-4	4	D
Regel's privet	Clipped	3	5	D
Dwarf honeysuckle	Unclipped	4	3	D
Tatarian honeysuckle	Unclipped	8	3	D
Pachistima canbyi	Either	1	6	E
Dwarf ninebark	Clipped	2	4	D
Colorado spruce	Either	5	3	E
Alpine currant	Either	3	2	D
Bridal wreath spirea	Unclipped	5	4	D
Persian lilac	Unclipped	8	3	D
Hicks yew	Either	4	6	E
American arborvitae	Clipped	5	3	E
Hemlock	Clipped	8	3	E
Viburnum opulus nanum	Unclipped	2	4	D

COMMON NAME	BOTANICAL NAME	STARTING TIME (WEEKS BEFORE LAST KILLING FROST)	COVERING FOR SEED
Ageratum	Ageratum mexicanum	8-12	Lightly
Amaranthus	Amaranthus	8-12	Lightly
Asters, Annual or Chinese	Callistephus chinensis	6-8	⅛"
Balsam	Impatiens balsamina	6-8	⅛"
Begonia, Wax or Annual	Begonia semperflorens	16-20	No cover
Carnation	Dianthus caryophyllus	8-12	Lightly
Cockscomb	Celosia plumosa and C. cristata	8-12	Lightly
Coleus*	Coleus blumei	8-12	Lightly
Dahlia, Annual	Dahlia pinnata	6-8	¼"-½"
Geranium	Carefree hybrids	12-16	Lightly
Gloriosa Daisy	Rudbeckia hybrid	8-12	⅛"
Heliotrope	Heliotropium arborescens	12-16	Lightly
Impatiens**	Impatiens sultani and I. holsti hybrids	12-20	Lightly
Marigold	Tagetes patula	6-8	¼"
Nicotiana or Flowering Tobacco	Nicotiana affinis	8-12	Lightly
Petunia	Petunia hybrida	10-12	No cover
Phlox	Phlox drummondi	10-12	⅛"
Salvia or Annual Sage	Salvia splendens	8-12	⅛"
Snapdragon	Antirrhinum majus	10-12	No cover
Verbena	Verbena hortensis	8-12	⅛"

Seeding temperature 65°-75° except where noted.
*Seeding temperature 70°-80°
**Seeding temperature 70°-75°

You beat the frost by starting flower seeds inside; the chart at left tells dates for planting various seeds *outside*. Types of hedges, how they are clipped, height, and other characteristics are shown in the chart above

THERE ARE THREE classifications of flowers: annuals, biennials and perennials. *Annuals* complete the entire cycle of growth in one year—including flowering and seeding. Zinnias, petunias, and marigolds are three of the most popular annuals. *Biennials* take two years to complete the cycle. Snapdragons, hollyhocks, and pansies are well-known *biennials. Perennials* last from three to five years without replanting. They include crocus, daylilies, poppies, iris, daffodils, tulips.

Flowers should be placed against a *dark background*—as a rule. *Also use curved lines.* Make sure the size of the individual flowers and the size of the flower mass are proportionate to the surroundings.

Rich soil of good texture is important. Texture refers to a soil that doesn't pack, holds sufficient moisture, and drains well. *Fertilizer* should be balanced (nitrogen, phosphorus and potash). Use it before planting. *Water flowers* to a depth of about 8 in. by soaking. Don't sprinkle. Both annuals and biennials have shallow roots that dry out quickly. Mulch helps.

Most perennials need full sun at least half of each day. Some, however, will tolerate partial shade.

Ground covers may be used where grass is difficult to grow or mow—as on a steep slope or in heavy shade.

For a wide range of soil and moisture conditions, three ground covers can be recommended: *myrtle, pachysandra,* and *English ivy.* Also excellent: *ajuga, Cornus canadensis, lily-turf, partridge-berry,* and *heather.*

To plant, prepare the soil as best you can with the time and money you have to spend. Adequate fertilizer is 3 to 6 pounds of a 5-10-5 to each 100 sq. ft. of area. Stir in plenty of peatmoss, well-rotted manure, leafmold or compost. Add extra humus to this, if the soil is sandy.

For quick ground cover, sink the plants close together—12 in. for English ivy and pachysandra. If you have very steep or difficult areas, it is wise to pick a creeper that roots at the nodes. Types include English ivy, a woody plant with an abundance of horizontal, ground-hugging stems. Hall's honeysuckle is good. If the soil is too rich, Hall's honeysuckle will become a pest because it will spread out of control.

Mealybugs have the appearance of tiny bits of cotton on the backs of leaves. Use malathion to dispatch them. If the infestation is small, you can touch individual bugs with a cotton swab dipped in nail-polish remover

Saw fly larvae attack pine and spruce. They are an inch long, and yellowish-green in color. They look like hairless caterpillars. Control them with rotenone in fruit trees. Use sevin in other plantings

Oyster-shell scale collect in clusters on stems and leaves. The result is discoloration and eventual death of the plant. Spray in the spring with dormant oil or lime-sulfur; or use malathion

Slugs chew away at foliage at night, then hide during the day. They look like little leeches and leave slimy trails. Stop them with bait containing metaldehyde. Keep careful plant sanitation

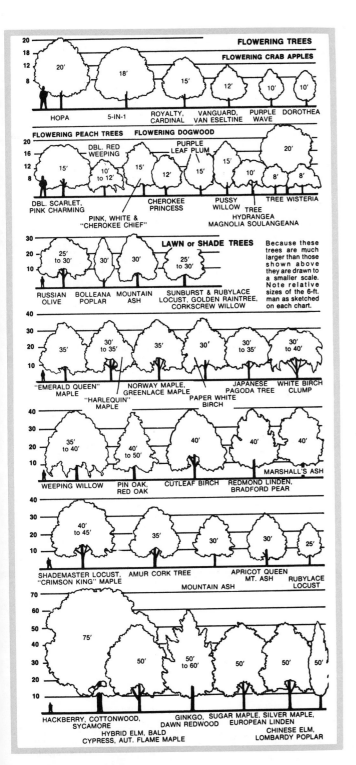

FLOWERING TREES

FLOWERING CRAB APPLES

20'	18'	15'	12'	10'	10'
HOPA	5-IN-1	ROYALTY, CARDINAL	VANGUARD, VAN ESELTINE	PURPLE WAVE	DOROTHEA

FLOWERING PEACH TREES   FLOWERING DOGWOOD

DBL. RED WEEPING   PURPLE LEAF PLUM

| 15' | 10' to 12' | 15' | 12' | 15' | 10' | 20' | 8' | 8' |

DBL. SCARLET, PINK CHARMING

PINK, WHITE & "CHEROKEE CHIEF"   CHEROKEE PRINCESS   PUSSY WILLOW   TREE HYDRANGEA   TREE WISTERIA

MAGNOLIA SOULANGEANA

LAWN or SHADE TREES

Because these trees are much larger than those shown above they are drawn to a smaller scale. Note relative sizes of the 6-ft. man as sketched on each chart.

25' to 30'	30'	30'	25' to 30'
RUSSIAN OLIVE	BOLLEANA POPLAR	MOUNTAIN ASH	SUNBURST & RUBYLACE LOCUST, GOLDEN RAINTREE, CORKSCREW WILLOW

35'	30' to 35'	35'	30'	30' to 35'	30' to 40'
"EMERALD QUEEN" MAPLE	"HARLEQUIN" MAPLE	NORWAY MAPLE, GREENLACE MAPLE	PAPER WHITE BIRCH	JAPANESE PAGODA TREE	WHITE BIRCH CLUMP

35' to 40'	40' to 50'	40'	40'	40'
WEEPING WILLOW	PIN OAK, RED OAK	CUTLEAF BIRCH	REDMOND LINDEN, BRADFORD PEAR	MARSHALL'S ASH

40' to 45'	35'	30'	30'	25'
SHADEMASTER LOCUST, "CRIMSON KING" MAPLE	AMUR CORK TREE	MOUNTAIN ASH	APRICOT QUEEN MT. ASH	RUBYLACE LOCUST

75'	50'	50' to 60'	50'	50'	50'
HACKBERRY, COTTONWOOD, SYCAMORE	HYBRID ELM, BALD CYPRESS, AUT. FLAME MAPLE	GINKGO, SUGAR MAPLE, SILVER MAPLE, DAWN REDWOOD EUROPEAN LINDEN	CHINESE ELM, LOMBARDY POPLAR		

Botritis blight disfigures gladiolus, lilies, peonies and tulips. Brown rot on petals and leaves, and soft stems are the clues. Spray or dust weekly with botran, ferbam, maneb or zineb. Also remove and burn infected parts

Leaf spot is a common fungus or bacterial disease. It appears when the humidity is high. Burn all infected leaves. Spray with pesticides to control insects, which may spread the disease

Trees are the most important plantings you'll make in your landscape. Because of the long-range effects of planting a tree, consider its overall shape and expected size at maturity before you plant it

281

HOW TO CONTROL COMMON LAWN WEEDS

WEED	BEST TIME TO TREAT	CONTROL	EFFECT
Bermudagrass	Spring or summer	Methyl bromide (kills all plants)	Good
Bindweed, field	Spring, fall	2,4-D; silvex; MCPA	Good
Chickweed, common	Spring, fall	Silvex	Good
Chickweed, mouse-eared	Spring, fall	Silvex	Good
Crabgrass	Winter, spring, summer	Dacthal, zytron, DMA	Fair to good
Dandelion	Spring and fall	2,4-D; MCPA; silvex	Good
Garlic, wild	Late fall, early spring	2,4-D	Good
Goosegrass	Spring, early summer	2,4-D	Poor
Ground-ivy	Spring, fall	Silvex	Good
Henbit	Spring, summer	Silvex	Good
Knotweed	Late winter, early spring	2,4-D; silvex	Good
Nimblewill	Spring	Zytron (repeated treatments)	Fair
Plantain, Buckhorn	Spring	2,4-D	Good
Plantain, rugel	Spring	2,4-D	Good
Quackgrass	Spring, summer, fall	Dalapon (kills all plants)	Fair
Sorrel, red	Spring	Silvex	Fair
Woodsorrel, yellow	Spring	Silvex	Good

NOTE: Many herbicides, including some above, are currently under review to determine their effects on both plant and animal life. Before you apply any weedkiller, check its possible environmental effects with a good nurseryman, who will have the latest information.

YOU CAN INSTALL a lawn sprinkling system. Do it in steps.

Step 1. Check local plumbing regulations. There may be regulations *against* lawn sprinkling systems. If not, determine the rate of water flow. If it flows at 9 gallons per minute, you can have 5 sprinkling heads in 1 full circle; 4 in 2 circles; 3 in 3 circles; or 1 in 1 circle. This data is usually contained with sprinkler-system kits.

Step 2. Prepare a plan of the area. Use graph paper.

Step 3. Locate the sprinkler heads on your plan. Nozzles have an adjusting screw to vary spray coverage up to 12-ft. radius to conform with the shape of the lot.

Step 4. Locate the control valves on the graph.

Step 5. Take the plan to a dealer and order the necessary materials to install the system.

Step 6. Uncoil the plastic pipe and let it soften in the sun so it is easy to handle. Then assemble the entire system and test it.

Step 7. Turn off the water at the main valve, and attach the control valve kit to the existing outlet pipe. Include an anti-siphon in the assembly.

Step 8. Connect the sprinkler pipe to the control valve.

Step 9. Mark the sprinkler head locations on the ground, and then connect all heads of one group together with the pipe. Do this above ground for testing.

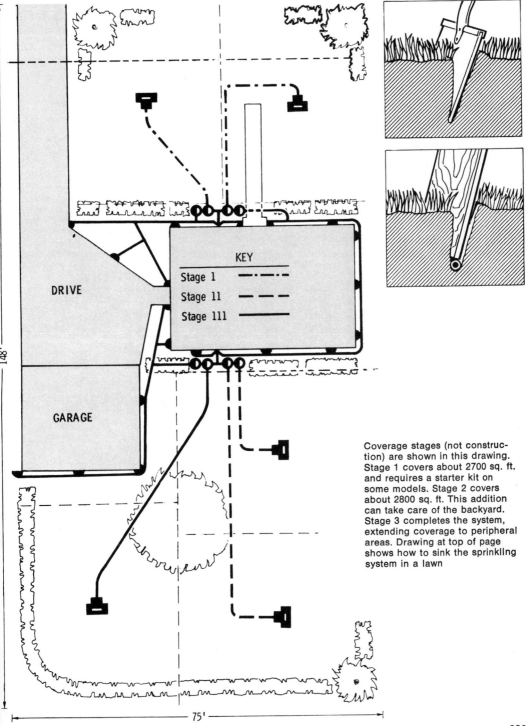

KEY

Stage 1	–·–·–
Stage 11	– – –
Stage 111	———

DRIVE

GARAGE

148'

75'

Coverage stages (not construction) are shown in this drawing. Stage 1 covers about 2700 sq. ft. and requires a starter kit on some models. Stage 2 covers about 2800 sq. ft. This addition can take care of the backyard. Stage 3 completes the system, extending coverage to peripheral areas. Drawing at top of page shows how to sink the sprinkling system in a lawn

Step 10. Water-test the entire sprinkling system before burying the pipe in the ground. You can balance the system by adjusting the screw in the sprinkler heads for the greatest water throw.

Step 11. Bury the entire system. Dig V-shaped trenches and save the sod so it can be replaced as soon as the pipe is underground.

If you have not allowed enough pipe at the control valve connection to lower the pipe into the trench, disconnect the pipe at the control, cut the right length, and connect the pieces with a plastic ell and clamps.

To go under walks and driveways, connect a hose to a piece of pipe, turn on the water, and use the water as a hydraulic ram or jet to wash out a tunnel under the obstruction.

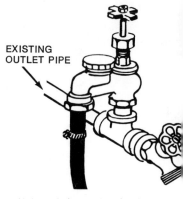

EXISTING OUTLET PIPE

If the existing outlet pipe in your home is ½ in., use a ¾ x ½-in. reducer bushing to make the proper connection to the tee

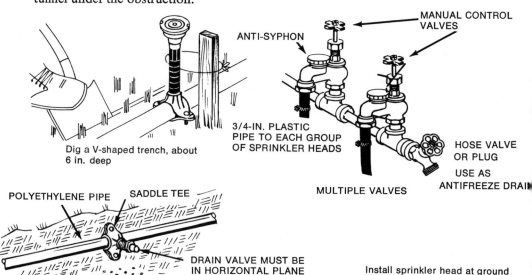

Dig a V-shaped trench, about 6 in. deep

ANTI-SYPHON

MANUAL CONTROL VALVES

3/4-IN. PLASTIC PIPE TO EACH GROUP OF SPRINKLER HEADS

HOSE VALVE OR PLUG

USE AS ANTIFREEZE DRAIN

MULTIPLE VALVES

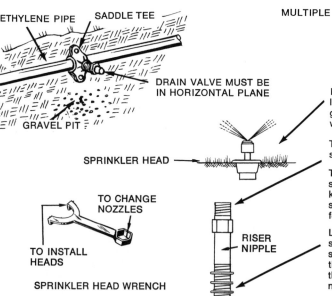

POLYETHYLENE PIPE   SADDLE TEE

DRAIN VALVE MUST BE IN HORIZONTAL PLANE

GRAVEL PIT

SPRINKLER HEAD

TO CHANGE NOZZLES

TO INSTALL HEADS

SPRINKLER HEAD WRENCH

RISER NIPPLE

Install sprinkler head at ground level. It will pop up above the grass level when you turn on the water pressure

This end is connected to the sprinkler head

This end of the riser fits into the saddle tee. You can cut it with a knife to the proper level of the sprinkler pipe and to compensate for unevenness of ground levels

Let set two weeks so ground settles. Inspect heads again to see if they are at ground level. If they are too high, simply unscrew the head and riser, cut off the nipple to fit, and replace

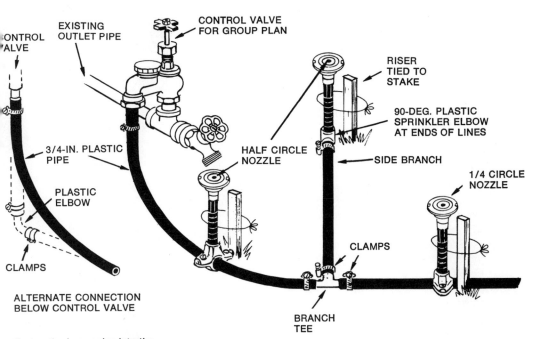

CONTROL
VALVE

EXISTING
OUTLET PIPE

CONTROL VALVE
FOR GROUP PLAN

RISER
TIED TO
STAKE

90-DEG. PLASTIC
SPRINKLER ELBOW
AT ENDS OF LINES

3/4-IN. PLASTIC
PIPE

HALF CIRCLE
NOZZLE

SIDE BRANCH

1/4 CIRCLE
NOZZLE

PLASTIC
ELBOW

CLAMPS

CLAMPS

ALTERNATE CONNECTION
BELOW CONTROL VALVE

BRANCH
TEE

Fasten the hose valve into the
tee. Use ¾-in. nipples. If the
valve is ½ in., then use a
¾ x ½-in. reducer bushing for
the connection. The anti-siphon
valve stops the system from
backflowing into your house
water system

1. Position saddle
tee on pipe.
Then tighten the
steel bolts

2. With torch, heat
bronze tool (on
some systems) to
a red heat

3. Put point of hot
tool in center of
outlet in saddle tee

4. Press heated
tool lightly through
the wall of the pipe

5. Remove the tool
by pulling it
straight out.
Don't twist

6. Replace tool on
torch to reheat it
while going to
next tee

edging techniques

YOU HAVE A BEAUTIFULLY landscaped lot, the trees and bushes are all located in just the right spots. The turf is the envy of the neighborhood—rich, full, weed-free, deep green. If this picture is not finished by proper edging around trees, shrubs, flowerbeds, driveways, etc., the total effort has been wasted.

On this and the opposite page, you'll find several different types of edging techniques for lawns. Other than a flat spade, mechanical equipment is used; most of it is inexpensive and can be purchased at nursery and garden centers, or in general merchandise stores.

Other edging methods involve metal and wooden strips, bricks, stone, chips, block and other materials positioned to give the finishing touch to lawn and garden.

Metal stripping is perhaps the most common edging method you can use. However, you do have to trim grass away from it with shears and be careful not to run over it with a lawnmower. The strips are manufactured from aluminum or galvanized metal usually in a corrugated pattern. They come in rolls in various widths; 4-in. widths generally are used around flowerbeds and trees. To position a strip, you simply cut a slot in the turf with a flat spade. Wiggle the spade back and forth to open the slot, and then pound in the edging until only about ½ in. shows. Do all digging at once. You'll need a long block of scrap wood to pound the metal stripping into the ground. (You'll bend the metal if you hit it with the face or side of a hammer.) Try to tap it into place evenly; the corrugations help the strip to follow gentle elevations and dips in the ground surface.

Wooden stripping is buried in small trenches in the ground. Generally, it has to be laid in straight lines or very broad curves, since it can't be bent to conform with the winding edges of some flowerbeds. Use redwood or cypress for the strips, which should be at least an inch thick and buried to a depth of 2 inches or so. Like metal, grass has to be trimmed away from the strips when they become covered.

Flat spade at about 60-degree angle removes grass along walks, driveways, patio edges. Dig to about a 2-in. depth

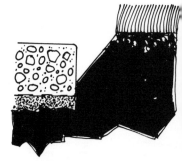

Groove left by flat spade edging technique should look similar to this when you're finished. Shallow and deep angle would hold water

204
414

Electric edger has a sharp blade
that cuts a slot between turf
and walk or driveway. Sharp,
metal disc does the job

Portable edger on shaft runs
on long-life, rechargable
batteries

Brick makes an excellent edger, since the units
are fairly short and the material doesn't usually
disintegrate from moisture. Set the bricks into the
ground in a trench; a 2-in. sand/gravel base
tamped down tightly makes a solid bed on which
the bricks rest. You can buy different colored
bricks—red, white, yellow—to accent the flower-
bed or the landscaping they border. You also have
to use grass shears to trim next to the brick border;
or you can buy mechanical clippers that are designed to trim right up to a flat surface.

Stone, chips, and rocks are a form of edging
since they are frequently used to keep down weeds
and stray blades of grass in flowerbeds and tree
borders. You have to have at least a 3-in.-deep
covering to prevent growth underneath.

Weed and grass growth between brick, block
and stone walkways, driveways and patios can be
deterred with special weed and grass killers you
can buy at lawn and garden centers. An application of such a product in early spring usually takes
care of weeds all season.

Inexpensive push-type edger
has sharp toothlike disc that
cuts away overlapping grass. To
operate, you simply push it along

how to plant a bush

BUSHES AND SHRUBS can screen a bad view, accent the architecture of your home, beautify your lot, stop soil erosion. And like most growing things, there are hundreds of varieties from which to choose. Pick the purpose; then pick the planting to serve it.

When you buy bushes from a nursery, make sure the plants are certified by the nursery to be free from disease and insects. And make your own examination; you can often spot cankers, galls on roots, leaf rot and spots, and bugs. If you do, keep your money in your pocket; such things may spell trouble later.

Here are some rules of thumb for planting:

1. Most plantings are packaged in burlap or a light metal container. When you get them home, plant the burlap ball (cut all binding twine after the root ball is in the hole) but completely remove any metal container.

2. Roots need room to grow; make sure the hole you dig is wide and deep enough, as explained elsewhere. Always spread out bare roots in the hole and cover them with good, rich soil.

3. Prune the stalks of most bushes back about a third of their length after they have been planted. Prune all broken and dead stalks.

4. Deep-water the roots and keep the soil moist until you notice growth on the planting. However, *don't saturate*. Feeding should be done only in accordance with the nursery's recommendation; ask when you purchase your particular bush. When you fill the hole, leave about a 3-in. depression around it. The depression serves as a saucer to hold water.

5. You can plant hedge in a trench; you don't have to dig individual holes for each planting. Make sure the trench is wide and deep enough to accept the root system. If you want the hedge to grow about 5 ft. high, space the plantings about 20 in. apart. If you want the hedge 6 ft. or more, space the plantings every 4 ft. apart.

Although it hurts to do so, trim the hedge down about three-quarters of its growth. This will insure a much thicker hedge when it is fully grown.

Hole should be about 6 in. wider and 4 in. deeper than balled roots. Sides of hole must not cramp the root system

Mix all-purpose peat with earth fill, and blend well. With conifers, you will probably need mulch. The nursery will tell you

If bush is potted or balled, set it into hole to determine correct depth. Planting should be set to about same level as balled

Remove metal container from roots and place planting into hole. If planting is balled and covered with burlap, cut cords

Fill hole with mixed soil; go completely around hole with mixture. Tamp soil lightly as you fill

Use a hose without nozzle to deep-water the planting. Keep the planting soil moist until you see growth

how to plant a rose

IN THE ROSE WORLD, there are literally hundreds of rose variations from which to choose.

The types of roses include **hybrid teas** (they take work); **hybrid perpetuals** (for the real rose lover); **floribundas** (easy to grow; lots of mass color); **grandifloras** (tops for the beginner in roses); **polyanthas** (very tough to grow for the beginner); **climbers** (early bloomers); **miniatures** (for pots and planters); **shrubs** (June bloomers, very large); **old-fashioned** (for hedges or borders).

Buy hybrid teas for all-summer blooming. Floribundas produce mass color in clusters for accents. Grandifloras have long-stemmed clusters, and are ideal for tall accent bushes. Polyanthas are low bushes; small blooms. Climbers bloom heavily early; scattered blooms late in the season. Miniatures are low bushes; seldom grow more than 12 in. in height. Shrub roses are hardy; go best with other type shrubs. Old-fashioned roses smell good, are very hardy, and resist disease.

Roses need room to grow, so don't neglect to provide the correct spacing. Separate hybrid teas and floribundas at least 2 ft.; space both grandifloras and shrub-type roses about 3 ft.; climbers should be spaced about 5 to 7 ft.

Roses are fairly delicate and are subjected to four common diseases: brown canker, crown gall, black spot, and a powdery mildew. To curb any of the four diseases, try using a multi-purpose rose fungicide. Container directions tell how.

Insects—beetles, leafhoppers, thrips, stem borers, and other bug types—love to eat roses. You can stop them with dusts and sprays you apply about every 10 days.

Water roses once a week. Before feeding, the earth should be soaked. Then water again, if you use a granular rose food. Mulch 2 in. in spring (corncobs, dry glass clippings). In the winter, mound the soil around the bushes about 10 in.; fill between the mounds with oak leaves, if you can get them. Sleeves of asphalt building paper (8-in. wide) also protect roses during the winter. Fill the sleeves with soil, after you pin the lap with nails or heavy staples.

Remove dead buds by breaking them off, as shown. Do this during the budding season. If canes are black, trim them back

Spread out the root system so
no roots overlap. If you live in
a cold climate, put graft knob an
inch below surface

Dig a hole wide enough and
deep enough to accept root
system to top of graft knob.
Make a mound of dirt in hole

Pack dirt around mound, covering the root system. Fill in
mound to ground level and
water the plant

When cutting flowers, leave at
least two healthy five-leaf
clusters on the stem. Cover the
cuts with special paint

Cut canes at an angle, not
straight across. On new plants,
prune canes back 6 in. on
hybrid teas and grandifloras

Measure and cut sod patch you need, digging deep enough to lift entire root system with the patch. Flat spade works best for this job

GRASS IS DIVIDED into two classifications: cold or cool-season, and warm-season. Cool-season grasses grow best above a line drawn roughly across the center of the United States—with the exception of the Southwest; warm season grasses grow best below this line. Northern grasses include bentgrass, rye, bluegrass and fescue; southern grasses include zoysia, St. Augustine, and Bermuda grass. And there are hybrids of these, making up over 1000 different kinds of grasses that grow in the United States and Canada.

The secret to a beautiful lawn is work. There are weeds and diseases to fight; the fight becomes easier with chemicals that do the work for you. Team chemicals with water and work, and you'll have a lawn that's the envy of the neighborhood.

Water and fertilizer. If you buy a good, automatic sprinkler, watering problems are solved. You should water your lawn about every seven days during the summer months when it doesn't rain. But, you must water the soil so it is moist to a depth of about eight inches. If your sprinkler isn't automatic, this means you pour on the water for about two to four hours for it to sink in to the right depth, depending upon your soil.

There are several different types of fertilizers and, unless you're a real green-thumb type, you should stick with an all-purpose mixture that can be used for both lawns and gardens. You can buy what are known as "quick fertilizers." These are good products, but you should use them with much caution. They are "hot"—that is, they have a heavy load of nitrogen—and will burn grass and plants quickly if they are not applied according to the manufacturer's recommendations.

280
286

297

Here's the easiest— and fastest—way to patch a bad spot in your lawn

Lift patch out carefully. If it is
a large one, cut it in two
sections, or use a piece of plywood to transport it to patch site

Use patch as template to cut
around bad spot in lawn. Dig
deep enough to slide the flat
spade under the root system

Test new patch in hole. If hole
is too deep, add more rich soil
to it so patch will be level with
the surrounding turf

293

If you don't know what grass type to use, run a soil test on your lawn. The test isn't expensive, and it will solve a lot of doubts—and work.

Generally, bluegrass, rye, and bentgrass do best in the north, while Bermuda, zoysia, and St. Augustine grass do best in the south. In shady areas, fescue is usually your best bet; bentgrass is tough to maintain—it requires a great deal of fertilizer and frequent mowing—so think twice before using it. If you have an all-day shady section on your lot, you should use a ground cover instead of grass.

According to most nurserymen, you waste your money if you try to sow seed over an existing lawn. The seed seldom germinates. A better way is to feed and water the lawn properly, and let the existing grass spread to produce new plants.

If you are starting a new lawn, here are several rules of thumb to follow:

1. Buy good grass seed, after you make a soil test. Cheap grass seed means trouble.

2. If your lot is clay, add from four to six inches of rich top soil.

3. Add fertilizer to the soil. You need about 10 pounds of fertilizer in a 1-1-1 (nitrogen, phosphorus, potash) ratio. If you are putting in the lawn in the fall, make it a 1-2-2 ratio.

4. Use a seed spreader to distribute the new seed; don't sow it by hand.

5. When you're through seeding, roll the lawn once with a *light* roller.

6. Lightly cover the new lawn with straw.

7. Water frequently. *The soil must be kept moist* until the seed starts to germinate. However, prior to germination you need not water deeply.

Sodding. The fast way to a new lawn is sodding, but it is quite expensive. If you have the money and not the time, buy the sod and lay it over the same type base as you prepare for seed. On slopes, stake the sod so it doesn't "sag." On level ground, remove all humps and dips; fertilize it with potash and phosphorous. Water it, and when the sod has rooted itself into the ground, add nitrogen food. Water more.

Patching. If you have a bad spot in your lawn, you can plug in a new section of grass cut from the edge of your lawn, or, you can buy single rolls of commercial sod. Spring or fall are the best times of the year to lay sod.

Place patch in hole and cover it with a piece of plywood or hardboard, as shown. Stand on it so patch is firmly embedded in the ground

Thoroughly water patch area.
Also water other, less prominent
area from where you took the
grass. Fertilize both areas lightly

Deep-water the patch and keep
soil moist for at least several
days. Hose set at "trickle" at
patch site does good job

295

With a rake, remove debris from bare spot in lawn. Rake also helps loosen dirt for seed. Add fertilizer to soil

If spot is clay, add rich topsoil you can buy at nursery. Thickness of topsoil should be from 4 to 6 in. for best results

IF SOD DOESN'T seem to be the answer to covering a bare spot in your lawn, you probably can seed the spot successfully. If you live in the southern tier of states, spring is the best planting time. Use Zoysias, Bermudagrasses, St. Augustines, Bahiagrass or Centipede grass. If you live in the northern tier of states, plant grass in the fall of the year. Use bluegrasses, the red fescues, and/or Astoria grass.

WEED CONTROL
Apply pre-emergent herbicides before weed seeds have a chance to germinate.

282

Rake lumps out of soil. Roll it with light roller, if you have one. Again loosen the soil with a rake for the grass seed

For crabgrass, use DMA (disodium monomethylarsonate) and PMA (phenylmercuric acetate). Apply in late spring and early summer. Two or three doses 10 days apart, or according to manufacturer's directions, usually will kill existing crabgrass plants.

Pre-emergent crabgrass killers are even better. They are applied in late winter or early spring. They include calcium arsenate, Dacthal, Zytron, Bestasan, and Azak.

Treat *dandelion weeds* in the spring and fall with 2, 4-D; MCPA; 2, 4, 5-T; silvex. For common and mouse-eared *chickweed,* use silvex or 2, 4, 5-T in the spring and fall months. In the spring, you can treat *nimblewill* with Zytron, and *Buckhorn* and *rugel plantain* with 2, 4-D. For *red sorrel* and *yellow woodsorrel,* use silvex in the spring.

Always follow manufacturer's recommendations when applying weed killers. And ask a local nurseryman for the latest recommendations.

If patch is large, use a spreader to sow seed. If small, use your hand. Roll spot once more. Cover with straw; water often

watering/feeding tips

SOME PLANTS RECEIVE WATER by drawing it in through the leaf structure. However, most plants take on water through the root system. The soil serves as a reservoir from which the plant draws water as it is needed.

For healthy plants you should water *thoroughly,* instead of frequently. If you don't use enough water, the plants will die. A skimpy watering simply draws the roots of the plants toward the surface and the sun kills them. So the key is to water thoroughly. You can buy sprinklers that measure the correct amount of water needed for any given area. Some are automatic so they shut themselves off when the correct amount of water is delivered.

If you are watering a deep-root system, you should water every 18 days in sandy soil, about a month in clay, and about 25 days in loam. If you are watering a sandy soil with shallow root depth, do so every four days. In loam, water every seven days; in clay, every 13 days. For plantings with medium root depth, water every eight days in sandy soil; 12 days in loam, and about 18 days in clay soil.

Feeding. Trees are the hardest to feed, and pouring fertilizer around the trunk of the tree is no assurance that the tree will benefit. A better way is to measure out from the trunk of the tree about half way to the outer branches. With the help of a soil auger you can sink the plant food in a ring around the tree at this distance.

Put evergreens on a regular feeding schedule, since they are susceptible to dry and windy weather. Dig or auger out about 3 ft. from the trunk of the evergreen or shrub to feed it.

For roses, a good rule of thumb is to water them in the cool of the evening and keep the water off the foliage. Don't spray or dust a dry plant; wait until it rains or you have fed the root system.

For lawns, the kind of fertilizer you use depends on the turf you have. Generally, the yearly nitrogen requirement is 1 pound of nitrogen per 1000 sq. ft. of turf per growing month. Quick fertilizer is "hot" and can burn the grass.

This feeding technique involves digging shallow hole for food. You can buy special tool for feeding shrubs, bushes, and trees

Place plant food into hole, as recommended by manufacturer. Special plantings require special food

fences, decks and patios

POET ROBERT FROST WROTE: "Good fences make good neighbors." The emphasis should be on the word *good*.

Fences, decks, and patios should be well planned for the job you want them to do; this is especially true for fences.

Fences can provide privacy, accent the architectural lines of your house, hide a bad view, capture the wind or block it, frame a landscape, or form a backdrop for plantings such as bushes, flowers and trees.

Consult any *local codes* that may restrict the height and style of fences in your area. Also, check your *property lines*. Decks and patios can be restricted by codes, too. And you may need a building permit.

HOW TO INSTALL FENCES

You have your choice of a very wide variety of fencing styles. These include chain link, redwood basketweave, stockade or picket, grape stake, board, rail, and western red-cedar townhouse fencing. In addition to various kinds of wood fencing, you can also choose fencing made of plastic, aluminum, plywood and fiberboard.

Fence-building tools include a level, tape measure, ball of strong twine, saw, hammer and nails. Digging postholes is almost impossible without a posthole digger. You can rent it. If you have a great many postholes to dig, consider renting a power posthole digger.

Decide on the type of fence you want, lay out its position on graph paper, buy the necessary fencing materials, and assemble the tools.

Start at an end post position. Do not dig all the holes in advance. Dig the first hole to a depth of about one-third the length of the post. As you dig, avoid disturbing any more soil than absolutely necessary.

When the end post has been positioned, pack its base with gravel or soil. The post must be plumb. Use a level for this, checking on two sides. Then tamp the soil and/or gravel around the post. A length of 2 x 4 makes a good tool for tamping.

Basketweave is popular fence style. It comes in sections that fit into slots in posts. Basketweave may be prefinished

Step-down installation can be used for basketweave sections on a sloping lot. Metal caps cover tops of posts

Texture 1-11 plywood forms
alternating panels. Top and
bottom rails are 2 x 4s; dividers
for plants also are 2 x 4s

Bamboo fencing is available in
rolls. You simply set the posts,
stretch the bamboo, and nail it
to the posts

Slats similar to venetian blind
slats can be woven into chain-
link fence. They provide a
privacy screen wherever needed

Low grape-stake fence hides garbage cans in front of higher fence. From a distance, both fences appear to be a unit

After you set the end post, install the first line post. Be sure that the distance between the posts is correct according to your plan. *If you make a mistake here, the mistake will be carried forward on all holes as you progress.*

If the ground is sandy, consider setting the posts in concrete. Do not pour the concrete into the hole first. Tamp gravel into the hole. It should form a 2-in. base. Then tamp gravel around the post to hold it. Line up the post and brace it. Then pour the concrete. Leave the braces in position until the concrete has set. Form a dome of concrete around the top of each hole to shed water.

If your fence has exposed back rails (stockade, grape stake, vertical boards), the tops of the posts should be even with the top of the back rail. If the fence is framed without back rails (basketweave or townhouse), install the posts flush with the top of the fence. If you wish, the posts can jut slightly above the fence.

Hang gates as you come to them. This is easier than trying to trim the gate later after the posts have been firmly set. The hinge post and gate should be set as a single unit. There should be about ½-in. clearance between the gate and post on each side of the gate. Allow at least 3-in. clearance at the bottom of the gate so it swings properly.

Most lots are graded so the ground slopes away from the house. You can "rack" sectional fencing to slope or follow the contour of the ground. Do this by pulling down on the free end of a fence section before it is nailed to the next post. Pull down easily so you don't split the fencing or posts.

Auger-type digger works like a screw. It is most efficient in soft ground, so soak the soil with water before you start

Clamshell digger either works by an auger principle (shown) or clamping action. Both tools are designed for harder soils

303

Auger digger is turned into the ground. When top is filled with dirt, the digger is pulled from the hole and emptied

Clamshell auger also is twisted into the ground. Other type has two handles you spread to trap dirt inside the jaws

If posts have not been pretreated with preservative, coat them with a penetrating sealer. This will help prevent rot

Exterior plywood fence sections are prefabricated. You simply nail them to posts—here double 2 x 4s. Posts are set in concrete

POSTS FOR BASKETWEAVE fences should be set so they are *inside* the fenced area. The fence sections are nailed to the outside face of each post; or the sections can slip into a groove in the fencepost. Where sections join, cover the joint with a face board.

Townhouse fencing is installed almost the same way as basketweave fencing. However, the first section laps over the front of an end post, and split-laps a line post. A face board is nailed over the joint. At corners, one section is overlapped so the adjoining section butts against it.

Grape-stake and board fencing should be positioned so the posts are on the inside. The bottom rail should be about 8 in. above the ground; the top rail should be parallel to the bottom rail with 24 to 48-in. spacing between the two, depending on the height of the fence. Be sure the first stake or board is absolutely vertical. The bottom of this component should be about 2 in. from the ground for ventilation. Check as you nail the stakes or boards to the rails to see that they are plumb. Boards should be double-nailed; stakes should be single-nailed.

For chain link and other metal fences, set the terminal posts first. Line them up. Centers should align. All posts should extend the proper height above grade (see next paragraph). Do this by first setting the bottoms of the posts in line; check for vertical plumb with a level; then use a taut line to check height.

Corner posts generally have two diagonal braces, while end or gate posts have one diagonal brace. All posts can be set in concrete for rigidity. The concrete for the footings should be 1 part cement, 2 parts sand, and 4 parts gravel. Set the posts according to the height of the metal fabric. End, gate and corner posts should be set so the top of the post is about 2 in. higher above ground than the fabric height. Line posts should be set so that the tops are 2 in. below the fabric height.

For erecting a metal fence you'll need a fence stretcher, which you can buy or rent. It is a block-and-tackle device. When the posts are in position, you anchor the fabric to an end, gate or corner post. Then use the stretcher to pull the fabric tight beyond the terminal post.

Some basketweave fence designs have a grooved post to accept the ends of the fence sections. The sections are toe-nailed into the posts

Gate is installed as shown at top right. Consider the gatepost and gate as a single unit. You can adjust the latch and lockpost to match. If your lot has a slope, center right, you can "rack" the fence to fit the contour of the ground. Pull down on free end of the fence section after the other end has been attached. Then fasten the free end. Townhouse and grapestake fences go together as shown at bottom right. Use galvanized or cement-coated nails

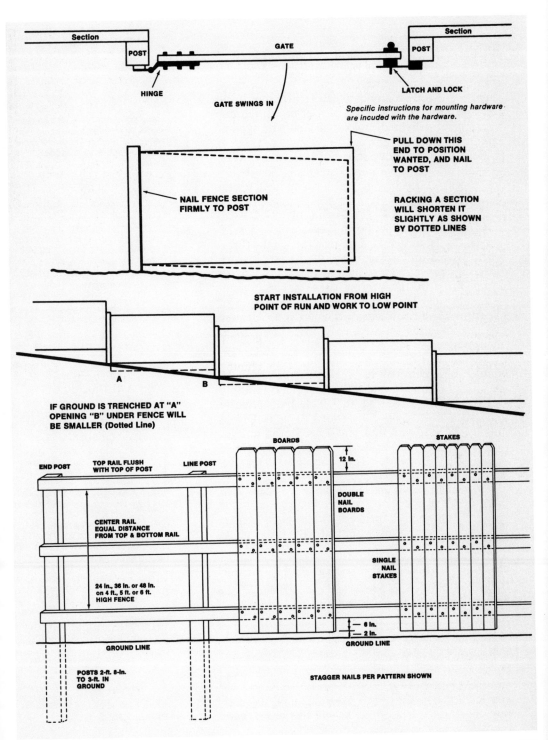

Section

POST

HINGE

GATE

Section

POST

LATCH AND LOCK

GATE SWINGS IN

Specific instructions for mounting hardware are incuded with the hardware.

PULL DOWN THIS
END TO POSITION
WANTED, AND NAIL
TO POST

NAIL FENCE SECTION
FIRMLY TO POST

RACKING A SECTION
WILL SHORTEN IT
SLIGHTLY AS SHOWN
BY DOTTED LINES

START INSTALLATION FROM HIGH
POINT OF RUN AND WORK TO LOW POINT

A   B

IF GROUND IS TRENCHED AT "A"
OPENING "B" UNDER FENCE WILL
BE SMALLER (Dotted Line)

BOARDS

STAKES

END POST

TOP RAIL FLUSH
WITH TOP OF POST

LINE POST

12 In.

DOUBLE
NAIL
BOARDS

CENTER RAIL
EQUAL DISTANCE
FROM TOP & BOTTOM RAIL

SINGLE
NAIL
STAKES

24 in., 36 in. or 48 in.
on 4 ft., 5 ft. or 6 ft.
HIGH FENCE

6 In.
2 In.

GROUND LINE

GROUND LINE

POSTS 2-ft. 8-in.
TO 3-ft. IN
GROUND

STAGGER NAILS PER PATTERN SHOWN

WHEN YOU HAVE A LOT of concrete work to do, it's best to order it ready-mixed. Concrete is sold by the cubic yard (27 cu. ft.) and a truck usually will deliver any quantity greater than 1 cu. yd. The cost varies with the size of order, the day you want it delivered, unloading time and type of mix.

Before you build a patio, deck, driveway, walk, or other surface from concrete, check local building codes. You probably will have to have a permit.

Forms can be 2 x 4s (or larger), plywood, hardboard, or metal strips. Form stakes can be 1 x 2s, 1 x 4s, 2 x 2s, or 2 x 4s. This depends on the formwork. With 1 in. lumber, space the stakes close together to prevent the concrete from bulging the forms. For 2-in.-thick forms, space stakes at about 4-ft. intervals. Drive the stakes below the top of the forms. Use double-headed nails driven through the stake into the form for easy disassembly when the concrete has set.

For amount of concrete needed, start with the number of square feet of area. To figure a slab 11 ft. wide, 41 ft. long and 4 in. thick, first multiply 11 by 41. This is 451 sq. ft. Divide by 3 because the slab is ⅓ ft. thick. This gives 150 cu. ft. Divide this by 27, and you find you'll need 5.55 cu. yd.

Use brick, stone, or broken concrete as a base inside the formwork. This cuts down on the amount of concrete needed.

Permanent forms are left in place for decorative purposes. Use 1 x 4 or 2 x 4 redwood, cypress, or cedar that has been primed with a clear sealer. Anchor outside forms with 16d galvanized nails.

Maximum-size aggregate, ins.	Minimum cement content, lb. per cu. yd.	Compressive strength at 28 days, lb. per sq. inch	Air content, percent by volume
⅜	610	3,500	7½ ± 1
½	590	3,500	7½ ± 1
¾	540	3,500	6 ± 1
1	520	3,500	6 ± 1
1½	470	3,500	5 ± 1

How to order ready-mix concrete for drives, walks and patios

Here are three types of control joints often used in walks, driveways and patios. The hand-tooled joint is done with an edger trowel

½" MAXIMUM RADIUS
+/5 MINIMUM

HAND-TOOLED
CONTROL JOINT

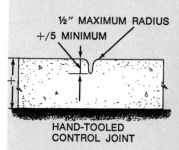

+/5 MINIMUM   ¼" MAXIMUM

SAWED CONTROL JOINT

16D GALVANIZED NAILS
AT 16" CENTERS FROM
ALTERNATE SIDES
½" MAXIMUM RADIUS

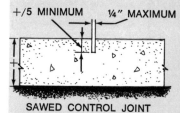

2x4 REDWOOD,
CEDAR, OR CYPRESS
WOOD DIVIDER STRIPS

* + = THICKNESS
EXAMPLE: +/5 = THICKNESS
DIVIDED BY 5, ETC.

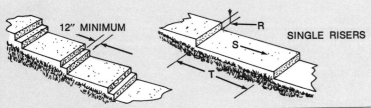

12" MINIMUM

SINGLE RISERS

PAIRED RISERS

Details for stepped ramps. Steps with risers as low as 4 in. and treads as wide as 19 in. are often built for appearance

	PAIRED RISERS		SINGLE RISERS	
	Min.	Max.	Min.	Max.
Riser Height (R)	4"	6"	4"	6"
Tread Length (T)*	3'0"	8'0"	5'6"	5'6"
Tread Slope (S)	⅛"/ft.	¼"/ft.	⅛"/ft.	¼"/ft.
Overall Ramp Slope	2⅛"/ft.	3¼"/ft.	15/16"/ft.	1-7/16"/ft.

* May be optional. Recommended values given provide 1 or 3 easy paces between paired risers and 2 easy paces between single risers

ISOLATION JOINT

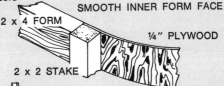

SMOOTH INNER FORM FACE

2 x 4 FORM

¼" PLYWOOD

2 x 2 STAKE

NOTE: BEVEL ON BOTTOM PERMITS FINISHING OF TREAD UNDER RISER FORM

Forming detail for steps. Rule of thumb: Sum of riser and tread should equal 17½ in. This is a good combination for most steps

PLYWOOD GRAIN VERTICAL

SUGGESTED DETAIL AT JOINT BETWEEN STRAIGHT AND CURVED FORMS

STAKES AT 1 TO 2 FT. INTERVALS

Horizontal curves are formed this way. Use plywood, hardboard, metal; stake forms with wood to prevent concrete pressure from bulging them

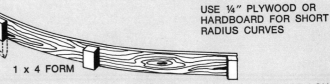

USE ¼" PLYWOOD OR HARDBOARD FOR SHORT RADIUS CURVES

1 x 4 FORM

STAKES AT 2 TO 3 FT. INTERVALS

USE 1" LUMBER FOR LONG RADIUS CURVES

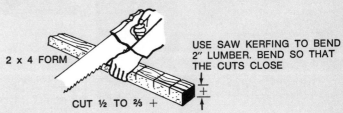

2 x 4 FORM

USE SAW KERFING TO BEND 2" LUMBER. BEND SO THAT THE CUTS CLOSE

CUT ½ TO ⅔ +

305

DESIGN INNOVATIONS have made wooden decks and patios popular. Industry statistics reveal that a wood deck made of 2 x 6s is one of the most common constructed; it is easy for a homeowner to build with hand tools.

One firm (Georgia-Pacific) prefabricates deck sections in two basic sizes: 3 x 3 and 4 x 4 ft. Redwood is used; it is stained at the factory.

You can build decks and patios with regular dimension lumber. The lumber should be redwood, cypress, or pretreated fir to deter rot.

Before you build a deck or patio, first consider its accessibility, traffic pattern, the availability of sunlight, shade and wind protection, and storage for tools and cookout equipment.

Concrete will give you the most design flexibility, although wood can be almost as flexible. If you are using concrete, you can tie the patio to the foundation of your house with #5 reinforcing rod. Anchor the rod with epoxy cement in holes drilled into the foundation. If the patio will "float," use

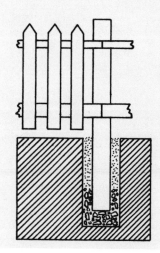

Decorative fencing around patios and decks should be anchored in concrete. Put 2-in. base of gravel in hole before pouring concrete

When laying prefabdecking over concrete, level decking with wood-shake shims. You also can use gravel or scrap wood for this

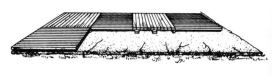

Alternating sections of decking provide architectural interest in this patio. Sections can be removed for special plantings

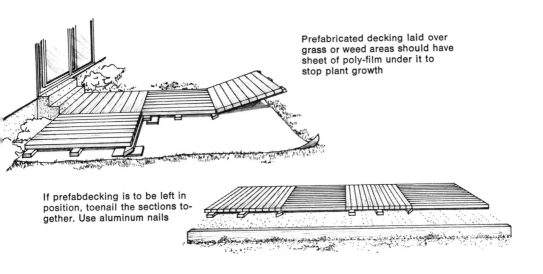

Prefabricated decking laid over
grass or weed areas should have
sheet of poly-film under it to
stop plant growth

If prefabdecking is to be left in
position, toenail the sections together. Use aluminum nails

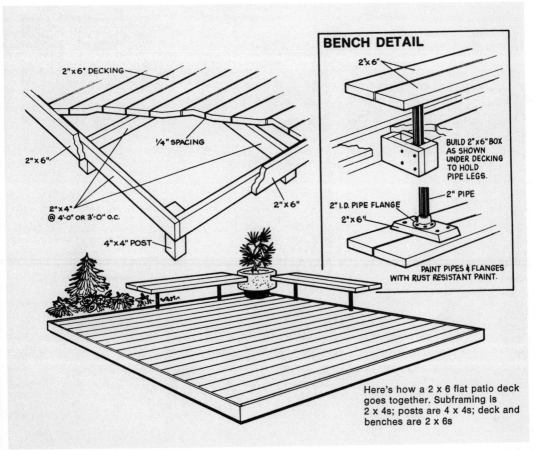

2"x6" DECKING

¼" SPACING

2"x6"

2"x4"
@ 4'-0" OR 3'-0" O.C.

2"x6"

4"x4" POST

BENCH DETAIL

2"x6"

BUILD 2"x6" BOX
AS SHOWN
UNDER DECKING
TO HOLD
PIPE LEGS.

2" PIPE

2" I.D. PIPE FLANGE

2"x6"

PAINT PIPES & FLANGES
WITH RUST RESISTANT PAINT.

Here's how a 2 x 6 flat patio deck
goes together. Subframing is
2 x 4s; posts are 4 x 4s; deck and
benches are 2 x 6s

expansion joints between the foundation and the patio. Wooden decks can be anchored to the house with ledger strips nailed to the studs or sill.

Patio roofs can be plastic, screening, plywood, and other water-resistant materials. The framing is simple: post-and-beam construction. If the roof must support a lot of weight, you should use 2 x 4 or 2 x 6 rafters or beams. Space them from 24 to 36 in. apart.

You can buy prefabricated metal/plastic frames for patio roofs. They hook to the house and are supported by metal rods or posts. Since the panels are light, they do not need large supporting members.

Louver-roof patio cover is installed this way. Wooden components should be redwood or cypress. To build, fasten ledger to siding. Set posts. Use 1 x 4 in. louvers. A 2 x 4 block makes a handy spacing tool. Toenail the louvers to the joists

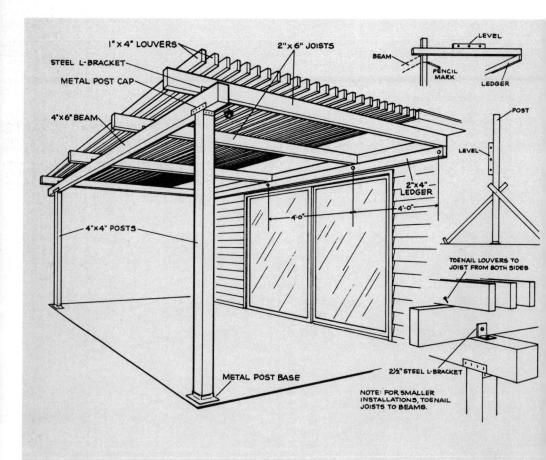

lawnmower maintenance

DIRT AND CORROSION are the biggest enemies of a power lawnmower. If the engine won't run, the chances are about 95 percent certain that dirt is causing the problem. For this section, we asked engineering experts how to keep power lawnmowers operating smoothly. You'll find their advice here; it is general in application, and the photos necessarily show only one make of mower.

Motor won't crank. If you have a self-start model, check to make sure there are no loose electrical connections. Also, see if the starter gears are engaged. If they're not, disconnect the sparkplug and turn the starter cup on the engine in a counterclockwise direction until the gears are free.

Engine won't start. Do not begin to make adjustments on the engine. Instead:

1. Make sure you have gas. If the lawnmower has set in storage all winter with gas in it, pour the old gas out and put in new fuel.

2. Is the throttle control lever in the proper position?

3. Check the sparkplug. Is the plug wire loose or disconnected? Is the plug faulty or improperly gapped?

4. The engine could be flooded. Take out the sparkplug, dry it with a soft cloth; crank the engine with the plug removed and the throttle off. Then replace the plug and lead wire, and start the mower.

Engine is tough to start and there seems to be a loss of power. This can be caused by dirt in the gas tank, a dirty air cleaner, water in the gas, or a clogged vent in the gas cap. Or the carburetor could be plugged.

Erratic operation. A dirty sparkplug is usually the reason. Also check the gap in the plug and the air cleaner, which may need cleaning service.

Engine skips at high speed. The sparkplug gap is probably too close. Clean the plug and reset.

Engine won't idle properly. Make sure there are no air passage obstructions and that the cooling fins are clean. Low oil level can cause this, too, so check the oil level in the crankcase.

Engine overheats. The sparkplug wire is prob-

Buying a new lawnmower? Pick one that mulches leaves and grass. Although more costly, it will save you time

ably loose. Also check the cutter blade bolt to make sure it is tight. A dirty air cleaner can cause overheating.

Excessive vibration. Check the cutter blade for looseness. BUT disconnect the sparkplug wire before you do this. A flip of the blade to test it may cause the engine to start. NEVER work on the engine unless the sparkplug is disconnected—with one exception: when you are attempting to make carburetor adjustments.

HOW TO MAKE CARBURETOR ADJUSTMENTS

Engine adjustments are usually made at the factory, so don't touch the engine if it is running smoothly. If you need adjustments, here are the procedures:

1. With your fingers, close the power adjusting needle. The drawing shows where it is on one make and model, and will help you locate the needle on your own mower. Close it all the way, then open it one turn.

2. With your fingers, close the idle adjusting needle. Then open it about ⅝ th of a turn.

3. Start the engine. Open the throttle to full power or fast position. Then adjust the power adjusting needle about ⅛ th turn at a time. Go forward and backward until the engine is running smoothly.

4. With the throttle lever closed, adjust the idle adjusting needle so the engine runs smoothly. To get the proper idling speed, you adjust this screw. Test it backward and forward to find the right position.

5. Don't rush the adjustment job. Give the engine time to adapt to each adjustment setting.

CUTTING BLADE MAINTENANCE

When the blades of grass in your lawn begin to look as if a sheep had eaten them off instead of your lawnmower cutting them off, chances are the blade of the mower needs sharpening. DO NOT ATTEMPT TO REMOVE THE BLADE OR SHARPEN IT UNTIL YOU DISCONNECT THE SPARKPLUG WIRE.

You can sharpen the blade while it's still on the mower with a file. Maintain the original bevel, and remove the same amount of metal from each side by counting the file strokes you make.

For adjusting throttle, move the throttle control lever as far to the rear as you can. It should be in an "off" position

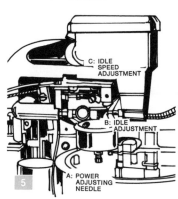
Main controls include: A—power adjusting needle; B—idle adjustment screw; C—idle speed adjustment

You remove blade by first removing a bolt or screw fitting. Some twist off, as shown here. ALWAYS disconnect sparkplug

With your fingers only (don't use pliers) close adjusting needle to right, or clockwise. Then open the needle one turn

If throttle still won't work, try tightening the throttle clamp. It sometimes works loose and slips in the clamp

If motor runs too fast or slow, adjust the idle speed until the engine runs smoothly. If motor stalls, enrich fuel mixture slightly

If engine won't start, check sparkplug connection. It must be clean. Make sure wire is firmly seated in connection

Check sparkplug at start of mowing season. If the plug is pitted or can't be cleaned easily, by all means replace it

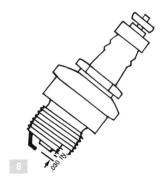

Clean and reset sparkplug gap about every 25 hours of mower use. On most models the gap should be .030 inches

If blade is stuck, twist it off, as shown. You can touch up the cutting edges with a metal file. Try to maintain the original bevel

If engine is stuck, disconnect sparkplug. Then turn starter cup on engine counterclockwise until the gears break free

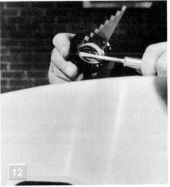

Gas caps have air vents that need to be cleaned about every third time you use the lawnmower

Air cleaners should be serviced about every 12 hours of motor operation. Wash cleaner, if it is polyurethane, in detergent

Power-driven mowers sometimes balk if V-belt is loose or worn. Tighten it so it can be compressed about ½-in. or so

On self-propelled models, check this gear case for leakage between it and the axle. If it is leaking, try tightening nuts

Bolt or lever adjusts cutting height for grass. Rule of thumb: set height at about 2 in. This helps promote dense growth

WHEN THE GROWING SEASON IS OVER and you put your lawnmower away for the winter,

1. Drain the fuel tank. If you don't, gum deposits can form on the carburetor, fuel line and gas tank. This can prevent the engine from starting in the spring. Run the engine until the gas is exhausted.

2. Drain the crankcase oil. Do this while it is still warm, and then fill it with new oil.

3. Unscrew the sparkplug, pour an ounce of 10-W-30 oil into the cylinder. Crank the engine once. This dispenses the oil. Then replace the plug.

4. Clean the lawnmower so all dirt and grass clippings are off the engine and the blade housing.

On most window air conditioners, you remove front to get at filters. Replace dirty throw-away filters; wash other types in water

AIR-CONDITIONING UNITS and heating plants are so designed that, as a general rule, you should call a serviceman to make major repairs. However, there are some repairs that you yourself can make in an emergency. There are also maintenance steps that you can follow to keep cooling and heating units in top working condition and avoid frequent breakdowns.

Before you attempt any repair jobs on heating and cooling units, obtain an owner's manual and if possible a service manual from a dealer or the manufacturer of your specific unit.

Window air conditioners operate similar to a refrigerator—without the freezing compartment. Basically, a refrigerant is boiled inside a coil. During this process, the refrigerant absorbs heat from the room. Then the refrigerant goes to a compressor. The compressor raises the temperature and pressure of the refrigerant. The refrigerant loses its heat to the outside air after it flows to a condensor coil. This causes the refrigerant to change to a liquid, which is piped back to a coil. The process repeats itself.

If the unit won't run, check the power source first. Use a test light. Start at the wall outlet and move to the main power entry at the fuse box or circuit breaker.

If the unit is operating at low capacity, low voltage may be the problem. The usual sign of low voltage is the dimming of lights when the air conditioner goes on.

You can test low voltage with a voltmeter. You can find the voltage for your specific window unit from the manufacturer's tag attached to it. The voltage probably will be 110 or 220 volts, although there are some models that operate on 208–220 volts.

Dirty filters can reduce air flow and affect the capacity of the unit. Some window units have throw-away filters; others have filters that can be

317
376
377

heating
and air
conditioning
repairs and
improvements

washed in a sink. Still others are washed, then coated with a filter coating that helps trap dirt. These filters are the metal mesh type; the coating comes in a spray can which you buy at a hardware store.

If the unit will not cool, first check the thermostat setting. It could be incorrect. Then check the filters to make sure they are clean. If this is not the trouble, the unit may have a refrigerant leak. This is sometimes indicated by an oily substance around tubing. If you find this situation, call a serviceman. Professional equipment is necessary to repair the trouble.

Noises and vibration can be caused by mountings that have become loose. You can tighten these with a screwdriver or wrench. If you determine that the noise is coming from inside the unit, check the fan blades to see if they are rubbing against their housing. On some models, you can adjust the blade or the housing with a screwdriver.

Mountings inside the unit are generally spring-loaded and preset at the factory. They are not too loose, not too tight, to prevent vibration. If the mountings on the compressor are loose—there are usually three of them—you can tighten them. Do not attempt to reset other mountings.

HEATING AND CENTRAL AIR CONDITIONING

Your furnace is powered by gas, electricity, or oil. A few coal-burners are still around, but they are rare in this day of laws against air pollution.

You should call in a serviceman annually to inspect your heating system. If you have central air conditioning, the same serviceman probably can check it, too. From these dealers, get an owner's manual and service guide for your specific equipment. Also watch the serviceman make the inspection, and ask questions. This will orient you to the equipment and may help if you have to make emergency repairs.

Furnace won't run. Check the power first. It may be off due to a *blown fuse* or *tripped circuit breaker.* If the fuse or circuit breaker continues to blow or trip, the trouble is probably a short inside the furnace. Call a serviceman.

Motors that drive furnace blowers sometimes

Thermostats can get dirty and malfunction. Remove cover yearly and brush away dirt. If thermostat is really old, have it replaced

If gas pilot light goes out on furnace and you smell gas, immediately shut off gas valve to furnace and get out of the house

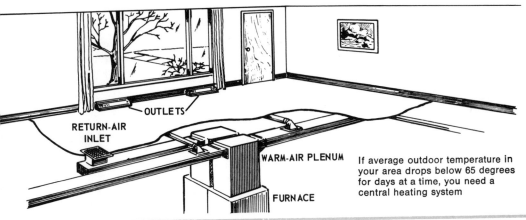

OUTLETS

RETURN-AIR INLET

WARM-AIR PLENUM

FURNACE

If average outdoor temperature in your area drops below 65 degrees for days at a time, you need a central heating system

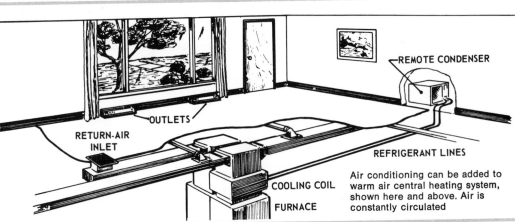

REMOTE CONDENSER

OUTLETS

RETURN-AIR INLET

REFRIGERANT LINES

COOLING COIL

FURNACE

Air conditioning can be added to warm air central heating system, shown here and above. Air is constantly circulated

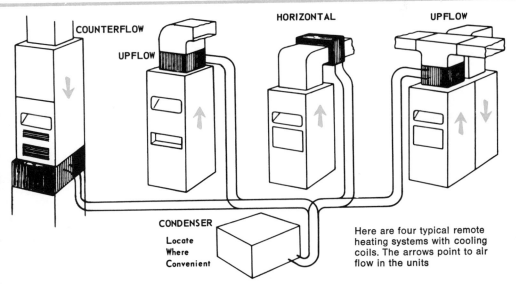

COUNTERFLOW

UPFLOW

HORIZONTAL

UPFLOW

CONDENSER

Locate Where Convenient

Here are four typical remote heating systems with cooling coils. The arrows point to air flow in the units

315

have *reset buttons*. Reset buttons act as circuit 369 breakers. Press this button for several seconds to reactivate the circuit. Also check the on/off switch that controls the furnace. It is usually located near or on the furnace and is marked "furnace." The switch could have been accidentally turned off.

The second checkpoint is the *thermostat*. Is it properly set? Turn the thermostat above normal room temperature. Listen for a click of the valve in the furnace. If there is no click, the thermostat is probably faulty and will have to be repaired or replaced by a professional.

If your furnace burns gas, check the pilot light. 320 If the light is out and there is a strong smell of gas, *turn off the gas supply immediately*. Raise a window in the basement or utility room and leave the house for an hour. Before you attempt to light the pilot, make sure all gas is out of the furnace. Turn on the gas valves again, and relight the pilot according to the manufacturer's instructions, usually embossed on a metal plate fastened to the unit near the pilot light. If the pilot doesn't burn, turn off the gas valves and call the serviceman.

If your furnace burns oil, and you have gone 322 through the systematic checklist above, try reacti- 323 vating the switch on the stack control box. It is usually located in back of the furnace. Flip this switch once. If the furnace doesn't come on, call the serviceman.

Other troubles may include:

Rapid cycling of the furnace. The furnace pops 319 on and off constantly. The thermostat is probably 321 faulty. If your furnace has an easily accessible *bonnet thermostat,* set it at a higher reading. Sometimes the blower starts before the air in the bonnet is warm enough. It usually runs after it has distributed the warm air.

Noisy blower. It may need oil. If there are oil holes present in the motor and blower, use lightweight oil for lubrication. Noise sometimes stems from misaligned pulleys or a worn V-belt. You will need an Allen wrench or screwdriver to reset the alignment or change the fan belt.

HEATING AND COOLING MAINTENANCE

Your heating and cooling system can be losing as much as 25 percent efficiency. Sometimes by

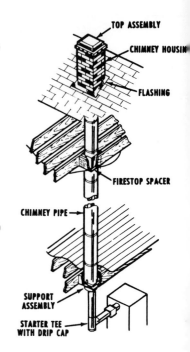

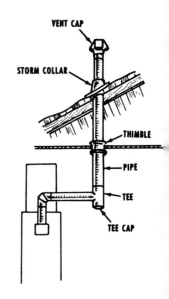

If you're remodeling your home and adding a heating system, it has to have a chimney or vent for the proper combustion. Prefabricated chimney is shown at top; prefabricated gas vent is at bottom

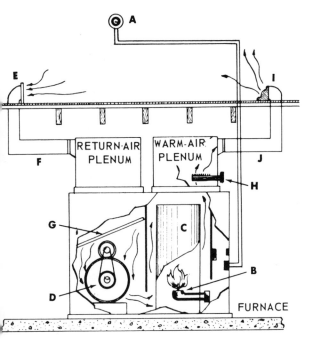

Forced-air systems work like this: (A) is thermostat. It starts the burner (B), which heats air around exchanger (C). Furnace blower (D) pulls in cool air, puffs out hot air through ducts

Furnace switch controls furnace. Check it first; it may have been accidentally turned off so furnace won't function. Also check switch on stack control box if unit burns oil, and check bonnet thermostat for proper setting

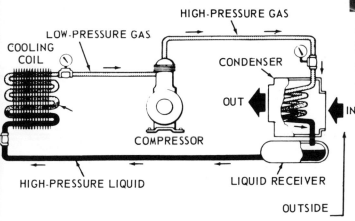

Here's how air conditioner works: Motor drives blower to circulate house air through cooling coil (motor not shown). Thermostat is used to control compresser/blower

317

simply vacuuming registers and changing the filters you can add greatly to the efficiency of your unit.

Clean filters regularly, or replace throw-away filters annually. If the furnace runs a lot during the heating season, clean or replace the filters at least twice during this period. Also do the same for air-conditioning filters during the cooling months.

Radiators on hot-water systems need bleeding yearly. A bleeder valve is located near the top of a radiator on one end. As you unscrew this valve, you will hear air hissing. Then water will seep out. Close the valve and move to the next radiator. The valves in some radiators may be faulty. To check them, interchange them with a valve you know is working. If faulty, try boiling the valve in washing soda and water for about 30 minutes. This will remove debris. Try the valve again. If it doesn't work, you will have to buy a new valve. *For leaky shut-off valves,* you can easily disassemble the unit and install new packing or a washer. Often, a wrench is all you need to tighten the collar around the valve stem.

Steam-heat troubles boil down to radiator valves and dirty boilers. Sometimes the pipes through which water and vapor pass become misaligned. They should slant downward from the radiators to the boiler. You can check these with a level and make corrections by adjusting pipes and hangers.

A dirty boiler is a job for a serviceman. You can drain it and flush it out according to the manufacturer's recommendations. If you use chemicals to clean the boiler, do so only once a year. The chemicals are injected into the boiler through a hole in which the safety valve is screwed. Make absolutely sure that there is no steam pressure in the boiler when you unscrew the valve.

Use a bucket or hose to direct the water you remove from the boiler through the drain valve. Flush the boiler by pouring more water into the safety valve opening. Do this until clean water flows out of the drain valve.

Gas burners require little service. You can tell if they are functioning properly by the flame. If it is blue with a small yellow tip on the end, the burner is working properly. If the yellow tip isn't there, there is not enough air mixed with the gas.

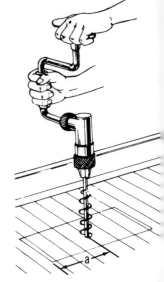

For new floor register, mark outline between joists. Drill hole and locate position from underneath floor to assure clearance

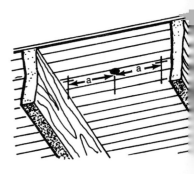

Measure from hole to sides of the opening. You may have to shift register slightly. If so, make measurement changes topside

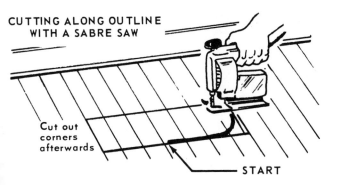

With keyhole saw or sabre saw, cut out flooring for register. Drill a probe hole on second floor installations

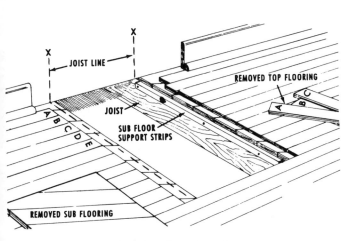

Some installations require running new ducts in second-floor joists. You have to remove flooring from this area

Change throw-away filters yearly —more often if heating season is long. Filters are marked as to air-flow direction

Blower speeds may be changed on some furnaces by switching the control wires. Speeds usually are marked in number sequence

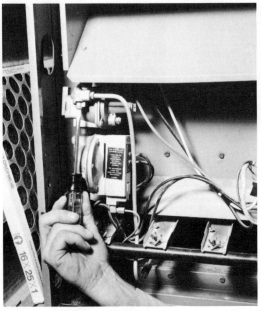

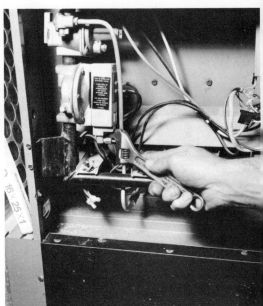

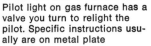

Pilot light on gas furnace has a valve you turn to relight the pilot. Specific instructions usually are on metal plate

If pilot won't stay lighted, it may be faulty thermocouple. To remove it, disconnect tube that runs from gas control valve to pilot on most models

If the flame appears to be too yellow, the trouble is too much air. You adjust the air intake shutter near the burner to correct this.

Functional fireplaces can present several problems; most are easy to solve:

Smoke won't go up chimney. Check to make sure the damper is open and that there are no obstructions in the chimney or above the chimney. A tree branch could be obstructing the draft. The chimney might be dirty.

Fire won't burn properly. Fire needs air to burn. Today's houses are built tightly, and the fireplace may not be getting enough air to function. Try cracking a window or door slightly to correct the problem. The fire should be centered in the fireplace. If it is too far forward, it does not properly heat the back of the fireplace for the necessary updraft. This also will cause the logs to smoke. Leave a bed of ashes under the andirons. If the hearth is cold, it can cause a down-and-out draft.

The fireplace opening may be too high. You can check this by holding a piece of metal or asbestos board over the opening at the lintel and lowering it. When smoking stops, you have the right height for the lintel.

You can make minor furnace repairs yourself, but if in doubt, always call a professional

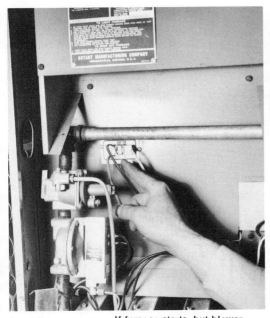

If furnace starts, but blower doesn't, limit control switch will turn off flame. Switch limits maximum temperature to deter fire

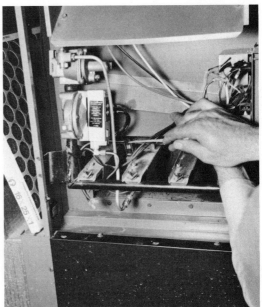

Gas pilot light on most furnaces is located near one of the main burners. You'll need fireplace matches or loop on long wire to hold match

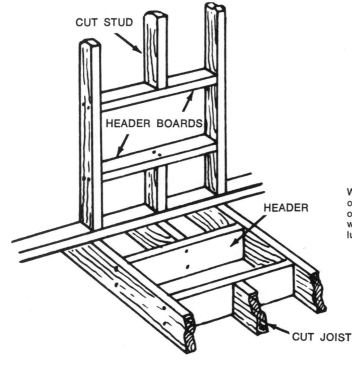

CUT STUD

HEADER BOARDS

HEADER

CUT JOIST

When you have to remove a stud or joist to install a register, tie off the end of the cut member with a header of the same size lumber

321

IF ROOMS FEEL COLD, and your home is equipped with a warm-air heating system, there are several methods of correcting the situation:

• 1. The thermostat may be improperly located, causing the corners of the room to be cold. Or the thermostat may be faulty.

• 2. The blower may be puffing air at too high a velocity. Even warm air swirling around your body can make you feel cold.

• 3. The registers may not be balanced properly. Air ducts have dampers in them which can be adjusted to balance the heating (or cooling) load. You adjust by a trial-and-error system. You also can adjust registers to balance the flow of heating or cooling. Do not shut off upper floor registers in an attempt to get more heat through the first floor registers. Instead, adjust the damper at the first floor level, just above the baseboard registers. This damper slows the flow of air to upper floors, and the lower floors are then heated.

• 4. If the relative humidity is low—below 40 percent—body moisture is lost quickly, and you feel cold although the temperature may be 80 degrees. Low relative humidity also can cause your home and furnishings to dry out. If the relative humidity is too high—over 60 percent—you will feel very warm. Windows will sweat and walls will become damp.

• 5. Since hot air rises and cool air drops, you may be getting cold drafts down a stairwell. Try shutting off this opening, if possible, or installing a return air-flow duct at the top of the stairs. Put the duct in the top step and vent it down under the stairs to the basement or furnace.

Emergency procedures usually are noted on an embossed plate fastened to your furnace. Also it's important to have an owner's manual

POSITION OF ELECTRODE TIPS AND GAP DISTANCE

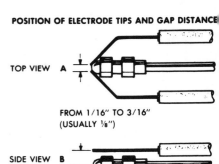

TOP VIEW   A

FROM 1/16″ TO 3/16″
(USUALLY ⅛″)

SIDE VIEW   B

FROM 3/8″ TO 9/16″
TO CENTER OF NOZZLE

ABOVE DISTANCES VARY
WITH DIFFERENT MAKES

Oilburner parts are similar; location in furnace may vary. You should replace nozzle annually with new one, same size and rating. To clean electrodes, remove them, wash in carbon solvent, polish the surface with emery cloth. Use #10 oil to lubricate motors

Forced-air furnace ducts in utility closets can rattle when furnace starts, stops. Styrofoam insulation can block some of this noise

Insulation fits over ductwork. Also make sure duct joints are properly taped. Joint tape is easy to use. Soak it in water and apply

Duct control is simple thumb-screw you turn to close damper. You can balance heat to registers with the damper. Use trial-and-error

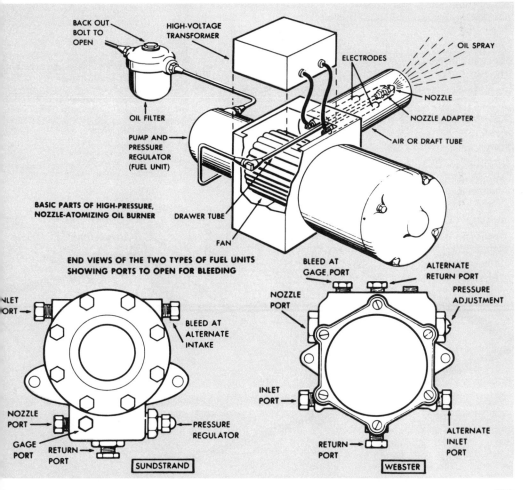

BACK OUT BOLT TO OPEN

HIGH-VOLTAGE TRANSFORMER

OIL SPRAY

ELECTRODES

NOZZLE

OIL FILTER

NOZZLE ADAPTER

PUMP AND PRESSURE REGULATOR (FUEL UNIT)

AIR OR DRAFT TUBE

BASIC PARTS OF HIGH-PRESSURE, NOZZLE-ATOMIZING OIL BURNER

DRAWER TUBE

FAN

END VIEWS OF THE TWO TYPES OF FUEL UNITS SHOWING PORTS TO OPEN FOR BLEEDING

BLEED AT GAGE PORT

ALTERNATE RETURN PORT

NOZZLE PORT

PRESSURE ADJUSTMENT

INLET PORT

BLEED AT ALTERNATE INTAKE

INLET PORT

NOZZLE PORT

PRESSURE REGULATOR

ALTERNATE INLET PORT

GAGE PORT

RETURN PORT

RETURN PORT

SUNDSTRAND

WEBSTER

WHEN REMODELING YOUR HOME, heating 251 and cooling units may be an important factor— especially if your present system can't handle an additional load. You may, however, be able to install a small, separate heating or cooling unit for a room addition or an attic conversion.

The deciding factors in selecting a separate system include fuel availability, cost, convenience and cleanliness.

The most popular type of heating is a central 257 forced-air system. Other types include hydronic 317 and electrical systems. Since codes are usually involved, you will have to consult a dealer for specific information for your area.

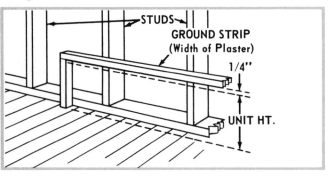

STUDS

GROUND STRIP
(Width of Plaster)

1/4"

UNIT HT.

For radiation units, you may have to open the wall. Saw off inside facing (plaster or gypsumboard) and install any necessary insulation

Series loop and monoflo system is shown at right. No air vents are used in radiation units for series loop; they are used for monoflo system. Cast-iron baseboard units are a single piece. To install loop, start at boiler, complete the loop to the return fitting at boiler

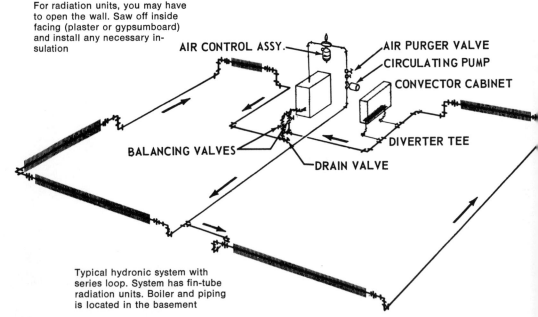

AIR CONTROL ASSY.

AIR PURGER VALVE

CIRCULATING PUMP

CONVECTOR CABINET

BALANCING VALVES

DIVERTER TEE

DRAIN VALVE

Typical hydronic system with series loop. System has fin-tube radiation units. Boiler and piping is located in the basement

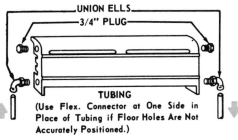

UNION ELLS
3/4" PLUG
TUBING
(Use Flex. Connector at One Side in Place of Tubing if Floor Holes Are Not Accurately Positioned.)

MAINS BELOW

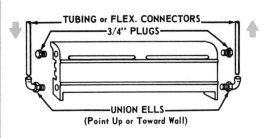

TUBING or FLEX. CONNECTORS
3/4" PLUGS
UNION ELLS
(Point Up or Toward Wall)

MAINS ABOVE

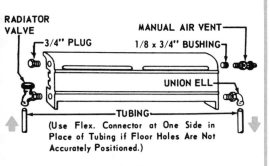

RADIATOR VALVE
3/4" PLUG
MANUAL AIR VENT
1/8 x 3/4" BUSHING
UNION ELL
TUBING
(Use Flex. Connector at One Side in Place of Tubing if Floor Holes Are Not Accurately Positioned.)

MAINS BELOW

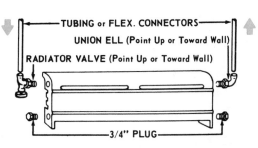

TUBING or FLEX. CONNECTORS
UNION ELL (Point Up or Toward Wall)
RADIATOR VALVE (Point Up or Toward Wall)
3/4" PLUG

MAINS ABOVE

NOTE
The two ends of each group are connected up like a single unit for system being used.

NOTE
A special Connector Kit includes 4 unions, 2 nipples and a cover that allows for 5½" spacing between units.

Use KIT Described in Note

PAIRING CAST-IRON UNITS ALONG A STRAIGHT WALL

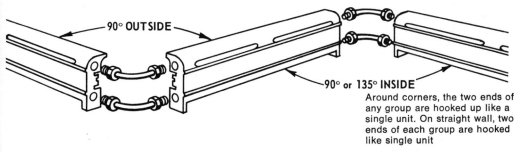

90° OUTSIDE

90° or 135° INSIDE
Around corners, the two ends of any group are hooked up like a single unit. On straight wall, two ends of each group are hooked like single unit

common plumbing problems

Typical faucet assembly looks like this. On chrome surfaces, use adjustable wrenches or smooth-jawed pliers. Or pad jaws with adhesive tape or cotton make-up pads. To remove handle, you may have to pry up with screwdriver

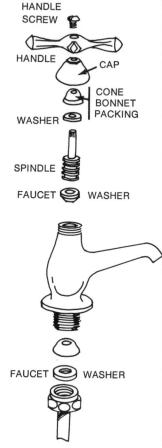

HANDLE SCREW

HANDLE — CAP

CONE
BONNET
PACKING

WASHER

SPINDLE

FAUCET — WASHER

FAUCET — WASHER

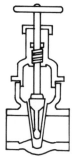

GATE VALVE

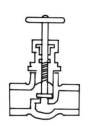

GLOBE VALVE

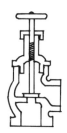

ANGLE VALVE

Common types of faucets are shown above. Some models have gate plates that are removed with a screwdriver. Plates may have gasket that can leak. If you're sweat-soldering joints in new construction, remove valves so heat from torch does not damage the valve or the gasket seals

Regular or Phillips head screw holds handle on; some are slip fit. Tightening this screw will not stop valve leak

Turn spindle with pliers or adjustable wrench. Just loosen it so you can back out spindle with your fingers. Never force

New washer fits on bottom of the spindle. It is held by a screw. You can buy inexpensive bags of assorted faucet washers

CLOGGED DRAINS AND PIPES are the most common plumbing problems, followed by flush tanks that won't work and leaky faucets. You can fix most of these problems.

212
448

Before you make most plumbing repairs, you must turn off the water. Do this at the main water entrance to your home (the valve will be near the water meter) or use the shut-off faucets that are located directly beneath the fixture that you'll be fixing.

Faucets that leak involve a three-step operation: 1. Remove the handle. 2. Remove the spindle; it is threaded and turns out of its fitting. 3. Remove the old washer at the bottom of the spindle and replace the washer with a new one.

Keep drains open by using chemical cleaner once every two weeks. If drain is slow, try chemical cleaner; however, it may not work. Chemical cleaners often are poison and some can irritate your skin, so be very careful in handling them

Plumber's friend works on suction principle to break obstruction in drain pipes. You push it up and down

Augers have off-set handle, spiral shaft, and a tip with mechanical "fingers" or corkscrew

Auger goes through trap like this. If trap is clean, remove it and thread auger into drain run to clean rest of pipe

Clean-out traps have plug you twist out with adjustable plumbing wrench. Here you may need long, flat "snake"

You may have to replace the screw that holds the washer. Spare screws come in boxes of washers.

Faucets that leak around the stem may be caused by a loose packing nut. Try tightening it very gently. If it still leaks, replace the packing. Packing looks like string, but it has been specially treated. Wind the new packing around the stem, filling the "threads." Replace the faucet; tighten the nut—turn it until it is snug. Do not overtighten.

A damaged valve seat can be repaired with a special tool you can buy that grinds the seat smooth again. However, you may want to replace the faucet instead of investing and working with a valve-seat dressing tool.

Faucets with a *single lever handle* don't often go bad, but when they do they usually are not easy to repair. We suggest you remove them and buy new ones.

Single handle *shower faucets* have a spindle that is laced with plastic O-rings. To repair them: 1. Remove the faucet handle. 2. Remove the cover plate. 3. Remove the spindle by lifting out a small "keeper" ring that you will find at the top of the spindle housing. 4. Twist out the spindle. A plumbing shop may be able to replace the rings. If not, buy a new spindle assembly.

Many modern faucets are equipped with an aerator. Dirt and lime deposits from water can clog its screen. You can take it apart by unscrewing the aerator and cleaning out the screen.

PUSH PLUMBER'S FRIEND DOWN TO APPLY PRESSURE AGAINST OBSTRUCTION

OBSTRUCTION

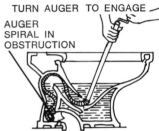

TURN AUGER TO ENGAGE

AUGER SPIRAL IN OBSTRUCTION

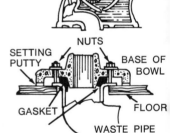

MECHANICAL GRIP PINCHES OBSTRUCTION SO IT CAN BE REMOVED

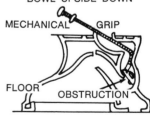

NUTS

SETTING PUTTY

BASE OF BOWL

GASKET

FLOOR

WASTE PIPE

BOWL UPSIDE DOWN

MECHANICAL GRIP

FLOOR

OBSTRUCTION

For clogged toilets, try plumber's friend first. Work the plunger up and down very fast to create a suction

Auger twists its own way to the obstruction in toilet bowl. You may want to don plastic sleeve to feed auger into outlet

Plumber's friend, auger work like this. In serious cases, bowl may have to be removed to reach obstruction

Shower heads fall into the aerator classification. The little holes can become clogged with dirt and lime. Remove the shower head, disassemble it by removing a couple of screws, or by simply un-twisting it (some have a thread fit), and clean the holes with fine steel wool or a needle.

Plastic or rubber hoses, such as those used for 339 rinsing dishes at the kitchen sink, can become damaged from hot water and kinking. Since there is no great expense involved, the entire hose should be replaced. You do it by disconnecting two clamp fittings.

HOW TO OPEN CLOGGED DRAINS

If the drain is slow but not completely clogged, 326 you may be able to open it with a chemical drain cleaner. Use the chemical cleaner when you first

Here's how flush tank works. The water in the flush tank is clean, so you do not have to worry about germs when you reach into the tank for repairs. With the exception of the flushing handle, all mechanical parts of a toilet are located in the flush tank. Look here for most problems: running toilet, leak, flusher won't work, tank won't fill with water

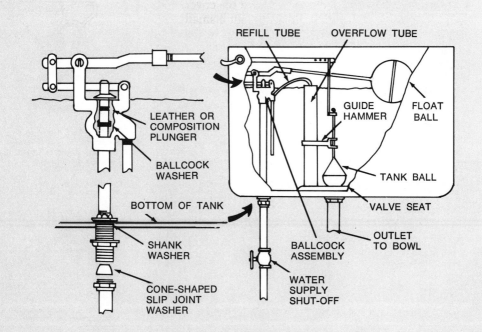

REFILL TUBE OVERFLOW TUBE

LEATHER OR COMPOSITION PLUNGER

BALLCOCK WASHER

BOTTOM OF TANK

SHANK WASHER

CONE-SHAPED SLIP JOINT WASHER

GUIDE HAMMER FLOAT BALL

TANK BALL

VALVE SEAT

BALLCOCK ASSEMBLY

OUTLET TO BOWL

WATER SUPPLY SHUT-OFF

notice the drain is becoming slow. If all the drains are running slow, check the lowest drain in the system. The trouble (blockage) usually can be found at this point.

Warning: chemical drain cleaners can injure your skin and most cleaners are poisonous. Use them according to directions on the container. If the drain is completely stopped, try using a plumber's friend first to break loose any obstruction. Then apply the chemical.

A plumber's friend is a friend indeed for clogged drainage systems. Before you use it, remove the mechanical stopper in the sink. Usually you do this by removing a nut on the end of a rod below the bottom of the sink. Pull the rod off the horizontal rod and push up. Twist the stopper, it will release itself. Also, stuff a cloth in the overflow drain of the sink or lavatory before you work the plumber's friend. This helps create more suction to break loose the obstruction in the pipe.

The secret to using a plumber's friend is not to give up too quickly. First, push the plunger up and down rapidly. Then, push it down easy and jerk it up with a snap.

If a sink or lavatory is clogged and chemicals or a plumber's friend won't unclog it, first try disassembling the U-shaped trap below. Bail out all the water you can from the sink first. Then put a pail under the trap. With an adjustable wrench (or plumber's pipe wrench with the jaws padded), remove the nuts, which are usually a slip fit. This

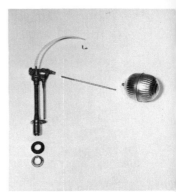

Disassembled, flushing valve on most toilets looks like this. Float simply lifts when water rises, closing the water valve

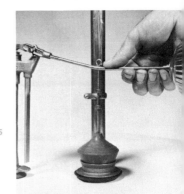

Water level in flush tank can be altered by bending the float rod. The rod is attached to the valve and the float

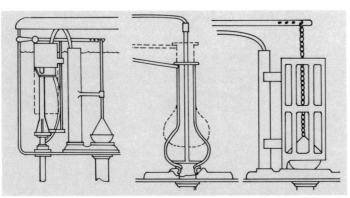

New type ball assembly in flush tank works in a cage guide. However, the same principle as used on older models applies

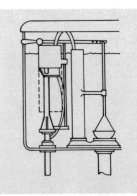

Plastic float on new valve assembly slides on rod; when toilet is flushed, float drops, then it floats up to turn off valve

Overflow tube assembly goes together in this fashion. Rubber ball fits into brass seat. If ball is worn, toilet may run or hiss

Adjust flushing handle assembly by adjusting chain or rod that is fastened to flushing handle and the tank ball lifting lever

Tank float rod assembly and lifting levers for rubber ball should be separated enough so units do not interfere

Refill tube goes from valve assembly to overflow tube. A tiny brass clip holds plastic tube in place

If toilet runs, rubber ball may be out of alignment. Realign guide as first step. Loosen set screw, twist guide, retighten

Leaky float may cause failure of flush tank to fill. You can check this by unscrewing the float. If it has any water in it, replace it

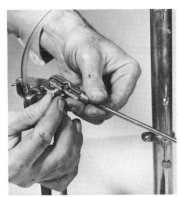

Valve is disconnected by first removing a screw on float arm. Then loosen thumb screw on back of arm and unscrew valve

Rubber washer in bottom of valve is replaced by prying it out and slipping in new one

Valve stem has a split washer that may be worn. It can be replaced by simply prying it out and inserting a new one

will drop the U-shaped piece of pipe from the other sections of pipe. Some U-sections have a plug in the bottom of them. Unscrew the plug to get at the obstruction, if possible.

Plumber's snakes and augers are the next step to unclogging drains—especially toilets—if the methods described above don't solve the problem.

Snakes and augers are fed into the pipes and twisted to remove the obstructions. If they come up against a T fitting with a very sharp bend, the ball game is over. Call the repairman; the clog is beyond your reach.

Clogged toilets. A plumber's friend sometimes works. Most often it doesn't; but it's worth a try. The next tool to try is a plumber's snake or auger.

If there isn't enough water in the toilet bowl, fill it to the normal level. Push the snake or auger through the drain channels. Push and pull so you ram the tool into the obstruction, hopefully breaking through it. If the obstruction is a toy, diaper, piece of cloth or similar material, the corkscrew type hook on the auger will snare it and you can pull the obstruction back out of the channel.

If the toilet is flooded, you frankly have a messy job. This means threading the auger or snake into the channels. Take a plastic clothes bag and wrap your hand and arm in the plastic wrap, making a watertight seal. Then insert the snake or auger. Usually, either will go through the channels to the vertical drop. No success? The next step is to call a plumber. He may have to remove the toilet bowl, turn it upside down, and remove the object from the underside.

Clean-out plugs go from top to bottom in T and Y sections. For blockage, you should start at the top and work down. A snake is the best tool for this since it has the length required to go the distance of the run. However, the runs are usually quite long; therefore, it is best to call in a professional rather than to buy or rent the necessary equipment.

For bathtubs that are clogged, remove the drain stopper, and try the plumber's friend treatment. If you don't have success, use an auger or snake which will go to the vertical pipe. Some bathtubs are installed against a wall that has a trapdoor on the opposite side. You may have to look carefully for the trap to find it. If you can, open it and rod out the vertical piping.

For any clogged drain, try the simplest solution first, then work toward the most difficult. Eventually you'll clear the clog

Septic systems are a job for a professional since most of the mechanical elements of the system are below ground in the form of a tank and drainfield. One common problem is bacteriological action in a tank that is flooded. This will cause a backup in the drain piping. If you notice that the grass is greener in the drainfield lines than in the rest of the lawn, chances are that nonsterile sewage is seeping upward from the draintiles.

FLUSH TANK REPAIRS

First, turn off the water and flush the toilet.

Valve won't shut. Bend float arm downward near the valve. Make a gentle bend. If this doesn't work, check the float, which may be half-filled with water. If so, replace it. If not, the valve may be faulty.

Toilet runs. Rubber tank ball is out of alignment or faulty. Or seat is damaged (try polishing with steel wool). The handle may not release the ball-guide rod. Try adjusting this.

Tank leaks at bottom. Probably faulty gaskets. Try tightening the nuts—very gently. If this won't stop it, you'll have to replace the gaskets. If so, consider replacing the entire valve system; it is inexpensive. But loosen nuts carefully; don't crack the ceramic tank.

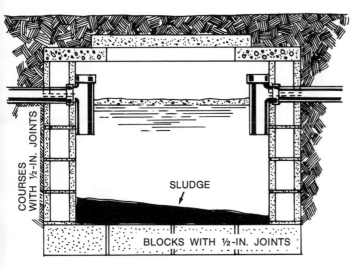

Septic systems are fabricated similar to this; some vary slightly as to construction. Septic system problems are best left to a professional. However, you can introduce chemicals into the standpipe that will deter root growth in the drainfield

Working with iron pipe

STANDARD SIZES of iron pipe are available—already threaded to match fittings. The trouble comes when you need nonstandard lengths. Here, you have to measure the length of pipe you need, buy it at a plumbing shop, and have the shop thread the ends for you. If you are doing a lot of iron-pipe work, you can rent threading equipment.

Measuring the pipe section you need is one key to working with iron pipe. Measure between the centers, then subtract for the fittings. The measurement should be that amount equal to the inside diameter of the pipe: if ¾-in., subtract ¾-in. for each of the fittings.

Assembly is the second key. Spread joint compound on the male threads of the pipe. Then screw on the fitting as far as it will go by hand. Tighten with pipe wrenches. To add the next section, you turn the pipe into the fitting with a wrench.

Fittings. Since it is very difficult to bend iron pipe (and you shouldn't try), you have to use fittings: 90- and 45-deg. elbows, tees, reducing tees, couplings and unions. Unions are vital to straight runs. You can join two sections of pipe without twisting either pipe. If the pipe is to go between fittings, it has to have a union. The union must be figured in the overall measurement for the correct fit. You can buy special fittings to join plastic and copper pipe to iron pipe.

To replace a section of pipe, measure as described above. Then shut off the water at a valve. Cut the old pipe between fittings with a hacksaw. Support the pipe so it doesn't damage any adjoining fittings or sag when the hacksaw slips through. Then, with pipe wrenches, unscrew each section of the pipe from its fitting. Put in two new pieces of pipe, measured to accept the union. Now install the union.

It's a good idea to "dry" assemble a pipe run before you install it. When you're satisfied everything fits, use joint compound on the male threads, and assemble.

It is not a good policy to fit new pipes to old, copper tubing to iron, or plastic pipe to either, without first checking the plumbing codes in your area.

340
341

Pipe-joint compound for iron-pipe fittings goes on the male threads of the pipe—not the female

With adjustable pipe wrench, turn the fitting onto the pipe until it's quite snug. Do not overtighten or you'll strip threads

Adjustable pipe wrench grips pipe tightly so you can turn it into fittings. If possible, work in a vise when fabricating "runs"

Working with copper tubing

WORKING WITH COPPER PIPE AND TUB-
ING is somewhat easier than handling iron pipe
mainly because it is lighter, needs no threading to
join it, and in some forms is flexible.

Rigid copper tubing is easier for a handyman
to use than flexible tubing, since the joints are always straight. Too, rigid tubing works well for
horizontal runs since it won't sag; flexible pipe is
better for vertical installations.

There are several important techniques to
master when working with copper pipe or tubing.
These are explained in the photographs in this
section, and below:

1. Clean the joint with steel wool. If you don't,
the solder will not hold.

2. Use 40/60 solder. 95/5 is better, but you
have to have a very hot gas torch for this material.
40/60 will work for most jobs.

3. Heat the connection, not the pipe, after you
coat the tip with flux and tin it with solder.

4. If you have a project where you can't use a
propane torch, use flare fittings to join the pipes.

5. Never mix metals: copper to iron, etc.

6. Check local codes before you use copper
tubing or pipe. Type K tubing can be used underground; type L is for residential plumbing. Type
M is used for waste lines, but you need a lot of
heat for this material.

PIPE PROBLEMS AND HOW TO SOLVE THEM

Pipes can break, freeze, drip, rattle and sweat.
Here are some of the more common problems and
how to fix them:

Dripping pipes in the summer months are
caused by condensation of moisture on the cold
surface of the metal—similar to a sweating glass
of ice water. You can cure this with a self-sticking insulation tape that is wrapped around the
pipe similar to electric tape.

Noisy pipes. Water hammer is probably the
most common. You can stop this by installing an
air cushion in the piping system. This consists of
a vertical pipe in the line that is about 3-ft. long.
It juts straight up off a tee connection. Put the air
cushion at the highest point of the plumbing run.

Fittings for copper tubing include
elbows, tees, connectors, and
threaded connectors. You'll
need a torch to sweat on fittings

If pipes squeak, block the sound by loosening the pipe hangers and inserting a pad of insulation. Plain loose wool insulation makes an ideal cushion. Then, retighten the hangers.

For pipes that bang, try padding the hangers with insulation, or add more hangers to the pipe runs.

Machine-gun rattle at faucets is not caused by the pipes. The faucet needs a new washer.

Frozen pipes froze because they were not properly insulated. You can thaw them out with an electric heating cable you can buy at building-supply stores. It simply is wrapped around the frozen pipe, plugged into an electrical outlet, and the cable heats up like a toaster.

If a pipe is frozen behind a wall where it is hard to get at with heating cable, try using a sunlamp over the spot. It will take some time, but it may work.

A leaking pipe can be a must-solve-right-now problem. First turn off the water at the main entrance, or at the nearest gate valve.

If the pipe is iron and it is leaking at the joint, try tightening the joint. Turn on the water. Still leak? Turn off the water. Disassemble the joint, coat the male threads with joint compound, and reassemble.

If an iron pipe is leaking along the run, replace it as mentioned above with new pipe.

Copper tubing can spring leaks at the joints. This is due to improper soldering. Or perhaps the pipe has moved slightly, breaking the joint.

To resolder the joint, you must drain the system. You can't resolder copper tubing with water in it. Heat the connection with a propane torch to disassemble the joint. Smooth it with steel wool, retin it with solder, and reassemble the joint. Sometimes, you can run another rim of solder around the joint to seal it—especially if it is the bottom of a vertical joint.

If the leak is in a run of copper tubing, you'll have to disassemble the joints and put in a new piece of tubing, using the same joining techniques described above.

Plastic pipe generally leaks at joints. First try screwing down the clamp that holds the pipe to the fitting. If this doesn't stop the leak, try adding another clamp to the fitting. In either case, shut off the water to reduce the pressure on the pipe. If all fails, you'll have to replace the pipe, which

Cutter is best to cut copper tubing. Tubing fits between rollers; sharp blade, turned down by handle, slices through

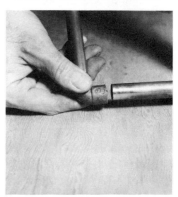

Always test connectors before you sweat joints. Connectors and tubing must be perfectly round for tight joint

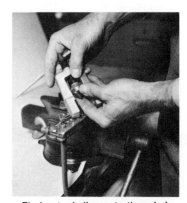

Flaring tool slips onto threaded spindle which, in turn, is fastened in the vise that holds the copper tubing

339

You also can use hacksaw to cut copper tubing. Remove burrs from cuts with file, but keep end of the pipe square

With steel wool, clean the end of the copper tubing where the tubing will go into the connector. It must be shiny bright

Coat end of copper tubing, after it is properly cleaned with steel wool, with soldering paste. Or you can tin end with hot solder

Hold flame of torch onto the connection, not the tubing. Hottest spot is at the tip of the flame. Solder will follow

Joint must be completely filled with solder. When you have finished the soldering operation, check the joint

Lock tubing in flaring vise and tighten the locknut as much as possible. Also, make sure the tubing is in the right hole

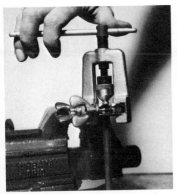

Turn spindle down to flare end of the copper tubing. Since copper is soft, it doesn't require much pressure

Flare looks like this. Tubing has been raised for illustration. Note how lips of the holes are countersunk to obtain the flare

Double flare is achieved with this attachment, which goes on spindle of vise. You insert it in tubing and turn down spindle

is probably damaged at the joint.

Special gadgets for sealing pinhole pipe leaks can be purchased at building-supply outlets. They include iron cement used with a pipe clamp. You fit the clamp around the pipe and hold it in position. The cement, which is in powder form, is mixed with water and tamped into the clamp, which has a groove in it for this purpose. When the cement hardens, you turn on the water—and hope.

Self-threading machine screws can stop a leak. Cut a rubber gasket about three times as large as the head of the screw. Coat the rubber and the pipe with iron glue, and drive the screw into the hole. This technique should be used for larger pipes, and is only a temporary stop-gap. Replace the pipe just as soon as possible.

For small pinhole leaks, you can cut a rubber gasket from an old inner tube, wrap it around the pipe and clamp it tight with a C-clamp.

Leaky garden hoses are easy to fix with tape (pinhole leaks) or with union clamps.

Metal union clamps fit into the hose section similar to the way plastic connectors are used to join two pieces of plastic pipe. Cut out the old leaky section of the hose. Insert the union and tap down the claws around it with a hammer. You can install a new end coupling in the same way. Trim off the old coupling and about 4 in. of the hose. Insert the new coupling, and tap down the clamps with a hammer to seal the joint.

Lawn sprinkler heads often become clogged with dirt and grass. To clean them, turn off the water. Then insert a screwdriver or special wrench to remove the core. Clean out the core with a fine wire. Then reassemble the unit.

Some sprinklers don't have this core. Loosen the top screw so the cap on the sprinkler head is loose. Then turn on the water. The water pressure should flush out the jets. When they are clean, re-tighten the cap.

Low water pressure can be caused by clogged pipes. You can clean them by flushing the system. Shut the valve that controls the run to be cleaned. Then open the faucet at the farthest point from the valve. Also open a second faucet nearer the valve. Slow the water in the second faucet with a rag. Now open the gate valve and let the water flow through until the sediment vanishes.

Wider flares are achieved with a broader-based fitting on the end of the spindle. Check size by matching coupling

Lock fitting in vise; coupling must be threaded on tubing before flare is made. Then match the fittings and tighten

Joint goes together like this. The smaller pipe is flared to take the connection; the larger pipe is sweated

plastic pipe know-how

PLASTIC PIPE is a handyman's dream. It goes together in a simple slip-joint fashion similar to a cane fishing pole. And it's almost as easy to assemble. It's fun to fabricate with the stuff. No special tools are necessary.

Plastic pipe is a relative newcomer on the residential construction scene. Because it is, some local areas prohibit its use. This is *not* to indicate that the plastic material is an inferior product; it isn't. But be sure you check your local building code before you use plastic pipe for any purpose other than as a drainline or for transporting water to a distant garden plot.

342
343
345

The CPVC (for chlorinated polyvinyl chloride) pipe shown in this section is typical of the plastic pipe now on the market. Most projects shown utilize ½-in. material, although larger sizes are available at many building supply outlets. You also can buy flexible plastic pipe; some of its uses are limited, so you should check with your dealer or local building code advisors before you purchase this product.

Advantages. Plastic pipe has several advantages over iron and copper piping. Perhaps, the biggest one is the ease of using it for almost any plumbing job.

It is extremely lightweight. According to Sears, Roebuck and Co., plastic pipe weighs about one-eighth as much as iron pipe and about one-third as much as copper tubing. For short runs you don't need hangers, as you sometimes do with iron pipe; you do need hangers, however, for long runs.

Plastic pipe is corrosion-proof. Acid, alkali, or corrosive water will not cause it to become rusty. It is not affected by electrolytic action. The pipe will not support scale build-up, and its natural insulation properties will keep hot water hotter and cold water colder. There also is a reduction in condensation on cold-water lines—often a summer problem.

Sizes/adapters/fittings. CPVC plastic pipe is usually available in ½- and ¾-in. sizes. The ½-in. material is generally used for supplying hot and cold water to individual fixtures. The ¾-in. pipe is for main distribution lines, although some ap-

Hacksaw is best tool for cutting plastic pipe. Assemble blade with teeth slanted forward. Use light forward cutting pressure

Use hacksaw for cutting *flexible* plastic pipe, too. Build a simple bench hook from scrap lumber to assure straight cut

plications may call for the larger pipe for individual fixtures. Pounds per square inch (psi) ratings usually are stamped on the pipe. If they are not, check the dealer for this rating. The rating should be matched with the water pressure in your area.

Fittings are available in both pipe sizes, and they include elbows, couplings, reducing bushings, tees and end caps. For both sizes of pipe, you can buy male and female iron-pipe adapters (mip/fip), elbow adapters, and copper-tubing adapters. These have metal fittings on one end, with the plastic pipe running out the other. In most installations, you can make the connections without having to thread pipe, soldering or "sweating" any fittings.

FABRICATION TECHNIQUES

Only basic hand tools are required for fabricating plastic pipe: a handsaw or hacksaw, miter box, emery cloth, pliers, screwdriver, wrench and, in some installations, a drill.

The first fabrication step is to find out if local building and plumbing codes permit the use of plastic pipe in your area. Your dealer should know.

Measure the amount of straight pipe you'll need, along with the different joints, fittings and adapters. Since plastic pipe comes in various lengths, you don't have to worry about buying a large amount of waste material to finish a job. You should, however, use the longest lengths available for the "run" you're making. This saves you the work of "slip" coupling joints.

If you have to go through walls, joists or studs with plastic pipe, drill the holes slightly larger than the pipe for easy fitting.

Assemble the job "dry." Do not cement it together until you are sure that everything fits correctly. Once the material has been joined with cement, you can't get it apart again unless you cut the joint and install a new piece of plastic material. This is not the case with flexible piping, since it goes together with slip-joints and clamps. However, once the joint is in position, it is very difficult to remove. You can "dry" test flexible material by loosely assembling it. Allow for the length of material necessary to slide onto the couplings or adaptors—usually ½-in. or so. Flexible plastic pipe can be curved, but do not bend or kink it.

334
335 With sharp knife, remove burrs from inside pipe, being careful not to slice plastic into walls of tubing. Twist pipe with one hand as you trim it

Lightly sand outside edge of pipe you've cut to remove the burrs. Emery cloth can be used for this, or fine sandpaper

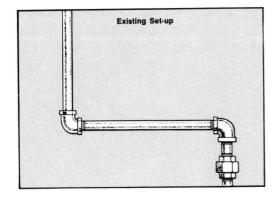

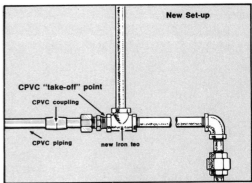

Typical metal joint system and how it can be adapted with the new plastic pipe. Check local codes before you use plastic

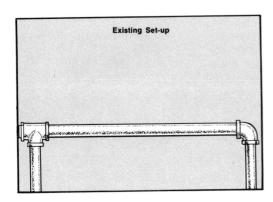

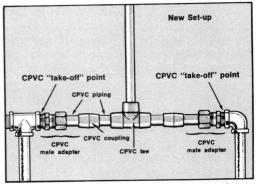

Take-off points are at metal pipe joints, as this drawing shows. If metal is old, you may need new metal fittings for plastic

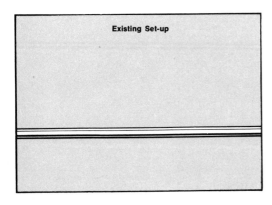

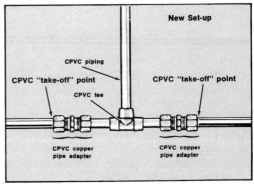

Straight pipe set-up shows how new plastic pipe can be fitted onto copper lines. Always "fit" new system before cementing it

341

You can cut CPVC pipe with a handsaw (combination or crosscut) or a hacksaw. A hacksaw is the best tool since it is small and easy to handle. Set the blade in the frame so the teeth point forward. The cutting stroke is made on the "push," not "pull," of the saw. If you use a regular handsaw, the teeth should be very sharp; use light pressure when cutting the plastic.

Keep the pipe square during your cuts. You can do this in a miter box or with a bench hook. A bench hook is a simple device: Use a piece of 1 x 4 or 1 x 6 and "cleat" one side of it with a 1 x 2, making sure it is fastened on squarely. On the opposite side—and on the other side of the board—fasten another cleat. This cleat is laid over the edge of your workbench or table to hold the hook in position while you are sawing. (See illustration on page 339.)

The cut should be smooth and square. *Remove all burrs inside and outside the pipe.* A sharp knife can be used for this, but avoid cutting the pipe as you remove the burr debris.

Clean the end of the pipe (both CPVC and flexible) with emery cloth or fine sandpaper. Just touch it up lightly for a little "tooth." Too much sanding will cause the pipe to go out of round and the joint may leak under water pressure.

With CPVC pipe, use CPVC adhesive or cement. Make sure the adhesive is the right type for the pipe you're using. Apply the CPVC cement to both the pipe and the fitting. Use a small brush for this, and smooth out the adhesive so it is evenly distributed. Do not stick the pipe or fittings into the cement.

Insert the plastic pipe immediately into the fitting after you apply the adhesive. Give the pipe a quarter turn into position. Allow for this as you join the sections. After you do a couple of them, the system will become almost automatic. With flexible pipe, you simply insert the fitting, twisting it as you force it into the pipe. You may need pliers here to assure a tight joint. If you use pliers, wrap the fitting in a piece of soft cloth to prevent the jaws of the pliers from marring the material. A screw clamp completes the job; make sure it is cinched tight, without stripping the threads as you turn the screw. If you do strip the threads, use another clamp.

Apply cement recommended only for use with the type of pipe you're fabricating. At shoulder of joint, cement must form bead

Flexible plastic pipe uses clamps for securing joints. You simply turn screw to tighten

Twist fitting into pipe, inserting clamp first on long runs. On CPVC pipe, give joint a quarter turn after you apply adhesive

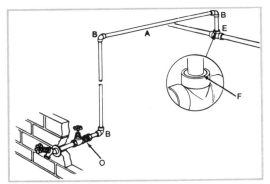

SUPPLY TO OUTSIDE SILL FAUCET

Letter Code	Type of Part	Size	Usual Quantity
A	CPVC pipe	½"	10'
B	90° ells	½"	3
E	Tee	¾"	1
F	Reducing bushing	¾ x ½"	1
O	MPI adapter	½"	1
—	Galv. nipple	½"	1
—	Valve shut-off	½"	1
—	Sill cock	½"	1

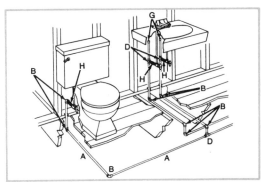

WATER SUPPLY FOR A HALF BATH

Letter Code	Type of Part	Size	Usual Quantity
A	CPVC pipe	½"	30'
B	90° ells	½"	9
D	Tees	½"	3
G	Caps	½"	2
H	FIP adapters	½ x ⅜"	3
—	Flexible supply pipes with angle valves		

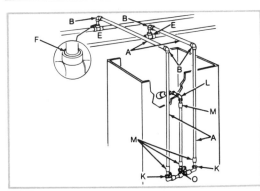

OVERHEAD WATER SUPPLY TO A BASEMENT SHOWER

Letter Code	Type of Part	Size	Usual Quantity
A	CVPC pipe	½"	20'
B	90° ells	½"	4
E	Tees	¾"	2
F	Reducing bushings	¾ x ½"	2
K	90° elbow adapter	½"	2
L	90° MIP elbow adapter	½"	1
M	Couplings	½"	4
O	MIP adapter	½"	1
—	Flexible supply pipes with angle valves		

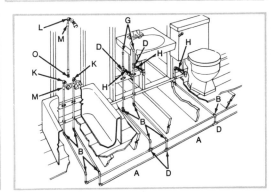

WATER SUPPLY FOR A FULL BATH

Letter Code	Type of Part	Size	
A	CPVC pipe	½"	40'
B	90° ells	½"	13
D	Tees	½"	5
G	Caps	½"	2
H	FIP adapters	½ x ⅜"	3
K	90° MIP elbow adapters	½"	2
L	90° FIP elbow adapters	½"	1
M	Couplings	½"	4
O	MIP adapter	½"	1
—	Flexible supply pipes with angle valves		

Remove any excess cement with a cloth after the fitting is in position. You should leave a continuous bead of cement at the shoulder of the joint, however, so it is thoroughly sealed.

The CPVC pipe shown in this section is rigid. It has some "give" to it, but the runs you make should be straight and the pipe should not be under bending stress or tension.

Flexible plastic pipe can be curved around objects in its way, but be very careful not to kink it as you make a gentle bend.

When using metal-to-metal adapters and connections, you should add joint compound to the threads before you tighten the assembly with a wrench. You can buy joint compound at plumbing shops and building material outlets.

Since plastic pipe (usually flexible) can be used outside without burying it, you should pre-plan the installation so the pipe won't be too conspicuous or in the path of lawn equipment. Plastic pipe will not deteriorate when it is frozen, while metal pipe must be buried below frost line.

You can bury plastic pipe just under the turf. Dig a shallow trench for the pipe, install it, and then replace the sod, tamping it firmly back into place.

If your home has a copper-tubing water system, you can interrupt this system almost anywhere to insert plastic piping. Simply use the correct adapters for the connections.

If your home has an iron-pipe water system, you should try to tie into lines just as close to a union as possible. This way, you disconnect the iron system back to an existing elbow, saving yourself time and material. If you have to cut into a straight section of iron pipe, try to pick a short section. The old iron section will have to be replaced with a new plastic section, with the fittings threaded onto the iron fittings. A plastic tee in the center of the run will serve as the take-off point in this type installation. Use joint compound ("pipe dope") for all metal-to-metal connections on iron pipe or threaded copper connections.

In assembly, you should attempt to work from the fixture back to the take-off point. And, as with any type of plumbing repair or improvement, be sure you *turn off the water* at the main meter before you start!

Typical fittings for flexible plastic pipe include tees, ells, and straight couples. Metal adapters also are available

CPVC fittings include ells, end caps, copper and iron adapters. Be sure fittings have same psi ratings as the pipe they fit

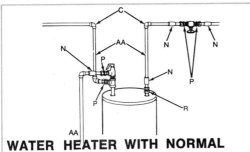

WATER HEATER WITH NORMAL RELIEF VALVE INSTALLATION

Letter Code	Type of Part	Size	Usual Quantity
AA	CPVC pipe	¾"	10'
C	90° ells	¾"	4
N	Couplings	¾"	4
P	MIP adapters	¾"	4
R	Relief valve (check codes)	—	1
—	Shut-off valve	¾"	1
—	Galvanized tee	¾"	1

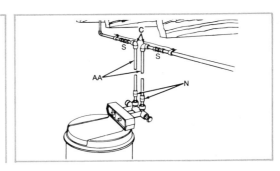

SUPPLY TO WATER SOFTENER

Letter Code	Type of Part	Size	Usual Quantity
AA	CPVC pipe	¾"	10'
C	90° ells	¾"	2
N	Couplings	¾"	2
S	Adapters to copper tubing	¾"	2

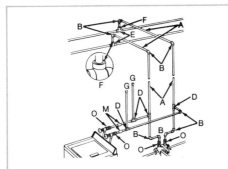

OVERHEAD WATER SUPPLY TO LAUNDRY TUBS/AUTOMATIC WASHER

Letter Code	Type of Part	Size	Usual Quantity
A	CPVC pipe	½"	20'
B	90° ells	½"	19
D	Tees	½"	2
E	Tees	¾"	2
F	Reducing bushings	¾ x ½"	2
G	Caps	½"	2
M	Couplings	½"	2
O	MIP adapters	½"	4
—	Sill cocks	½"	2

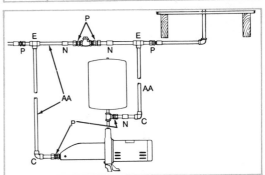

BOOSTER PUMP INSTALLATION

Letter Code	Type of Part	Size	Usual Quantity
AA	CPVC pipe	¾"	20'
C	90° ells	¾"	2
E	Tees	¾"	2
N	Couplings	¾"	3
P	MIP adapters	¾"	6
—	Check valve	1¼ x ¾"	1
—	Bushing	¾"	1
—	Tee	¾"	1
—	Nipple	¾"	1
—	Shallow well pump (jet type)		

electrical switches and outlets

Typical circuit breaker looks like this. When line is overloaded, circuit breaker snaps open. Flip switch "on" to reset

Top left is time-delay fuse for overload-motor starts; center is regular fuse; bottom is Fustat, with reduced-size base. Adaptor makes it tamper-free

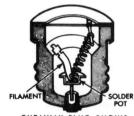  

HERE'S HOW TWO TYPES OF PLUG FUSES OPERATE

	NEW FUSES	BLOWN BY OVERLOAD	BLOWN BY SHORT
ORDINARY	THIN METAL FILAMENT PASSES CURRENT, BUT IS DESIGNED TO FAIL BEFORE WIRING GETS TOO OVERHEATED	FILAMENT OVERHEATS AND MELTS AT WEAKEST POINT, BREAKING FLOW OF CURRENT TO OVERLOADED CIRCUIT	SUDDEN SURGE OF CURRENT VAPORIZES FILAMENT INSTEAD OF MELTING IT, SO MICA WINDOW BLACKENS
TIME-DELAY	FILAMENT — SOLDER POT. CUTAWAY PLUG SHOWS STRETCHED SPRING ATTACHED TO END OF FILAMENT THAT'S EMBEDDED IN SOLDER	FILAMENT PULLED FREE. WHEN PROLONGED OVERLOAD SOFTENS SOLDER, SPRING JERKS FILAMENT FREE, BREAKING HOT CIRCUIT	FILAMENT VAPORIZED. AS WITH ORDINARY FUSE, FILAMENT VAPORIZES AT WEAKEST POINT, CLOUDING WINDOW WITH SMOKE

Cut BX across fat part of spiral; it cuts best if looped slightly. Lock BX in vise, or use loose C-clamp to hold it

Bend BX back to snap it open. Make cut about 8-inches from end to expose wires. Use side-cutters to snip remaining metal

Tiny plastic inserts slip around the wires to protect them from sharp edges. BX has two in-sulated wires and a ground

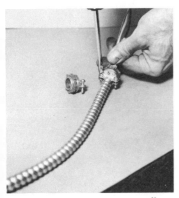

BX connector serves as a collar and is simply slipped over the end of the armor shield and clamped tightly to it

In junction box, another metal collar, similar to a flat washer that is threaded, is turned down on the BX connector to hold it

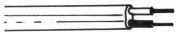

Interior plastic-sheathed cable is flat. It's easy to pull and strip; it has solid copper wire conductors

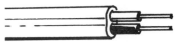

Multi-purpose plastic-sheathed cable can be used indoors and out. It also can be buried in the ground

Flexible armored cable—or BX—is used for exposed or open installations in dry locations. Use with junction boxes. Do not use BX in damp indoor in-stallations, outdoors, under-ground

ELECTRICITY HAS ITS OWN safety require-ments. Follow them!

The techniques and systems are simple; the only tools required, usually, are pliers and a set of screwdrivers, although other tools may be help-ful, particularly an inexpensive circuit tester.

Fuses. Use the correct size fuse for its specific circuit. Do not, for example, put a 30-amp fuse in a 15-amp circuit. Always remove defective fuses by holding onto the glass collar of the fuse. *Do not touch the socket.*

In new construction and remodeling when you are installing new wiring, follow all local codes. Never work with the electricity turned on. Make

192

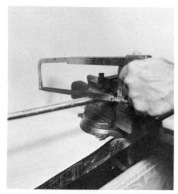

Thin-wall conduit is rigid; it is generally used in new construction. Also, it is required by many electrical codes

Connectors are threaded onto conduit for fitting into junction boxes. Threaded collar—similar to BX—locks conduit and box

Special curved tool is used to bend conduit without kinking it. Benders are fairly inexpensive; you also can rent them

certain that the power on the circuit on which you are working is off. The only exceptions are explained in the general wiring section that follows this section.

For any electrical breakdown, follow a system. If a lamp won't work, for example, first check the bulb in another lamp, then the lamp in another outlet. If it still won't work, check the fuses or circuit breaker. Then take off the wall plate and test the circuit with a circuit tester. Put one wire of the tester on the black wire and the other on the side of the box. Turn on the electricity. *If the tester light goes on,* the switch or outlet is faulty. At this point, turn off the power again and install a new switch or outlet.

When you open the box, you may find only two connecting wires. This means that the box is at the end of the circuit line. If you find two white and two black wires, this means that the circuit continues on down the line from this box. If you find a third wire—usually red—consider it a "hot" —or black wire.

In some installations, you may find the white wire hooked onto the white connector. The black wire may be spliced onto one of two wires leading out of the junction box. This is called a "switch leg." It operates a separate wall switch.

To replace a two-way switch—it turns on a light from two different points—you will find multiple sets of wires. Note how they came off the old switch by marking each with different colored tape as a key (or use paper and Scotch tape). Replace them exactly the same way.

Conduit can be prefitted in new construction and remodeling; notch framing members. Also support open runs of conduit every 6 ft. with hangers

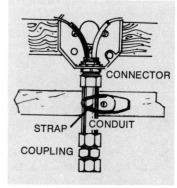

Wires are threaded through conduit after it is in position. Wires must be insulated. Support concealed runs of conduit

348

TWO SPECIALTY SWITCHES you may want to consider are *dimmers* and *mercury switches*. Dimmers are usually installed the same way as regular wall switches: Remove the plate; remove the old switch; put in the dimmer switch. If there are special instructions—such as in a three-phase dimmer switch (low, medium, high) these will be noted on the packaging in which the switch is sold.

Mercury switches are silent switches—there is no audible click when the switch is operated. This makes a mercury switch an excellent choice for the bedroom of a small child.

Always wire in a switch with the toggle in the "up" position when the switch is on.

"Three hole" outlets are used to ground appliances and tools. Two of the prongs look like

240
241

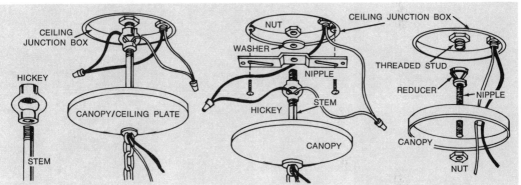

Typical ceiling fixture is mounted in any one of the three ways shown here. Stem (above) releases the canopy

For a standard ceiling junction box, special adapters are necessary to support the additional weight of heavy lighting fixtures

Shallow fixture has a canopy or decorative ceiling plate; the light globe is attached to it with setscrews

To change ceiling fixture, remove old one (see drawings above). New wires are spliced to wires in junction box with solderless connectors; twist them on

Screws in new fixture are threaded directly into screw holes in junction box. Holes are slotted so fixture can be turned

Ceramic type fixtures generally are used for basement lighting installations. Special metal adaptor is used for mounting fixture on junction box

slots in a normal outlet. A third slot is round to accept a round prong on the cord. This is the grounding line. The round prong slips into a metal clip. The clip in turn is fastened to a flange in the outlet which is fastened to a green screw on the junction box by a shiny uninsulated wire.

If you can't find this wire, you may assume that the wires have been grounded elsewhere in the wiring system. To test it, use the electrical tester. Put one point on the black wire and the other on the wall of the junction box. Turn on the current. *If the light in the tester goes on,* the wire is grounded.

To change wall switch, cut paint seal around switch plate with sharp razor-knife. This prevents paint from peeling

Remove old wall switch, put in new one. Connect black wire to brass-colored pole; white to white pole

To install new outlet or switch, use junction box as marking guide. Cut wall material with razor knife or sabre saw

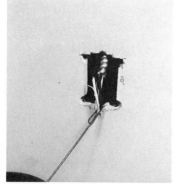

Pull wire to junction box location with "fish" wire. If wall is lath and plaster, use box as template

Thin metal locking strips sandwich between plaster and junction box. Turn over tabs into junction box to hold it rigid

Make necessary wire/junction box connections. Then hook on wires to poles

minor electrical problems

ELECTRICAL WIRING CODES are tough, and they should be. Electricity is a power that always has to be reckoned with; improper installations not only can kill, but faulty electrical wiring is the most frequent cause of fires. *Check with local codes before you do your own wiring even if you are especially skilled at it.*

If you are not skilled in electrical work, do not attempt to take on complicated projects.

There are, however, many minor electrical jobs you can do: change a plug, tap a wire, renew a cord. The basics are in this section. And in making most minor repairs, you don't have to worry about breaking codes.

Before you start any project, other than changing a plug, make sure the electricity is turned off at the main power source. Since this involves multiple circuits, you only have to switch off the circuit on which you'll be working. Plug in a dropcord or lamp exactly where you'll be working, and watch it while a helper flips the circuit breakers or unscrews the fuses in the fuse box at the main entry. When the light goes off, you can safely assume that that one outlet—*but only that one*—is disconnected. *Don't* assume that every other outlet in that room is disconnected, too.

A couple of more "don'ts" before you start: Do not work with wet or sweaty hands; do not work if the surface on which you are standing is wet.

If you own a new home, it probably is adequately wired to accept most modern appliances— dishwashers, washing machines, mixers, television, and sundry gadgets. Airconditioning and major appliances are generally on separate circuits because of their large power requirements.

If you live in an older home, it may lack the housepower necessary for increasingly bigger loads. When this happens, the fuses blow or the wires get hot because of the added amperes that flow through them. When the wire gets hot, the insulation melts, and this can cause a fire. Fuses of the right size will prevent this; that is why it is important that you *never put a large capacity fuse into a small capacity line.*

346
347

356

354

You can make many minor electrical repairs yourself—but don't forget to turn off the current!

ELECTRICITY HAS ITS OWN TERMS, and you should know them before you attempt to purchase any materials or tools for repairs. The most common terms include:

Watt. This is simply a unit of electric power required to do a certain amount of work. Light bulbs, for example, are marked in watts—100 watts, 300 watts, etc. The power company bills you on the number of kilowatt-hours you use over a given period of time. One thousand watts make one kilowatt. A kilowatt-hour thus is the energy expended by 1000 watts for one hour.

Current. There are two types of current: direct (DC) and alternating (AC). *Direct current* is a straight shot of electricity from the power source to the object—light bulb, dryer, toaster, etc. As a rule, direct current is from a generator or battery source. *Alternating current* is a reverse flow system that "alternates" in cycles—usually 60 cycles per second. Most homes are served by alternating current.

Ampere. The shortened version of this term is "amp," and you'll find this marked on most appliances and fuses. An amp is a unit of electrical current.

Voltage is electrical pressure, or the force which causes current to flow through a conductor.

TOOLS FOR MINOR ELECTRICAL REPAIRS

For minor household electrical repairs, you don't need a collection of fancy tools. Only the basics are required; these include a wire stripper, pliers, side cutters, screwdrivers, electrical tape, soldering gun and solder.

Wire is measured on a standard (but arbitrary) scale. A No. 14 wire is used in most circuits in the home. As a rule of thumb, you shouldn't use any wire smaller than No. 14 for wiring. Larger sizes —No. 12, 10, 8 (wire diameter gets *larger* as the number size *decreases*)—are for heavy appliances and usually take a 30-amp fuse. No. 14 wire takes a 15-amp fuse—or 1750-watt capacity.

In most minor repairs you'll be working with lamp cord covered with rubber, plastic or rayon insulation. Most cord is approved by Underwriters' Laboratory, which certifies it to be adequate *for the job it's designed to do.*

402
404
405

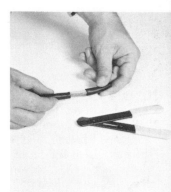

Wire strippers are inexpensive—under $2 for these. If you do many wiring repairs, they'll make your work much easier

Underwriters' knot is tied like this. It prevents wire from being jerked out of plug. Tie it and slip the knot tight

DIRECTION
SCREW TURNS

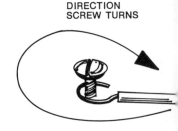

Twist wires around poles the way the screws tighten. This helps tighten wires, instead of loosen them

Sharp wire strippers are notched to fit diameter of the wire. Squeeze handles lightly to cut insulation

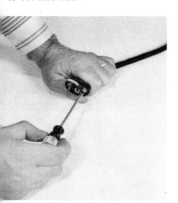

If wires have many fine strands, it sometimes is best to twist them, then coat tips with solder to prevent stray wires

Always wrap splices with electrical tape. Do not use adhesive, masking or other tapes

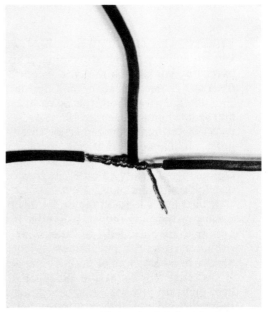

Tie-in wire is joined in pig-tail fashion. Remove only as much insulation as necessary for a tight joint

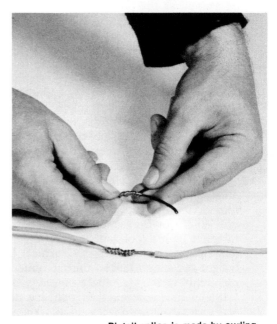

Pigtail splice is made by curling one wire around the other. This makes a very tight splice. If possible, solder the splice

353

THE MOST COMMON household wiring problem probably is a pulled-off plug. This usually is caused by yanking on the cord to release the plug from the outlet instead of pulling the plug itself. The wires untwist from the poles, there's a spark and sputter, and a fuse may blow.

When you make the repair, be sure the plug has not been damaged. If it has, replace it. For appliance cords, see the appliance chapter in this section. They involve a different type of wire and, usually, a different plug.

If the plug is loose in the outlet, try bending the prongs of the plug outward slightly. If the prongs appear to be corroded (and they usually are after a sputter), you can polish them bright again with a piece of emery cloth or fine sandpaper.

Defective wiring at the plug can cause great heat build-up just before a fuse blows. Sometimes this will weld the plug into the outlet. If so, turn the current off at the main fuse box before you attempt to pull the plug out of the outlet. Upon inspection, you may have to replace the wall outlet as well as the plug. If you're in doubt, buy a new outlet.

Broken light bulbs in sockets are another common problem. Turn off the current at the main fuse box. Then push a bar of hand soap into the broken socket and twist out the broken stub.

Worn cords are another common problem. These can be caused by kinking or heat build-up from lights. It's a good idea to check the cords on your lamps and appliances once a year to make sure the insulation is not cracked, broken or hardened through heat.

Don't overload circuits with multiple outlet plugs and extension cords. It's better to have a new circuit installed, since the overload can cause fire. When you do use an extension cord—such as to run a power tool—make sure the cord is adequate to carry the necessary current. If the cord is light and the distance from the outlet to the appliance is great, the power output can drop and cause undue wear on the appliance motor. You can make your own heavy-duty extension cords; use heavy-duty cord with a heavy plug and outlet (female plug). If the extension will be used outside, make sure it is grounded.

Replacing lamp cords usually is easy. If lamp has fibre pad, remove pad to get at wire. Wire is threaded through base to the light socket

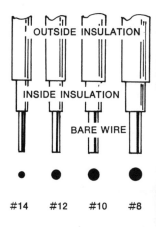

Use the right wire size for the job, or you'll have voltage drop or wire will get hot. The bigger the wire diameter, the smaller the number

Most lamp sockets are this type. You squeeze base to disassemble socket to change the wires

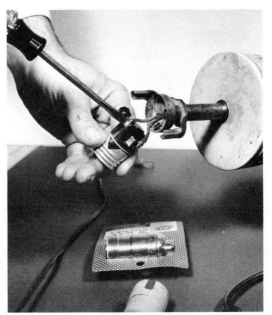

Remove old cord from socket poles; pull it out of lamp; insert new cord, stripping off insulation

New socket? Turn a set-screw on base of one you'll replace. Then twist the old socket off the threaded spindle

New socket goes on base like the one you removed. Twist wires around the poles in direction screws turn

appliance repairs

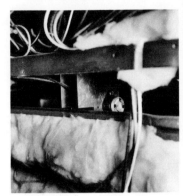

Many electric and gas ranges have fuses that serve as circuit breakers for the heating elements and the control panels

A SYSTEMATIC APPROACH is the key to solving most appliance problems.

First, determine whether the trouble is electrical or mechanical.

An open circuit is the most common electrical problem, followed by a short circuit and ground.

1. Make sure the appliance is getting power. Start at the outlet and work back to the fuse box or circuit breaker. If the appliance has a fuse, which acts as a circuit breaker (or a reset button), check this. A reset button is similar to a fuse. It breaks the circuit mechanically when there is an overload on the circuit. You push a button to reset it. With a tester you can buy for about $1, you can find out whether there is current to the outlet box.

2. Is there a short circuit? This problem can be caused by a faulty plug. It also can be caused by bare wires touching each other.

3. Grounding is caused when a conductor that carries current to the appliance touches grounded metal. This is a dangerous situation; you can suffer a serious shock. You usually can spot a ground or

346
348
369

352

To get at control panel, remove controls, which can be push fit or held by set screw. Then service the component

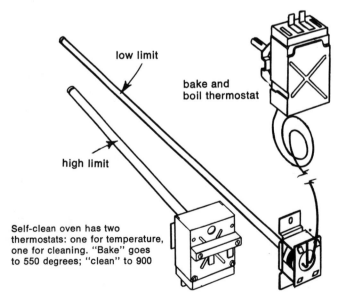

Self-clean oven has two thermostats: one for temperature, one for cleaning. "Bake" goes to 550 degrees; "clean" to 900

low limit

bake and boil thermostat

high limit

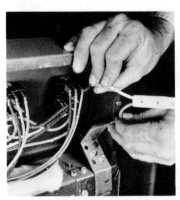

Test light determines whether control element is receiving current. If not, you often can replace the faulty component

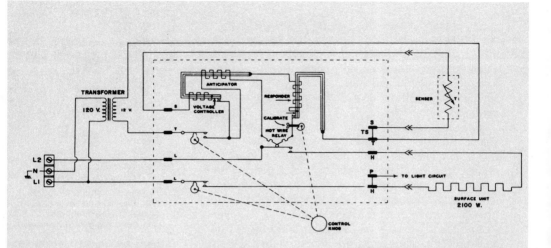

Typical wiring diagram of control circuits. Your range may be slightly different; there are two separate circuits here

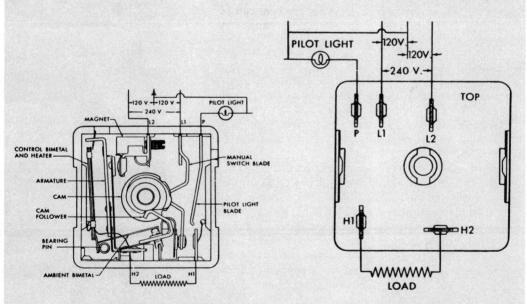

Heat switch regulates flow of current to elements. Contacts shown here (L2) will cut off current when correct heat is obtained

With power off, use ohmmeter to check line current; follow your service manual for hook-up. Reading should be same. No? Change switch

357

short circuit because the fuse has blown or a circuit breaker has tripped. Try another fuse or reset the breaker. If the same thing happens to them again, you have a short or ground that has to be located. You can tell this, usually, by a black smudge on a wall outlet, switch, or the plug on the appliance.

If there is current to and through the appliance and it still doesn't function, the problem probably is mechanical—a faulty component, a clogged drain pipe, low water pressure, worn brushes in motors, a broken drive belt. You also should take a systematic approach to mechanical problems. This is basically done through testing.

Appliance repair tools. Regular hand tools can be used for making most appliance repairs. These include screwdrivers, box-end wrenches, pliers and wire cutters.

For testing, you will need a test light, or you can make your own with a light socket that has been prewired. Strip off the insulation from the end of each wire. One end is inserted into the power source; the other end is grounded.

An ohmmeter sounds like a professional piece of equipment, and it is. But the cost is not prohibitive—from about $15. An ohmmeter can be used to check resistance and continuity. On a scale, the meter reads high ohms at the left and low, or zero ohms, at the right. If the prods are shorted, the needle goes to zero. When the prods are on an exceptionally low resistance path, the needle will go almost to zero.

Basically, when you use your ohmmeter—as in the case of a check for continuity—the needle will go from one end to the other: left is open, right is for short or continuous. You will need to know the ohm rating for appliance you are testing (you can get it from a dealer), and the meter should read within 10 percent of the expected ohm value. For example, a toaster element has a normal ohm rating of 10. If you get a reading of 9 or 11, the toaster element is working properly.

Some testers can read the voltage, current or amperes, resistance or ohms, power or watts, and leakage. Different scales are printed on the face of the meter for making these measurements. Connections for the measurements are made by turning a selector switch.

350

366

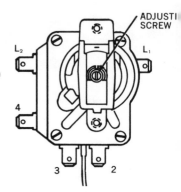

To change temperature calibration, remove control dial. Turn adjusting screw *clockwise* if you want to *lower* the temperature

Components have push-fit terminals on many range models; if component is faulty, remove wires. Mark them for replacement

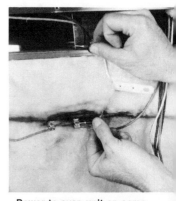

Power to oven unit on some models can be checked with test light. Hold one probe to terminal, and ground the other

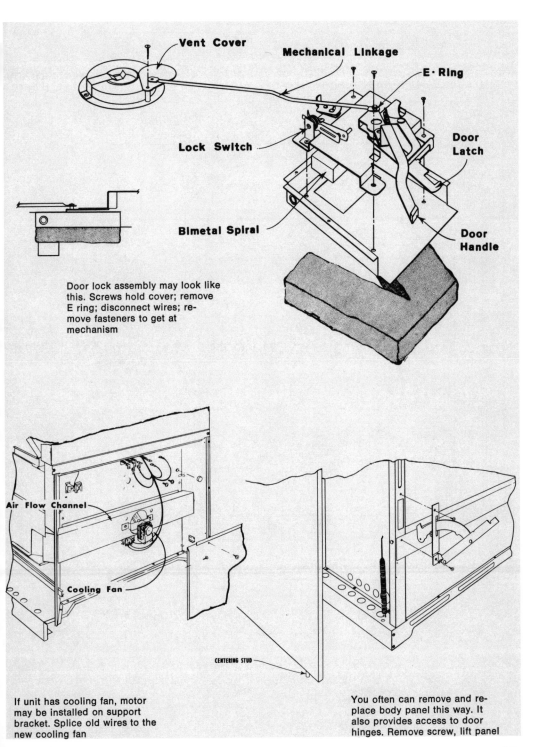

Vent Cover

Mechanical Linkage

E·Ring

Lock Switch

Door Latch

Bimetal Spiral

Door Handle

Door lock assembly may look like this. Screws hold cover; remove E ring; disconnect wires; remove fasteners to get at mechanism

Air Flow Channel

Cooling Fan

CENTERING STUD

If unit has cooling fan, motor may be installed on support bracket. Splice old wires to the new cooling fan

You often can remove and replace body panel this way. It also provides access to door hinges. Remove screw, lift panel

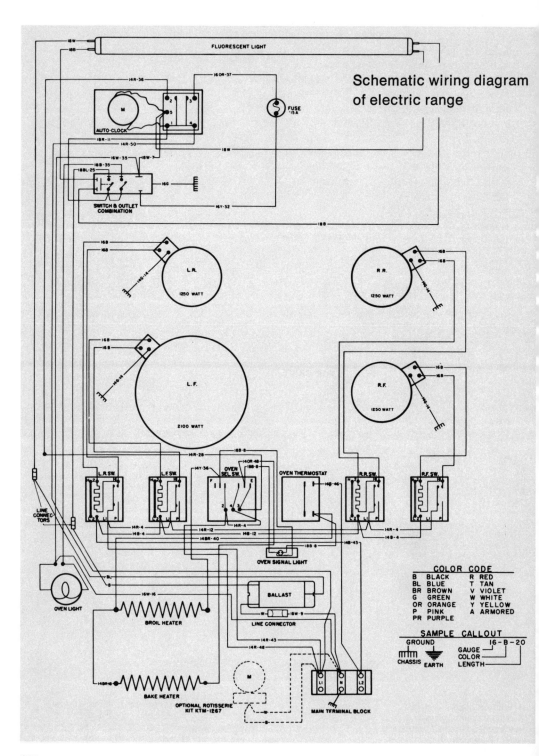

Schematic wiring diagram of electric range

RANGE REPAIRS

Gas ranges require electrical grounding since many range accessories are operated by electricity. If the range has a three-prong grounded supply cord and plug, it requires a grounded outlet.

Pilot lights. If the gas pilot constantly goes out, the problem could be improper ventilation. Make sure ventilation holes are not blocked. The surface burner pilot should have a flame about ⅛ in. high. If the flame is too high, the combustion of the gas may be incomplete. In this case, you'll find soot around the pilot. The flame also will burn yellow for more than half its length. Oven pilots should be about ½ in. in length. Adjust the pilot in accordance with the manufacturer's instructions for your particular model.

Surface burners. Properly adjusted, the burners should have a clean-burning flame with the inner cone about ½ in. in length. To adjust, turn the burner valve handle to its full "on" position. The

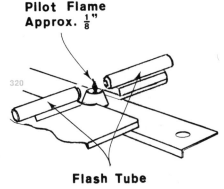

Pilot Flame Approx. ⅛"

Flash Tube

Pilot flame should be adjusted to about ⅛ in. high. Soot around the pilot flame area may indicate improper ventilation

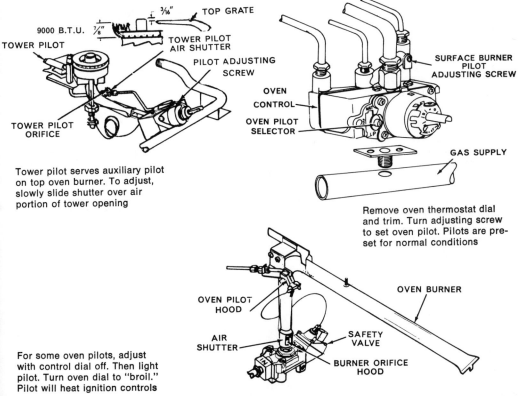

Tower pilot serves auxiliary pilot on top oven burner. To adjust, slowly slide shutter over air portion of tower opening

Remove oven thermostat dial and trim. Turn adjusting screw to set oven pilot. Pilots are pre-set for normal conditions

For some oven pilots, adjust with control dial off. Then light pilot. Turn oven dial to "broil." Pilot will heat ignition controls

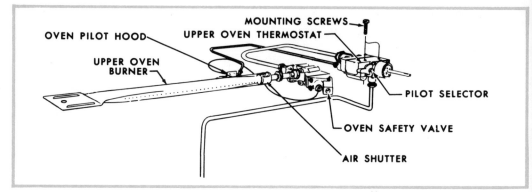

Upper oven burner system may look similar to this. Adjust air shutter to produce a sharp, almost invisible, flame

burner should light easily from the pilot. If it doesn't, adjust the air shutter for a medium-sharp flame.

On controlled top burners, the flame should be adjusted to a ⅞ in. blue cone. To adjust:

1. Rotate dial to high position.
2. Light burner.
3. Remove the trim and dial.
4. Turn the pilot-flame adjusting screw clockwise to decrease the flame; counterclockwise to increase it. If needed, adjust the sensing head to 3/16 in. above the surface of the top grate.

A controlled burner is a burner which has a thermostatic element to control its heat intensity. This is regulated by the heat reflectance on the bottom of the utensil. A sensing head regulates the flow of gas to the burner by monitoring the temperature of the flame at the burner.

Dirty burners. Food and soot can clog the flash tubes and ports on gas surface burners. You can wash the flash tubes to clean them. Check the hole or orifice at the end of the tube. If it is clogged, use a needle to open it. You also can clean the ports around the gas ring with a needle. On some ranges, the entire burner assembly can be lifted away from the main gas jets so you can wash it in the kitchen sink with a mild detergent. Thoroughly dry the burner assembly or the gas will not burn properly. Note: Do not adjust the screws at the end of the gas jets while you are cleaning the assembly.

Control problems in ovens. Generally, oven control problems stem from a misadjusted control knob, incorrect thermostat setting or a failed thermocouple. Thermostats should be adjusted only after you have consulted the repair manual.

In a gas range, make sure the burners and pilots are properly adjusted

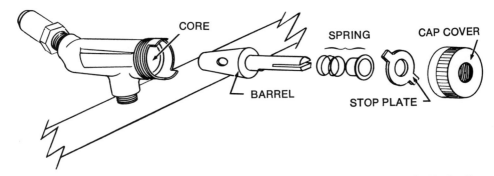

CORE

SPRING

CAP COVER

BARREL

STOP PLATE

Here's how typical hydraulic oven control is assembled. It adjusts the oven burner to the setting of the temperature dial

To clean standard valve, first turn off gas; lift off top of range. Typical valve system comes apart as shown in this diagram

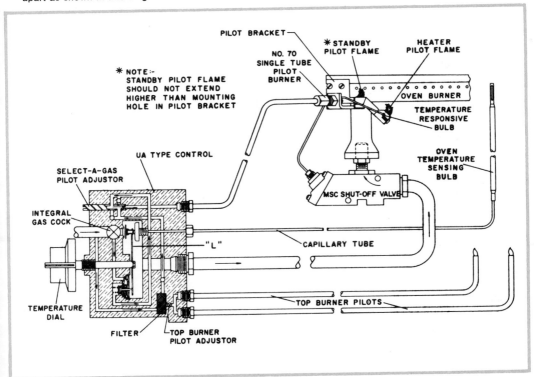

PILOT BRACKET

NO. 70 SINGLE TUBE PILOT BURNER

* STANDBY PILOT FLAME

HEATER PILOT FLAME

OVEN BURNER

* NOTE:-
STANDBY PILOT FLAME SHOULD NOT EXTEND HIGHER THAN MOUNTING HOLE IN PILOT BRACKET

TEMPERATURE RESPONSIVE BULB

UA TYPE CONTROL

OVEN TEMPERATURE SENSING BULB

SELECT-A-GAS PILOT ADJUSTOR

MSC SHUT-OFF VALVE

INTEGRAL GAS COCK

"L"

CAPILLARY TUBE

TEMPERATURE DIAL

TOP BURNER PILOTS

FILTER

TOP BURNER PILOT ADJUSTOR

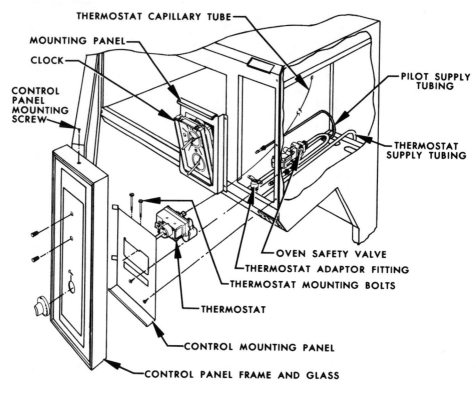

THERMOSTAT CAPILLARY TUBE

MOUNTING PANEL

CLOCK

CONTROL PANEL MOUNTING SCREW

PILOT SUPPLY TUBING

THERMOSTAT SUPPLY TUBING

OVEN SAFETY VALVE

THERMOSTAT ADAPTOR FITTING

THERMOSTAT MOUNTING BOLTS

THERMOSTAT

CONTROL MOUNTING PANEL

CONTROL PANEL FRAME AND GLASS

You can adjust the thermostatic setting in an oven this way:

1. Position an accurate thermometer at the center of the oven. If the door has a window, place the thermometer so you can read it without opening the door.

2. Set the oven at 350 degrees for 30 minutes.

3. Jot down the high and low points for the length of three oven cycles. The flame in the course of operation should go on and off three times. Each time denotes a cycle.

4. If the *variation* in the high and low readings is less than 50 percent, try resetting the control knob. If the variation is more than 50 percent, the thermostat and thermocouple should be checked by a repairman. The thermostat control knob can be adjusted with a screwdriver for minor variations.

Electric ranges and ovens. If neither the top nor bottom oven elements work with the thermostat in an operating position and the selector switch set at preheat, you should:

1. Turn off the current.

2. Inspect the heater terminal and leads for a loose or broken connection. If you can't find the

To replace gas oven thermostat, remove mounting bolts; disconnect gas tubing nuts. Electric connections? Insulator must cover tubing

347

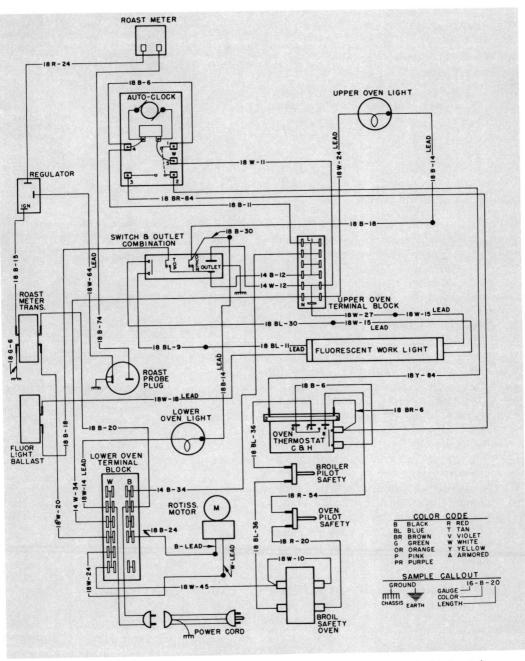

Wiring diagram of typical gas range with accessories is shown at right. Similar diagram may be mounted on your range; look on back. If it's not there, remove the rear panel to locate it. Letters here are color codes, numbers are wire designation for this specific model

trouble, remove the leads from the heater and check the heating element resistance with the chart below. The readings should be within 10 percent of the figures.

Heater Wattage	Cold Ohms Resistance
1500	38.4
1650	35.0
2000	28.8
2200	26.2
2400	24.0
3000	19.2
3200	18.0
3600	16.0

If the meter reads an infinite resistance, the element is "open," and must be changed.

To replace a surface unit: Disconnect the power. Remove the faulty unit from the opening in the main top. Disconnect or cut the unit lead wires back from the unit or terminal block. All damaged insulation should be removed. Strip leads, make splices, strip on insulation of the new unit.

Self-cleaning ovens. You can pin down problems with self-cleaning ovens by the visible soil.

If the soil is brown and soft, there is no heat in the oven during the cleaning cycle. If the soil is dark brown and hard, the oven heated to only about 600 degrees. If some of the soil is left, the cleaning time was not long enough; the soil was unusually heavy; one of the oven units was open; the high-limit thermostat cycles were at too low a temperature; or the line voltage was too low.

Checkpoints for soil include these:

Fuses; timer contacts; relay coil; locking switch; door switch; high-limit thermostat; selector switch; catalyst heating element; door.

Use the proper utensils. The bottoms of utensils used on electric ranges should be flat so they make good contact with the unit and sensor head. On surface heating units, *do not use aluminum foil in the drip bowl.* It can cause a short.

(*Note: All repair data in this section applies to appliances in a general way. Specific brands will vary depending on the manufacturer. If possible, obtain an owner's manual and repair manual for your appliances—especially if the data here does not seem to apply to your appliances.*)

To replace coffee-maker element, detach wires, marking them for reconnection. Most heating elements simply screw out and in

Damaged plug can be removed and replaced on coffee-maker. This one fits in slot in base; you remove terminal wires by removing two taps or nuts

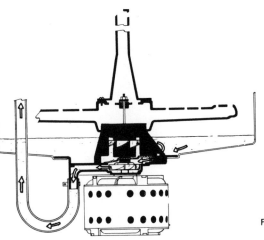

When motor runs, upper impeller of this dishwasher windmills. Lower impeller pumps water and food particles out the drain hose

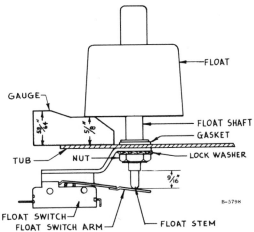

Typical float-switch test. Switches vary. Consult your service manual. When float is raised, switch should have continuity

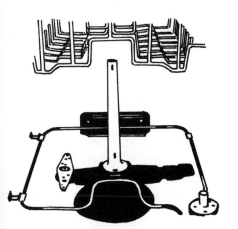

To test heating element, remove electrical leads; check ohms. Check wattage against recommendations for your model

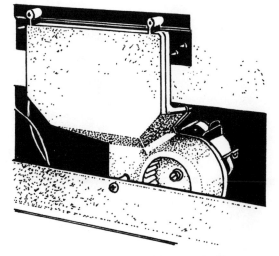

To clean blower assembly on some model dishwashers, remove rear panel, motor, housing. Fan is fastened to motor shaft with clip

FOOD DISPOSERS generally are maintenance free. The most common problem is a jammed grinder. Free this with a length of wood, after you disconnect the power. Preventative maintenance includes:

327
329

1. Use a steady flow of *cold* water, allowing the unit to run long enough to do a thorough job.

2. Do not put metal in the disposer.

3. Do not put glass or crockery in the disposer, since ground glass does not float and will clog household plumbing.

4. Do not put lye or drain-cleaning chemicals in the disposer. If the disposer drain is clogged, you will have to remove the pipes to clean it.

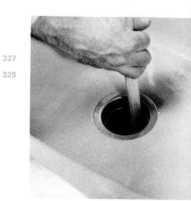

If grind ring and turntable won't turn, try breaking it free with wooden pole. *Don't* stick your hand into the ring

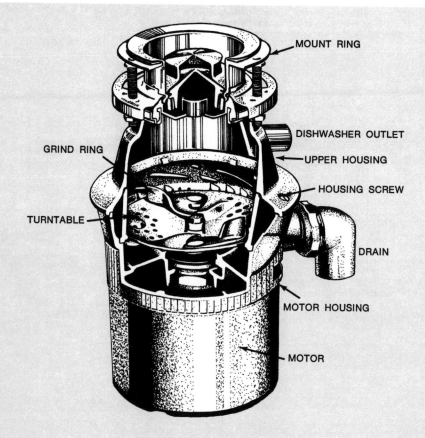

MOUNT RING

DISHWASHER OUTLET

GRIND RING

UPPER HOUSING

HOUSING SCREW

TURNTABLE

DRAIN

MOTOR HOUSING

MOTOR

Reset button serves as circuit breaker on some disposers. If power goes off, push this before checking fuses

Test light determines whether disposer is getting current. Do this after you check reset button, fuses, or circuit breakers

If disposer won't empty, clogged drain may be problem. Disassemble it like sink drain; use auger to clean out debris

COMPLAINT	CAUSE	REMEDY
Water leak around bottom of sink flange.	Sink flange not properly sealed.	Remove the flange and apply plumber's putty or preferably the plumber's mastic as described under installation instructions.
Water drains slowly when the motor is not operating.	Food waste already in the disposer is covering the major portion of the water drain holes.	Turn on the water, flip the switch and run the food waste down.
	Partially clogged drain line.	Clean with a plumber's snake.
	Insufficient slope in the drain line.	Increase slope to at least 1 in. per 4 ft. run.
Excessive vibration when the motor is running without a load.	The lower mounting stud nuts on the mounting stud are too tight, removing resilience from the mounting.	Loosen these mounting stud nuts slightly.
Excessive noise.	The lower mounting stud nuts on the sink flange stud are too tight, removing resilience from the mounting.	Loosen these mounting stud nuts slightly.
Disposer won't start and makes no humming noise.	Motor overload protector open.	Press the red reset button at the bottom of the motor firmly until it clicks and starts the disposer.
	Fuse—a fuse burned out.	Check fuse box and replace burned out fuses.
Disposer won't start and makes a humming noise.	Turn table assembly will not rotate.	Turn switch off. Free turn table and check for foreign metal in disposer.
	Grounded or burned out motor field.	Repair or replace motor field.
	Inoperative starting relay.	Replace.
	Loose terminal connections.	Tighten connections and check motor field for continuity.
Clogged drain line.	Drain line was not cleaned out properly before installation.	Clean out the drain line mechanically with a plumber's snake.
	Insufficient slope in line.	Increase to at least one 1 in. per 4 ft. run.

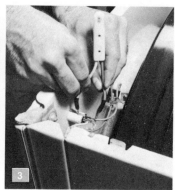

If the drier is drying too slowly, first clean lint trap. This should always be done before a load is run through

Drier door won't latch? You can replace lock by removing a couple of screws. Control switch may be operated by catch

Light inside drier won't work? Test connection. Top lifts off most units after you remove screws from underside

DIRT AND LINT are the biggest enemies of clothes driers. Driers must be properly vented or they will not function properly. Take time to clean out lint traps; vacuum the inside of the unit every six months or so to minimize problems.

Minor problems include broken or loose belts, loose pulleys, and broken motor tension springs. If the drum doesn't turn at all, or it is noisy, check the belt tension, tighten loose pulleys, and look for a broken motor tension spring where the belt and motor converge.

Another common source of trouble is the timer. If you find it faulty, remove it this way:

1. Disconnect the electric power.

2. Pull the timer knob, and peel off the tape holding the wires together. Disconnect the timer wires from the harness.

3. Remove the screws or bolts holding the mounting plate to the control panel; remove the grounding wire.

4. Remove the bolts that hold the timer to the mounting plate.

To install the new timer, reverse the above procedure.

Gas drier checkpoints include the gas burner and pilot light. Most pilot lights work from an electrical igniter. You can usually determine what the problem is by tracing the gas power source, testing the igniter, and testing the electrical power source at the wall outlet. Consult your owner's manual or service guide for specific repairs.

Individual drier components can be tested to see if current is reaching them. Most are easy to take out by removing screws

361
363

Belt is held under spring tension in pulley and motor connection. Make sure pulley is tight and in correct alignment

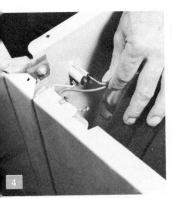

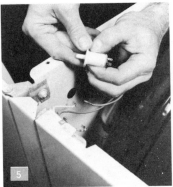

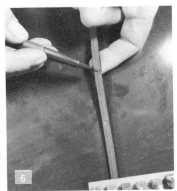

Terminals are removed from switch; mark them for hook-up later. Switch may be held in place by spring which must be compressed

New switch goes in from front. On some models, it is held in place with tiny screws you remove from the rear

Drier belt may be conventional V-belt, although some models may vary slightly. Belt should have moderate tension

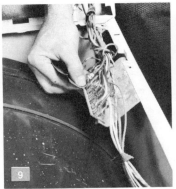

Timers and switches on many electric driers are wired into junction box. Wires are color-coded

Terminals should be free of corrosion and dirt. To remove corrosion, use piece of fine emery cloth on all contacts

If you have to change a drier belt, slip on new one and hold it with tape while you turn drum to align it with pulleys

Most driers should be vented. You can vent through a floor, sidewall or ceiling, depending on location of the drier

Get more headroom in basement by running vent pipe between joists. Also, remount pipes so dissimilar materials do not touch

Electrical current enters drier at junction box similar to this. Faulty cord can be replaced by loosening terminals

WASHING MACHINE breakdowns (the minor 326 ones) and their remedies include these:

No water enters the tub, or little water enters it. Check the water supply and operation of the wash timer; fill valve; and the water-level switch. Faulty timers, fill valves and water-level switches should be replaced. You can use a circuit tester to check these. Clean the fill-valve filter screens if they are clogged.

Water won't stop running and impeller will not start. Check the water-level switch with a circuit

Belt drive system on spin drier and washer combination looks like this on some models. Other models have gear type drive

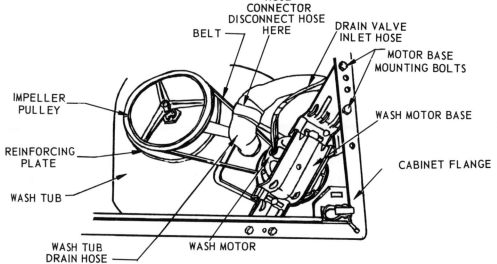

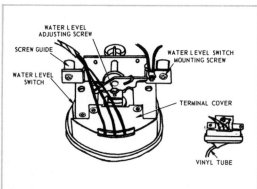

Water-level switch on spin drier and washer combination. You turn screw (shown) to adjust the water level in the washer's tub

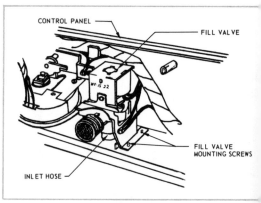

Fill valve on spin drier and washer combination. Check inlet screen annually for lint and lime deposits

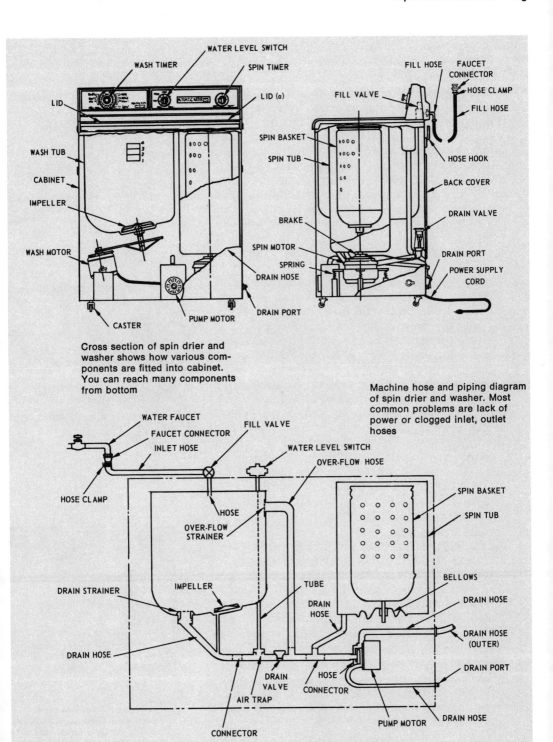

WATER LEVEL SWITCH

WASH TIMER

SPIN TIMER

LID

FILL HOSE

FAUCET CONNECTOR

HOSE CLAMP

FILL HOSE

FILL VALVE

LID (a)

SPIN BASKET

SPIN TUB

WASH TUB

CABINET

IMPELLER

HOSE HOOK

BACK COVER

DRAIN VALVE

WASH MOTOR

BRAKE

SPIN MOTOR

SPRING

DRAIN HOSE

DRAIN PORT

POWER SUPPLY CORD

CASTER

PUMP MOTOR

DRAIN PORT

Cross section of spin drier and washer shows how various components are fitted into cabinet. You can reach many components from bottom

Machine hose and piping diagram of spin drier and washer. Most common problems are lack of power or clogged inlet, outlet hoses

WATER FAUCET

FAUCET CONNECTOR

INLET HOSE

FILL VALVE

WATER LEVEL SWITCH

OVER-FLOW HOSE

HOSE CLAMP

HOSE

OVER-FLOW STRAINER

SPIN BASKET

SPIN TUB

DRAIN STRAINER

IMPELLER

TUBE

DRAIN HOSE

BELLOWS

DRAIN HOSE

DRAIN HOSE (OUTER)

DRAIN HOSE

DRAIN VALVE

HOSE CONNECTOR

DRAIN PORT

AIR TRAP

CONNECTOR

PUMP MOTOR

DRAIN HOSE

tester. If inoperative, replace the switch. Check the water-level tube for air leaks; reglue it, or replace it with a new tube, if you can't fix it.

No water discharge through outlet hose. The drain strainer could be plugged with lint; the drain hose might be restricted, plugged or kinked. Check the drain valve coil operation; check the drain pump motor and impeller unit. In both cases, the coil may be disconnected or burned, or there may be a broken wire. Also, the impeller may be jammed, worn or broken. Also check the wash and spin timers for an open circuit caused by internal contacts that don't operate properly.

Slow water pump drain. The drain hose is too high above the washer, or it is blocked with lint.

Water leaks. Inspect the hoses, tub, bellows, top of outer tub seals, drain valve, water-supply valve and pump assembly. In most cases, the hoses and other parts will have to be repositioned, retightened or replaced.

Washer vibrates. This can be caused by worn or high spots on the belt; an out-of-round pulley or a loose pulley set screw; a faulty wash or spin-motor shaft; motor cushions hardened from age; washer not level or not resting on all four feet.

Water overflows the top of the wash tub at rinse time. This can be caused by an open motor coil; a worn, broken or loose impeller; plugged hoses or strainers; internal water fill-valve contact is inoperative, or a wire is disconnected.

REFRIGERATOR AND FREEZER REPAIRS

Refrigerators and freezers are difficult for a homeowner to service because many of the parts are permanently sealed and should not be disassembled without professional service equipment. However, there are several checks you can make.

If the compressor won't run, unplug the line cord from the wall outlet. Then remove any shields necessary to expose the compressor controls.

Connect ohmmeter leads across the control terminals and check for continuity. If the instrument indicates continuity, check the defrost timer and cabinet wiring for any defects.

If the compressor runs continuously, turn the control knob to "off." If it still runs, unplug the

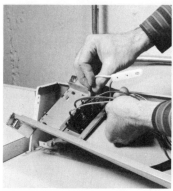

Control panel comes off so you can test controls for power entry. Use a test light, grounding one leg, to locate trouble

Faulty drain valve sometimes can be detected with tester. If new one is needed, first disconnect the inlet and drain hose

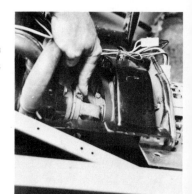

Make sure pulleys, belts and clutches are tight. Fibre clutch is used here. Belts too loose or tight can damage bearings

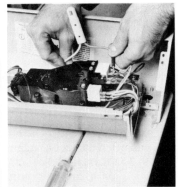

If component is faulty, you first have to remove knobs in front of panel. Wires then are removed and faulty part replaced

Water temperature and spin cycle switches should be checked along with the others. One faulty part may affect others

Check each sequence with bulb tester. With new "plug-in" units you may have to replace entire component, not just single part

If water runs slowly into the tub, hose may be clogged. Check screens in hot and cold lines for lime deposits and dirt

If motor won't run, check current at the motor, not controls above. Keep motor and drive unit clean by vacuuming away dirt

Spring clips hold drain hose in position. Some models have clamps. If water runs slowly from tub, check drain hose

line cord. Then remove either the red or blue wire from the control terminals. (The colors may differ as to model or make of the unit; consult a service manual for the color of yours.)

Plug in the line cord. If the compressor doesn't start, the control has to be replaced. If the compressor runs, there is a short in the cabinet wiring. Also, don't overlook the possibility of a malfunctioning freezer fan or defective fan blade. Both can reduce the air flow, causing the compressor to run all the time.

You can check the operating temperatures of the cold control on many refrigerators by securely attaching the bulb of a remote-reading thermometer to the control housing. The cut-in temperature will be about ½ degree higher than the specified temperature given in the specifications chart for your appliance.

Door alignment. If your refrigerator isn't functioning properly, always check door alignment and the gasket seal:

1. Make sure the refrigerator is level.

2. By adjusting the hinge-side front leveler, you can often correct a sagging door.

3. Oversize holes in the cabinet permit sideways or in-and-out adjustments of the hinge or hinges.

4. You can raise the top hinge by placing a 1/32 in. washer or shim under it.

5. The lower hinge can be moved out by adding a 1/32 in. shim between it and the cabinet.

On most models, the lower hinge can't be adjusted up or down or sideways. However, a special spacer on some models can be inserted under the bearing surface of the hinge pin to raise the door. If you insert a spacer under this surface, make sure it doesn't raise the door too high. This operation could cause an out-of-alignment condition in the door trim. Adjust the upper hinge to provide an even space between doors on combination refrigerator-and-freezer models.

Knowing how a refrigerator and/or freezer is wired may help you pinpoint trouble areas. The diagram shown on Page 379 is typical of these units. However, the wires on your specific model may be a different color than those indicated. If at all possible, buy a service manual for your appliance.

REPAIRS FOR ELECTRIC MOTORS

There are two types of electric motors used in appliances: *Induction motors,* and *universal* or *series* motors. The universal motor has brushes. The induction motor has a rotor, but no direct electric connection to the source of electric power. The current is induced into the rotor by a magnetic field. This part of the motor is called the stator, or field windings.

In most cases, you can identify universal motors from the brush mountings on the outside or housing of the motor. Some may be stamped as to type.

You can repair many motors without taking them apart. You can replace brushes from the

Check faulty light switch in refrigerator like this. Since compressors are sealed, most repairs have to be made by pro

Keep coils clean with vacuum; dirt can cut efficiency. Also make sure unit is level and the cooling controls properly set

Refrigerator wiring diagram— usually pasted on rear panel— can help spot problems if you have checking equipment

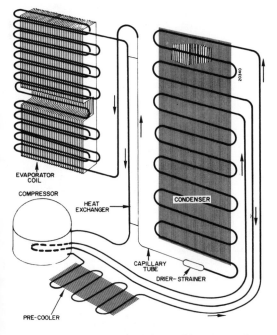

Here's how refrigerator works through refrigerant flow pattern. Evaporator absorbs heat. Condensor removes heat

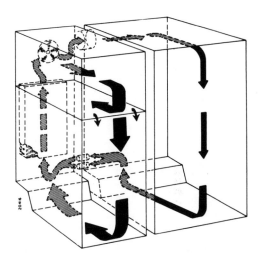

Air circulation in both compartments of a refrigerator-freezer. Units have single evaporator. One fan circulates air through both

outer housing of some motors, and you can test for continuity outside. Use an ohmmeter for this. Connect it to the two power leads with the electric power turned off.

Unless you have equipment and special know-how, it is best to let a professional rewind a field or remove and replace a bearing. You can, however, replace some bearings. Bearings are the support points on the rotating shaft. An arbor press is generally used to replace sleeve bearings; you sometimes can do the job by tapping in the new bearings, using a block of wood.

SMALL APPLIANCE REPAIRS

Since small appliances usually have universal-type motors, you can make many repairs yourself—especially replacement of brushes. Modern appliances have components that simplify repairs. With a tester, you can quickly find out what parts are faulty, and replace them.

Before you attempt to repair any small appliance, first determine if it is worth the repair. Mass production sometimes makes it possible to replace

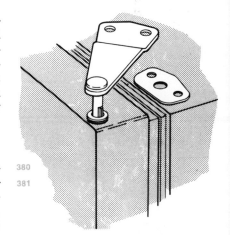

Refrigerator-freezer door hinges are easy to replace by removing two screws and hinge pin which, on most models, is a slip-fit

a small appliance for less money than repairing it.

Cords. You can repair a damaged cord where it
enters the appliance. Most cords have clamp
terminals instead of wrap-around terminal poles.
Remove two screws and the old cord, and replace
it. Cords on irons are wrapped with asbestos which
protects them from heat. When you replace an iron
cord, make sure that the asbestos insulation covers
the wires to protect them properly.

Irons. Trouble frequently stems from the cord
and its plug; the thermostat; or the heating element. If a check shows the problem is the thermostat, you can sometimes clean the breaker points
with fine emery paper and make it functional.
Most often, however, a faulty thermostat has to be
replaced.

To get at the terminals and thermostat on some
irons you have to remove a cover plate. You test
for continuity through the line cord while you re-
volve the shaft of the thermostat from off to on.

You also can test the heating element with a
meter to see whether it is functioning. Some elements are replaceable. If the element in your iron
is, you will see the connections. Take care to make
good, clean connections when installing the new
element, which may smoke a bit when you first
plug in the iron. A steam iron is similar to a
regular iron. Use distilled water to prevent hard-
water scale. If the seals leak, you have to replace
them by first disassembling the iron.

Fans. The most frequent troubles are: Fan
won't run; fan runs too slowly; fan is noisy. For
the first problem, check the power supply with a
tester. This will pinpoint where the trouble is—
cord or motor. If the fan runs slowly, check the
speed control and its connections for defects. If the
fan is noisy, the motor components or the safety
guard over the blades may be loose.

Bent blades also can cause noise. If the blades
are out of symmetry, the entire fan will vibrate.
The speed of the fan also can be affected. Attic
fan blades are especially critical; the drive power
is so great a bent blade can roar like a freight
engine.

Waffle-makers and sandwich grills. Waffle-
makers and sandwich grills usually have a coiled
wire as a heating element. Ceramic spacers keep

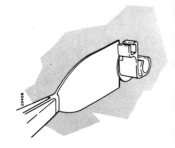

Some shelf brackets have twist-in
studs. If you want to rearrange
shelves, you pry out studs with
a stiff-bladed puttyknife

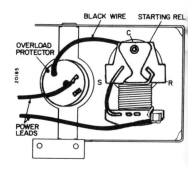

Relay and overload terminals for
refrigerator-freezer. To check
relay, momentarily short
terminals. If compressor won't
run, it's faulty

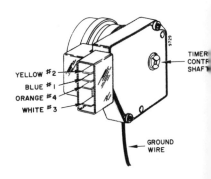

Defrost timer terminal locations
are similar on many models.
Check your service manual to
determine where and how to
run test meter

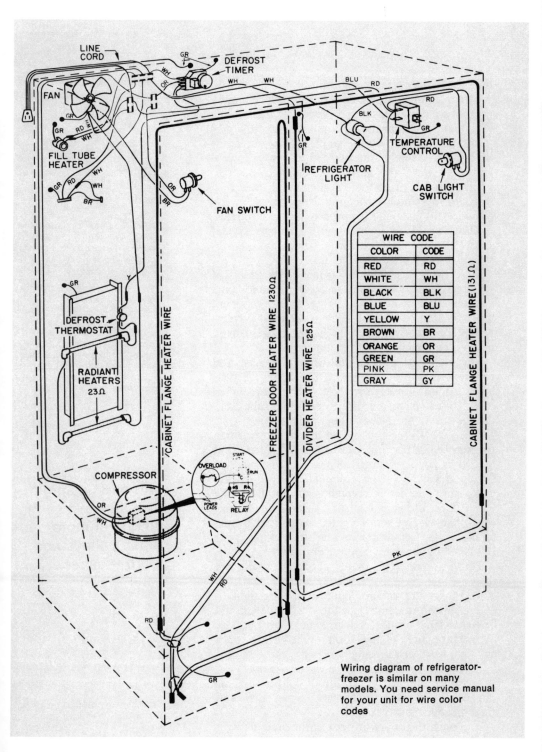

Wiring diagram of refrigerator-
freezer is similar on many
models. You need service manual
for your unit for wire color
codes

the wire in the correct position.

Other than a worn cord, the most common 384 trouble spot is an insulated section of the heating 385 wire that runs from the bottom section of the grill to the top section. As the waffle-maker (or sandwich grill) is opened and closed, this wire is subject to bending and kinking that can cause it to break inside its insulation. You can usually replace this wire by simply switching a new wire for the old one and fastening it properly to the terminals.

Other problems include loose connections and shorts at thermostat terminals. Check the thermostat; if it is defective, replace it.

Television sets. The electronic parts of a TV set are relatively complex and often require professional equipment for testing and component replacement. You can re-activate a circuit breaker or replace a fuse on a set; the locations are usually marked on the chassis of the unit.

On some older black-and-white TV sets, you can replace tubes, using the tube tester at your local drugstore or supermarket. When you remove tubes to test them, be sure to code the tubes and the spot from which they came.

On color TV sets, it is best to call a repairman for service. But before you call him, be sure that the set is properly tuned. These instructions can be found in your owner's manual. And, of course, make sure the set is receiving current from the wall outlet. Industry statistics show that 20 percent of television service calls are caused by the failure of the set owner to read the tuning guide furnished by the manufacturer or dealer.

TV antennas. The major checks to make are 384 these:

1. Make sure antenna connections are tight.

2. All lead-in connections to the TV set should be tight. Tiny strands of wire should not overlap.

3. Make sure the insulation on the lead-in is not cracked, worn or exposing bare wire.

If you are installing a new antenna, *do not:*

1. Splice the lead-in outside of the house. This can cause impedance changes, signal loss and ghost-producing waves.

2. Touch the boom or mast of the antenna with the lead. Always use high-quality stand-offs to

Loose pulleys on any motor cause loss of power, wear out motor parts and drive belts. Allen wrench tightens, loosens set screws

The most common problems with electrical motors are loose pulleys and worn brushes

Remove cover plate to expose motor terminals and wire connections. You can reverse direction of some motors

Wiring diagram on back of cover plate usually shows how to reconnect wires to reverse direction motor shaft turns

Here are the terminals. You usually reverse leads, as shown on diagram. Wires are generally color-coded

Use screwdriver and socket set to disassemble motor for new bearings or brushes. You have to remove pulley before disassembly

If housing is stuck, use a wooden block and hammer to tap it. Both ends of the housing come off like this, exposing brushes

New bearings are usually job for pro. If *you* change them, use block of wood to protect metal when you tap bearings in place

381

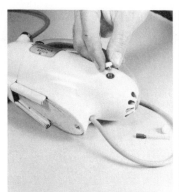

Changing brushes in mixer motors is simple screwdriver job. Brushes are spring-loaded

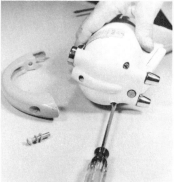

To service gearbox of most mixers, remove screws on front end. Housing pops off, exposing gears

Use gear lube recommended and inspect gears yearly, more often if mixer is used a lot

Switch problems are most common on vacuum cleaners. Housing generally is removed by unscrewing it

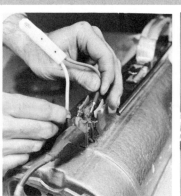

Test light can be used to see if switch is getting power. New switches usually are in components, so you replace the unit

Brushes are replaced similar to other motors. If suction is bad, check for blockage or air leakage in tank seals or bag unit

space away from masts, gutters, downspouts, metal siding, telephone and power lines.

3. Enter buildings through metal window frames, metallic screening, or other conductive material.

4. Use metal tacks or staples to fasten leads inside the house. Instead, use plastic-headed tacks.

5. Make sharp bends in the lead-in wire. Twist a flat lead-in wire to avoid pickup of stray signals.

6. Forget to ground the antenna mast and provide a lightning arrestor for the transmission line.

When buying a new antenna, keep these comparisons in mind:

Gain. The better the gain, the stronger the signal it will intercept. If you are in a fringe area, you need an antenna with very high gain.

Remove crumb pan from toaster every month or so and clean up crumbs, which can burn and cause odors

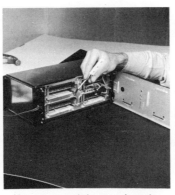

If toaster won't heat and cords are okay, use a test light to see if elements are getting current. You can replace switch

If element is burned out, you will have to disassemble the toaster. Take out screws at bottom and remove lever controls

Remove switch in order to take out frame which helps hold elements in position. Also remove "light and dark" toast lever

Power cord is hooked to terminals. Here's how to replace it. You'll also have to remove it to replace bad element

Disassemble toaster. Joints are usually slip-fit; you simply push up and pull out to remove the metal side panels

Thin strip of metal holds elements in position. Carefully unscrew it after the sides of the toaster have been removed

Most elements look like this. They are fragile, so be careful. Lock tabs hold elements in position inside the toaster shell

Directivity. Antennas can be designed to have high gain in the forward direction and little or no gain to the sides or back. This helps reduce or eliminate unwanted signals.

Orientation. A directional antenna must be basically oriented precisely to the station being received. Rotate the antenna until it faces the direction of incoming signals. You'll know this by picture results.

Transmission cable. It should be television cable, not an insulated electric wire.

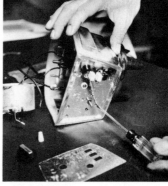

To disassemble a blender, remove the knobs on the control panel and the bottom of the blender

You can install a master TV antenna that utilizes a wall outlet similar to a regular electrical outlet. Antenna can be inside

Tiny strands of lead-in wire shouldn't overlap different connections. Do not splice lead-in wire; keep it uncut

Annually inspect lead-in wire for damaged insulation. Also make sure all connections from the antenna to the set are tight

Iron repairs are usually confined to changing a cord, which has asbestos insulation

Clean out ports. Nail makes a good tool for this. If lime is really bad, try leaving vinegar inside iron overnight

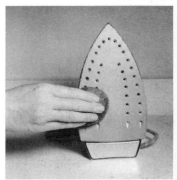

Clean sole of regular iron with steel wool to remove starch, etc. If sole is coated with special plastic, do not use abrasive

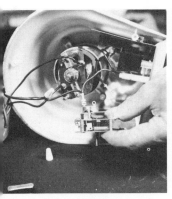

Timers and switches are in units —similar to other appliances manufactured today. You unclip terminal wires and remove bolt

Brushes are changed the same way as on other motors. If the commutator is burned, use fine sandpaper to shine it

If cord is damaged, you replace it by removing the bottom plate, disconnecting the wires, and reconnecting new ones

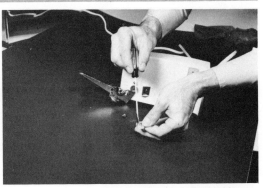

Cutter is usually first part to fail on electric can opener. It is held with single screw. You can resharpen or replace it

Keep cutter wheel clean; chip off dried food with knife or screwdriver; polish with steel wool. If cutter is nicked, replace

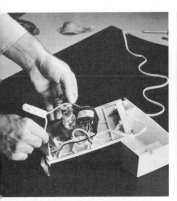

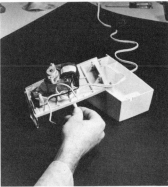

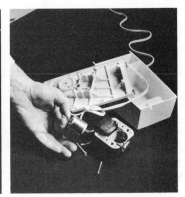

With test light, check wiring, switch, motor—if lack of power in opener is problem. If opener grinds, gears may need grease

Use wire nuts to splice new cord to inside wires. Wire nuts do better job than electrical tape, which can gather grease

Motor looks like this; drive shaft is keyed to accept gears and cutter. New can opener may be cheaper than a new motor

YOU DO NOT NEED A BASEMENT FULL OF TOOLS to accomplish most home-maintenance jobs. You do, however, need a kit of basic hand tools to which you can add more tools as you tackle more complicated projects. A basic selection of tools will cost you about $30. They include a 13-ounce hammer; pliers; a set of three screwdrivers, one of which is a Phillips screwdriver; a medium-sized adjustable wrench; a tape measure; a combination saw; a multibladed forming plane; razorknife and spare blades; countersink; combination square; level; push drill and bits.

As you progress in maintenance and improvement projects, you will want to add more tools to the basics. These should include a rip and crosscut saw; a selection of files and rasps; a chisel set; adjustable pipe-wrench set; a vise; hacksaw and blades; sharpening stone; vise-grip pliers; brace-and-bit set; propane torch outfit; needle-nose pliers.

At this point, you will have enough tools to do most household chores. However, there is a third and fourth phase to consider. Each phase makes projects a bit easier, since some tools are designed for specific jobs, and others take the muscle out of hard jobs.

Phase three tools should include C-clamps; a framing square; channel pliers; a heavy-duty stapler and staples; a ¼-in. portable electric drill; a power sander; block and jack planes; tack hammer; socket set; spiral ratchet screwdriver; marking gauge; bevel gauge; stud finder; dividers.

Phase four tools you might consider include portable electric saws; a router; bench grinder; and so-called stationary equipment such as a bench saw, jointer, drill press, drum and belt sander. By phase four, you will have the experience necessary to pick out the type of tools that are most needed for the jobs you do.

Always buy quality tools. Good tools will last a lifetime; they are expertly balanced and precision machined. These built-in features will help you do any job easier, faster and better.

391
400

Start saw on marked line with knuckle of your thumb. Pull the first stroke to seat the saw; keep your knuckle against blade until slot is started

For straight-line cuts on long boards, clamp a straightedge on the board to help guide the saw. Never use a metal straightedge

As final saw strokes are made, hold cut-off piece to prevent it from splitting good stock. Rock saw slightly as you cut

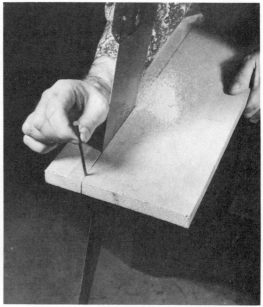

On long ripcuts, the saw won't bind in its kerf if you spread the kerf with a nail or wooden wedge. Move either with the saw as you cut

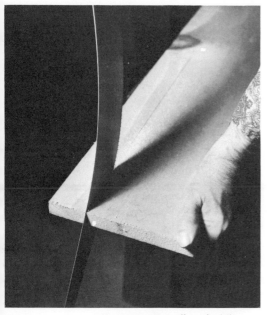

If saw wanders off marked line, you can twist the saw slightly to bring it back square . Use a rip saw for cutting with the grain

tools and materials

For some straight-across cuts and all angle cuts, you need a miter box. These sell for about $2; most are made of hardwood

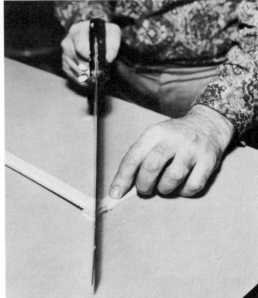

If you don't have a miter box and you want to saw a 45-degree angle, lap the wood as shown and saw it across the lap. Pieces will match very closely

SAW SAVVY can save you lots of time and lots of wood.

Crosscut saws have more teeth to the inch than rip saws, so they make smoother cuts across the grain of the wood and don't tear and splinter it.

Rip saws have wide-set chisel-like teeth; they are made to saw *with* the grain.

If money is a consideration, buy the crosscut saw first. In a pinch it can be used for ripping. A combination saw is a cross between a crosscut and rip saw. It also is an excellent basic hand tool.

The key to sawing is to have a sharp saw—even more than knowing the proper technique of using the saw, which is explained below. Unless you have the know-how, let a professional sharpen and set your saws.

The saw stroke is a rocking motion from the shoulder down through the arm. Make the stroke smooth; don't jerk it. Work out a cutting rhythm. As you stroke, check the angle of the saw frequently. It should be absolutely square with the material you are cutting. Think of it as a carpenter's square; one leg of the square is the saw at right angles to the material, which is the other leg of the square.

Hacksaws cut on the forward stroke, so insert the blade in the saw frame so the teeth of the blade slant forward

When cutting thin metal with a hacksaw, sandwich between two pieces of scrap wood and clamp in a vise. Saw through wood

For hard-to-get-at spots, you can remove the hacksaw blade, tape one end, and make the cut. Use a light, steady stroke

To cut tubing with a hacksaw, sandwich the tubing between two sponges and clamp it in a vise. Nick with a file to start

SPECIAL JOBS require special saws. Here are types you may want to add to your basic tool kit:

Keyhole saws have long tapered blades. They are used for cutting *within* a piece of wood or metal. To start them, you have to first drill a hole in the material you will cut. Then insert the point of the blade and cut out the marked area.

Cabinet saws look like backsaws, which are designed for miterboxes. Cabinet saws are made for cutting dadoes, tenons, rabbets. The teeth are closely set for very fine cutting—especially across grain.

Coping saws have very deep-throated frames. The blade is very thin, since the saw is basically used for cutting curves. You can make inside cuts with a coping saw. First, drill a hole in the material. Then remove the saw blade from its frame. Poke the blade through the hole and reassemble the saw. Tension on the blade should be enough to prevent it from twisting and binding.

For cutting glass you can buy a special round blade to fit a hacksaw frame. This blade also will cut tile, slate, marble and other ceramic materials.

Portable electric saws are ideal for cutting large sheet materials such as plywood and hardboard. If you have a lot of sawing to do, it probably will pay you to invest in this piece of equipment. A 7-in. blade size usually is adequate for a handyman; it will cut 2 x 4s easily; it also will make angle cuts.

A portable saber saw is the power-driven counterpart of a keyhole saw. It also can be used—with the proper blade—for cutting metal and plastics.

Stationary power saws are manufactured in two types: a table (bench) saw, and a radial-arm saw. The choice is really preference, although the radial-arm saw is an excellent tool for crosscutting, if this is a consideration. If you buy a bench model, look at the 10-in. size. It will cost you less than the floor model, if you build the stand.

Saw attachments are made for ¼-in. portable electric drills. You can buy a circular saw or hacksaw attachment. There is, of course, some limit to both attachments as compared to their counterparts in single-purpose power tools.

Chain saws can be used for construction, as well as cutting down trees and grubbing out underbrush. They will cut timber stock; use them for fencing, decks, patios.

164
165

Damaged screw slot? Back out screw as far as you can. Then cut new slot with hacksaw. Lightly stroke blade forward; lift on return stroke

In tight quarters, you can reverse
a hacksaw blade on its frame to
make cutting stroke. Remove
blade; reassemble saw around
the material

Portable electric saw has guide
for ripping; blade can be set to
depth necessary. You can buy
table to convert it into small
bench saw

Portable saw can be adjusted
for angle cuts. You can buy a
variety of blades: Teflon coated;
carbide-tipped for masonry

Circular saw attachment for ¼
in. drill can be adjusted for
depth and angles. Capacity of
saw is somewhat limited

PLANES ARE USED for cutting and smoothing. For most handyman type jobs, a low-angle block plane is satisfactory. A jack plane should be your next choice.

Like all cutting tools, the blade must be kept sharp. A sharp tool is actually safer than a dull one—and it does a better job more easily and quickly.

To use a plane, keep most of the pressure on the knob on the forward stroke. Balance the pressure at midstroke and the rest of the way through it. The plane should be set on the wood at a slight angle so it shaves the material. Check for depth on a piece of scrap wood. The blade must be set parallel with the bed or bottom of the plane. You can make this adjustment with a lever located behind the blade.

180
181

Plane parts (from left) are plane iron and plane iron cap; and the lever cap, which supports the iron and cap. The blade-adjusting lever is next to the handle; the depth adjustment for the blade, a knurled metal disc, is located under this lever

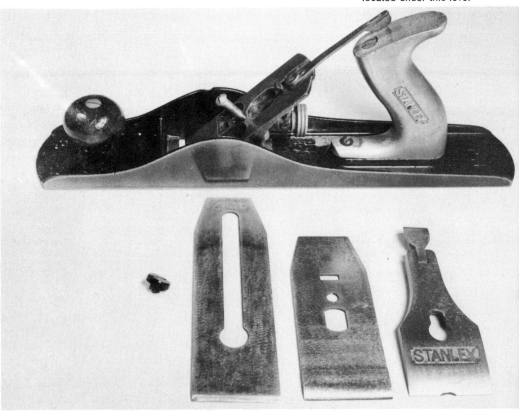

Run plane across stock at a slight angle so you get a shave cut. Use even strokes, lifting the plane off the stock on the return stroke

Apply pressure on the front of the plane at the start of the stroke, then balance the pressure as you complete stroke

Chamfer (angle) cuts are made this way—with the plane at a slight angle. Stroke is even with most pressure on front

When using a plane against or across the grain of the wood, cut a slight bevel (angle) at end. This will help prevent splitting

CHISELS ARE FIRST COUSINS to knives. The best first sizes are ¼ in., ½ in., ¾ in., and 1 in. If you buy chisels that have metal caps on the handles, you can tap them with either a wooden mallet or hammer. Otherwise, you should use only a wooden mallet to strike the handles.

Chisels are used much like planes. Cuts are at an angle across the stock in a shaving motion. Use one hand to guide the blade; use the other hand to apply pressure to the blade near the cutting edge.

Cold chisels and *brick chisels* are used for chipping and cleaning masonry, while wood chisels should be used only on wood. However, an old wood chisel makes an excellent tool for rough work such as prying loose old roof coating, slotting thin metal, notching timbers, and scraping dried glue off pieces of lumber.

Chisel should go into the grain, not with it, in a shaving angle cut. Take small cutting bites when smoothing wood, similar to a plane cut

Multibladed Surform tool works similar to a plane chisel, and knife for smoothing or cutting flat, convex, and concave surfaces

Mortise cuts with chisel should be a series of slightly angled downward cuts. Excess wood is then shaved away, and new downward cuts are made until proper depth is reached. Chisel with thick blade should be used for deep cuts

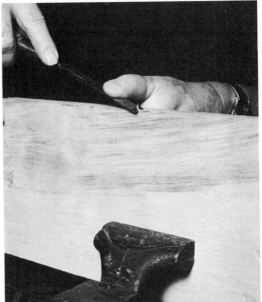

If chisel can't rest on its flat side for recessed cuts, hold it at a slight angle with the beveled edge down. You have better control over the chisel's angle by using this technique. For cross grain, keep flat side toward shoulder of the wood

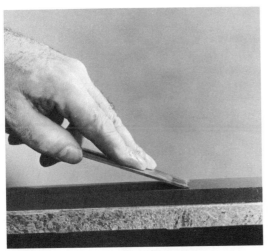

To sharpen chisel or plane blade, rock blade slightly on oilstone. Heel and toe of the edge must be in contact with the sharpening surface

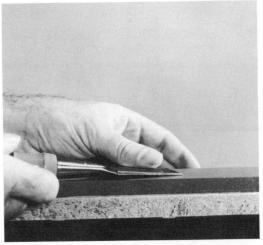

When you've finished honing the bevel side, turn the blade over and "touch" the back edge of the blade against the oilstone to remove any burrs

	Aluminum oxide Silicon carbide Garnet	Emery	Flint
Very fine	600		
	500		
	400 (10/0)		
	360		
	320 (9/0)		
	280 (8/0)		
	240 (7/0)		
	220 (6/0)		Very fine
Fine	180 (5/0)	3/0	
	150 (4/0)	2/0	
	120 (3/0)	1/0	
			Fine
Medium	100 (2/0)	1/2	
	80 (1/0)	1	
			Medium
	60 (1/2)	1-1/2	
Coarse	50 (1)	2	Coarse
	40 (1-1/2)	2-1/2	
	36 (2)	3	
			Very
Very coarse	30 (2-1/2)		coarse
	24 (3)		
	20 (3-1/2)		
	16 (4)		
	12 (4-1/2)		

Type of abrasive, grit size, and backing is printed on the back of abrasive paper. Use chart at right to determine the type you need

PICK THE RIGHT ABRASIVE and you have a tool instead of just sandpaper. As a rule of thumb, use a closed-coat paper for fast cutting; use an open-coat paper on materials that tend to clog the abrasive.

There are many types of abrasive available; they include garnet for wood, emery paper for metal; aluminum oxide for both wood and metal; crocus cloth for metal; silicon carbide for glass; flint for materials that are gummy. The backing for abrasives is manufactured in two types: paper and cloth. The weight of the paper is classified by letter: A is light, while D is heavy for machine-sanding. For cloth, J is lightweight; X is heavy.

Steel wool also is considered an abrasive, and it is available in fine, medium, and coarse.

Your basic tool kit should have at least one sheet of very fine to very coarse abrasive and a tube of medium steel wool.

FILES AND RASPS are smoothing tools for either metal or wood. If the file has a single row of teeth it is called a single-cut file. If a second row of teeth cross the first row, the file is a double-cut file.

You can buy files in four different types: a coarse (bastard) file is used for rough work; a second-cut file is for smoothing rough work; a smooth-cut file is for smoothing surfaces to a fine finish; a rasp is used for wood only.

For most jobs, you can get by with an 8-in. mill file and a wood rasp. Some wood rasps have a combination of teeth—from very coarse to fine. These are called combination shoe rasps.

Always use a sanding block when you work on flat surfaces. A piece of 1 x 4 scrap is adequate. If you don't use block, abrasive can cup surface

Slightly rounded edges take finish better than perfectly square edges. Hit them very lightly with fine abrasive stretched over sanding block

Power sanders are inexpensive and can save you muscle if you have much sanding to do. Orbital or reciprocal models both work well

Disc-sander attachment is available for ¼-in. drill. It is best used for rough sanding where a lot of wood must be removed

Files cut on the forward stroke; lift file off work on return stroke. Grip the file with both hands to apply hard, even pressure

File card has series of tiny wires that go into the teeth of files to clean them. When teeth begin to clog, clean them

A HAMMER IS THE HOMEOWNER'S basic tool—even if it's just used for cracking walnuts. The basic type is a claw hammer; the 13-ounce weight is probably the easiest one for you to swing, although 16- and 20-ounce hammers are generally used by professional carpenters.

Specialty hammers include *tack hammers* with the head or claw magnetized so tacks and brads will be easier to start; *ball peen hammers* for working with metal and masonry; and *mason's hammers* for brick, stone and concrete work.

Good hammers have good balance. Buy a good hammer and you will get more driving power and not tire as quickly. You can tell a good hammer by how well the face of the hammer and the claws are machined. The face should be slightly crowned. The crown lets you drive nails flush; it will not leave hammer marks in softer materials. The claws should be sharp so you can grip the *body* or *shank* of a nail and pull it—not just pull on the head of the nail.

To properly use a hammer, grip the handle near its end. Do not choke up on the handle. Swing it freely, keeping the face of the hammer square with the head of the nail. You should, however, choke up on the handle a bit to start the nail. Give it a couple of easy taps; then swing hard for the proper leverage.

For metal working, a ball peen hammer is designed to flare rivets. *Rubber hammers* also are designed for metal working, while *wooden mallets* are used for chisels. If you don't want to invest in a rubber hammer or wooden mallet, you can adapt a regular claw hammer for these jobs with a rubber crutch tip. Simply slip the tip over the face of the hammer.

Other "driving" tools include *hatchets* and *heavy-duty staplers.* A light hatchet with a blade on one end and a flat face on the other is the best all-round driving and chopping tool for lawn and garden projects. A stapler can substitute for a hammer and nails for many light fabrication jobs. There are several types of staplers available; one type has an adjustable spring drive for both light and heavy work.

Picks are generally classified as garden tools, although they are used mostly for breaking out concrete, prying up bricks, and lifting slabs.

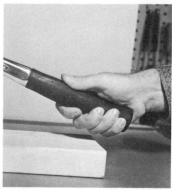

Grip a hammer handle this way— at the end of the handle—for easier swinging through balance. Start nails by choking up on the handle

To clinch a nail, hit the very tip of it with the hammer. Don't smack it midway down the shank. Use light taps to bend the nail

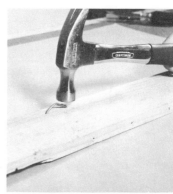

If you've hit the nail properly to clinch it, the nail will be slightly curved in the center. Then hit tip to sink it into wood

Clinch nails against grain if possible. This prevents splitting. Another trick to prevent splitting is to blunt point with hammer

Block of wood gives hammer more leverage for pulling nails. It also protects the wood from damage. For tough pulls, use a wrecking bar

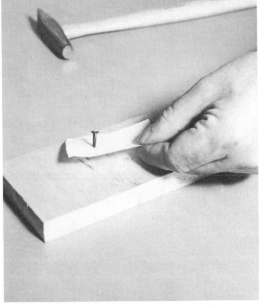

Start tacks without hitting your fingers by sticking them through a slip of paper. Or you can use a bobby pin to hold the tack

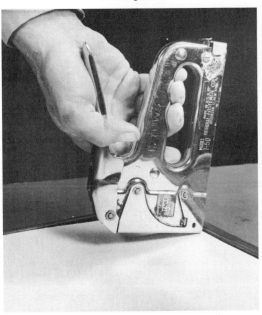

Heavy-duty stapler can replace tacks and hammer for many household jobs—from mending screens to reupholstery

FOR THOSE BORING JOBS, you'll need a drill and assorted bits for wood and metal. There are several drill variations: the *push-pull type* for small holes; the *crank type* for small holes; the *brace type* which accepts expansion bits for cutting holes up to 3 in. in diameter; portable and stationary *electric drills.*

A good brace should have a spring-type chuck and an adjustable ratchet. The chuck will accept bits from ¼ in. to 1⅛ in. in diameter. You also can buy an expansion bit (adjustable) for boring holes from 1 to 3 in. in diameter. For holes larger than this, you can buy power-driven hole saws.

Auger bits are for boring holes in wood; *twist drills* are for boring holes in either wood or metal. Special bits and drills include *masonry bits* for holes in brick, stone, concrete, etc.; *countersinks* for beveling the edges of a hole to drive a flathead screw flush with the material; *reamers* for smoothing holes basically in metal; and *screwdriver bits.*

The quarter-inch portable electric drill has become a basic tool because of its versatility. With special attachments, you not only can drill holes but saw wood, sand, drive and draw screws, grind, shape wood and some metals, polish, buff, trim hedges, and even set up simple lathe jobs.

Using any boring tool takes practice. There are two tricks: Keep the bit or drill square to the material you are boring or drilling; do not over-force the cutting action of the bit or drill. Start bits and drills with a pilot hole you can make with an awl or centerpunch. This way, the bit or drill won't wander across the surface of the material.

When using auger bits, bore through the wood until the lead screw of the bit peeks out the other side. Then remove the bit from the hole and bore from the other side to complete the job. This prevents the wood from splitting when the bit breaks through.

Portable electric drills have become popular, but not necessarily for just drilling holes. Versatility of the different attachments is probably the reason why this is the most popular of all power tools.

The most practical accessories include disc sanders and buffers; a speed-reducing gear, which will double the torque of the drill; and the screwdriver attachment, which will drive and draw screws.

Use your body to help steady, guide, and apply pressure to brace. Keep drill or bit square to the material you are working

Special wood bits for power outfit have pilot hole starter, cutter, and countersink built into them; they also come with a depth gauge

Screws let you remove housing to repair electric drills. Make sure power cord is removed from outlet before you start any repairs

Auger bits are for wood; don't use them in metal. Sizes run from 1/16 in. to 1¼ in.; lengths go from 1⅞ in. to 6½ in.

Expansion bits have an adjustment screw to extend the cutter. You can bore holes up to 3 in. Make sure screw is tight

"Fly-cutters" are made for electric drills. They have a built-in pilot-hole cutter on the tip. Use them only on wood

"Screwmates" are designed for drilling holes for screws; they are made in the shape of a screw. For hand drills, use a regular countersink bit

Holes in masonry are easy to drill with masonry bits in electric drills. If you must punch holes in masonry by hand, use a star drill and hammer

Brushes in drills are spring-loaded and are removed by twisting out screw. Brushes should be changed yearly

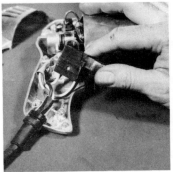

Trigger switch is a single unit in many drills and can be replaced. Also replace insulation around wires after making repairs

Gears in drills need annual inspection, and probably lubrication. Use grease recommended by the manufacturer for this job

IF YOU HAVE EVER HAD to use the edge of a dime to tighten a screw, you know how important the proper screwdriver can be for a potpourri of home-maintenance jobs.

There is a wide range of screwdrivers and screwdriver combinations you can buy—hand and power operated. The basics, however, include short, medium and long-bladed screwdrivers, and a screwdriver with a Phillips blade. A Phillips head screw has a crossed slot.

In selecting a screwdriver for a specific job, make sure the blade of the driver fits the screw slot perfectly. If it doesn't, you can mar the surface of the surrounding material or break the slot of the screw when you twist it in or out of the material.

To use a screwdriver, grip the handle so it seats firmly in the palm of your hand. With thumb and index finger, grip the bottom part of the handle. Keep the screwdriver blade square in the screw.

If you have a lot of screws to drive, consider buying a spiral ratchet screwdriver. It is reversible so you can both drive and draw screws. You also can buy a screwdriver attachment for a ¼-in. drill that drives and draws screws.

Screwdriver maintenance is important. Keep the tip square with a file or grinding wheel. Also, do not use good screwdrivers as levers, chisels, paint paddles or hole-punchers. Since they do these jobs so well, keep an old screwdriver handy for them.

For special jobs, you can buy screwdrivers with clamp-type screw holders, and offset screwdrivers for spaces too cramped for long-bladed drivers.

For screws broken off in holes, you can drill into the screw with a drill the same size. If you can't match the screw size with a drill, use a smaller drill. Drill into the screw a short way, and use a screw extractor to remove it. If a screw extractor isn't available, you can tap a small nail into the hole and use it like an Allen wrench to back out the screw.

When drilling pilot holes in softwoods, drill just half as deep as the threaded portion of the screw. If you are working with hardwoods, the pilot hole should be as deep as the entire length of the screw. Pilot holes also should be equal in diameter to the screw shank. If you are counterboring for a plug, do this first with an auger bit. Then finish drilling the hole with a twist drill.

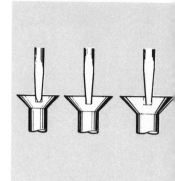

Tip of blade must fit the screw slot. If it doesn't, the screwdriver can break the slot and damage the material below

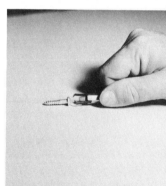

Springlike jaws on screw holder are pressed apart to accept the head of the screw. The holder slips along the blade of the screwdriver

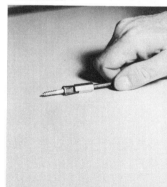

Screw holder keeps tip of screwdriver blade in screw slot. After the screw is started in the hole, flick blade to release holder

Spiral ratchet screwdriver is an
excellent tool for driving lots of
screws. An adjustment locks it
in forward, reverse and neutral

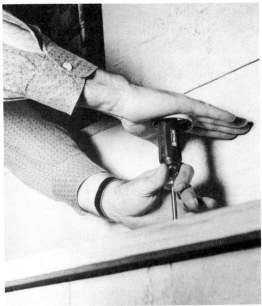

You can get more pressure for
driving and drawing screws with
lid from a jar. It distributes
pressure across palm

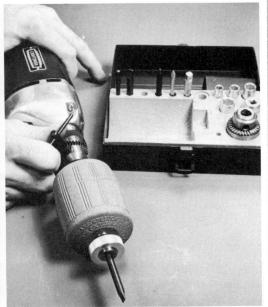

Screwdriver attachment for
power drill includes different
types of blades , and socket sets for
tightening and loosening bolts

DRILLING LEAD HOLES

SCREW SIZE (No. and Diameter)	DRILL SIZE (No. and Diameter)	
	HARDWOODS	SOFTWOODS
0 (.060″)	70 (1/32″)	
1 (.073″)	66 (1/32″)	71 (1/32″)
2 (.086″)	56 (3/64″)	65 (1/32″)
3 (.099″)	54 (1/16″)	58 (3/64″)
4 (.112″)	52 (1/16″)	55 (3/64″)
5 (.125″)	49 (5/64″)	53 (1/16″)
6 (.138″)	47 (5/64″)	52 (1/16″)
7 (.151″)	44 (3/32″)	51 (1/16″)
8 (.164″)	40 (3/32″)	48 (5/64″)
9 (.177″)	37 (7/64″)	45 (5/64″)
10 (.190″)	33 (7/64″)	43 (3/32″)
12 (.216″)	30 (1/8″)	38 (7/64″)
14 (.242″)	25 (9/64″)	32 (7/64″)
16 (.268″)	18 (5/32″)	29 (9/64″)
18 (.294″)	13 (3/16″)	26 (9/64″)
20 (.320″)	4 (13/64″)	19 (11/64″)
24 (.372″)	1 (7/32″)	15 (3/16″)

NOTE: Lead holes aren't usually required for
Nos. 0 and 1 screws. For sizes smaller than No.
6, lead holes can be eliminated in softwoods,
except near the edges and ends of boards.

PLIERS ARE EXTENSIONS of your fingers—holding tools—and the home-maintenance jobs they can do are countless.

Like other tools, you should buy good pliers; the best ones are still inexpensive and have precision-machined jaws with serrations to hold and firmly grip the work. Good pliers also have pivot bolts that are machined so they won't slip under pressure.

Pliers can bend strips of light metal, strip insulation from wires, cut light wire, serve as a clamp and/or vise, reach into tight spots where your fingers can't go, turn bolts and screws, etc.

Selection, other than the basic types, depends on the work to be done. Pincers are used to pull nails and cut wire; needle-nose pliers are used mainly for electrical work. Vise-grip pliers have a screw adjustment at the end of one handle so the jaws can be firmly locked on the work.

Pliers require little maintenance. Sometimes the pivot bolt will become loose. You can fix this by tightening the bolt so it doesn't wobble in the hole. Then, with a punch, bend a thread on the bolt to keep the nut firmly in place. You can clean serrations with a file card or one edge of a three-cornered file.

Tinsnips are scissors, but they can substitute for pliers in bending metal, stripping insulation and cutting wire, and similar jobs. Use standard snips for light sheet metal. Duckbill snips have more leverage for tougher metals. You can buy these snips with a right or left cut.

Wire strippers operate like scissors, too, to strip insulation off 8 to 22-gauge wire without damage to the wire. Some even cut small bolts. If you do any electrical home maintenance, you should add wire strippers to your tool kit. The price is under $7 for top quality.

Other handy gripping tools include beauty tweezers; arc-joint pliers for use on pipe, conduit, couplings, and castings; bent needle-nose pliers for working in cramped spaces, and "mini" precision pliers for very delicate work. For lawn and garden work, fence pliers are handy to have. Some types have a combination staple puller, wire splicer, pincer, cutter and hammer in a single unit.

An ordinary pair of pliers is much more versatile than you might think

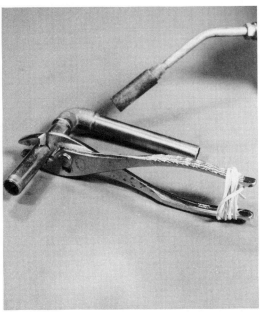

With rubber band around handles, pliers make fine clamp for holding light work. Use them to clamp glue joints, too

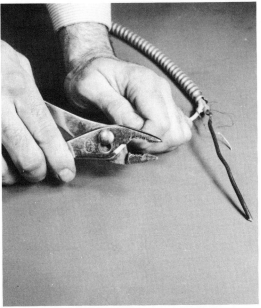

Wire cutters on pliers are at base of jaws. The cutters also can be used to strip insulation if you don't have a stripper

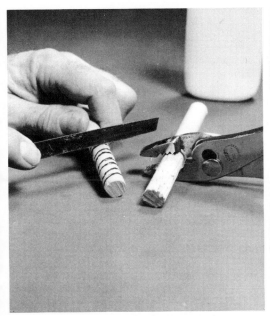

Serrations in jaws of pliers can score wood that will be used for glue dowels. You also can score dowels with edge of file

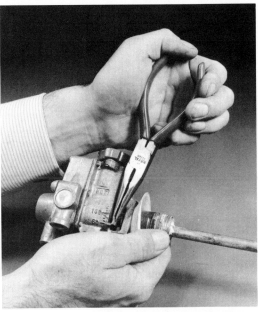

Needle-nose pliers reach spots that other pliers can't go. Use them for electrical work and delicate assembly projects

FOR PLUMBING REPAIRS, you'll require several gripping tools. Most of them sell for under $10.

Reversing chain pipe wrenches are for use in tight places on pipe and conduit. The jaws of the wrench actually consist of the links in the chain. Thus they will fit irregular shapes.

For sink and toilet repairs, adjustable slip and locknut wrenches fit slip-type nuts on sink traps and locknuts on toilet connections. Buy the wrench that adjusts from ⅜ to 3 in.

Pipe vises can be used for holding any round material—even wooden dowels, if they are cushioned so the jaws of the vise won't damage the wood.

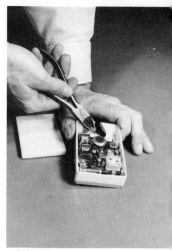

Sidecutters are for cutting wire, and are made for electrical work. Keep the edges sharp with an oilstone

SUPPORT TOOLS

As any experienced homeowner will tell you, there is a collection of support tools that will help you do certain jobs other tools can't do as easily. These can be employed in several different ways:

Ice picks can start pilot holes, scratch a mark for sawing or snipping, hold a piece of light material in position while you fasten it to a floor, wall or ceiling.

Paint paddles make excellent shims and wedges; cut in small pieces, you can use them as cushions for clamps.

Adhesive bandages and cotton make-up pads can be used to pad the jaws of clamps and pliers to prevent damage to finished materials.

Scraps of used sandpaper are excellent for restoring a point on marking pencils; for scouring cement trowels, tuckpointing strikes, shovels and hoes. Worn abrasive won't scratch these tools.

Penknives make substitute insulation strippers, mark materials for cutting, and serve as adhesive spreaders for small patching jobs.

Old hacksaw blades with wide teeth can be used for spreading adhesive over small areas.

Use cotton swabs for applying finishes to small areas. They work best with stains.

Old combs work well to comb paint out of an old brush, after hardened paint has been softened with paint remover. After the loose paint has been combed out, soak the brush in soapy water.

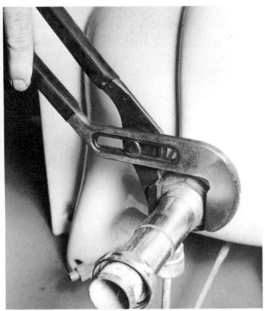

Use adjustable pliers to turn fittings on plumbing runs. You can buy them with serrated or smooth jaws

Wire strippers cut wire, strip insulation from it, and cut small screws and bolts used in electrical repairs

Adjustable pipe wrenches are made especially for working with iron pipe. The serrated jaws bite into the pipe

Some vises have special inserts below jaws to hold pipe. The inserts can be padded when you work with wooden dowels

MEASURING AND MARKING TOOLS can be classed among the most important of all for basic home repair and improvements. Nothing fits without them!

Such tools include a *square, level, tape measure, plumb bob, and chalkline.*

If you are beginning to assemble a basic tool kit, buy a combination square, instead of the large carpenter's square. It is easier to handle and will do most jobs you want it to do, including marking miters. A small torpedo level also is satisfactory, although a longer level is essential for extensive remodeling work.

For measuring and marking *inside* and *outside* dimensions, you need a 12-ft. measuring tape. Buy a good one with a tape stiff enough to make vertical measurements without bending.

A plumb bob provides a true vertical line; a *chalkline* is used to suspend the plumb bob. You also use the chalkline—saturated with chalk—for marking horizontal and vertical lines for installing paneling, fenceposts, framing walls, and a host of other jobs.

Secondary measuring and marking tools include a *marking gauge, outside calipers, dividers, bevel gauge* and *caliper rules.*

A marking gauge is used to scribe a mark along the face of a board for cutting. The head of the gauge is adjustable along a rule, which has a scribing pin inserted in the end of the rule. As it is pulled along the material, it scribes a line.

Outside calipers and *caliper rules* help you find inside and outside dimensions of cylinders, while *dividers* can mark circles and small arcs. Dividers also can be used to step off a series of preset measurements along a scribed line.

For duplicating angles, a bevel gauge works best. A sliding blade, locked in position by a thumbscrew, can be set from 0 to 180 degrees.

Also handy is a *folding rule.* It can be adjusted for many angle cuts. Accuracy, however, is somewhat limited because of the large folding joints.

Maintenance of measuring and marking tools involves wiping the tools occasionally with an oil-soaked cloth. Always keep the tools out of the way of any damage. The least little jar on a level, for example, can ruin its accuracy.

Plumb bob establishes a true vertical line. It is suspended from a nail with chalkline, which can leave a vertical mark

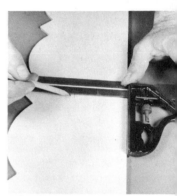

Combination square is large enough for most maintenance jobs. It can be used as a marking gauge and to scribe miters

Marking gauge scribes a line along the length of a board. Head of gauge is adjustable; pin in end of rule marks the stock

Tape can be used for inside and outside measurements. It should be heavy enough to make vertical measurements

If you are undertaking extensive remodeling, use a framing square for squaring panels, studs, joists

For narrow dimension lumber, a combination square is accurate. The blade of the square is adjustable; lock it with thumbscrew

Accurate cuts can be marked with framing square. It can be utilized for scribing notches in rafters and joists

When bubble in level is between the lines, the surface below is level. A similar bubble is used for a true vertical line

For notching material to go around pipes and other obstructions, a marking gauge is the tool to mark the cut

Pointed dividers are accurate for making inside and outside measurements of round and irregular objects

Keep metal marking tools like new with a light coating of oil or plastic. Steel wool removes any rust from metal

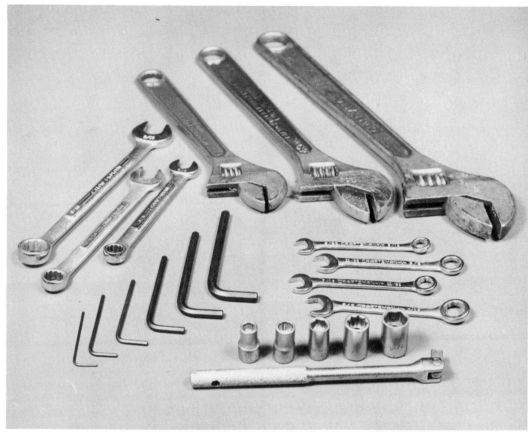

Types of wrenches include adjustables, at top; open and box-end at left; Allen wrenches, below left; and socket wrenches at bottom

WRENCHES, like some other tools, are available in hundreds of different sizes and shapes to turn nuts and bolts, pipes, fittings, screws, etc.

Your first buy should be a good set of adjustable wrenches—small, medium, and large. When you add to this set, first choose a set of socket wrenches; then go on to box-end wrenches to complete the set.

To use a wrench, make sure it fits the fastener it is to turn. Otherwise, you will strip the metal edges, and the fastener will become round.

Pull the wrench toward you when working; don't push it. If the wrench slips while you're pushing it, you can skin a knuckle or two, or hurt your wrist. Always pull against the fixed jaw of an adjustable wrench.

There is little or no *maintenance* involved with wrenches. Keep them free of grease and oil so they don't slip in your hand.

Adjustable wrenches are adaptable to most home-maintenance.

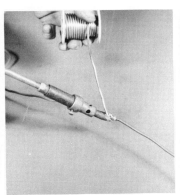

Fastening tools include a heavy-duty stapler for upholstery. Best buy for all-around use is stapler for 9/16-in. staples

Soldering iron is ideal for small jobs such as electrical splices. For big jobs—sweating copper tubing, etc.—use propane torch

Soldering gun is similar to a soldering iron, and might be easier for you to use. You pull trigger to quickly heat tip

Often overlooked method of fastening is rivets. Properly peened, rivets have amazing strength. They're even used to fabricate jet planes

A vise can serve as a clamp for small glue jobs; it distributes all the pressure needed. Use scrap stock to protect surfaces

Bar clamps are for big jobs such as edge-gluing wide pieces of hardwood. You buy the clamps and install them on ¾-in. pipe

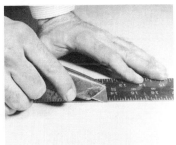

With clamping blocks, you can hold together miters while the glue dries. Spring clamps look like clothespins; use for small jobs

Razor or utility knife has a razor-type blade inside a handle. This tool is excellent for many jobs— here cutting wallboard

Pull scrapers work best for removing paint; flat scrapers trowels and for light scraping. Putty knife is all-around tool

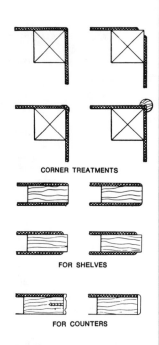

CORNER TREATMENTS

FOR SHELVES

FOR COUNTERS

FOR UNSUPPORTED PANELS

EDGE TREATMENTS

Hardboard finishing treatments include these for raw edges. You can buy many different types of metal mouldings to hide edges, too. These include division strips, inside corners, outside corners, caps and edgings

Selecting for appearance

Use these symbols when you specify plywood	Description and Most Common Uses	Face	Back	Inner
INTERIOR TYPE				
N-N, N-A, N-B, N-D INT-DFPA	Natural finish cabinet quality. One or both sides, select all heartwood or all sapwood veneer. For furniture having a natural finish, cabinet doors, built-ins. Use N-D for natural finish paneling.	N	N,A B or D	
A-A INT-DFPA	For interior applications where both sides will be on view. Built-ins, cabinets, furniture and partitions. Face is smooth and suitable for painting.	A	A	
A-B INT-DFPA	For uses similar to Interior A-A but where the appearance of one side is less important and two smooth solid surfaces are necessary.	A	B	
A-D INT-DFPA	For interior uses where the appearance of only one side is important. Paneling, built-in, shelving, partitions.	A	D	
B-B INT-DFPA	Interior utility panel for use where two smooth sides are desired. Permits circular plugs. Paintable.	B	B	
B-D INT-DFPA	Interior utility panel for use where one smooth side is required. Good for backing, sides or built-ins. Industry: shelving, slip sheets, separator boards and bins.	B	D	D
DECORATIVE PANELS	Rough-sawn, brushed, grooved or striated faces. Good for interior accent walls, built-ins, counter facing, displays and exhibits.	C or btr.	D	
PLYRON INT-DFPA	Hardboard face on both sides. For countertops, shelving, cabinet doors, flooring. Hardboard faces may be tempered, untempered, smooth or screened.			C &
EXTERIOR TYPE				
A-A EXT-DFPA*	Use where the appearance of both sides is important. Fences, built-ins, signs, boats, cabinets, commercial refrigerators, shipping containers, tote boxes, tanks and ducts.	A	A	
A-B EXT-DFPA*	For use similar to A-A EXT panels but where the appearance of one side is less important.	A	B	C
A-C EXT-DFPA*	Exterior use where the appearance of only one side is important. Sidings, soffits, fences, structural uses, boxcar and truck lining and farm buildings. Tanks, trays, commercial refrigerators.	A	C	
B-B EXT-DFPA*	An outdoor utility panel with solid paintable faces for uses where higher quality is not necessary.	B	B	C
B-C EXT-DFPA*	An outdoor utility panel for farm service and work buildings, boxcar and truck linings, containers, tanks, agricultural equipment.	B	C	
HDO EXT-DFPA*	Exterior type High Density Overlay plywood with hard, semi-opaque resin-fiber overlay. Abrasion resistant. Painting not ordinarily required. For concrete forms, signs, acid tanks, cabinets, countertops.	A or B	A or B	C Plugged
MDO EXT-DFPA*	Exterior type Medium Density Overlay with smooth, opaque resin-fiber overlay heat-fused to one or both panel faces. Ideal base for paint. Usually recommended for siding and other outdoor applications. Also good for built-ins, signs and displays.	B	B or C	C
303 SPECIAL SIDING EXT-DFPA	Grade designation covers proprietary plywood products for exterior siding, fencing, etc., with special surface treatment such as V-groove, channel groove, striated, brushed, rough sawn.	B or btr.	C	
T 1-11 EXT-DFPA	Exterior type, sanded or unsanded, shiplapped edges with parallel grooves ¼″ deep, ⅜″ wide. Grooves 2″ or 4″ o.c. Available in 8′ and 10′ lengths and MD Overlay. For siding and accent paneling.	C or btr.	C	
PLYRON EXT-DFPA	Exterior panel surfaced both sides with hardboard for use in exterior applications. Faces are tempered, smooth or screened.			
MARINE EXT-DFPA	Exterior type plywood made only with Douglas fir or Western larch. Special solid jointed core construction. Subject to special limitations on core gaps and number of face repairs. Ideal for boat hulls. Also available with overlaid faces.	A or B	A or B	
SPECIAL EXTERIOR	Premium Exterior panel similar to Marine grade but in other species covered under new grading system.	A or B	A or B	

*Also available in Structural I (face, back and inner plies limited to Group 1 species).

Selecting for construction

Use these symbols when you specify plywood (1) (2)	Description and Most Common Uses	Veneer Grade Face	Back	Inner Plies
INTERIOR TYPE — STANDARD INT-DFPA (4)	Unsanded Interior sheathing grade for floors, walls and roofs. Limited exposure crates, bins, containers and pallets.	C	D	D
STANDARD INT-DFPA (4) (with Exterior glue)	Same as Standard sheathing but has Exterior glue. For construction where unusual moisture conditions may be encountered. Often used for pallets, crates, bins, etc. that may be exposed to the weather.	C	D	D
STRUCTURAL I and STRUCTURAL II INT-DFPA	Unsanded structural grades where plywood strength properties are of maximum importance. Structural diaphragms, box beams, gusset plates, stressed skin panels. Also for containers, pallets, bins. Made only with Exterior glue. Structural I limited to Group 1 species for face, back and inner plies. Structural II permits Group 1, 2, or 3 species.	C	D	D
UNDER-LAYMENT INT-DFPA (4)	For underlayment or combination subfloor-underlayment beneath resilient floor coverings, carpeting. Used in homes, apartments, mobile homes, commercial buildings. Ply beneath face is C or better veneer. Sanded or touch-sanded as specified.	C Plugged	D	C & D
C-D PLUGGED INT-DFPA (4)	For utility built-ins, backing for wall and ceiling tile. Not a substitute for Underlayment. Ply beneath face permits D grade veneer. Also for cable reels, walkways, separator boards. Unsanded or touch-sanded as specified.	C Plugged	D	D
2-4-1 INT-DFPA (5)	Combination subfloor-underlayment. Quality base for resilient floor coverings, carpeting, wood strip flooring. Use 2-4-1 with Exterior glue in areas subject to excessive moisture. Unsanded or touch-sanded as specified.	C Plugged	D	C & D
EXTERIOR TYPE — C-C EXT-DFPA (4)	Unsanded grade with waterproof bond for subflooring and roof decking, siding on service and farm buildings. Backing, crating, pallets, pallet bins, cable reels.	C	C	C
C-C PLUGGED EXT-DFPA (4)	Use as a base for resilient floors and tile backing where unusual moisture conditions exist. For refrigerated or controlled atmosphere rooms. Also for pallets, fruit pallet bins, reusable cargo containers, tanks and boxcar and truck floors and linings. Sanded or touch-sanded as specified.	C Plugged	C	C
STRUCTURAL I C-C EXT-DFPA	For engineered applications in construction and industry where full Exterior type panels made with all Group 1 woods are required. Unsanded.	C	C	C
PLYFORM CLASS I & II B-B EXT-DFPA	Concrete form grades with high re-use factor. Sanded both sides. Edge-sealed and mill-oiled unless otherwise specified. Special restrictions on species. Also available in HDO.	B	B	C

Notes: (1) All Interior grades shown also available with Exterior glue.
(2) All grades except Plyform available tongue and grooved in panels 1/2" and thicker.
(3) Panels are standard 4x8-foot size. Other sizes available.
(4) Available in Group 1, 2, 3 or 4. (5) Available in Group 1, 2 or 3 only.

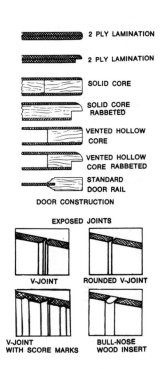

DOOR CONSTRUCTION

- 2 PLY LAMINATION
- 2 PLY LAMINATION
- SOLID CORE
- SOLID CORE RABBETED
- VENTED HOLLOW CORE
- VENTED HOLLOW CORE RABBETED
- STANDARD DOOR RAIL

EXPOSED JOINTS

V-JOINT   ROUNDED V-JOINT

V-JOINT WITH SCORE MARKS   BULL-NOSE WOOD INSERT

Hardboard can be laminated to itself with glue, or fastened to other types of wood. It can not be mechanically fastened to itself, since it has no grain

Plywood panels have been standardized so you can easily select a panel for a specific job. The most common panel width is 4 ft.; length most often used is 8 ft. Lengths run 8, 10 and 12 ft. Thicknesses are 3/16, then 1/4 to 3/4 in. in 1/8-in. jumps. Letters designate the veneer grades. The species group number is an indication of panel stiffness: the lower the number, the stiffer the panel will be

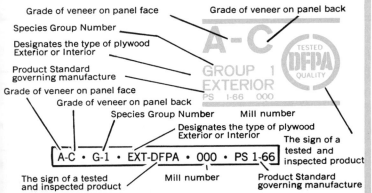

Grade of veneer on panel face
Grade of veneer on panel back
Species Group Number
Designates the type of plywood Exterior or Interior
Product Standard governing manufacture
Grade of veneer on panel face

A-C GROUP 1 EXTERIOR PS 1-66 000 DFPA QUALITY TESTED

Grade of veneer on panel back
Species Group Number   Mill number
Designates the type of plywood Exterior or Interior
The sign of a tested and inspected product

A-C · G-1 · EXT-DFPA · 000 · PS 1-66

The sign of a tested and inspected product   Mill number   Product Standard governing manufacture

the properties of common woods

Notes on working properties and finishing

These data on working and finishing properties of woods are based on results of experimental work at Forest Products Laboratory. Entries and remarks are only average. As an example, pounds-per-cubic-foot are given for samples of dry wood. The figure can vary, even in samples cut from the same tree and reduced to the same moisture content. Figures under "Sanding" refer generally to grades of sandpaper that will not leave scratches on the surface when smooth-sanding as the final step. These, too, are variable values. On some samples of a given wood, you may have to go to an even finer grade of paper to achieve desirable results. Figures given under the heading "Planing and Jointing" refer to cutting angles of edge tools that have been found generally best, especially for power tools with cutters such as a jointer or moulding head. Of course, these values are not critical except, perhaps, in some phases of factory production. As another example, finishing data given for Douglas fir states under "Stain" that the color may be brown. This can be any shade of brown from light to dark. But few samples of fir, either of plywood or solid stock, are pleasing to the eye when stained —possible exceptions being a very light or very dark stain. This wood generally appears at its best when sealed, with a special sealer provided for the purpose, and painted or enameled. In entries "Oil" refers to a penetrating oil stain; "Wiping" refers to a wiping stain, usually an oil stain. Bleaching is not always necessary except, possibly, for uniforming the color of a given piece of wood.

Name of Wood	Weight Per Cubic Foot	Hardness	Planing and Jointing	Turning	Sanding	Natural Color
Ash (U.S.A.)	35	Med.	Good 10-25	Fair	Best 2/0	White to Brown
Basswood	24	Soft	Good 20-30	Poor	Poor 4/0	Cream
Birch	39	Hard	Good 15-20	Good	Fair 4/0	Cream
Butternut	25	Soft	Good 10-25	Good	Fair 4/0	Heart: Amber Sap: Cream
Cherry	36	Med.	Best 10-25	Best	Best 4/0	Red to Brown
Cedar (Aromatic Red)	23	Soft	Poor 5-15	Fair	Good 3/0	Heart: Red Sap: Cream
Chestnut	27	Soft	Good 15-20	Best	Best 3/0	Gray-Brown
Cypress	29	Soft	Good 15-25	Poor	Fair 2/0	Heart: Brown Sap: Cream
Elm (Southern)	34	Med.	Poor 15-20	Poor	Good 2/0	Brown to Cream
Fir (Douglas)	26	Soft	Fair 10-25	Poor	Fair 3/0	Cream to Red
Gum (Red)	33	Med.	Fair 10-20	Best	Fair 4/0	Heart: Br. Red Sap: Cream
Hickory	42	Hard	Good 10-25	Good	Best 2/0	White to Cream
Holly	33	Hard	Good 10-25	Good	Best 3/0	Silver White
Mahogany	35	Med.	Good 5-25	Best	Good 4/0	Brown to Red-Brown
Mahogany (Philippine)	33	Med.	Good 5-25	Good	Poor 3/0	Brown to Red-Brown
Maple	41	Hard	Fair 15-20	Good	Good 4/0	Cream
Oak (English Brown)	40	Hard	Best 10-20	Good	Good 2/0	Deep Brown
Oak (Red)	39	Hard	Best 10-25	Good	Best 2/0	Red-Brown
Oak (White)	40	Hard	Best 10-20	Good	Best 2/0	White to Light Brown
Pine (White)	25	Soft	Good 10-25	Good	Fair 2/0	White to Cream
Poplar	29	Soft	Good 5-20	Good	Poor 4/0	White to Cream
Redwood	29	Soft	Good 10-25	Fair	Poor 2/0	Red
Sycamore	35	Med.	Poor 5-15	Good	Poor 3/0	White to Pink
Walnut	36	Med.	Good 15-20	Best	Best 4/0	Heart: Brown Sap: Cream

(Table spans: General Characteristics)

Note: NGR = Non-Grain Raising (Applies to stain)

Usual Grain Figure	Stain		Filler Color	Bleach	Paint	Natural Finish	Remarks
	Type	Color					
Plain or Fiddleback	Any	Any	White or Brown	Yes	Yes. Fill First	Yes	A tough, grainy wood quite uniform in color. Bends quite easily when steamed. Will take stain, but finishes best in natural color
Very Mild	NGR	Red or Brown	None	Not Nec.	Yes	No	Light, softwood usually uniform in color. Fine texture, fairly strong, takes paint well. Used for drawing boards and as veneered core stock
Mild	Any	Walnut or Mahogany	Natural or Brown	Yes	Yes. Interior	Yes	Similar in texture to hard maple. Takes the maple finish well. Widely used in furniture construction. Fairly uniform color
Like Walnut	Water	Walnut or Oak	Medium Brown	Yes	No	Yes	Similar in grain and texture to black walnut. Relatively easy to work with hand and power tools, except as noted
Good	Water	Red or Brown	Red to Black	No	No	Yes	One of the finest domestic cabinet woods. Fine texture, dense grain, often wavy or curly. Takes natural, stain, fine enamel finishes
Knotty	None		None	No	No	Yes. Pref.	Universally used for cedar chests and clothes-closet linings, also novelties. Finishes best in its natural color
Heavy Grain	Oil or Wiping	Red or Brown	Red or Brown	No	Yes	Yes	Rather coarse grained, often worm-holed. Used as picture frames and sometimes as random paneling. Machines well, takes novelty finishes
Plain or Figured	Water, Oil or Wiping	Red or Brown	None	No	Yes	Yes	Tends to splinter when worked by hand or machine. Most durable in outdoor exposures. Will take natural or novelty finishes quite well
Heavy Grain	Water	Red or Brown	Dark Brown	No	Yes	Yes	A good furniture wood but difficult to work either by hand or machine. Takes stain fairly well. Some pieces attractively grained
Plain or Wild	Wiping or Oil	Brown	None	No	Yes	No	Widely used in home construction, especially framing. Universally available as plywood in varying thicknesses. Best sealed and painted
Plain or Figured	Any	Red or Brown	Match Wood	Yes	Yes	Yes	Dense-grained wood, smooth texture. Occasional attractive figure in heartwood, easily worked. Widely used in furniture construction
Usually Straight	Water	Red or Brown	Brown	Yes	No	Yes	Among best domestic woods for steam bending, tool handles. Usually straight grained and of a fairly uniform color and texture
Mild	Water	Amber	None	Not Nec.	Yes	Yes	Similar to basswood in color and texture. Works easily. Can be stained. Once widely used in inlay and marquetry in early construction
Stripe	Water	Red or Brown	Red to Black	Yes	No	Yes	One of the choicest cabinet woods. Select pieces beautifully grained. Works easily. Takes both red and brown stains. An imported wood
Stripe	Water or Wiping	Red or Brown	Red to Black	Yes	No	Yes	Similar to true mahoganies but coarser in grain and softer. Serves well as boat planking, also used as trim and in core-door construction
Varied	Water and Wiping	Maple	None	Yes	No	Yes	One of the best domestic hardwoods. Widely used in fine furniture construction, also as flooring, turnings, bowling pins
Plain, Flake or Swirl	NGR	Brown	Brown to Black	Yes	No	Yes	One of the finest of the oaks. An imported wood, most commonly available as veneer. Very attractively grained. Takes stains well
Plain or Flake	NGR	Green Toner	Brown	Yes	Yes	No	Perhaps the most common of the domestic oaks. Heavy, strong and tough. Open-grained, used in furniture where durability comes first
Plain or Flake	NGR	Brown	Brown	Yes	Yes	Yes	Perhaps the finest domestic oak of exceptional strength and durability. Beautiful graining when quarter-sawed. Takes fine finishes
Mild	Water or Oil	Brown Only	None	No	Yes	No	One of the most popular woods almost universally used for trim, paneling and furniture. Perhaps the best all around domestic softwood
Occ. Dark Stripe	NGR	Brown	None	No	Yes	No	Another of the most useful domestic softwoods. Widely used as a secondary wood in both early and late furniture construction
Mild St. Grain	Red only for toning		None	No	Yes	Yes	An exceptionally durable softwood when used in outdoor applications as house siding, outdoor furniture, fencing, industrial applications
Flake	Water	Amber or Brown	None	Seldom	Yes	Yes	Difficult to work with either hand or power tools. Beautiful, flaky grain when quarter-sawed. Most attractive in natural finish
Varied	Water	Walnut	Brown to Black	Yes	No	Yes	Rated by most as the finest domestic cabinet wood. Used by best cabinetmakers from earliest times. Has every desirable feature

BY MEASUREMENT, a 2 x 4 is not 2 x 4 in. It actually measures 1½ x 3½ in. However, 2 x 4s and other lumber goes by nominal size, not actual size.

Lumber grading methods can vary; they usually follow numbers, names, and/or letters. No. 1 is construction grade; No. 2 is standard grade; No. 3 is utility grade; No. 4 is economy grade. The best quality lumber is termed 1 and 2 clear; B and better has small imperfections; C select has limited imperfections; D select has imperfections that may be covered with paint.

Structural dimension lumber must be at least 4 in. thick. *Select lumber* is the strongest, while *common lumber* may have weaknesses.

Five-quarter lumber is about 1¼-in. thick. Lumber is sold by the board foot; panels are sold by the panel size, grade and type of panel

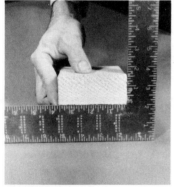

Nominal size is 2 x 4. Actual size is about 1½ x 3½ in. Softwood is usually sold in multiples of 2 lineal ft.

Nominal size is 1 x 3. Actual size is about ¾ x 2½ in. Hardwood is sold in odd and even foot lengths.

STANDARD LUMBER SIZES		
TYPE OF LUMBER	NOMINAL SIZE IN INCHES	ACTUAL SIZE SURFACED 4 SIDES DRY*
Boards	1 x 2	¾ x 1½
	1 x 3	¾ x 2½
	1 x 4	¾ x 3½
	1 x 5	¾ x 4½
	1 x 6	¾ x 5½
	1 x 7	¾ x 6½
	1 x 8	¾ x 7½
Dimension	2 x 4	1½ x 3½
	2 x 6	1½ x 5½
	2 x 8	1½ x 7¼
	2 x 10	1¼ x 9¼
Timbers	5 and thicker	½ off
Shiplap ⅜-inch lap	1 x 4	¾ x 3⅛
	1 x 6	¾ x 5⅛
	1 x 8	¾ x 6⅞

* Dry lumber allows 19 percent moisture content or less. The standards in this table were issued by The Department of Commerce for Softwood Lumber. You may find some lumber the dimensions of the old standards, ie.: 1 x 4—25/32 x 3⅝; 2 x 4 —1⅝ x 3⅝. Boards less than the minimum thickness for 1 inch nominal but ⅝-inch or greater thickness dry may be regarded as American Standard Lumber, but such boards shall be marked to show the size and condition of seasoning at the time of dressing. They shall also be distinguished from 1-inch boards on invoices and certificates.

moulding patterns and sizes

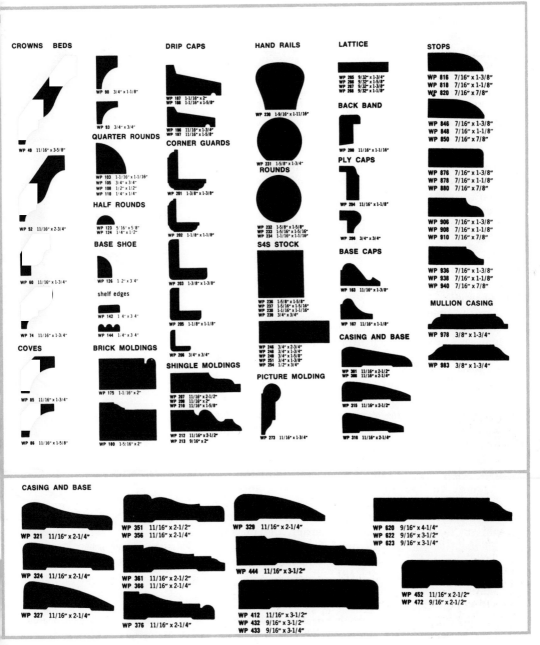

CROWNS   BEDS

WP 49   11/16" x 3-5/8"

WP 52   11/16" x 2-3/4"

WP 60   11/16" x 1-3/4"

WP 74   11/16" x 1-3/4"

COVES

WP 85   11/16" x 1-3/4"

WP 86   11/16" x 1-5/8"

WP 90   3/4" x 1-1/8"

WP 93   3/4" x 3/4"

QUARTER ROUNDS

WP 103   1-1/16" x 1-1/16"
WP 105   3/4" x 3/4"
WP 108   1/2" x 1/2"
WP 110   1/4" x 1/4"

HALF ROUNDS

WP 123   5/16" x 5/8"
WP 124   1/4" x 1/2"

BASE SHOE

WP 126   1 2" x 3 4"

shelf edges

WP 142   1 4" x 3 4"
WP 144   1/4" x 3 4"

BRICK MOLDINGS

WP 175   1-1/16" x 2"

WP 180   1-5/16" x 2"

DRIP CAPS

WP 187   1-1/16" x 2"
WP 188   1-1/16" x 1-5/8"

WP 196   11/16" x 1-3/4"
WP 197   11/16" x 1-5/8"

CORNER GUARDS

WP 201   1-3/8" x 1-3/8"

WP 202   1-1/8" x 1-1/8"

WP 203   1-3/8" x 1-3/8"

WP 205   1-1/8" x 1-1/8"

WP 206   3/4" x 3/4"

SHINGLE MOLDINGS

WP 207   11/16" x 2-1/2"
WP 208   11/16" x 2"
WP 210   11/16" x 1-5/8"

WP 212   11/16" x 2-1/2"
WP 213   9/16" x 2"

HAND RAILS

WP 230   1-9/16" x 1-11/16"

WP 231   1-5/8" x 1-3/4"

ROUNDS

WP 232   1-5/8" x 1-5/8"
WP 233   1-5/16" x 1-5/16"
WP 234   1-1/16" x 1-1/16"

S4S STOCK

WP 236   1-5/8" x 1-5/8"
WP 237   1-5/16" x 1-5/16"
WP 238   1-1/16" x 1-1/16"
WP 239   3/4" x 3/4"

WP 246   3/4" x 2-3/4"
WP 240   3/4" x 1-3/4"
WP 240   3/4" x 1-5/8"
WP 251   3/4" x 1-3/8"
WP 254   1/2" x 3/4"

PICTURE MOLDING

WP 273   11/16" x 1-3/4"

LATTICE

WP 265   9/32" x 1-3/4"
WP 266   9/32" x 1-5/8"
WP 267   9/32" x 1-3/8"
WP 268   9/32" x 1-1/8"

BACK BAND

WP 290   11/16" x 1-1/16"

PLY CAPS

WP 294   11/16" x 1-1/8"

WP 296   3/4" x 3/4"

BASE CAPS

WP 163   11/16" x 1-3/8"

WP 167   11/16" x 1-1/8"

CASING AND BASE

WP 301   11/16" x 2-1/2"
WP 306   11/16" x 2-1/2"

WP 315   11/16" x 2-1/2"

WP 316   11/16" x 2-1/4"

STOPS

WP 816   7/16" x 1-3/8"
WP 818   7/16" x 1-1/8"
WP 820   7/16" x 7/8"

WP 846   7/16" x 1-3/8"
WP 848   7/16" x 1-1/8"
WP 850   7/16" x 7/8"

WP 876   7/16" x 1-3/8"
WP 878   7/16" x 1-1/8"
WP 880   7/16" x 7/8"

WP 906   7/16" x 1-3/8"
WP 908   7/16" x 1-1/8"
WP 910   7/16" x 7/8"

WP 936   7/16" x 1-3/8"
WP 938   7/16" x 1-1/8"
WP 940   7/16" x 7/8"

MULLION CASING

WP 978   3/8" x 1-3/4"

WP 983   3/8" x 1-3/4"

CASING AND BASE

WP 321   11/16" x 2-1/4"

WP 324   11/16" x 2-1/4"

WP 327   11/16" x 2-1/4"

WP 351   11/16" x 2-1/2"
WP 356   11/16" x 2-1/4"

WP 361   11/16" x 2-1/2"
WP 366   11/16" x 2-1/4"

WP 376   11/16" x 2-1/2"

WP 329   11/16" x 2-1/4"

WP 444   11/16" x 3-1/2"

WP 412   11/16" x 3-1/2"
WP 432   9/16" x 3-1/2"
WP 433   9/16" x 3-1/4"

WP 620   9/16" x 4-1/4"
WP 622   9/16" x 3-1/2"
WP 623   9/16" x 3-1/4"

WP 452   11/16" x 2-1/2"
WP 472   9/16" x 2-1/2"

417

DADO

Plywood sheets have different types of cores to which the face veneers are bonded. Lumber-core plywood is the most expensive

Hardboard and particleboard panels are actually wood ground into a fine pulp and pressed into sheets under great pressure and heat

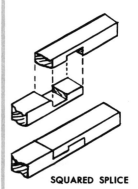

SQUARED SPLICE

UNLESS YOUR FRIENDLY lumber dealer lets you go through the lumber stacks and choose your own boards there is no way to be sure that every piece of lumber that you buy will be clear, straight, and lumber-mill clean. However, you usually get what you pay for, and that is why it is important to plan a project from the studs to the trim mouldings. For example, don't buy No. 1 stock if No. 4 will do.

Lumber is sold by the board foot. Rather than take the time to figure out "board feet," give the dealer the running feet, width and thickness of the lumber you need. He'll transfer it into board feet and charge you accordingly. A "board foot" is equivalent to a board (nominal) 1 in. wide, 12 in. thick, and 12 in. long.

If the project you are planning is a large one, don't overlook the possibility of buying used lumber. Such boards are salvaged by wrecking companies.

Trim pieces and dowels are sold by the lineal foot, while shingles are sold by the "square." A "square" equals 100 sq. ft. of shingles applied. Sheet materials such as plywood and hardboard are sold by the sheet or square foot. Some dealers will cut the sheets in half or quarter for you and sell them to you at half or quarter price.

Simulated stone and decorative panels are usually sold by the panel or piece.

Bricks, concrete block, patio block, and other masonry products are usually sold by the unit. If you buy enough units, the dealer may give you a special price.

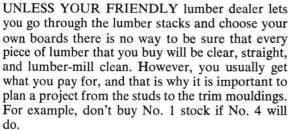

HALF LAP

rabbet and dado

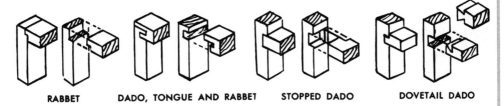

RABBET   DADO, TONGUE AND RABBET   STOPPED DADO   DOVETAIL DADO

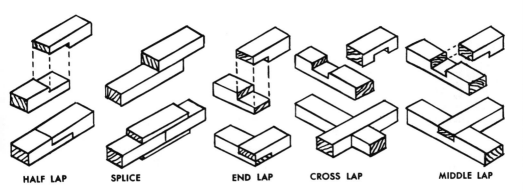

HALF LAP   SPLICE   END LAP   CROSS LAP   MIDDLE LAP

splice and lap joints

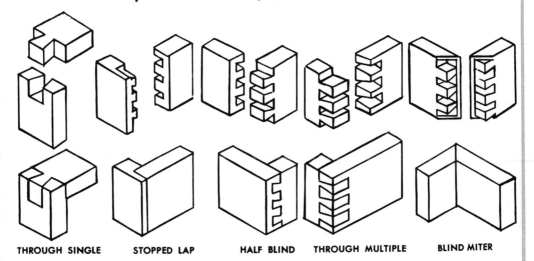

THROUGH SINGLE   STOPPED LAP   HALF BLIND   THROUGH MULTIPLE   BLIND MITER

dovetail joints

WORKING WITH WOOD and other building materials really presents no obstacles to a homeowner. Most building materials are modular; they are standardized as to thickness, width, length, and shape.

By buying good tools at the outset and learning the techniques of using them, you will be surprised how quickly you can fabricate a stud wall, put up paneling, build a patio or deck, enclose a carport, or remodel a garage into living space—even add a new room to the back or side of your home.

The key to building is fastening and joining two pieces of material. You first have to decide what type joint is best. Then, you have to choose the right fasteners. These may be nails, screws, bolts or anchors—or a combination of all these mechanical devices. Tools, actually, only bring you to the point of fastening the materials together. Do it the right way and you will have a job that not only is strong enough to withstand the elements and daily wear-and-tear, but looks professional from every angle.

Butt joints are the most common of joints. Mechanical fasteners can include nails, screws, glue, bolts, anchors and rivets

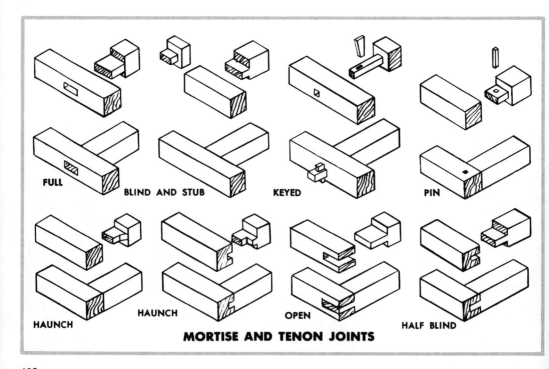

FULL

BLIND AND STUB

KEYED

PIN

HAUNCH

HAUNCH

OPEN

HALF BLIND

MORTISE AND TENON JOINTS

Rabbet joint is easy to make with a power saw; it produces a strong joint when used with nails or screws and the proper kind of glue

Miter joint is not exceptionally strong unless it is beefed-up with glue blocks or metal angle brackets. Miters should be glued, too

Plywood corner brace, glued and nailed to small strips of lumber, will strengthen a butt or miter joint in any type of construction

WOODWORKERS' GLUING CHART

TYPE OF WORK	GLUE FOR LOW-COST WATER-RESISTANT JOINT (In order of preference)	TYPE OF WORK	GLUE FOR LOW-COST WATER-RESISTANT JOINT (In order of preference)
All general gluing of hard and softwoods	Plastic resin glue Casein glue Polyvinyl glue	End-wood joints, mitered joints, scarf joints	Polyvinyl glue Casein glue (heavy mix)
Particle and chip boards to wood	Plastic resin glue Casein glue Contact cement Polyvinyl glue	Loose-fitting joints, relatively rough surfaces	Polyvinyl glue Casein glue (heavy mix)
Plywood to decorative plastic laminates	Casein glue Contact cement Plastic resin glue	Doweling	Plastic resin glue Polyvinyl glue
Laminating heavy framing members	Casein glue	Hardboard to plywood, wood or itself	Plastic resin glue Casein glue Polyvinyl glue Contact cement
Veneering, inlays, cabinet work	Plastic resin glue (extended) Polyvinyl glue	Porous materials, such as linoleum and canvas to wood	Plastic resin glue Casein glue Contact cement
Bonding oily woods (teak, pitch pine, osage, yew)	Casein glue (sponge surface with dilute caustic soda solution 1 hour before gluing)	Plastics, metal and foil to wood	Epoxy glue

Solid corner brace fastened with nails and glue has the advantage of not adding thickness to joint, as plywood brace (above) does

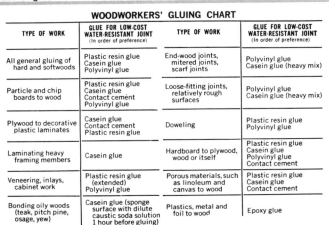

Dowels can be used to join two pieces of wood. This makes an exceptionally strong butt joint. Dowels also can be used as trim

Cabinet-making requires different joints for strength, and to hide raw edges . Butt, dado, rabbet joints are used in this drawer

Nails in nearly any finish work should be countersunk and the holes filled with wood putty. Screws also can be countersunk

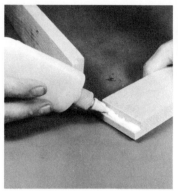

Polyvinyl is good glue for many wood joints. Always cover all the surface with a thin coating; then clamp the job until glue sets

Triangular glue blocks strengthen any construction where one piece of wood overlaps another.

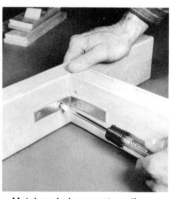

Metal angle braces strengthen butt joints. The angle must be fastened to both sides of the joint for the best holding strength

Get a tighter joint by inserting thin cardboard under one side. Run screws in other side, then remove shim. Fasten other side

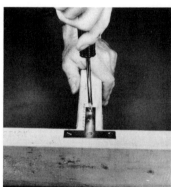

T-shaped mending plates provide same strength to butt joints as metal angles. Position plates so screws are away from the joint

Corner plate for butt joints. If metal strength is needed, but you don't want it to show, you can mortise plate and cover it

Wood tape in grain patterns hides raw edges of plywood. The tape is actually wood veneer; it is applied with contact adhesive

New epoxy glues are excellent for joining metals—especially delicate work—where solder can't be used

HOME IMPROVEMENT and maintenance projects are good investments. Not only do they improve the livability of your home, but the money spent on well-conceived projects usually comes back to you in one of two ways: 1. lower operating costs; 2. an increased return at the time you sell your home.

This is especially true of maintenance projects. Let the little things go to pot—holes in the gutters, a leaky roof, a broken driveway—and soon the entire house looks as if it will come tumbling down. One wag expressed it completely: "You use up a house—like food, almost. If you don't constantly replenish the larder, it soon will be empty."

This is true, and good evidence can be found in the slum areas of large cities—and some smaller ones, too. Of course, in many instances the homeowners—or landlords—either don't have the money to spend on maintenance or they don't care. This is not the point here; the point is that homes are indeed "devoured like food" unless they are kept in shape by a proper maintenance and improvement schedule.

Since home improvement and maintenance projects are good investments, virtually all financial institutions dealing with the public offer some form

Where do you get the money?

of home-improvement loan program. Lenders like dealing with homeowners, who tend to be stable borrowers. For example, the Federal Housing Administration (FHA) reports its losses since 1934 on almost $21 billion in remodeling loans runs less than 2 per cent.

At first look, the variety of ways to finance remodeling projects—and the larger maintenance jobs—may seem confusing. Actually, they are not, although there are many ways to "skin the cat." This section is *not* a course on financing techniques. However, it does describe some of the basics—simplified greatly—to acquaint you with the kind of programs that are available to you and how you can best take advantage of them.

Financing can be expensive, and the difference between the various plans can mean hundreds and even thousands of dollars to you in the final payoff. As in any business dealing, you should always go to a reputable lending institution for a home improvement or maintenance loan. Stay away from the quick-buck artists and the suede-shoe operators; the money they loan is easy to get but very hard to repay.

BECAUSE MOST REMODELING LOANS require interest rates of 10, 11, 12 per cent or more, it suddenly becomes obvious that if you can afford it, a straight cash payment is the best arrangement you can make. However, this might not be practical for you—as with many homeowners. However, there are several other possibilities open to you.

When you are comparison-shopping these different programs, listed and discussed in this section, you should always keep in mind the *real interest* you must pay. The Federal Truth in Lending Act, which went into effect in 1970, requires all lenders to specify exactly what the financing charges will be in terms of both *dollars* and *true interest*. If the lender does not provide you with this information right off the bat, run—don't walk —to the nearest exit. And, if you want to be a good citizen, report that "lender" to the Better Business Bureau, the Federal Reserve Board or one of the other federal agencies dealing with money and loans.

Shop for money as you would anything else. You may be surprised at some of the bargains you'll find

LOAN CHART		Type of Structure	Maximum Loan Exclusive of Financing Charges	Maximum Maturity of Note
Class of Loan	Purpose of Loan			
Class 1 (a)	Finance alterations, repairs, and improvements upon or in connection with existing structures, which substantially protect or improve the basic livability or utility	All structures[1]	$5,000	7 years and 32 days[2]
Class 1 (b)	Same as above	Structure used or to be used as dwelling for two or more families[1]	Average of $2,500 per unit not exceeding $15,000	7 years and 32 days[2]
Class 2 (a)	Finance construction of proposed structures	Nonresidential or non-farm structure	$5,000	7 years and 32 days[2]
Class 2 (b)	Finance construction of proposed structures	Nonresidential farm structure	$5,000	7 years and 32 days, or 15 years and 32 days if secured by first lien[2]

[1] If advance, exclusive of financing charge, exceeds $600 and is to finance improvements to a residential structure, the structure must have been completed and occupied for at least 90 days, unless the loan is for the construction of a civil defense shelter or for repair of a structure damaged in a major disaster.

[2] The added 32-day period is provided in order to permit the maximum of 84 or 180 monthly payments, as the case may be (in the event there should be two calendar months to the first payment).

Your first step toward borrowing money is to shop potential lenders you might deal with on a regular basis. These might include insurance companies, banks, savings and loan associations, and the credit union where you work—if your firm has one. An increasing number of credit unions have established home-improvement loan programs with interest rates substantially lower than independent or private lending institutions.

SHORT TERM/REVOLVING CREDIT

If the project in which you're involved could be considered "maintenance" (roof repairs, new gutters, paint, concrete work, screening, etc.) don't overlook the possibility of a "30-day charge" arrangement with your local building-supply outlet. As a general rule, "maintenance" materials are not very costly since you don't use a really large amount of them—150 feet of new gutters; 10 gallons of paint, and so forth. If you don't have the ready cash but know it's coming in, many dealers will postpone billing you for 30 days or so for the material. But, of course, you have to pay the full amount at that time.

In an attempt to keep up with the changing times, many building-material dealers are offering "revolving" charge accounts similar to the large general merchandise outlets. Here, you are permitted to charge up to a certain amount at the store—usually from $300 to $500—and pay it back in installments. For example, if you charge $100 worth of materials, you pay back $10 per month, plus interest, on the unpaid balance. As your balance drops, you can re-charge more materials up to the top amount. But be advised that the interest rate on this type arrangement can be very high. Usually it is 18 per cent per year—or 1½ per cent of the unpaid balance per month. Again, the Truth in Lending Act comes into play here; the dealer has to tell you exactly the amount of interest you are paying for, in effect, using his money. If you pay the bill in full before the specified pay-back time, there usually is no interest charge.

Since there are so many specialized programs these days, it is impossible to pinpoint for you here what the current practice is in your area. Generally, the above statements are true, but be sure to check carefully any financing arrangements with a building-material dealer before you sign any paper.

Your building-supply dealer may be an overlooked source of credit

INSURANCE LOANS

Don't overlook your own life-insurance policy as a possibility for a home improvement loan. It can provide you with an attractive, low-cost source of money that can be used for remodeling purposes.

Many insurance companies will loan you 95 per cent of the *cash value* (*not* the face value) of your policy at interest rates not exceeding 6 per cent—the legal limit (1971) they can charge. Your insurance agent or broker should be able to provide you with answers to your questions on amounts, rates, and terms within a day or two after he is contacted.

Maximum Maturity of Refinanced Note	Maximum Financing Charge (including FHA insurance charge)[3]	Insurance Premium (to be included in maximum financing charge)
7 years and 32 days (not more than 12 years from date of original note)	$5.50 discount per $100 of face amount per year on first $2500 $4.50 on amount above $2500	0.50% per year of amount advanced
7 years and 32 days (not more than 12 years from date of original note)	$5.50 discount per $100 of face amount per year on first $2500 $4.50 on amount above $2500	0.50% per year of amount advanced
7 years and 32 days (not more than 12 years from date of original note)	$5.50 discount per $100 of face amount per year on first $2500 $4.50 on amount above $2500	0.50% per year of amount advanced
7 years and 32 days (not more than 12 years from date of original note), or 15 years and 32 days if original and refinanced note are both secured by first lien (not exceeding 25 years from date of original note)	$5.50 discount per $100 of face amount per year on first $2500 $4.50 on amount above $2500 $3.50 on loans having a maturity over 7 years and 32 days	0.50% per year of amount advanced

3 If insured takes security, borrower may be required to pay recording fees and cost of title search, but these may not be paid out of proceeds of loan or included in face amount of note.

OPEN-END MORTGAGES

You may have an "open-end clause" in your original house mortgage. If you do, it can provide you with a ready and, often, a low cost source of remodeling funds.

Open-end provisions normally allow you to re-borrow money *equal to the mortgage principal* you have paid off. This money generally is available at the original interest rate of the mortgage, which can save you a significant amount of money.

For example, if you took an open-end mortgage of $20,000 on your home initially, but have reduced it to $13,000, this means that the same lender will allow you to borrow $7,000, restoring the mortgage to its original amount of $20,000 outstanding.

DISBURSEMENT OF ELIGIBLE LOANS

FH-1
Rev. 8/68

U.S. DEPARTMENT OF HOUSING AND URBAN DEVELOPMENT
FEDERAL HOUSING ADMINISTRATION

Form Approved
Budget Bureau No. 63–R037.10

CREDIT APPLICATION FOR PROPERTY IMPROVEMENT LOAN

This application is submitted to obtain credit under the provisions of Title I of the National Housing Act
(PLEASE ANSWER ALL QUESTIONS)

TO: Lending Institution which will provide the funds: **The Doe Bank**	Date **10-15-68**

1. Do you have any past due obligations owed to or insured by any agency of the Federal Government? *(If the answer is "Yes", you are not eligible to apply for an FHA Title I Loan until the existing debt has been brought current.)*   ☐ Yes ☐ No

2. Have you any other application for an FHA Title I Improvement Loan pending at this time? ☐ Yes ☒ No *(If yes, with whom-name and address.)*

3. I hereby apply for a loan of: $ **3,500** *(Net)*
To be repaid in **84** Months

4. APPLICANT ➔

Name **John Smith**	Age **35**	Marital status **Married**		Number of dependents **2**
Address **000 A Street Washington, D.C.**	How long **7**	Name—Wife/Husband **Mary**	Age **28**	Home phone **734-7956**
Previous address **000 3rd Street Washington, D. C.**	How long **3**	Name and address of nearest relative not living with you **Allen Smith 000 B Avenue, Wash. D.C.**		Relationship **Father**

5. EMPLOYMENT AND SALARIES: *(If applicant self-employed, submit current financial statement.)*

Employer—Name and business address **Universal Gear Co 000 42nd Street, Wash. D.C.**	Type of work or position **Gear Mfg. Assistant Eng.**	No. of years **8**	Business phone **894-4000**	Salary *(Week/Month)* **$1,000 per Mo.**
Previous employer—Name and business address **Dorks Electric Co. 000 5th Street, Washington D. C.**				
Wife's employer—Name and business address **None**	Type of work or position	No. of years	Business phone	Salary *(Week/Month)* **$ per**
Other income—Source *(List)* **None**				Amount *(Week/Month)* **$**

6. BANK ACCOUNT:

☒ Yes ☐ No   ☒ Checking   ☐ Savings   Name and address—Bank or branch **ABC Bank**

7. CREDIT ACCOUNTS: *(Give name and address of finance companies or stores which have extended credit and which you have paid in full.)*

a. **Allied Furniture Co.**	b. **Jones Department Store**
c. **Atlas Drug Company**	d.

8. DEBTS. List all fixed obligations, installment accounts, FHA loans, and debts to banks, finance companies, and Government agencies. *(If more space needed, list all additional debts on an attached sheet)*

FHA ins. Yes	FHA ins. No	To whom indebted *(Name)*	City and State	Date incurred	Original amount	Present balance	Monthly payments	Amount past due
		Mortgage/Contract						
	X	American Mortgage	Washington, D.C.	5-'60	$ 14,000	$ 11,500	$ 98	$ none
	X	Personal Loan Company	Washington, D.C.	1-'68	$ 300	$ 210	$ 10	$ none
					$	$	$	$
					$	$	$	$
					$	$	$	$
Auto		Lien holder **East Side Bank**		Year and make **1965 Ford**		$ 730	$ 30	$ none

(Reserved for use of Lending Institution.)

Term *(In Months)*	_____
No. of payments	_____
Amt. of mo. payts.	$ _____
Amount of note	$ _____
Discount	$ _____
Net proceeds	$ _____

APPENDIX 2.   FH-1   CREDIT APPLICATION FOR PROPERTY IMPROVEMENT LOAN (REVERSE)

DISBURSEMENT OF ELIGIBLE LOANS

FH-1 Rev. 8/68

9. PROPERTY TO BE IMPROVED

If this is a residential structure, has it been completed and occupied for 90 days or longer?   ☒ Yes   ☐ No

Address (Number, street, city and State)		Type—(Home) apt., store, farm, etc., (If apt., no. of units)	Date purchased
000 A Street Washington, D. C.			May, 1960

FILL IN ONE

Is owned by:	Name of title holder: John and Mary Smith		Date of mortgage: May 1960	Price paid: $ 14,500
Is being bought on installment contract by:	Name of purchaser	Name and address of title holder		Price paid: $
Is leased to:	Name of lessee			Date lease expires
Name of landlord		Address		Rent per month: $

10. PROCEEDS OF THIS LOAN WILL BE USED TO IMPROVE THE DESCRIBED PROPERTY AS FOLLOWS:

Describe each improvement planned	Name and address contractor/dealer	Estimated cost
Build additional room	A B C Improvement Company	$ 3,500
	Washington, D.C.	$

Maximum charges for Title I loans are fixed by law. Interest and insurance premium charges may not exceed (A) an amount with respect to so much of the net proceeds thereof as does not exceed $2,500, equivalent to $5.50 discount per $100 of original face amount of a 1-year note payable in equal monthly installments, plus (B) an amount, with respect to any portion of the net proceeds thereof in excess of $2,500, equivalent to $4.50 discount per $100 of original face amount of such note. These charges should not be interpreted as simple interest charges, examples of which are set out in the following table based on monthly payments, the first payment being due 1 month from the date of the note.

Title I Property Improvement Loans With Equal Monthly Payments to Principal and Interest

AMOUNT OF ADVANCE	12 MONTH LOAN			24 MONTH LOAN			36 MONTH LOAN			48 MONTH LOAN			60 MONTH LOAN			72 MONTH LOAN			84 MONTH LOAN		
	Monthly payment	Equiv-alent interest rate	Total cost of interest	Monthly payment	Equiv-alent interest rate	Total cost of interest	Monthly payment	Equiv-alent interest rate	Total cost of interest	Monthly payment	Equiv-alent interest rate	Total cost of interest	Monthly payment	Equiv-alent interest rate	Total cost of interest	Monthly payment	Equiv-alent interest rate	Total cost of interest	Monthly payment	Equiv-alent interest rate	Total cost of interest
$500	$44.10	10.57%	$29	$23.17	10.40%	$56	$16.19	10.24%	$83	$12.71	10.09%	$110	$10.61	9.94%	$137	$9.22	9.81%	$163	$8.22	9.68%	$190
$1,000	88.19	10.57	58	46.34	10.40	112	32.38	10.24	166	25.41	10.09	219	21.22	9.94	273	18.43	9.81	327	16.44	9.68	381
$1,500	132.29	10.57	87	69.51	10.40	168	48.57	10.24	248	38.12	10.09	329	31.83	9.94	410	27.65	9.81	490	24.66	9.68	571
$2,500	220.46	10.57	146	115.83	10.40	280	80.95	10.24	414	63.51	10.09	548	53.05	9.94	683	46.08	9.81	817	41.09	9.68	951
$5,000	438.61	9.58	263	229.44	9.44	506	159.71	9.30	749	124.85	9.18	992	103.93	9.06	1,236	89.99	8.94	1,479	80.03	8.83	1,722

WARNING

Any person who knowingly makes a false statement or a misrepresentation in this application or causes such a false statement or misrepresentation to be made shall be subject to a fine of not more than $5000 or by imprisonment for not more than 2 years, or both, under provisions of the United States Criminal Code.

IMPORTANT—APPLICANT READ BEFORE SIGNING

The selection of a Contractor or Dealer, acceptance of materials used, and work performed is your responsibility. Neither the FHA nor the Financial Institution guarantees the material or workmanship nor inspects the work performed.

I (We) certify that the above statements are true, accurate, and complete to the best of my (our) knowledge and belief. This application shall remain the property of the Lending Institution to which submitted for the purpose of obtaining a loan.

I (We) hereby consent to and authorize the Lending Institution or the FHA, after the giving of reasonable notice, to enter the improved property for the purpose of determining that the improvements specified in this application have been completed.

Name *John Smith* (LS)   Name *Mary Smith* (LS)
(Applicant)   (Applicant)

NOTE TO SALESMEN: If proceeds will be disbursed to the Contractor/Dealer, the person(s) selling the above described improvements must sign the following certification.

I (We) certify that: 1—I (We) am (are) the person(s) who sold the job. 2—The Contract contains the whole agreement with the borrower. 3—The borrower has not been given or promised a cash payment or rebate nor has it been represented to the borrower that he will receive a cash bonus or commission on future sales as an inducement for the consummation of this transaction; that the improvements have not been misrepresented; that there are no guarantees beyond those of the manufacturer; no promises impossible of attainment; no encouragement of trial purchases; no promise that the improvements will be used as a model for advertising or other demonstration purposes; and no offer of debt consolidation.

(LS) Name *Joseph Brown*
(My true name and signature are as shown above)

If application is prepared by one other than the applicant, the person preparing the application must sign below. I (We) certify that the statements made herein are based upon information given to me (us) by the borrower(s) and are accurate to the best of my (our) knowledge and belief.

Prepared by: _____   Address _____
(Signature of preparer other than borrower)

Representing: _____
(Name of Dealer/Contractor)

Where Does the Remodeling Dollar Go?

	% of Loans	% of Dollars	Average Total
Additions & Alterations	20.9%	28.6¢	$2,007
Exterior Finishing	16.4	19.8	1,765
Interior Finishing	14.4	17.0	1,731
Roofing	6.4	4.4	1,005
Plumbing	9.8	5.6	838
Heating & Air Conditioning	13.6	11.2	1,201
Insulations	6.2	2.9	686
Miscellaneous & Non-Residential	12.3	10.5	1,436
	100.0%	$1.00	$1,463*

* A sign of the inflationary trends in building is revealed by the fact that in 1950 the average loan was for $479.

RECASTING EXISTING MORTGAGES

Many lenders take a favorable look at a home-owner refinancing his present mortgage—especially for a sound home-improvement program.

Here, the cost of the project is normally added to the *outstanding balance* (principal) of the old mortgage. However, a new mortgage, complete with a new schedule of payments and interest rates, usually is created.

In this situation you should *carefully* evaluate the impact of this arrangement on your present mortgage. That mortgage probably carries a lower interest rate—especially if it is several years old—than you would have to pay for the same mortgage today. If your present mortgage is relatively small, and if your project is relatively large, recasting can offer you definite savings advantages.

CONVENTIONAL HOME-IMPROVEMENT LOANS

Savings and loan associations, commercial, and mutual savings banks usually provide a variety of remodeling loan programs. The programs can vary widely from one lender to another, however. All are influenced by the general availability of money and related economic conditions.

One good way to scout the availability of money for remodeling loans is to check financial advertising in your local newspaper. As a rule, if the

Check your present mortgage; you may be able to refinance it for further improvements

goose hangs high, the savings associations and banks blast away about how great their individual home-improvement loan departments are. If money is tight, you won't see much advertising to this effect.

Even so, you should always investigate several different lending institutions personally, and compare their home-improvement loans in detail. Although money may be tight at the time, your individual circumstances and particular home improvement may be the type a lender is looking for at that specific time.

BANK LOANS/CONTRACT FINANCING

Two other common forms of financing are the *personal* (secured and unsecured) *loan* from a bank and a *contract* or arranged financing program. Both of these tend to be higher in cost (interest) than the other loan forms listed in this section.

However, both types usually offer you a high degree of convenience and a minimum of red tape. *Know this:* Remodeling industry experts warn you to avoid consolidation of any other existing loans with a home-improvement loan. And be very, very cautious about allowing a contractor to place a lien on the property when arranging any financing for you. Both are common techniques for defrauding homeowners, and you can be in a trap before you realize what has happened.

LOANS FROM GENERAL MERCHANDISE STORES

Such merchandising greats as Montgomery Ward and Sears, Roebuck and Co., have a form of home-improvement "loan" which can be very valuable to you for small repairs and some big-ticket projects.

Generally (and we'd like to underline "generally" since the plans do vary somewhat), you can take advantage of a revolving charge account, a payment plan program, and a modernizing credit plan.

The revolving charge account is similar to many others now in operation. You have charge privileges and there is no finance charge if the bill is paid within 25 days of the store's billing date. Or,

Americans Are Taking a Longer Time to Pay Off Home Improvement Loans

	Number of Loans		
	1968	1960	1950
6 Payments	0.3%	0.5%	0.8%
12 Payments	6.1	8.8	10.1
18 Payments	2.9	5.0	6.0
24 Payments	11.9	13.0	10.2
30 Payments	1.5	2.1	9.8
36 Payments	24.2	44.2	62.5
48 Payments	5.7	2.6	0.1
60 Payments	45.5	23.3	0.4
60 Plus	1.9	0.5	0.2
Median	48.5 Payments	36.7 Payments	36.4 Payments

you can spread the payments over many months—with a financing charge—usually 1½ per cent per month—or 18 per cent per year.

The so-tagged *"easy payment plan"* actually *is* an easy payment plan—giving you up to 36 months to pay, depending upon what you purchase. Home appliances and some building materials are usually included in this package; you have to check it out, however.

One plan (Sears) is called the *Modernizing Credit Plan*. This gives you up to five years to pay back the money when you use the merchandise to repair and improve your home. A bonus feature is the opportunity of adding home-modernizing merchandise to your account at any time without having to go through ribbons of red tape.

THE FEDERALLY-INSURED LOAN

If your remodeling project can be handled for $5000 or less, you should investigate the possibility of getting an *FHA Title Insured Loan*. Under Title I of the National Housing Act, FHA is authorized to insure up to 90 per cent of remodeling loans that make homes "more useful or habitable."

In addition to the obvious eligible additions and alterations, other improvements such as grading, landscaping, permanent sprinkler systems, driveways, and sidewalks also qualify in the eyes of the federal government. Luxury improvements, such as a swimming pool, tennis court, outdoor

You can't get a government-insured loan for a swimming pool, but you can for a good many other improvement projects

barbecue, your own golf putting green, etc., are not eligible.

The Title I program is available through 8200 federally approved lenders in all areas of the United States; it can offer you many advantages. Here are some of the features:

• Loans are usually made solely on your signature basis—without additional security or cosigners.

• There is no reason to adjust or disturb any existing mortgage loans on your property.

• You must meet only three simple requirements: you must own your own property or hold a long-term lease that extends at least six months beyond the loan payment period . . . have income sufficient to handle payments . . . have a satisfactory credit rating.

• Loan coverages can be flexible covering only materials, if desired, and they also can be extended to the architectural and engineering fees as well as building permits. This can be a very important feature to you in large remodeling such as a room addition or carport conversion.

• Only three forms are necessary for complete processing of your loan. These are an application form, the note itself, and a completion form, if the work or materials are furnished by a dealer or contractor. Authorized lenders can normally approve a loan within a matter of several days; you don't have to spend weeks waiting, as some persons believe.

• You are protected by FHA requirements, which force the lender to screen and approve the contractor, if you're using a contractor for part of the work. And, if there is a problem, you can take your problem directly to FHA's Title I Consumer Protection Division, which has been known to call in the Federal Bureau of Investigation (FBI) to probe instances of federal fraud.

As a piece of background, the Title I program has proved remarkably successful since it was initiated in 1934. Through the first half of 1971, FHA had insured more than 30 million remodeling loans worth almost $21 billion to American homeowners. In recent years, however, activity has declined because of the ceiling of 10.57 per cent interest allowed on the loans.

Please note that you *don't borrow money*

U. S. DEPARTMENT OF HOUSING AND URBAN DEVELOPMENT
FEDERAL HOUSING ADMINISTRATION

COMPLETION CERTIFICATE FOR PROPERTY IMPROVEMENT LOAN

(UNDER FHA TITLE I)

WORK DONE OR MATERIALS DELIVERED

TO: (Financial Institution)   Address

The Doe Bank   *Washington, D.C.*

In accordance with my (our) credit application dated *October 15, 1968* , for a loan pursuant to the provisions
Title I of the National Housing Act:

I (We) certify that I (we) have not been given or promised a cash payment or rebate nor has it been represented to me (us) that I (we)
will receive a cash bonus or commission on future sales as an inducement for the consummation of this transaction.

I (We) understand that the selection of the dealer and the acceptance of the materials used and the work performed is my (our) responsibility and that neither the FHA nor the financial institution guarantees the material or workmanship or inspects the work performed.

CHECK HERE IF LOAN IS TO PAY FOR COST OF MATERIALS AND INSTALLATIONS.

[☑] I (We) hereby certify that all articles and materials have been furnished and installed and the work satisfactorily completed on prem-
ises indicated in my (our) credit application.

CHECK HERE IF LOAN COVERS ONLY THE PURCHASE OF MATERIALS

[ ] I (We) hereby acknowledge receipt in satisfactory condition of the materials described in my (our) credit application.

		SIGNATURES OF BORROWERS	DATE SIGNED
NOTICE **TO** **BORROWER**	<u>DO NOT SIGN</u> THIS CERTIFI-CATE UNTIL THE DEALER HAS COMPLETED THE WORK AND/OR DELIVERED THE MATERIALS IN ACCORDANCE WITH THE TERMS OF YOUR CONTRACT OR SALES AGREEMENT.	*(Read Before Signing)* *John Smith* *(Read Before Signing)* *Mary Smith*	*11/15/68* *11/15/68*

For the purpose of inducing the payment of proceeds of this loan and the insurance thereof by the FHA the undersigned certifies and
warrants that:

(1) The above work or materials constitute the entire consideration for which this loan is made.

(2) A copy of the contract or sales agreement has been delivered to the borrower and the above financial institution.

(3) This contract contains the whole agreement with the borrower.

(4) As an inducement for the consummation of this transaction, the borrower has not been given or promised a cash payment or rebate
nor has it been represented to the borrower that he will receive a cash bonus or commission on future sales.

(5) The work has been satisfactorily completed or materials delivered.

(6) The above certificate was signed by the borrower after such completion or delivery.

(7) The signatures hereon and on the note are genuine.

(8) All bills for labor or materials have been or will be paid within 60 days and that the improvements had not been misrepresented
to the borrower.

If any of the above representations prove incorrect, the undersigned agrees to promptly repurchase the note from the financial institution or from the FHA as the case may be.

	Name of Dealer	Date
DEALER **SIGN** **HERE**	*P. B. C. Improvement Co.* Signature *J. B. Stone*	*11/15/68* Title *Owner*

WARNING

Any person who knowingly makes a false statement or a misrepresentation in this certificate shall be subject to a fine of not more
than $5,000 or to imprisonment for not more than 2 years, or both, under provisions of the United States Criminal Code.

434

directly from the government. Instead, you borrow it from a government-approved lender. The government simply guarantees that you'll pay back the money. Therefore the risk to the lender is lower, and he should be willing to loan money at a lower interest rate.

However, many lenders, especially in higher interest areas such as the West, feel the interest ceiling is too low after they deduct ½ per cent to pay the insurance premiums, which cannot be passed on to the borrower in any form. If you are interested in getting a Title I loan, contact any one of the 72 FHA field offices for a list of approved lenders in this area. You'll find the listing in the telephone book. Or ask directory assistance.

If you do not want, or you cannot qualify for, a Title I loan, the FHA cautions that you should make sure exactly what interest you will be paying on another type loan, and if it exceeds the FHA ceiling, find out why it does.

In addition, FHA recommends that you be able to answer these questions:

1. What is the total cost of the job?

2. What is the interest rate and what does it total?

3. What service charges or fees are involved?

4. How many payments of what size will be needed to pay off the loan?

Here are four questions that the FHA suggests you be ready to answer

CONSTRUCTION LOANS AND MORTGAGES

Generally speaking, a construction loan is money that is loaned by a savings and loan association, bank, or other financial institution to a *builder*—not a homeowner. The builder uses this money to purchase the materials he needs to build a house and pay his crew wages during the building period.

When the house is completed, the builder puts it up for sale. He has an "asking price" for the house and lot, and when he makes a sale, he takes the money from the sale and repays the construction loan. If there is any money left over, this is the builder's profit. When the homeowner buys the house and lot from the builder, he receives a *mortgage* from the bank, savings and loan association, insurance firm, or other lender. The mortgage money is repaid to the lender over a period of time—usually 20–30 years in equal installments.

Therefore, *construction loans* are indeed construction loans; mortgages are loans on real property that are repaid over a long period of time. Construction loans are paid in one lump payment.

BORROWING MONEY

For many persons, borrowing money from a savings and loan association, bank, or other type of lending institution is a very apprehensive thing to do.

Many persons would rather go to the dentist or have open-heart surgery than go into a bank and ask for a loan of $2500 to fix up the house or put on a room addition.

This, generally speaking, is an image that has grown up through the Great Depression days. You get a mental picture of some banker in a stovepipe hat knocking at the door to foreclose on the mortgage, while the kids are half-starving in the kitchen.

This, of course, is not a true image, but the image is so strong that many persons will pay extra, super interest rates to somewhat shady loan companies to finance a project simply because they are frightened to go to a qualified savings and loan or bank. Many loan companies have really "merchandised" the fact that "money is easy to borrow from us," and the fact is that it usually *is* easy to borrow the money—but at very high interest rates. This, however, is not *always* the case. Shop around.

William D. McGuire, Assistant Vice President of the Lake View Trust and Savings Bank of Chicago, sums it up this way:

"Banks and other financial institutions that loan money are in the *business* of loaning money. It is how we make our money—loaning it out. It pays our salaries, pays our overhead, and pays our savers a dividend or earnings on their savings accounts, certificates of deposit, etc."

McGuire adds that any homeowner who has a project he wants to complete should not be frightened to talk with any financial institution about it.

Banks and other lending institutions are in the business of lending money; don't hesitate to approach them

YOU'RE DEEP INTO A REMODELING PROJECT and you run into a special materials problem. The clerk at your local lumberyard can't solve the problem—he doesn't even know what you're talking about.

This is not an uncommon situation for the do-it-yourselfer today—especially since there are more than 500,000 different building products manufactured and distributed in the United States.

Although you will find most of the answers to your maintenance and improvement problems in this book, you may suddenly find yourself with a unique problem requiring specialized information.

This section is devoted to helping solve such problems; it lists manufacturers of various building materials; and the brand and or trade names of specific products.

Space here, of course, prohibits the listing of every manufacturer. We have, however, attempted to compile a composite listing that is representative.

When writing to a manufacturer, address your letter to "Director of Customer Relations." The state abbreviations shown below are those recommended by the Federal Government for use with zip codes.

Where to go to solve special problems

ABRASIVES

American-Lincoln Corp., 518 S. St. Clair St., Toledo, OH 43603

Armour Industrial Products Co., Abrasives Division, 16123 Armour St., NE, Alliance, OH 44601

Carborundum Co., Box 477, Niagara Falls, NY 14302

Red Devil, Inc. 2400 Vauxhall Rd., Union, NJ 07083

3M Company, 3M Center, St. Paul, MN 55101

United Mineral & Chemical Corp., 129 Hudson St., New York, NY 10013

Williams Co., 251 W. High St., London, OH 43140

ACCESS DOORS

Advance Metal Products, Inc., 2445 N.W. 76th St., Miami, FL 33147

Bilco Co., P.O. Box 1203, New Haven, Conn. 06505

Challenger Mfg. Co. 342 N. Royal St., Jackson, TN

Leigh Products, Inc., 1969 Lee St., Coopersville, MI

Majestic Co., Inc. 516 Erie St., Huntington, IN

Miami-Carey Div., Philip Carey Corp., 320 S. Wayne Ave., Cincinnati, OH 45215

Republic Steel Corp., Mfg. Div., 1315 Albert St., Youngstown, OH 44505

Superior Fireplace Co., 4325 Artesia Ave., Fullerton, CA 92633

Weyerhaeuser Co. (Wood Prods. Group) Tacoma Bldg., Tacoma, WA 98401

ACCESSORIES, BATHROOM

Aetna Plumbing Industries, Inc., 4701 W. Augusta Blvd., Chicago, IL 60651

American Standard, 40 W. 40th St., New York, NY

Barclay Industries, Inc., 65 Industrial Rd., Lodi, NJ 07644

Crane Co., 4100 S. Kedzie Ave., Chicago, IL 60632

General Bathroom Products Corp., 2201 Touhy, Elk Grove Village, IL 60007

Hall Mack (A Textron Co.) 801 W. 8th St., Cincinnati, OH 45203

Hirsh Co. (The) 8051 Central Park, Skokie, IL

Hoover Bathroom Accessories, 425 Frank St., Fowlerville, MI

Miami-Carey Div., Philip Carey Corp., 320 S. Wayne Ave., Cincinnati, OH 45215

Mirro-Chrome Co., Inc., P.O. Box 315, Garnerville, NY

Mosaic Tile Co., P.O. Box 999, Florence, AL 35630

Plumb Shop, 620 Fisher Bldg., Detroit, MI 48202

Schaul Mfg. Co., 796 E. 105th St., Cleveland, OH

Ador-Hilite (Sub Rusco Industries, Inc.) 2401 W. Commonwealth Ave., Fullerton, CA 92634

Filon Div., Vistron Corp., 12333 S. Van Ness Ave., Hawthorne, CA 90250

Basement repairs, new partition walls, retaining walls, borders, and other projects are possible with "hard materials" such as concrete blocks, cinder blocks, stone, bricks, cement. Buy individual units for your small requirements; buy pallets for large jobs

K-Lux Products Div., KSH, Inc., 10091 Manchester Rd., St. Louis, MO 63122

Rusco Industries, Inc. 1100 Glendon Ave., Los Angeles, CA 90024

Shower Door Co. of America, P.O. Box 20202, Atlanta, GA

Showerfold Div., Kinkead Industries, Inc., 5858 N. Pulaski Rd., Chicago, IL 60646

Tub-Master Corp., 413 Virginia Dr., Orlando, FL

Weather-Tile/Aristocrat Divs., Pacific Coast Co., 7103 Krick Rd., Cleveland, OH 044146

ACOUSTICAL BOARD AND TILE

Armstrong Cork Co., 6402 Roosevelt, Lancaster, PA

Barclay Industries, Inc., 65 Industrial Rd., Lodi, NJ 07644

Bestwall Gypsum Div., Georgia-Pacific Corp., P.O. Box 311, Portland, OR 97207

Celotex Corp., 1500 N. Dale Mabry, Tampa, FL

Certain-Teed Products Corp., 120 E. Lancaster St., Ardmore, PA 19003

Conwed Corp., 332 Minnesota St., St. Paul, MN

Cook Paint & Varnish Co., 1412 Knox, North Kansas City, MO 64116

Evans Prods. Co., Fiber Prods. Div.,

P.O. Box E, Corvallis, OR 97330

Flintkote Co., 400 Westchester Ave., White Plains, NY

Insulite Div. of Boise Cascade Corp., Northstar Center, Minneapolis, MN 55402

Johns-Manville Corp., 22 E. 40th St., New York, NY

K-Lux Products Div., KSH, Inc. 10091 Manchester Rd., St. Louis, MO 63122

Macklanburg-Duncan Co., 4041 N. Sante Fe, Oklahoma City, OK 73125

Marlite Division of Masonite Corp., Dover, OH

National Gypsum Co., 325 Delaware St., Buffalo, NY

Pacesetter Products, Inc. 1515 Spring St., Houston, TX 77001

Simpson Timber Co., 2000 Washington Bldg., Seattle, WA

U. S. Gypsum Co., 101 S. Wacker Dr., Chicago, IL

BOARD/TILE, DECORATIVE

Artcrest Products Co., Inc., 401 W. Ontario St., Chicago, IL 60610

B & L Lighting Co., P.O. Box 71, Blue Hills Sta., Hartford, CT 06112

Barclay Industries, Inc., 65 Industrial Rd., Lodi, NJ 07644

Certain-Teed Products Corp., 120 E. Lancaster St., Ardmore, PA 19003

Diffusa-Lite Co., 1 Forrest St., Conshohocken, PA

Emerson Electric Co., 8100 W. Florissant St., St. Louis, MO 63136

Filon Div., Vistron Corp., 12333 S. Van Ness Ave., Hawthorne, CA 60250

General Plastics Corp., 1400 N. Washington St., Marion, IN

Hastings Aluminum Products, 429 S. Michigan St., Hastings, MI 49058

Kemlite Corp., 101 N. Republic Ave., Joliet, IL

K-Lux Products Div., KSH, Inc., 10091 Manchester Rd., St. Louis, MO 63122

Laminated Plastics, Inc., 1610 S. Buder Industrial Drive, St. Louis, MO 63144

Metallic Plastics Corp., 300 Madison Ave., New York, NY 10017

National Gypsum Co., 325 Delaware St., Buffalo, NY

Owens-Corning Fiberglas Corp., P.O. Box 901, Toledo, OH 43601

Pacesetter Products, Inc., 1515 Spring St., Houston, TX 77001

ACOUSTICAL PLASTER

Bestwall Gypsum Div. Georgia-Pacific Corp., P.O. Box 311, Portland, OR 97207

Larsen Products Corp., Box 5938, Bethesda, MD 20014

Perlite Institute, Inc., 45 W. 45th St., New York, NY 10036

U. S. Gypsum Co., 101 S. Wacker Dr., Chicago, IL

ADHESIVES

Afco Products, Inc., 44 Park St., Somerville, MA

Anti-Hydro Waterproofing Co., 265 Badger Ave., Newark, NJ 07108

Armstrong Cork Co., 6420 Roosevelt, Lancaster, PA

Azrock Floor Products, Box 531, San Antonio, TX

Barclay Industries, Inc., 65 Industrial Rd., Lodi, NJ 07644

Bestwall Gypsum Div. Georgia-Pacific Corp., P.O. Box 311, Portland, OR 97207

Borden, Inc., Chemical Div., 350 Madison Ave., New York, NY 10017

Bruce (E. L.) Co., Box 397, Memphis, TN 38101

Carey (Philip) Corp., 320 S. Wayne Ave., Cincinnati, OH

Celotex Corp., 1500 N. Dale Mabry, Tampa, FL 33607

Consoweld Corp., 700 Hooker St., Wisconsin Rapids, WI

DAP, Inc., 5300 Huberville Rd., Dayton, OH 45401

Dow-Corning Corp., Consumer Products Division, P.O. Box 592, Midland, MI 48641

DuPont (E. I.) de Nemours & Co., Product Info Section, Wilmington, DE 19898

Formica Corp., 4614 Spring Grove Ave., Cincinnati, OH

Franklin Glue Co., 2020 Bruck St., Columbus, OH

Fuller (H. B.) Co., 2400 Kasota Ave., St. Paul, MN

GAF Corporation, Building Products Div., 140 W. 51st St., New York, NY 10020

General Electric Co., Silicone Prods. Dept., Waterford, NY

Goodrich (B. F.) Co., 500 S. Main St., Akron, OH

Goodyear Tire & Rubber Co., 1144 E. Market St., Akron, OH

Grace (W. R.) & Co. (Construction Products Div.) 62 Whittemore Ave., Cambridge, MA 02140

Larsen Products Corp., Box 5938, Bethesda, MD 20014

Macco Adhesives Div., The Glidden-Durkee Co., 30400 Lakeland Blvd., Wickliffe, OH 44092

National Casein Co., 601 W. 80th St., Chicago, IL

PPG Industries, Inc., Adhesive Products, 225 Belleville Ave., Bloomfield, NJ 07003

Standard Dry Wall Prods., 7800 NW 38th St., Miami, FL

Technical Adhesives, Inc., 315 S. Hicks Rd., Palatine, IL

3M Company, 3M Center, St. Paul, MN 55101

Wilhold Glues, Inc., 8707 Millergrove Dr., Santa Fe Springs, CA 90670

Woodhill Chemical Co., 18731 Cranwood Parkway, Cleveland, OH 44128

AEROSOL PAINTS

Bruning Paint Co., Inc., Fleet and Haven Sts., Baltimore, MD 21224

Cook Paint & Varnish Co., 1412 Knox, North Kansas City, MO 64116

DuPont (E. I.) de Nemours & Co.,

Product Info. Section, Wilmington DE 19898

Enterprise Paint Mfg. Co., 2841 S. Ashland Ave., Chicago, IL 60608

Illinois Bronze Powder & Paint Co., 300 E. Main St., Lake Zurich, IL 60047

Lowe Bros. Co., 424 E. 3rd, Dayton, OH 45402

Martin-Senour Co., 2500 S. Senour Ave., Chicago, IL 60608

O'Brien Corp., 2001 W. Washington St., South Bend, IN 46621

Pratt & Lambert, 75 Tonawanda St., Buffalo, NY

Rust-Oleum Corp., 2301 Oakton St., Evanston, IL

AGGREGATES, PERLITE

Grace (W. R.) & Co., (Construction Products Div.) 62 Whittemore Ave., Cambridge, MA 02140

Johns-Manville Corp., 22 E. 40th St., New York, NY

Perlite Institute, Inc., 45 W. 45th St., New York, NY

AGGREGATES, VERMICULITE

Grace (W. R.) & Co., (Construction Products Div.) 62 Whittemore Ave., Cambridge, MA 02140

Zonolite-W. R. Grace & Co., P.O. Box 14279, Phoenix, AZ 85031

ANCHOR NAILS AND BOLTS

Armco Steel Corp, 7000 Roberts St., Kansas City, MO

Bethlehem Steel Corp., 701 E. Third St., Bethlehem, PA

Cleveland Steel Specialty Co., 14435 Industrial Ave., S., Cleveland, OH 44137

Hilwood Mfg. Co., 21700 St. Clair St., Cleveland, OH

Precut lumber is offered by most building-material outlets: You don't have to buy a 2 x 6 x 8-ft. piece of board to get a 2 x 6 x 6-ft. piece, for example. If possible, pick and choose the lumber by piece so you can eliminate twists, warps, knots and blemishes

Independent Nail, Inc., 106 Hale St., Bridgewater, MA

Ramset Fastening Systems, Winchester Group Olin, 289 Winchester Ave., New Haven, CT 06504

Rawlplug Co., Inc., 200 Petersville Rd., New Rochelle, NY

Redi-Bolt, Inc., 5334 Indianapolis Blvd., East Chicago, IN 46312

Star Expansion Industries, Mountainville, NY

USM Corp., Consumer Prods. Center, 221 Oley St., Reading, PA 19601

Wilmod Co., Inc., 200 W. 57th St., New York, NY

ANCHORS, PLASTIC

AEG Tool Div., (Ferrostaal Overseas Corp.) 37–26 13th St., Long Island City, NY 11101

Holub Industries, 473 Elm St., Sycamore, IL 60178

Jordan Industries, Inc., 3030 N.W. 75th St., Miami, FL

Miracle Adhesives Corp., 250 Pettit Ave., Bellmore, L.I., NY

U. S. Expansion Bolt Co., 500 State St., York, PA

USM Corp., Consumer Prods. Center, 221 Oley St., Reading, PA 19601

ANCHORS, POST

Advance Metal Prods., Inc., 2445 N.W. 76th, Miami, FL

Cleveland Steel Specialty Co., 14435 Industrial Ave., S, Cleveland, OH 44137

United Steel Products Co., 8400 Pillsbury Ave., Minneapolis, MN 55420

Weatherguard Service, Inc. 2339 Chatterton Ave., New York, NY 10462

ANCHORS, STONE AND BRICK

A A Wire Products Co., 6100 S. New England Ave., Chicago, IL 60638

Bieler National Industries, 45-B Gilpin Ave., Haupauge, NY 11787

Cleveland Steel Specialty Co., 14435 Industrial Ave., S., Cleveland, OH 44137

Decor Mfg. Co., Box 264, Alliance, OH 44601

Dur-O-Wal National, Inc., 650 Twelfth Ave., S.W., Cedar Rapids, IA 52404

Harris, Inc., 200 E. Long, Columbus, OH 43215

Kees (F. D.) Mfg. Co., P.O. Box 523, Beatrice, NE

Lustre Line Prods. Co., Richmond & Norris St., Philadelphia, PA 19125

Ten Point Trim Corp., 1200 E. 52nd St., Indianapolis, IN

ANGLES AND CHANNELS

Armco Steel Corp., 7000 Roberts St., Kansas City, MO

C F & I Steel Corp., Box 1920, Denver, CO 80201

Heltzel Steel Form & Iron Co., 1750 Thomas Rd., Warren, OH 44481

Jones & Laughlin Steel Corp., 3 Gateway Ctr., Pittsburgh, PA

Northwestern Steel & Wire Co., Ave. B & Wallace St., Sterling, IL

Specialty and accent building products such as shutters, plastic panels, simulated brick and stone, false beams are all on a module system of measurement, as are major building materials: plywood, hardboard, dimension lumber

APPLICATORS, WALLBOARD

Goldblatt Tool Co., 503A Osage St., Kansas City, KS

Wallboard Tool Co., 1708 Seabright St., Long Beach, CA

Warner Mfg. Co., 801 16th Ave., S.W., Minneapolis, MN

ARCHES AND COLUMNS, FIBERGLASS

Medow Industries, Inc., 2051 N.E. 160th St., Miami, FL

ARCHES, LAMINATED

Anthony Forest Products Co., P.O. Box 1877, El Dorado, AR 71730

Koppers Co., Inc. (Forest Prods. Div.) Koppers Bldg., Pittsburgh, PA 15219

Laminated Rafters Corp., Box 706, Warsaw, IN 46580

Weyerhaeuser Co. (Wood Prods. Group) Tacoma Bldg., Tacoma, WA 98401

ARCHES. METAL LATH

Ceco Corp., 5601 W. 26th St., Chicago, IL 60650

National Gypsum Co., 325 Delaware St., Buffalo, NY

U. S. Gypsum Co., 101 S. Wacker Dr., Chicago, IL

AUGERS, POST HOLE

Seymour Mfg. Co., 520 N. Broadway, Seymour, IN

True Temper Corp., 1623 Euclid Ave., Cleveland, OH

AWLS

Black & Decker Mfg. Co., Joppa Rd., Towson, MD

Estwing Mfg. Co., 2647 8th St., Rockford, IL 61101

Millers Falls Co., 57 Wells St., Greenfield, MA

Nicholson File Co., 676 Waterman Ave., E., Providence, RI 02914

Plumb (Fayette R.) Inc., 4837 James St., Philadelphia, PA

Rockwell Mfg. Co., (Power Tool Div.) 676 N. Lexington Ave., Pittsburgh, PA 15208

Stanley Tools Div., The Stanley Works, 600 Myrtle St., New Britain, CT 06050

True Temper Corp., 1623 Euclid Ave., Cleveland, OH

AWNINGS AND CANOPIES

American Aluminum Window Co., 767 Eastern Ave., Malden, MA 02148

Arrow Metal Products Corp., Third Ave., Haskell, NJ

Barclay Industries, Inc., 65 Industrial Rd., Lodi, NJ 07644

Chamberlain Mfg. Corp., 845 Larch Ave., Elmhurst, IL

Filon Div., Vistron Corp., 12333 S. Van Ness Ave., Hawthorne, CA 90250

Florida Industries, Inc., P.O. Box 15175, Tampa, FL

Hastings Aluminum Products, 429 S. Michigan St., Hastings, MI 49058

Homeshield Industries, Inc., Chatsworth, IL 60921

Kinkead Industries, Inc., 5860 N. Pulaski Rd., Chicago, IL 60646

Security Aluminum Co., 385 Midland St., Detroit, MI

U. S. Aluminum & Chemical Corp., 11440 W. Addison St., Franklin Park, IL 60131

Weather-Tile/Aristocrat Divs., Pacific Coast Co., 7103 Krick Rd., Cleveland, OH 44146

BASEBOARD, RUBBER

Jarrow Building Prods., Inc., 2000 N. Southport Ave., Chicago, IL 60614

Musson (The R. C.) Rubber Co., 1322 E. Archwood, Akron, OH 44306

Tilemaster Corp., 4400 N. Harlem Ave., Chicago, IL

BASEMENT STAIRS, STEEL

Bilco Co. (The) P.O. Box 1203, New Haven, CT 06505

Decatur Iron & Steel Co., 21 S.W. Second St., Decatur, AL

Metal Crafters, Box 577, Cedar Rapids, IA 52406

Potomac Iron Works, Inc., 4711 Rhode Island Ave., Hyattsville, MD

BASEMENT WINDOWS AND SASH

Acorn Products Co., 12620 Westwood Ave., Detroit, MI

Amco Aluminum Corp., 8501 Hegerman St., Philadelphia, PA

Architectural Aluminum Mfrs. Assn., One E. Wacker Dr., Chicago, IL 60601

Kawneer Co., 1105 N. Front St., Niles, MI 49120

Reynolds Metals Co., Building Products & Supply Div., 325 W. Touhy

Ave., Park Ridge, IL

Rusco Industries, Inc., 1100 Glendon Ave., Los Angeles, CA 90024

Stanley-Artex Windows (Div. of The Stanley Works) 1890 N.E. 146th St., North Miami, FL 33161

Weather-Tite/Aristocrat Divs., Pacific Coast Co., 7103 Krick Rd., Cleveland, OH 44146

Wepco Div. Weatherproof Co., P.O. Box 45, Litchfield, IL

BATHTUB SEAL, PLASTIC

Calbar, Inc., 2626 N. Martha St., Philadelphia, PA

DAP, Inc., 5300 Huberville Rd., Dayton, OH 45401

Dow-Corning Corp., Consumer Products Division, P.O. Box 592, Midland, MI 48641

General Electric Co., Silicone Prods. Dept., Waterford, NY

Macklanburg-Duncan Co., 4041 N. Santa Fe, Oklahoma City, OK 73125

Miracle Adhesives Corp., 250 Pettit Ave., Bellmore, LI, NY

Savogran Co., P.O. Box 130, Norwood, MA 02062

BEAMS

K-Lux Products Div., KSH, Inc., 10091 Manchester Rd., St. Louis, MO 63122

Marvel Wood Corp., 110 E. Industry Ct., Deer Park, LI, NY 11729

Panelmatch, P.O. Box 234, Chelsea, MA 02150

Reichhold Chemicals, Inc., (Reinforced Plastics Div.) 20545 Center Ridge Rd., Cleveland, OH 44116

Stonier (Russ), Inc., 1375 Merchandise Mart, Chicago, IL 60654

Ten Point Trim Corp., 1200 E. 52nd St., Indianapolis, IN 46205

Urethane Fabricators Lite Beams, Haddon & Line St., Camden, NJ 08103

BELLS, DOOR

Bevin Bros. Mfg. Co., East Hampton, CT

General Electric Wiring Device Dept., 95 Hathaway St., Providence, RI 02904

NuTone Div., Scovill Mfg. Co., Madison and Red Bank Rd., Cincinnati, OH 45227

Thomas Industries, Inc., 207 E. Broadway, Louisville, KY

BENCHES, WORK

Acme Steel Co., 135th & Perry Ave., Chicago, IL

Michigan Ladder Co., Forest at River, Ypsilanti, MI

Nelson Industries, 115 E. Carson, Pittsburgh, PA

Republic Steel Corp., Mfg. Div., 1315 Albert St., Youngstown, OH 44505

Weatherguard Service, Inc., 2339 Chatterton Ave., New York, NY 10462

BLACK TOP MIX

Carey (Philip) Corp., 320 S. Wayne Ave., Cincinnati, OH

Meadows (W. R.) 22 Kimball St., Elgin, IL 60120

Sakrete, Inc., Fischer & B & O RR, Cincinnati, OH

BLADES, SAW, HAND/POWER

Graham (John H) & Co., 105 Duane St., New York, NY

Hardware & Industrial Prods. (Div. H. K. Porter Co.) Porter Bldg., Pittsburgh, PA 15219

Millers Falls Co., 57 Wells St., Greenfield, MA

Nicholson File Co., 676 Waterman Ave., E., Providence, RI 02914

P & C Tool Co., Box 22066, Portland, OR 97222

Sandvik Steel, Inc., Finished Prods. Div., 1701 Nevins Blvd., Fairlawn, NJ 07710

Simonds Saw & Steel Div., Wallace-Murray Corp., Intervale Rd., Fitchburg, MA 01420

Black & Decker Mfg. Co., Joppa Rd., Towson, MD

Buzzmaster, Inc., 606 Hartrey, Evanston, IL 60202

DeLuxe Saw & Tool Co., 500 E. Main St., Louisville, KY

Portable Electric Tools Div., G. W. Murphy Ind., 1200 E. State St., Geneva, IL 60134

Power Tools, Inc., 500 Hicks Rd., Palatine, IL

Shopmaster Division (Shopco, Inc.) 6600 S. County Rd. 18 (Eden Prairie) Minneapolis, MN 55343

Skil Corp., 5033 N. Elston Ave., Chicago, IL

Stanley Power Tools Div. of the Stanley Works, 480 Myrtle St., New Britain, CT 06050

BOLTS

Adjusta-Post Mfg. Co., 605 W. Bowery St., Akron, OH

Aluminum Co. of America, 1501 Alcoa Bldg., Pittsburgh, PA 15219

Bolt Master Corp., 119 Bond St., Elk Grove Village, IL

Jordan Industries, Inc., 3030 N.W. 75th St., Miami, FL

Larson (Charles O.) Co., Box E, Sterling, IL

Paine Co., 501 Westgate Rd., Addison, IL 60101

Ramset Fastening Systems, Winchester Group Olin, 289 Winchester Ave., New Haven, CT 06504

Rawlplug Co., Inc. 200 Petersville Rd., New Rochelle, NY

Redi-Bolt, Inc., 5334 Indianapolis Blvd., East Chicago, IN 46312

Stanley Hardware Div. of the Stanley Works, 195 Lake St., New Britain, CT 06050

Wilmod Co., Inc., 200 W. 57th St., New York, NY

BONDING AGENTS, CONCRETE/ PLASTER

American Sta-Dri Co., 4019 38th St., Brentwood, MD

Borden, Inc., Chemical Div., 350 Madison Ave., New York, NY 10017

Camp Co., Inc., 9300 S. Sangamon St., Chicago, IL

Evans Adhesive Corp., 925 W. Henderson Rd., Columbus, OH

Fritz Chemical Co., P.O. Box 17087, Dallas, TX

Grace (W. R.) & Co., (Construction Products Div.) 62 Whittemore Ave., Cambridge, MA 02140

Macco Adhesives Div., The Glidden-Durkee Co., 30400 Lakeland Blvd., Wickliffe, OH 44092

Standard Dry Wall Prods., 7800 N.W. 38th St., Miami, FL 33166

Technical Adhesives, Inc., 315 S. Hicks Rd., Palatine, IL

U. S. Protective Coatings, Inc., 1200 Court Square Bldg., Baltimore, MD 21202

Valspar Corp., 200 Sayre St., Rockford, IL 61101

BRICK, FACE
Evans Brick & Pipe Co., Inc., Uhrichsville, OH

Kraftile Co., P.O. Box 2907, Fremont, CA

Miami Brick & Stone Co., P.O. Box 879, Miami, FL

Z-Brick Co., 2834 N.W. Market St., Seattle, WA

BRICK, FIRE
Babcock & Wilcox Refractories Div., Old Savannah Rd., Augusta, GA 30903

C-E Refractories, 101 Ferry St., St. Louis, MO

Gladding McBean & Co., 2901 Los Feliz St., Los Angeles, CA

Johns-Manville Corp., 22 E. 40th St., New York, NY

North American Refractories Co., National City Bank Bldg., Cleveland, OH

Porter (H. K.) Co., Inc., Refractories Div., Porter Bldg., Pittsburgh, PA 15219

BRICK, PLASTIC
Bolen International, Inc., 7800 N. Milwaukee Ave., Niles, IL 60648

Dacor Mfg. Co., Inc. 65 Armory St., Worcester, MA

Decro-Wall Corp., 375 Executive Blvd., Elmsford, NY

General Plastics Corp., 1400 N. Washington St., Marion, IN

Marvel Wood Corp., 110 E. Industry Ct., Deer Park, LI, NY 11729

Woodcraft Millwork, P.O. Box 231, Moonachie, NJ

BRUSHES, PAINT
Baker Brush Co., Inc., 83 Grand St., New York, NY

Devoe Paint Div., (Celanese Coatings Co.) 224 E. Broadway, Louisville, KY 40202

E-Z Paintr Corp., 4051 S. Iowa St., Milwaukee, WI

Fuller-O'Brien Corp, 4115 W. Artesia St., Fullerton, CA

Hanna Paint Mfg. Co., 1313 Windsor St., Columbus, OH

Lowe Bros. Co., 424 E. 3rd, Dayton, OH 45402

Muralo Co., Inc., E. 5th & Hobart Ave., Bayonne, NJ 07002

Rubberset Co., Crisfield, MD 21817

Sherwin-Williams Co., 101 Prospect Ave., N.W., Cleveland, OH 44101

Wooster Brush Co., 604 Madison Ave., Wooster, OH

CASING BEADS
Alabama Metal Industries Corp., P.O. Box 3928, Birmingham, AL 35208

Bostwick Steel Lath Co., 102 W. Federal St., Niles, OH

National Gypsum Co., 325 Delaware St., Buffalo, NY

U. S. Gypsum Co., 101 S. Wacker Dr., Chicago, IL

CAULKING COMPOUNDS
Anti-Hydro Waterproofing Co., 265 Badger Ave., Newark, NJ 07108

Cook Paint & Varnish Co., 1412 Knox, North Kansas City, MO 64116

DAP, Inc., 5300 Huberville Rd., Dayton, OH 45401

DuPont (E. I.) de Nemours & Co., Product Info. Section, Wilmington, DE 19898

Lustre Line Products Co., Richmond & Norris Sts., Philadelphia, PA 19125

Macklanburg-Duncan Co., 4041 N. Santa Fe, Oklahoma City, OK 73125

Marlite Division of Masonite Corp., Dover, OH

Miracle Adhesives Corp., 250 Pettit Ave., Bellmore, LI, NY

Rutland Products, 96 Curtis Ave., Rutland, VT

Stay-Tite Prods., Inc. 2889 E. 83rd St., Cleveland, OH

3M Company, 3M Center, St. Paul, MN 55101

Woodhill Chemical Co., 18731 Cranwood Parkway, Cleveland, OH 44128

Elco Mfg. Co., 111 Third St., Pittsburgh, PA 15215

Miraplas Tile Co., 980 Parsons Ave., Columbus, OH

Process Solvent Co., Inc. 1041 Chelsea Trfwy., Kansas City, KS 66104

U. S. Protective Coatings, Inc., 1200 Court Sq. Bldg., Baltimore, MD 21202

CAULKING, PREMOLDED
Chicago Adhesive Products Co., 4658 W. 60th St., Chicago, IL 60629

DAP, Inc., 5300 Huberville Rd., Dayton, OH 45401

Johns-Manville Corp., 22 E. 40th St., New York, NY

Macklanburg-Duncan Co., 4041 N. Santa Fe, Oklahoma City, OK 73125

Re-Nu-It Corp., 424 W. 42nd St., New York, NY

Tapco Prods. Co., Inc., 9240 Hubbell, Detroit, MI

CEILINGS, LUMINOUS
American Louver Co., 7700 N. Austin, Skokie, IL

Armstrong Cork Co., 6402 Roosevelt, Lancaster, PA

Artcrest Products Co., Inc., 401 W. Ontario St., Chicago, IL 60610

Barclay Industries, Inc., 65 Industrial Rd., Lodi, NJ 07644

Sheet-metal components—tees, elbows, registers for ductwork—are standardized to conform with other building modules. However, you can also buy off-sizes. Do not mix metals, i.e., galvanized steel with aluminum; aluminum with copper, etc.

442

Celotex Corp., 1500 N. Dale Mabry, Tampa, FL 33607

Certain-Teed Products Corp., 120 E. Lancaster St., Ardmore, PA 19003

Conwed Corp., 332 Minnesota St., St. Paul, MN

Diffusa-Lite Co., 1 Forrest St., Conshohocken, PA

Emerson Electric Co., 8100 W. Florissant St., St. Louis, MO 63136

Filon Div., Vistron Corp., 12333 S. Van Ness Ave., Hawthorne, CA 90250

Flintkote Co., 400 Westchester Ave., White Plains, NY

General Plastics Corp., 1400 N. Washington St., Marion, IN

Hastings Aluminum Products, 429 S. Michigan St., Hastings, MI 49058

Kemlite Corp., 101 N. Republic Ave., Joliet, IL

K-Lux Products Div., KSH, Inc., 10091 Manchester Rd., St. Louis, MO 63122

Laminated Plastics, Inc., 1610 S. Buder Industrial Drive, St. Louis, MO 63144

Leigh Products, Inc., 1969 Lee St., Coopersville, MI

National Gypsum Co., 325 Delaware St., Buffalo, NY

Owens-Corning Fiberglas Corp., P.O. Box 901, Toledo, OH 43601

CEILINGS, SUSPENDED

American Louver Co., 7700 N. Austin, Skokie, IL

Armstrong Cork Co., 6402 Roosevelt, Lancaster, PA

Barclay Industries, Inc., 65 Industrial Rd., Lodi, NJ 07644

Celotex Corp., 1500 N. Dale Mabry, Tampa, FL 33607

Certain-Teed Products Corp., 120 E. Lancaster St., Ardmore, PA 19003

Conwed Corp., 332 Minnesota St., St. Paul, MN

Cook Paint & Varnish Co., 1412 Knox, North Kansas City, MO 64116

Diffusa-Lite Co., 1 Forrest St., Conshohocken, PA

Eastern Products Corp., 1601 Wicomico St., Baltimore, MD 21230

Florida Industries, Inc., P.O. Box 15175, Tampa, FL

Insulite Div. of Boise Cascade Corp., Northstar Center, Minneapolis, MN 55402

Johns-Manville Corp., 22 E. 40th St., New York, NY

Kemlite Corp., 101 N. Republic Ave., Joliet, IL

K-Lux Products Div., KSH, Inc., 10091 Manchester Rd., St. Louis, MO 63122

Leigh Products, Inc., 1969 Lee St., Coopersville, MI

Leslie Building Prods., Inc., 11550 W. King St., Franklin Park, IL 60131

Macklanburg-Duncan Co., 4041 N. Santa Fe, Oklahoma City, OK 73125

National Gypsum Co., 325 Delaware St., Buffalo, NY

Owens-Corning Fiberglas Corp., P.O. Box 901, Toledo, OH 43601

Pacesetter Products, Inc., 1515 Spring

Boards are lumber less than 2 in. thick; a board-foot is equivalent to a board that is 1 ft. square and 1 in. thick. Boards are usually sold by the board-foot; occasionally by the piece. Piece prices are usually higher, so shop before you buy

St., Houston, TX 77001

Panelboard Mfg. Co., 100 James St., Somerville, NJ

Regal Products Corp., P.O. Box 1508, Harrisburg, PA

Temple Industries, Diboll, TX 75941

U. S. Gypsum Co., 101 S. Wacker Dr., Chicago, IL

CEMENT, CONCRETE FLOOR REPAIR

Anti-Hydro Waterproofing Co., 265 Badger Ave., Newark, NJ 07108

Armstrong Cork Co., 6402 Roosevelt, Lancaster, PA

California Products Corp., 169 Waverly St., Cambridge, MA 02139

Consumers Glue Co., 1515 Hadley St., St. Louis, MO

DAP, Inc., 5300 Huberville Rd., Dayton, OH 45401

Evans Adhesive Corp., 925 W. Henderson Rd., Columbus, OH

Flintkote Co., 400 Westchester Ave., White Plains, NY

Glidden-Durkee (Div. of SCM Corp.) 900 Union Commerce Bldg., Cleveland, OH 44115

Larsen Products Corp., Box 5938, Bethesda, MD

Macco Adhesives Div., The Glidden-Durkee Co., 30400 Lakeland Blvd., Wickliffe, OH 44092

Penn Crete Prods. Co., Inc., 2745 N. Amber St., Philadelphia, PA 19134

Pennsalt Chemicals Corp., 3 Penn Ctr., Philadelphia, PA

Sherwin-Williams Co., 101 Prospect Ave., N.W., Cleveland, OH 44101

Sike Chemical Corp., 875 Valley Brook Ave., Lyndhurst, NJ 07071

Tamms Industries Co., 8000 Joliet Rd., Lyons, IL

Wilhold Glues, Inc., 8707 Millergrove Dr., Santa Fe Springs, CA 90670

CEMENT, HOUSEHOLD REPAIR

Borden, Inc., Chemical Div., 350 Madison Ave., New York, NY 10017

Camp Co., Inc., 9300 S. Sangamon St., Chicago, IL

Consumers Glue Co., 1515 Hadley St., St. Louis, MO

DuPont (E. I.) de Nemours & Co., Product Info. Section, Wilmington, DE 19898

Franklin Glue Co., 2020 Bruck St., Columbus, OH

Fuller (H. B.) Co., 2400 Kasota Ave., St. Paul, MN

Miracle Adhesives Corp., 250 Pettit Ave., Bellmore, LI, NY

National Starch and Chemical Corp., 750 3rd Ave., New York, NY

Sherwin-Williams Co., 101 Prospect Ave., N.W., Cleveland, OH 44101

U. S. Plywood Div. of U. S. Plywood-Champion Papers, Inc., 777 Third Ave., New York, NY 10036

Wide range of patterns is now available in wall coverings, including contact papers, which can be used for accents in any room. Basically you pay for the *design* and the *surface*. Choose the right surface (waterproof, etc.) for the particular room

Wilhold Glues, Inc., 8707 Millergrove Dr., Santa Fe Springs, CA 90670

CEMENT, MASONRY
Penn-Dixie Cement Corp., 60 E. 42nd St., New York, NY
Universal Atlas Cement Div., United States Steel Corp., 112 Washington Place, Pittsburgh, PA 15230
Medusa Portland Cement Co., Monticello & Lee Blvd., Cleveland Heights, OH
Trinity White Dept., General Portland Cement Co., P.O. Box 324, Dallas, TX 75221
Marquette Cement Co., 20 N. Wacker Dr., Chicago, IL

CEMENT, TILE GROUT
Anti-Hydro Waterproofing Co., 265 Badger Ave., Newark, NJ 07108
Atlas Minerals & Chemicals Div., ESB, Inc., 141 Elm St., Mertztown, PA 19539
Burco Products, Inc., 1100 High Ridge Rd., Stamford, CT 06904
Chicago Adhesive Products Co., 4658 W. 60th St., Chicago, IL 60629
Fritz Chemical Co., P.O. Box 17087, Dallas, TX
Glidden-Durkee (Div. of SCM Corp.) 900 Union Commerce Bldg., Cleveland, OH 44115
Larsen Products Corp., Box 5938, Bethesda, MD
Macco Adhesives Div., The Glidden-Durkee Co., 30400 Lakeland Blvd., Wickliffe, OH 44092
Miracle Adhesives Corp., 250 Pettit Ave., Bellmore, LI, NY
National Floor Prods. Co., Inc., Box 354, Florence, AL
Oxford Tile Co., Inc. Woodlawn Ave., Cambridge, OH
Pecora Chemical Corp., 300 W. Sedgley Ave., Philadelphia, PA 19140
Rutland Products, 96 Curtis Ave., Rutland, VT
Savogran Co., P.O. Box 130, Norwood, MA 02062
Tamms Industries Co., 8000 Joliet Rd., Lyons, IL

CEMENT, WALLBOARD JOINT
Armstrong Cork Co., 6402 Roosevelt, Lancaster, PA
Barclay Industries, Inc., 65 Industrial Rd., Lodi, NJ 07644
Borden, Inc., Chemical Div., 350 Madison Ave., New York, NY 10017
Flintkote Co., 400 Westchester Ave., White Plains, NY
GAF Corporation, Building Products Div., 140 W. 51st St., New York, NY 10020
Glidden-Durkee (Div. of SCM Corp.) 900 Union Commerce Bldg., Cleveland, OH 44115
Macco Adhesives Div., The Glidden-

Durkee Co., 30400 Lakeland Blvd., Wickliffe, OH 44092

National Gypsum Co., 325 Delaware St., Buffalo, NY

Stay-Tite Prods., Inc., 2889 E. 83rd St., Cleveland, OH

Tamms Industries Co., 8000 Joliet Rd., Lyons, IL

United Gilsonite Laboratories, 1396 Jefferson Ave., Scranton, PA 18501

Wilhold Glues, Inc., 8707 Millergrove Dr., Santa Fe Springs, CA 90670

CLAMPS, WOODWORKERS

Adjustable Clamp Co., 409 N. Ashland Ave., Chicago, IL

Knape & Vogt Mfg. Co., 2700 Oak Industrial Dr., Grand Rapids, MI 49505

Stanley Tools Div., The Stanley Works, 600 Myrtle St., New Britain, CT 06050

Wing Prods. Co., Inc., 807 Farmer Ave., Tempe, AZ

CLEANERS, BRICK AND MASONRY

American Calmal Corp., 2540 W. 6th Lane, Hialeah, FL

DuPont (E. I.) de Nemours & Co., Product Info. Section, Wilmington, DE 19898

Elco Mfg. Co., 111 Third St., Pittsburgh, PA 15215

Goldblatt Tool Co., 503A Osage St., Kansas City, KS

Klean Strip Co., Inc., 2340 S. Lauderdale, Memphis, TN

United Gilsonite Laboratories, 1396 Jefferson Ave., Scranton, PA 18501

CLEANERS, FLOOR

American Biltrite Rubber Co., Perrine Ave., Trenton, NJ

Armstrong Cork Co., 6402 Roosevelt, Lancaster, PA

Azrock Floor Products, Box 531, San Antonio, TX

Congoleum-Nairn, Inc., 195 Belgrove Dr., Kearny, NJ

Elco Mfg. Co., 111 Third St., Pittsburgh, PA 15215

Grace (W. R.) & Co., (Construction Products Div.) 62 Whittemore Ave., Cambridge, MA 02140

Johnson (S. C.) & Son, Inc., 1525 Howe St., Racine, WI

Miraplas Tile Co., 980 Parsons Ave., Columbus, OH

Pennsalt Chemicals Corp., 3 Penn Ctr., Philadelphia, PA

PPG Industries, 632 Fort Duquesne Blvd., Pittsburgh, PA 15222

Technical Adhesives, Inc., 315 S. Hicks Rd., Palatine, IL

CLEANERS, PAINT AND VARNISH

Cabot (Samuel), Inc., 246 Summer St., Boston, MA

Devoe Paint Div., (Celanese Coatings Co.) 224 E. Broadway, Louisville, KY 40202

Enterprise Paint Mfg. Co., 2841 S. Ashland Ave., Chicago, IL 60608

Klean Strip Co., Inc., 2340 S. Lauderdale, Memphis, TN

Woodhill Chemical Co., 18731 Cranwood Parkway, Cleveland, OH 44128

CLEANERS, PAINT BRUSH

Cabot (Samuel), Inc., 246 Summer St., Boston, MA

Chemical Products Co., P.O. Box 400, Aberdeen, MD

Consumers Glue Co., 1515 Hadley St., St. Louis, MO

DuPont (E. I.) de Nemours & Co., Product Info. Section, Wilmington, DE 19898

Fuller-O'Brien Corp., 4115 W. Artesia St., Fullerton, CA

Glidden-Durkee (Div. of SCM Corp.) 900 Union Commerce Bldg., Cleveland, OH 44115

Lowe Bros. Co., 424 E. 3rd, Dayton, OH

PPG Industries, 632 Fort Duquesne Blvd., Pittsburgh, PA 15222

Savogran Co., P.O. Box 130, Norwood, MA 02062

Sherwin-Williams Co., 101 Prospect Ave., N.W., Cleveland, OH 44101

Wilson-Imperial Co., 115 Chestnut St., Newark, NJ

CLIPS, FLOOR

Advance Metal Products, Inc., 2445 N.W. 76th St., Miami, FL 33147

Spotnails, Inc., 1100 Hicks Rd., Rolling Meadows, IL

Weatherguard Service, Inc., 2339 Chatterton Ave., New York, NY 10462

CLIPS, ROOFING

Alpine Engineered Prods., Inc., P.O. Box 927, Pompano Beach, FL 33061

Panel Clip Co., Box 423-D, Farmington, MI 48024

Spotnails, Inc., 1100 Hicks Rd., Rolling Meadows, IL

Timber Engineering Co., 1619 Massachusetts Ave., N.W., Washington, DC 20036

COATINGS, ALUMINUM AND ASPHALT

Al-Chroma Paint Co., 2701 Chamber St., Stevens Point, WI 54481

Alumi-Gard Co., 1638 W. 79th St., Chicago, IL

Bird & Son, Inc., Washington St., East Walpole, MA

Borden, Inc., Chemical Div., 350 Madison Ave., New York, NY 10017

Celotex Corp., 1500 N. Dale Mabry, Tampa, FL 33607

Flintkote Co., 400 Westchester Ave., White Plains, NY

Gibson-Homans Co., 2366 Woodhill Rd., Cleveland, OH

Hartline Products Co., Inc., 2186 Noble Rd., Cleveland, OH 44112

Kol-Tar, Inc., 699 Adams St., N., Abington, MA 02351

Rust-Oleum Corp., 2301 Oakton St., Evanston, IL

Stanchem, Inc., 641 Berlin St., East Berlin, CT

3M Company, 3M Center, St. Paul, MN 55101

U. S. Gypsum Co., 101 S. Wacker Dr., Chicago, IL

Valspar Corp., 200 Sayre St., Rockford, IL 61101

COLUMN AND WALL TIES

Advance Metal Products, Inc., 2445 N.W. 76th St., Miami, FL 33147

Ceco Corp., 5601 W. 26th St., Chicago, IL 60650

Cleveland Steel Specialty Co., 14435 Industrial Ave., S., Cleveland, OH 44137

COLUMNS, METAL

Acosta Awning Corp., 823 Maria St., Kenner, LA

Bethlehem Steel Corp., 701 E. Third St., Bethlehem, PA

Deslauriers Column Mould Co., Inc., 5036 W. Lake St., Chicago, IL 60644

Jack-Post Corp., P.O. Box 252, Galien, MI 49113

Keystone Building Products, Box 1449, Harrisburg, PA

Logan Company, 200 Cabel St., Louisville, KY

Superior Aluminum Prods., Inc., Box 445, Russia, OH

Yeck Mfg. Corp., 579 Tecumseh St., Dundee, MI

COLUMNS, WOOD

Bendix Mouldings, Inc., 1112 E. Tremont Ave., Bronx, NY 10460

California Redwood Assn, 617 Montgomery St., San Francisco, CA 94111

Federal Millwork Corp., 3300 S. Federal Highway, Fort Lauderdale, FL

Stonier (Russ), Inc., 1375 Merchandise Mart, Chicago, IL 60654

COMPOUNDS, ANTI-DRIP

Calbar, Inc., 2626 N. Martha St., Philadelphia, PA

Presstite Div., Interchemical Corp., 3738 Chouteau Ave., St. Louis, MO 63110

CONNECTORS, TIMBER

Advance Metal Products, Inc., 2445 N.W. 76th St., Miami, FL 33147

National Mfg. Co., One 1st Ave., Sterling, IL

Panel Clip Co., Box 423-0, Farmington, MI 48024

Sanford Industries, Inc., P.O. Box 1177, Pompano Beach, FL 33061

Timber Engineering Co., 1619 Massachusetts Ave., N.W., Washington, DC 20036

CORNER BEAD, DRYWALL/PLASTER

National Gypsum Co., 325 Delaware St., Buffalo, NY

3M Co., 3M Center, St. Paul, MN 55101

Casings, Inc., West Middlesex, PA 16159

Georgia-Pacific Corp., P.O. Box 311, Portland, OR

Keystone Steel & Wire Co., 7000 S. Adams St., Peoria, IL

COVE BASE
American Biltrite Rubber Co., Perrine Ave., Trenton, NJ

Armstrong Cork Co., 6402 Roosevelt, Lancaster, PA

Crane Plastics, Inc., 2141 Fairwood Ave., Columbus, OH 43216

Kentile Floors, Inc., 58 Second Ave., Brooklyn, NY

National Gypsum Co., 325 Delaware St., Buffalo, NY

Potlatch Forests, Inc., Southern Div., Wood Products Group, P.O. Box 390, Warren, AR 71671

Selck (Walter E. & Co.) 7125 W. Gunnison, Chicago, IL

CUTTERS, TILE
Burco Products, Inc., 1100 High Ridge Rd., Stamford, CT 06904

Consumers Glue Co., 1515 Hadley St., St. Louis, MO

DAMPPROOFING COMPOUNDS
Anti-Hydro Waterproofing Co., 265 Badger Ave., Newark, NJ 07108

Atlas Minerals & Chemicals Div., ESB, Inc., 141 Elm St., Mertztown, PA 19539

Cabot (Samuel), Inc., 246 Summer St., Boston, MA

Camp Co., Inc., 9300 S. Sangamon St., Chicago, IL

Dow Chemical Co., P.O. Box 426, Midland, MI 48640

Glidden-Durkee (Div. of SCM Corp.) 900 Union Commerce Bldg., Cleveland, OH 44115

Lehon Co., 320 S. Wayne Ave., Cincinnati, OH 45215

Meadows (W. R.), 22 Kimball St., Elgin, IL 60120

DOORS, ACCESS
Bilco Co. (The), P.O. Box 1203, New Haven, CT

Challenger Mfg. Co., 342–46 N. Royal St., Jackson, TN

Long-Bell Div. (International Paper Co.) Box 579, Longview, WA 98632

Majestic Co., Inc., 516 Erie St., Huntington, IN

Panelboard Mfg. Co., 100 James St., Somerville, NJ

Superior Fireplace Co., 4325 Artesia Ave., Fullerton, CA 92633

DOORS, COMBINATION
Alside, Inc., 3773 Akron-Cleveland Rd., Akron, OH

"One-stop" building-supply outlets

American Aluminum Window Co., 767 Eastern Ave., Malden, MA 02148

Architectural Aluminum Mfrs. Assn. One E. Wacker Dr., Chicago, IL 60601

Hines (Edward) Lumber Co., 200 S. Michigan Ave., Chicago, IL 60604

Marvin Windows, Warroad, MN 56763

Phenix Mfg. Co., Inc., 625 Elizabeth St., Shawano, WI

Reynolds Metals Co., Building Products & Supply Div., 325 W. Touhy Ave., Park Ridge, IL

Season-All Industries, Inc., Box 371, Indiana, PA

Security Aluminum Co., 385 Midland St., Detroit, MI

Weather-Tite/Aristocraft Divs., Pacific Coast Co., 7103 Krick Rd., Cleveland, OH 44146

Wepco Div., Weatherproof Co., P.O. Box 45, Litchfield, IL

DOORS, GARAGE
Anchor Sales Corp., 205 Bush St., Brooklyn, NY

Berry Doors Div. of The Stanley Works, 2400 E. Lincoln Rd., Birmingham, MI 48012

Crawford Door Co., 4270 High St., Ecorse, MI

Frantz Mfg. Co., 301 W 3rd St., Sterling, IL

Rowe Mfg. Co., 614 W. 3rd St. Galesburg, IL 61401

DRAINS, FLOOR AND ROOF
Donley Bros. Co., 13940 Miles Ave., Cleveland, OH

Empire-Reeves Steel Div., Cyclops Corp., 913 Bowman St., Mansfield, OH 44901

Majestic Co., Inc., 516 Erie St., Huntington, IN

Vestal Mfg. Co., Box 420, Sweetwater, TN 37874

ENTRANCES, DOOR, WOOD
Burton Woodwork Div., Klein Industries, Mac Arthur Ave., Cobleskill, NY 12043

Cupples Products Corp., 2654 S. Hanley Rd., St. Louis, MO

Georgia-Pacific Corp., Box 311, Portland, OR

Shingles are sold by the "square," or enough shingles to cover 100 sq. ft. Some dealers will sell shingles and other roofing by the piece for small maintenance jobs. Roofing colors are sometimes tough to match; bring along sample when you go shopping

ll everything from asphalt to wooden brick. Frequently a cash-and-carry system helps you save money

Long-Bell Div. (International Paper Co.) Box 579, Longview, WA 98632
Marvin Windows, Warroad, MN 46763
Morgan Co., 601 Oregon St. Oshkosh, WI 54901
Ponderosa Pine Woodwork, 39 S. LaSalle St., Chicago, IL

EXPANSION FASTENERS
AEG Tool Div. (Ferrostaal Overseas Corp.) 37–26 13th St., Long Island City, NY 11101
National Lead Co., 111 Broadway, New York, NY
Omark Industries, 9701 S.E. McLoughlin Blvd., Portland, OR 97222
Philips Drill Co., U.S. Rte. #12, Michigan City, IN
Ramset Fastening Systems, Winchester Group, Olin, 289 Winchester Ave., New Haven, CT 06504
Rawlplug Co., Inc., 200 Petersville Rd., New Rochelle, NY
Star Expansion Industries, Mountainville, NY

EXPANSION JOINTS
Afco Products, Inc., 44 Park St., Somerville, MA
Bostwick Steel Lath Co., 102 W. Federal St., Niles, OH
Fel-Pro Building Prods., Inc., 7450 McCormick Blvd., Skokie, IL 60076
Meadows (W. R.), 22 Kimball St., Elgin, IL 60120
Presstite Div., Interchemical Corp., 3738 Chouteau Ave., St. Louis, MO 63110
Weatherguard Service, Inc., 2339 Chatterton Ave., New York, NY 10462

FASTENERS, FIBRE WALLBOARD
Independent Nail, Inc., 106 Hale St., Bridgewater, MA
Jordan Industries, Inc., 3030 N.W. 75th St., Miami, FL
National Lock Co., 1902 7th St., Rockford, IL
Paslode Co., Div. of Signode Corp., 8080 McCormick Blvd., Skokie, IL 60076
Spotnails, Inc., 1100 Hicks Rd., Rolling Meadows, IL

U. S. Expansion Bolt Co., 500 State St., York, PA
Wilmod Co., Inc., 200 W. 57th St., New York, NY

FAUCETS
Aetna Plumbing Industries, Inc., 4701 W. Augusta Blvd., Chicago, IL 60651
Crane Co., 4100 S. Kedzie Ave., Chicago, IL 60632
Elkay Mfg. Co., 2700 17th Ave., Broadview, IL
General Bathroom Prods. Corp., 2201 Touhy, Elk Grove Village, IL 60007
Peerless Faucet Co., Div. Masco Corp., 21001 Van Born Rd., Taylor, MI 48180
Plumb Shop, 620 Fisher Bldg., Detroit, MI 48202

FENCE AND GATES
Armco Steel Corp., 7000 Roberts St., Kansas City, MO
Atlantic Steel Co., Box 1714, Atlanta, GA 30301
Filon Div., Vistron Corp., 12333 S. Van Ness Ave., Hawthorne, CA 90250
Gilbert & Bennett Mfg. Co., Georgetown, CT 06829
Hallinan Lumber Co., 1202 S.W. 19th, Portland, OR
Keystone Building Products, Box 1449, Harrisburg, PA
Metal Crafters, Box 577, Cedar Rapids, IA 52406
Nichols-Homeshield, Inc., 15 Spinning Wheel Rd., Hinsdale, IL 60521
Potomac Iron Works, Inc., 4711 Rhode Island Ave., Hyattsville, MD 20781
Union Lumber Co., 120 Montgomery St., San Francisco, CA 94104
U. S. Steel Corp., 525 Wm Penn Pl., Pittsburgh, PA
Wood Products Co., 1533 Laskey Rd., Toledo, OH
Robot Industries, Inc., 7041 Orchard Ave., Dearborn, MI 48126
California Redwood Assn, 617 Montgomery St., San Francisco, CA 94111

FILLERS, CRACK & JOINT
Atlas Minerals & Chemicals Div., ESB,

Inc., 141 Elm St., Mertztown, PA 19539
Camp Co., Inc., 9300 S. Sangamon St., Chicago, IL
Consumers Glue Co., 1515 N. Hadley St., St. Louis, MO
Penn Crete Prods. Co., Inc., 2745 N. Amber St., Philadelphia, PA 19134

FILM, PLASTIC
Borden, Inc., Chemical Div., 350 Madison Ave., New York, NY 10017
Eastman Kodak Co., 343 State St., Rochester, NY
Ethyl Corp. (Visqueen Div.) P.O. Box 2422, Baton Rouge, LA 79821
Mobil Chemical Co., (Mobil Packaging Dept.) Macedon, NY 14502
Sisalkraft Div., St. Regis Paper Co., 55 Starkey Ave., Attleboro, MA
3M Company, 3M Center. St. Paul, MN 55101
Warp Bros., 1100 N. Cicero Ave., Chicago, IL 60651

FINISHES, WOOD
Cabot (Samuel), Inc., 246 Summer St., Boston, MA
Deft, Inc., 612 Maple Ave. Torrance, CA 90503
DuPont (E. I.) de Nemours & Co., Prod. Info. Section, Wilmington, DE 19898
Kurfees Coatings, Inc., 201 E. Market St., Louisville, KY 40202
Magic American Chemical Corp., 14215 Caine Ave., Cleveland, OH 44128
Minwax Co., Inc., 72 Oak St., Clifton, NJ 07014
Protection Prods. Div., (U. S. Plywood-Champion Papers) 2305 Superior St., Kalamazoo, MI 49001
Rez Co. (The), P.O. Box 142, Springdale, PA
Stanchem, Inc., 641 Berlin St., East Berlin, CT
Valspar Corp., 200 Sayre St., Rockford, IL 61101

FIREPLACES, PREFAB
Condon-King Co., 5611 208th Ave., S.W., Lynnwood, WA

447

Fasco Industries, 255 N. Union, Rochester, NY 14602
Leslie Building Prods., Inc., 11550 W. King St., Franklin Park, IL 60131
Majesitc Co., Inc., 516 Erie St., Huntington, IN
Readybuilt Products Co., 1705–23 McHenry St., Baltimore, MD 21223
Thulman-Eastern Corp., 3485 Chevrolet Dr., Ellicott City, MD 21043
Vega Industries, Inc., 402 E. Brighton Ave., Syracuse, NY

FIXTURES, LIGHT
Angelo Bros. Co., 159 W. Allegheny Ave., Philadelphia, PA 19133
Artcrest Products Co., Inc., 401 W. Ontario St., Chicago, IL 60610
Corbett Lighting, Inc., 2955 Anode Ln., Dallas, TX
Dura Steel Products Co., P.O. Box 54175, Los Angeles, CA 90054
Emerson Electric Co., 8100 W. Florissant St., St. Louis, MO 63136
Grote Mfg. Co., Inc., P.O. Box 766, Madison, IN
Miami-Carey Div., Philip Carey Corp., 320 S. Wayne Ave., Cincinnati, OH 45215
NuTone Div., Scovill Mfg. Co., Madison and Red Bank Rd., Cincinnati, OH 45227
Progress Lighting Div., Lighting Corp. of America, Box 12701, Philadelphia, PA 19134

FIXTURES, PLUMBING
Aetna Plumbing Industries, Inc., 4701 W. Augusta Blvd., Chicago, IL 60651
Borg-Warner Corp., Plumbing Products Div., 207 E. 5th, Mansfield, OH
Briggs Mfg. Co., 6600 E. 15-Mile Rd., Warren, MI
Crane Co., 4100 S. Kedzie Ave., Chicago, IL 60632
Hoover Bathroom Accessories, 425 Frank St., Fowlerville, MI 48836
Kohler Co., Kohler, WI 50344
Plumb Shop, 620 Fisher Bldg., Detroit, MI 48202

FLASHING
Advance Metal Products, Inc., 2445 N.W. 76th St., Miami, FL 33147
Aluminum Co. of America, 1501 Alcoa Bldg., Pittsburgh, PA 15219
Anaconda-American Brass Co., 414 Meadow St., Waterbury, CT 06720
Howmet Corp. (Building Products Div.) Box 1167C, Lancaster, PA 17604
Keystone Roofing Mfg. Co., P.O. Box 1549, York (Windsor Park), PA 17405
Revere Copper & Brass, Inc., 230 Park Ave., New York, NY
Reynolds Metals Co., Building Products & Supply Div., 325 W. Touhy Ave., Park Ridge, IL
Colonial Plastics Mfg. Co., 8107 Grand Ave., Cleveland, OH 44104
Rutland Products, 96 Curtis Ave., Rutland, VT 05702

FLOOR FINISHES
American-Lincoln Corp., 518 S. St.

Lawn and garden equipment has moved into building-supply outlets, which have become "home centers." Include a broom rake, weeder, grass shears, garden spade and hand trowel in your basic gardening tool kit. Also handy: spading fork, pruning shears, and a hoe

Clair, Toledo, OH 43603
Cabot (Samuel), Inc., 246 Summer St., Boston, MA
Camp Co., Inc., 9300 S. Sangamon St., Chicago, IL
Cook Paint & Varnish Co., 1412 Knox, North Kansas City, MO 64116
DAP, Inc., 5300 Huberville Rd., Dayton, OH 45401
DuPont (E. I.) de Nemours & Co., Product Info Section, Wilmington, DE 19898
Fritz Chemical Co., P.O. Box 17087, Dallas, TX
Lowe Bros. Co., 424 E. 3rd, Dayton, OH 45402
Macco Adhesives Div., The Glidden-Durkee Co., 30400 Lakeland Blvd., Wickliffe, OH 44092
O'Brien Corp., 2001 W. Washington St., South Bend, IN 46621
PPG Industries, 732 Fort Duquesne Blvd., Pittsburgh, PA 15222

Rez Co. (The), P.O. Box 142, Springdale, PA
Rutland Products, 96 Curtis Ave., Rutland, VT
Steelcote Mfg. Co., 3148 Gratiot St., St. Louis, MO
Valspar Corp., 200 Sayre St., Rockford, IL 61101

FLOORING, FIR
Hines (Edward) Lumber Co., 200 S. Michigan Ave., Chicago, IL 60604
Long-Bell Div., (International Paper Co.) Box 579, Longview, WA 98632
Pacific Lumber Co., 1111 Columbus-Ave., San Francisco, CA 94133
Weyerhaeuser Co., (Wood Prods. Group), Tacoma Bldg., Tacoma, WA 98401

FLOORING, WOOD
Anchor Sales Corp., 205 Bush St., Brooklyn, NY

Bruce (E. L.) Co., Box 397, Memphis, TN 38101

National Oak Flooring Mfrs. Assn., 814 Sterick Bldg., Memphis, TN

Potlatch Forests, Inc., P.O. Box 3591, San Francisco, CA 94119

Wood-Mosaic Corp., P.O. Box 21066, Louisville, KY

Hardwood Plywood Manufacturers Association, 2310 S. Walter Reed Dr., Arlington, VA 22206

GLASS

Pittsburgh Corning Corp., 1 Gateway Ctr., Pittsburgh, PA

PPG Industries, 632 Fort Duquesne Blvd., Pittsburgh, PA 15222

Arvey Corp., 3462 N. Kimball Ave., Chicago, IL

Barclay Industries, Inc., 65 Industrial Rd., Lodi, NJ 07644

Filon Div., Vistron Corp., 12333 S. Van Ness Ave., Hawthorne, CA 90250

K-Lux Products Div., KSH, Inc., 10091 Manchester Rd., St. Louis, MO 63122

Acorn Products Co., 12620 Westwood Ave., Detroit, MI

GRILLES, DOOR/WINDOW

Alsco, Inc., 225 S. Forge St., Akron, OH 44308

Clark Aluminum, 13131 Almeda Rd., Houston, TX

Croft Metal Prods., Inc., Aluminum Bldg-24th St., McComb, MS 39648

Duncan-Morris Co., 48 N. Valley Ave., Akron, OH

Ideal Security Hardware Corp., 215 E. 9th St., St. Paul, MN

Superior Aluminum Prods., Inc., Box 445, Russia, OH

Weather-Tite/Aristocraft Divs., Pacific Coast Co., 7103 Krick Rd., Cleveland, OH 44146

Andersen Corp., Bayport, MN 55003

GUTTERS

Air-King Mfg. Corp., Box 6302, Tigard, OR 97223

Cleveland Dowel and Wood Turning Co., 20950 Center Ridge Rd., Cleveland, OH 44116

HANGERS

Adjusta-Post Mfg. Co., 605 W. Bowery St., Akron, OH

Duratile of Ohio, 2240 Hayes Ave., Fremont, OH

Panel Clip Co., Box 423-D, Farmington, MI 48024

Reddi-Bolt, Inc., 5334 Indianapolis Blvd., East Chicago, IN 46312

Weatherguard Service, Inc., 2339 Chatterton Ave., New York, NY 10462

HARDBOARD

Abitibi Corp., 1400 N. Woodward Ave., Birmingham, MI

American Hardboard Association, 20 N. Wacker Dr., Chicago, IL 60606

Armstrong Cork Co., 6402 Roosevelt, Lancaster, PA

Barclay Industries, Inc., 65 Industrial Rd., Lodi, NJ 07644

Bowaters Southern Paper Corp., Calhoun, TN

Celotex Corp., 1500 N. Dale Mabry, Tampa, FL 33607

Conwed Corp., 332 Minnesota St., St. Paul, MN

Evans Products Co., Building Products Group, P.O. Box 880, Corona, CA 91720

Evans Prods. Co., Fiber Prods. Div., P.O. Box E, Corvallis, OR 97330

Georgia-Pacific Corp., P.O. Box 311, Portland, OR

Hardboard Fabricators Corp., 79 Empire St., Newark, NJ

Johns-Manville Corp., 22 E. 40th St., New York, NY

Masonite Corp., 29 N. Wacker Dr., Chicago, IL

Panelboard Mfg. Co., 100 James St., Somerville, NJ

U. S. Gypsum Co., 101 S. Wacker Dr., Chicago, IL

U. S. Plywood, Div. of U. S. Plywood-Champion Papers, Inc., 777 Third Ave., New York, NY 10036

Weyerhaeuser Co., (Wood Prods. Group) Tacoma Bldg., Tacoma, WA 98401

HARDWARE, CABINET

Ajax Hardware Corp., 825 S. Ajax Ave., City of Industry, CA 91747

Amerock Corp., 4000 Auburn St., Rockford, IL 61101

Corbin/Safe, (Div. of Emhart Corp.) 102 Washington St., New Britain, CT 06050

Faultless Caster Co., 1421 Garvin St., Evansville, IN

Grant Pulley & Hardware Corp., 17 High St., West Nyack, NY

Hager Hinge Co., 139 Victor St., St. Louis, MO

Hardware Designers, Inc., Kisco Ave., Mt. Kisco, NY

Ideal Security Hardware Corp., 215 E. 9th, St. Paul, MN

Knape & Vogt Mfg. Co., 2700 Oak Industrial Dr., Grand Rapids, MI 49505

Kwikset Sales & Service Co., 615 E. Santa Ana St., Anaheim, CA 92805

Macklanburg-Duncan Co., 4041 N. Santa Fe, Oklahoma City, OK 73125

National Lock Co., 1902 7th St., Rockford, IL

Stanley Hardware Div. of The Stanley Works, 195 Lake St., New Britain, CT 06050

Weslock Co., 13344 S. Main St., Los Angeles, CA

Yale Lock & Hardware Div., Eaton Yale & Towne, Inc., 401 Theodore Fremd Ave. Rye, NY 10580

HOOKS AND BRACKETS

Add Sales Co., Inc., 403 N. 9th St., Manitowoc, WI

Knape & Vogt Mfg. Co., 2700 Oak Industrial Dr., Grand Rapids, MI 49505

Masonite Corp., 29 N. Wacker Dr., Chicago, IL

INSECTICIDES

Borden, Inc., Chemical Div., 350 Madison Ave., New York, NY 10017

California Chemical Co., Ortho Div., Lucas & Ortho Way, Richmond, CA

Dow Chemical Co., P.O. Box 426, Midland, MI 48640

DuPont (E. I.) de Nemours & Co., Product Info. Section, Wilmington, DE 19898

INSULATION

Flintkote Co., 400 Westchester Ave., White Plains, NY

GAF Corporation, Building Products Div., 140 W. 51st St., New York, NY 10020

Midwest Insulations, P.O. Box 336, Wabash, IN 46992

Pittsburgh Corning Corp., 1 Gateway Ctr., Pittsburgh, PA

Celotex Corp., 1500 N. Dale Mabry, Tampa, FL 33607

Armstrong Cork Co., 6402 Roosevelt, Lancaster, PA

Dierks Div.-Weyerhaeuser Co., 810 Whittington St., Hot Springs, AR

Bird & Son, Inc., Washington St., East Walpole, MA

IRON, ORNAMENTAL

Alco Engineering Co., P.O. Box 12640, Charleston, SC

Keystone Building Products, Box 1449, Harrisburg, PA

Locke Mfg. Co., 300 Ohio St., Lodi, OH 44254

Logan Company, 200 Cabel St., Louisville, KY

Metal Crafters, Box 577, Cedar Rapids, IA 52406

Tennessee Fabricating Co., 2366 Prospect, Memphis, TN

Versa Products Co., Billman St., Lodi, OH 44254

JALOUSIES

Alsco, Inc., 225 S. Forge St., Akron, OH 44308

Anderson (V. E.) Mfg. Co., 1515 E. 18th St., Owensboro, KY

Continental Aluminum Products Co., P.O. Box 208, McHenry, IL 60050

Duo-Temp Corp., 786 Terrace Blvd., Depew, NY 14043

Howard Industries, Inc., 6721 N.W. 36th Ave., Miami, FL

Rusco Industries, Inc., 1100 Glendon Ave., Los Angeles, CA 90024

Stanley-Artex Windows (Div. of The Stanley Works) 1890 N.E. 146th St., North Miami, FL 33161

Weather-Tite/Aristocraft Divs., Pacific Coast Co., 7103 Krick Rd., Cleveland, OH 44146

LACQUER

Cook Paint & Varnish Co., 1412 Knox, North Kansas City, MO 64116

Deft, Inc., 612 Maple Ave., Torrance, CA 90503

O'Brien Corp., 2001 W. Washington St., South Bend, IN

Sherwin-Williams Co., 101 Prospect Ave., N.W., Cleveland, OH 44101

Valspar Corp., 200 Sayre, Rockford, IL 61101

LADDERS

Babcock (W. W.) Co., Inc., Delaware Ave., Bath, NY

Duo-Safety Ladder Corp., 513 W. 9th Ave., Oshkosh, WI 54901

Michigan Ladder Co., Forest at River, Ypsilanti, MI

LATH, GYPSUM

Bestwall Gypsum Div., Georgia-Pacific Corp., P.O. Box 311, Portland, OR 97207

Celotex Corp., 1500 N. Dale Mabry, Tampa, FL 33607

Flintkote Co., 400 Westchester Ave., White Plains, NY

LATH, INSULATING

CPR Div., (The Upjohn Co.) 555 Alaska Ave., Torrance, CA 90503

National Gypsum Co., 325 Delaware St., Buffalo, NY

U. S. Gypsum Co., 101 S. Wacker Dr., Chicago, IL

LATH, METAL

Alabama Metal Industries Corp., P.O. Box 3928, Birmingham, AL 35208

Bostwick Steel Lath Co., 102 W. Federal St., Niles, OH

C. F. & I. Steel Corp., Box 1920, Denver, CO 80201

Mid States Steel & Wire Co., 510 S. Oak St., Crawfordsville, IN 47933

LEGS

All-Luminum Products, Inc., Tulip & Westmoreland Sts., Philadelphia, PA 19134

Angelus Consolidated Industries, Inc., 2911 Whittier Blvd., Los Angeles, CA 90023

Emco Specialties, Inc., 300 New York Ave., Des Moines, IA

Gerber Wrought Iron Prods., Inc., 1510 Fairview Ave., St. Louis, MO 63132

Metalcraft Engineering Co., 3625 N. 48th St., Lincoln, NE

Tennessee Fabricating Co., 2366 Prospect, Memphis, TN 38106

LUBRICANTS, HOME

American Grease Stick Co., 2651 Hoyt St., Muskegon, MI 49443

Cabot (Samuel), Inc., 246 Summer St., Boston, MA

DuPont (E. I.) de Nemours & Co., Product Info. Section, Wilmington, DE 19898

Miracle Adhesives Corp., 250 Pettit Ave., Bellmore, LI, NY

Norton Co., Coated Abrasive & Tape Divs., Dept. 6865, Troy, NY 12181

MANTELS, WOOD

Angel Co., Inc., 340 Broad St., Fitchburg, MA 01420

Hewnrite Industries, Inc., 5 Picone Blvd., Farmingdale, NY 11735

Olinkraft Wood Prods. Div., Olinkraft, Inc., P.O. Box 488, West Monroe, LA 71291

Potlatch Forests, Inc., P.O. Box 3591, San Francisco, CA 94119

Westchester Timber Corp., 47 McClellan St., Newark, NJ

MIRRORS

Bache (Semon) & Co., 636 Greenwich St., New York, NY

Curtis-Electro Lighting, Inc. (NATCCO Div.) 1536 S. Paulina Ave., Chicago, IL 60608

Hall Mack (A Textron Co.) 801 W. 8th St., Cincinnati, OH 45203

Kidde (Walter) & Co., Inc., 798 Main St., Belleville, NJ

Libbey-Owens-Ford Co., 811 Madison Ave., Toledo, OH

PPG Industries, 632 Fort Duquesne Blvd., Pittsburgh, PA 15222

Regal Prods. Corp., P.O. Box 1508, Harrisburg, PA

MOULDINGS AND TRIMS

Anthony Forest Products Co., P.O. Box 1877, El Dorado, AR 71730

Boise-Cascade Corp., P.O. Box 923, Boise, ID

Cannon Craft Co., P.O. Box 307, Sulphur Springs, TX

Colombia Moulding Co., 1408 Standard Oil Bldg., Baltimore, MD 21202

Evans Products Co., Building Products Group, P.O. Box 880, Corona, CA 91720

Hardboard Fabricators Corp., 79 Empire St., Newark, NJ

Marvin Windows, Warroad, MN 56763

Masonite Corp., 29 N. Wacker Dr., Chicago, IL

Potlatch Forests, Inc., Southern Div., Wood Products Group, P.O. Box 390, Warren, AR 71671

St. Regis Paper Co., Forest Products Div., 1019 Pacific Ave., S. Tacoma, WA 98401

Western Wood Prods. Assn., 710 Yeon Bldg, Portland, OR 97204

Woodtape, Inc., 3911 Airport Way, S, Seattle, WA

OPERATORS, ELECTRIC DOOR

Berry Doors Div. of The Stanley Works, 2400 E. Lincoln Rd., Birmingham, MI 48012

Chamberlain Mfg. Corp., 845 Larch Ave., Elmhurst, IL

Crawford Door Co., 4270 High St., Ecorse, MI 48229

Frantz Mfg. Co., 301 W. 3rd St., Sterling, IL

Kawneer Co., 1105 N. Front St., Niles, MI 49120

Norton Door Closer Div., Eaton Yale & Towne, Inc., 372 Meyer Rd., Bensenville, IL 60106

Overhead Door Corp., 8600 S. Central Expressway, Dallas, TX

Raynor Mfg. Co., E. River Rd., Dixon, IL 61021

Rowe Mfg. Co., 614 W. Third St. Galesburg, IL

OUTDOOR FIREPLACE EQUIPMENT

Bennett Ireland Co., 23 State St., Norwich, NY

Ductless Hood Co., 151 Haven Ave., Port Washington, NY 11050

Majestic Co., Inc., 516 Erie St., Huntington, IN

Vestal Mfg. Co., Box 420, Sweetwater, TN 37874

PAINTS, COLDWATER

Devoe Paint Div. (Celanese Coatings Co.) 224 E. Broadway, Louisville, KY 40202

National Gypsum Co., 325 Delaware St., Buffalo, NY

PPG Industries, 632 Fort Duquesne Blvd., Pittsburgh, PA 15222

Republic Powdered Metals, Inc., 2628 Pearl Rd., Medina, OH 44256

Sherwin-Williams Co., 101 Prospect Ave., N.W., Cleveland, OH 44101

U. S. Protective Coatings, Inc., 1200 Court Square Bldg., Baltimore, MD 21202

PAINTS, EPOXY

Anti-Hydro Waterproofing Co., 265 Badger Ave., Newark, NJ 07108

Cook Paint & Varnish Co., 1412 Knox, North Kansas City, MO 64116

DuPont (E. I.) de Nemours & Co., Prod. Info. Section, Wilmington, DE 19898

Enterprise Paint Mfg. Co., 2841 S. Ashland Ave., Chicago, IL 60608

Fuller-O'Brien Corp., 4115 W. Artesia, Fullerton, CA

Jewel Paint & Varnish Co., 345 N. Western Ave., Chicago, IL 60612

Martin-Senour Co., 2500 S. Senour Ave., Chicago, IL

O'Brien Corp., 2001 W. Washington St., South Bend, IN 46621

Pratt & Lambert, 75 Tonawanda St., Buffalo, NY

Rust-Oleum Corp., 2301 Oakton St., Evanston, IL

Sherwin-Williams Co., 101 Prospect Ave., N.W., Cleveland, OH 44101

3M Company, 3M Center, St. Paul, MN 55101

PAINTS, LATEX

Bruning Paint Co., Inc., Fleet and Haven Streets, Baltimore, MD

Calbar, Inc., 2626 N. Martha St., Philadelphia, PA

Cook Paint & Varnish Co., 1412 Knox, North Kansas City, MO 64116

Devoe Paint Div. (Celanese Coatings Co.) 224 E. Broadway, Louisville, KY 40202

Elliott Paint & Varnish Co., 4525 W. Fifth Ave., Chicago, IL 60624

Foy-Johnston, Inc., 1776 Mentor Ave., Cincinnati, OH

Hanna Paint Mfg. Co., 1313 Windsor St., Columbus, OH

Klee Chemical Coatings, 4011 Red Bank Rd., Cincinnati, OH 45227

Plywood and hardboard paneling are popular wall coverings; prices range from very low to ultrahigh, depending on type of wood and how the panels are matched. Most panels are prefinished; you simply apply them to the wall over furring strips, or directly to sound walls with adhesive. You can buy panels of high-pressure laminates for accent walls, special effects

Kyanize Paints, Inc., 2nd & Boston St., Everett, MA

Lowe Bros. Co., 424 E. 3rd, Dayton, OH 45402

Masury Paint Co., Div. of Conchemco, Inc., Bayard & Seven St., Baltimore, MD 21230

Monroe Co., 10707 Quebec Ave., Cleveland, OH 44106

National Lead Co., 111 Broadway, New York, NY

Pabco Bldg. Materials Div. (Fibreboard Corp.) 475 Brannan St., San Francisco, CA 94119

PPG Industries, 632 Fort Duquesne Blvd., Pittsburgh, PA 15222

Pratt & Lambert, 75 Tonawanda St., Buffalo, NY

Sherwin-Williams Co., 101 Prospect Ave., N.W., Cleveland, OH 44101

PAINTS, METAL

Al-Chroma Paint Co., 2701 Chamber St., Stevens Point, WI 54481

Alumatone Corp., 1523 Grande Vista Ave., Los Angeles, CA 90023

Cabot (Samuel), Inc., 246 Summer St., Boston, MA

Cook Paint & Varnish Co., 1412 Knox, North Kansas City, MO 64116

Enterprise Paint Mfg. Co., 2841 S. Ashland Ave., Chicago, IL 60608

Glidden-Durkee (Div. of SCM Corp.)

900 Union Commerce Bldg., Cleveland, OH 44115

Lucas (John) & Co., 1617 J. F. Kennedy Blvd., Philadelphia, PA 19103

Martin-Senour Co., 2500 S. Senour Ave., Chicago, IL 60608

Rust-Oleum Corp., 2301 Oakton St., Evanston, IL

PAINTS, METALLIC

Alumatone Corp., 1523 Grande Vista Ave., Los Angeles, CA 90023

Cabot (Samuel), Inc., 246 Summer St., Boston, MA

Cook Paint & Varnish Co., 1412 Knox, North Kansas City, MO 64116

DuPont (E. I.) de Nemours & Co., Product Info. Section, Wilmington, DE 19898

Glidden-Durkee (Div. of SCM Corp.) 900 Union Commerce Bldg., Cleveland, OH 44115

Lowe Bros. Co. 424 E. 3rd, Dayton, OH 45402

Martin-Senour Co., 2500 S. Senour Ave., Chicago, IL

PPG Industries, 632 Fort Duquesne Blvd., Pittsburgh, PA 15222

Rust-Oleum Corp., 2301 Oakton St., Evanston, IL

Sherwin-Williams Co., 101 Prospect Ave., N.W., Cleveland, OH 44101

Valspar Corp., 200 Sayre St., Rockford, IL 61101

PAINTS, OIL

Alumi-Gard Co., 1638 W. 79th St., Chicago, IL

Cabot (Samuel), Inc., 246 Summer St., Boston, MA

Devoe Paint Div. (Celanese Coatings Co.) 224 E. Broadway, Louisville, KY 40202

Elliott Paint & Varnish Co., 4525 W. Fifth Ave., Chicago, IL 60624

Enterprise Paint Mfg. Co., 2841 S. Ashland Ave., Chicago, IL 60608

Glidden-Durkee (Div. of SCM Corp.) 900 Union Commerce Bldg., Cleveland, OH 44115

Hanna Paint Mfg. Co., 1313 Windsor St., Columbus, OH

Jewel Paint & Varnish Co., 345 N. Western Ave., Chicago, IL 60612

Lowe Bros Co., 424 E. 3rd, Dayton, OH 45402

Sherwin-Williams Co., 101 Prospect Ave., N.W., Cleveland, OH 44101

PANELING

Fuller (H. B.) Co., 2400 Kasota Ave., St. Paul, MN

Sanspray Industries, Inc., 515 Madison Ave., New York, NY 10022

Abitibi Corp., 1400 N. Woodward Ave., Birmingham, MI 48011

451

Barclay Industries, Inc., 65 Industrial Rd., Lodi, NJ 07644
Celotex Corp., 1500 N. Dale Mabry, Tampa, FL 33607
Conwed Corp., 332 Minnesota St., St. Paul, MN
Evans Products Co., Building Products Group, P.O. Box 880, Corona, CA 91720
Evans Prods. Co., Fiber Prods. Div., P.O. Box E, Corvallis, OR 97330
Forest Fiber Products Co., Box 68-B, Forest Grove, OR
Georgia-Pacific Corp., P.O. Box 311, Portland, OR
Hardboard Fabricators Corp., 79 Empire St., Newark, NJ
Johns-Manville Corp., 22 E. 40th St., New York, NY
Marlite Division of Masonite Corp., Dover, OH 44622
Masonite Corp. 29 N. Wacker Dr., Chicago, IL 60606
Panelboard Mfg. Co., 100 James St., Somerville, NJ
Superior Wall Prods. Co., 4401 N. American, Philadelphia, PA 19140
Weyerhaeuser Co. (Wood Prods. Group) Tacoma Bldg., Tacoma, WA 98401
American Plywood Association, 1119 A St. Tacoma, WA 98401
California Redwood Assn., 617 Montgomery St., San Francisco, CA 94111

PANELS, GLASS FIBER, PLASTIC
Artcrest Products Co., Inc., 401 W. Ontario St., Chicago, IL 60610
Bolen International, Inc., 7800 N. Milwaukee Ave., Niles, IL 60648
Filon Div., Vistron Corp., 12333 S. Van Ness Ave., Hawthorne, CA 90250
General Electric Co., Laminated Prods. Dept., Plastics Ave., Coshocton, OH 43812
K-Lux Products Div., KSH, Inc., 10091 Manchester Rd., St. Louis, MO 63122
Masonite Corp., 29 N. Wacker Dr., Chicago, IL 60606
Owens-Corning Fiberglas Corp., P.O. Box 901, Toledo, OH 43601
Reichhold Chemicals, Inc. (Reinforced Plastics Div.) 20545 Center Ridge Rd., Cleveland, OH 44116
Town & Country Reproductions, Inc., 90-28 Van Wyck Expressway, Jamaica, NY 11418
U. S. Plywood, Div. of U. S. Plywood-Champion Papers, Inc., 777 Third Ave., New York, NY 10036

PARTICLEBOARD
Barclay Industries, Inc., 64 Industrial Rd., Lodi, NJ 07644
Celotex Corp., 1500 N. Dale Mabry, Tampa, FL 33607
Duraflake Co., P.O. Box 428, Albany, OR 97321
Formica Corp., 4614 Spring Grove Ave., Cincinnati, OH
Long-Bell Div. (International Paper

Co.) Box 579, Longview, WA 98632
Masonite Corp., 29 N. Wacker Dr., Chicago, IL 60606
National Particleboard Assn., 711 14th St., N.W., Washington, DC 20005

PIPE, METAL
Aluminum Co. of America, 1501 Alcoa Bldg., Pittsburgh, PA 15219
Anaconda American Brass Co., 414 Meadow St., Waterbury, CT 06702
Nichols-Homeshield, Inc., 15 Spinning Wheel Rd., Hinsdale, IL 60521
U. S. Steel Corp. 525 Wm. Penn Pl., Pittsburgh, PA

PIPE, PLASTIC
Can-Tex Industries (Div. of Harsco Corp.) P.O. Box 340, Mineral Wells, TX 76067
Celanese Plastics Co., 4550 Cemetery Rd., Hilliard, OH
Colonial Plastics Mfg. Co., 8107 Grand Ave., Cleveland, OH 44104
Cresline Plastic Pipe Co., Inc., 955 Diamond, Evansville, IN 47717
DuPont (E. I.) de Nemours & Co., Product Info. Section, Wilmington, DE 19898
Ethyl Corp. (Visqueen Div.) P.O.

Box 2422, Baton Rouge, LA 79821
Flintkote Co. (Pipe Products Group) Orangeburg, NY
Kyova Pipe Co., 1912 S. 1st St., Ironton, OH 45638
Phillips Prods. Co., Inc., P.O. Box 66, Titusville, PA 16354
Thermoplastics Corp., P.O. Box 15694, Charlotte, NC

PIPE, VITRIFIED CLAY
Amvit, 24480 Lakeland Blvd., Euclid, OH 44132
Lehigh Sewer Pipe & Tile Co., Box 728, Fort Dodge, IA
National Clay Pipe Institute, 1130 17th St., N.W., Washington, DC

PLASTER, GYPSUM
Flintkote Co., 400 Westchester Ave., White Plains, NY
GAF Corporation, Building Products Div., 140 W. 51st St., New York, NY 10020
U. S. Gypsum Co., 101 S. Wacker Dr., Chicago, IL

PLASTER, LIME
Bestwall Gypsum Div., Georgia-Pacific Corp., P.O. Box 311, Portland, OR 97207

Plastic pipe is newcomer to building construction. Before you purchase any for a plumbing project, check your local code. Some areas do not yet permit the use of plastic pipe, although it has many advantages

Flintkote Co., 400 Westchester Ave., White Plains, NY

Ohio Lime Co., Woodville, OH

PLASTER, PATCHING

DAP, Inc., 5300 Huberville Rd., Dayton, OH 45401

GAF Corporation, Building Products Div., 140 W. 51st St., New York, NY 10020

Macco Adhesives Div., The Glidden-Durkee Co., 30400 Lakeland Blvd., Wickliffe, OH 44092

Magic American Chemical Corp., 14215 Caine Ave., Cleveland, OH 44128

Penn Crete Prods. Co., Inc., 2745 N. Amber St., Philadelphia, PA 19134

Rutland Products, 96 Curtis Ave., Rutland, VT 05702

Sakrete, Inc., Fischer & B & O RR, Cincinnati, OH

Tuff-Kote Co., 214 Seminary Ave., Woodstock, IL

PLASTIC LAMINATES

Conolite Div., Woodall Industries, Inc., 425 Maple Ave., Carpentersville, IL 60110

Consoweld Corp., 700 Hooker St., Wisconsin Rapids, WI

Formica Corp., 4614 Spring Grove Ave., Cincinnati, OH

Pioneer Plastics Corp., Pionite Road, Auburn, ME

U. S. Gypsum Co., 101 S. Wacker Dr., Chicago, IL

PLYWOOD

Anchor Sales Corp., 205 Bush St., Brooklyn, NY

Brown Co., Building Materials Div., 277 Park Ave., New York, NY 10017

Evans Products Co., Building Products Group, P.O. Box 880, Corona, CA 91720

Georgia-Pacific Corp., P.O. Box 311, Portland, OR

Jones Veneer & Plywood Co., P.O. Box 789, Eugene, OR

Long-Bell Div. (International Paper Co.) Box 579, Longview, WA 98632

Pascagoula Veneer Co., P.O. Box 612, Pascagoula, MS

Simpson Timber Co., 2000 Washington Bldg., Seattle, WA

Abitibi Corp., 1400 N. Woodward Ave., Birmingham, MI

Boise-Cascade Corp., P.O. Box 923, Boise, ID

Bruce (E. L.) Co., Box 397, Memphis, TN 38101

General Plywood Corp., 417 S. 32nd St., Louisville, KY

Hardwood Plywood Manufacturers Association, 2310 S. Walter Reed Dr., Arlington, VA 22206

American Plywood Association, 1119 A St. Tacoma, WA

POSTS, ADJUSTABLE

Adjusta-Post Mfg. Co., 605 W. Bowery St., Akron, OH

Dorfile Mfg. Co., 3800 S.E. Naef Rd., Portland, OR

Jack-Post Corp., P.O. Box 252, Galien, MI 49113

POSTS, CLOTHES, STEEL

Hy-Ko Prods. Co., 24001 Aurora Rd., Bedford Heights, OH 44146

Wolfe Steel Products Corp., P.O. Box 20065, Cleveland, OH

POSTS, FENCE

Armco Steel Corp., 7000 Roberts St., Kansas City, MO

C. F. & I. Steel Corp., Box 1920, Denver, CO 80201

Keystone Steel & Wire Co., 7000 S. Adams St., Peoria, IL

Northwestern Steel & Wire Co., Ave. B & Wallace St., Sterling, IL

Air-King Mfg. Corp., Box 6302, Tigard, OR 97223

California Redwood Assn., 617 Montgomery St., San Francisco, CA 94111

Dierks Div.-Weyerhaeuser Co., 810 Whittington St., Hot Springs, AR 71901

Hewnrite Industries, Inc., 5 Picone Blvd., Farmingdale, NY 11735

Weyerhaeuser Co., (Wood Prods. Group) Tacoma Bldg., Tacoma, WA 98401

PUMPS, SUMP

Barnes Mfg. Co., 651 N. Main St., Mansfield, OH

Crane Co., 4100 S. Kedzie Ave., Chicago, IL 60632

Dayton Electric Mfg. Co., 5959 W. Howard St., Chicago, IL 60648

Flint & Walling, Inc., 95 Oak St. Kendallville, IN

Milwaukee Faucets, Inc., 4250 N. 124th St., Milwaukee, WI 53201

Tait Mfg. Co., 500 Webster St., Dayton, OH

PUTTY

Atlas Minerals & Chemicals Div., ESB, Inc., 141 Elm St., Mertztown, PA 19539

Cabot (Samuel), Inc., 246 Summer St., Boston, MA

Chicago Adhesive Products Co., 4658 W. 60th St., Chicago, IL 60629

Cook Paint & Varnish Co., 1412 Knox, North Kansas City, MO 64116

DuPont (E. I.) de Nemours & Co., Product Info. Section, Wilmington, DE 19898

PPG Industries, 632 Fort Duquesne Blvd., Pittsburgh, PA 15222

Rutland Products, 96 Curtis Ave., Rutland, VT 05702

RAILINGS

Bel-Met, Inc., 439 S. Maple Ave., Greensburg, PA

Hollaender Mfg. Co., 3841 Spring Grove Ave., Cincinnati, OH 45223

Metal Crafters, Box 577, Cedar Rapids, IA 52406

Nichols-Homeshield, Inc., 15 Spinning Wheel Rd., Hinsdale, IL 60521

Shower Door Co. of America, P.O. Box 20202, Atlanta, GA

Tennessee Fabricating Co., 2366 Prospect, Memphis, TN 38106

RAIN CARRYING EQUIPMENT

Alabama Metal Industries Corp., P.O. Box 3928, Birmingham, AL 35208

Alcan Aluminum Corp., Building Products Division, Jacobus Ave., South Kearny, NJ 07032

Aluminum Co. of America, 1501 Alcoa Bldg., Pittsburgh, PA 15219

Amax Aluminum Bldg. Products, Inc., 820 E. Columbia St., Evansville, IN 47711

Kaiser Aluminum & Chemical Sales, 300 Lakeside Dr., Oakland CA 94604

Nichols-Homeshield, Inc., 15 Spinning Wheel Rd., Hinsdale, IL 60521

Reynolds Metals Co., Building Products & Supply Div., 325 W. Touhy Ave., Park Ridge, IL

Weather-Tite/Aristocraft Divs., Pacific Coast Co., 7103 Krick Rd., Cleveland, OH 44146

REMOVERS, PAINT

Chemical Products Co., P.O. Box 400, Aberdeen, MD

Deft, Inc. 612 Maple Ave. Torrance, CA 90503

DeMert & Dougherty, Inc., 5000 W. 41st St., Chicago, IL

Hyde Mfg. Co., 54 Eastford Rd., Southbridge, MA

Klean Strip Co., Inc., 2340 S. Lauderdale, Memphis, TN

Masury Paint Co., Div. of Conchemco, Inc., Bayard & Severn St., Baltimore, MD 21230

Pratt & Lambert, 75 Tonawanda St., Buffalo, NY 14207

Sherwin-Williams Co., 101 Prospect Ave., N.W., Cleveland, OH 44101

RIMS, SINK

Aetna Plumbing Industries, Inc., 4701 W. Augusta Blvd., Chicago, IL 60651

Kinkead Industries, Inc., 5860 N. Pulaski, Chicago, IL

Macklanburg-Duncan Co., 4041 N. Santa Fe, Oklahoma City, OK 73125

Youngstown Mfg., Inc., 700 Shepherd St., Hendersonville, NC 28739

ROLLERS, PAINT

Bestt Tollr, Inc., 160 S. Brooke, Fond du Lac, WI

Cook Paint & Varnish Co., 1412 Knox, North Kansas City, MO 64116

DeMert & Dougherty, Inc., 5000 W. 41st St., Chicago, IL

E-Z Paintr Corp., 4051 S. Iowa St., Milwaukee, WI

Fuller-O'Brien Corp., 4115 W. Artesia, Fullerton, CA

Lucas (John) & Co., 1617 J. F. Kennedy Blvd., Philadelphia, PA 19103

Rubberset Co., Crisfield, MD 21817

Sherwin-Williams Co., 101 Prospect Ave., N.W., Cleveland, OH 44101

Wooster Brush Co., 604 Madison Ave., Wooster, OH

ROOF EDGING
Alabama Metal Industries Corp., P.O. Box 3928, Birmingham, AL 35208
Cincinnati Sheet Metal & Roofing Co., 1725 Eastern Ave., Cincinnati, OH 45202
Modern Materials Corp., 16000 W. Nine Mile Rd., Southfield, MI 48075
Reynolds Metals Co., Building Products & Supply Div., 325 W. Touhy Ave., Park Ridge, IL
Wolverine Aluminum Corp., 1650 Howard, Lincoln Park, MI

ROOF VALLEY
Aluminum Co. of America, 1501 Alcoa Bldg., Pittsburgh, PA 15219
Anaconda American Brass Co., 414 Meadow St., Waterbury, CT 06702
Ceco Corp., 5601 W. 26th St., Chicago, IL 60650
Howmet Corp. (Building Products Div.) Box 1167C, Lancaster, PA 17604
Inland-Ryerson Construction Prods. Co., P.O. Box 393, Milwaukee, WI 53201
Lifeguard Inds., Inc., 4460 W. Mitchell Ave., Cincinnati, OH
Perry Metal Starting Strip, Inc., P.O. Box 222, Perry, IA

ROOFING MATERIALS
Aluminum Co. of America, 1501 Alcoa Bldg., Pittsburgh, PA 15219
Craver Industries, Inc., Craver Industrial Park, P.O. Box 10027, Charleston, SC 29411
Hartline Products Co., Inc., 2186 Noble Rd., Cleveland, OH 44112
Howmet Corp. (Building Products Div.) Box 1167C, Lancaster, PA 17604
Reynolds Metals Co., Building Products & Supply Div., 325 W. Touhy Ave., Park Ridge, IL
Carey (Philip) Corp., 320 S. Wayne Ave., Cincinnati, OH
GAF Corporation, Building Products Div., 140 W. 51st St., New York, NY 10020
Johns-Manville Corp., 22 E. 40th St., New York, NY
Supradur Corp. of New York, 122 E. 42nd St., New York, NY 10017
Bird & Son, Inc., Washington St., East Walpole, MA
Flintkote Co., 400 Westchester Ave., White Plains, NY
Fry (Lloyd A.) Roofing Co., 5818 Archer Rd., Summit, IL
Keystone Roofing Mfg. Co., Box 1549, York (Windsor Park), PA 17405
Pabco Bldg. Materials Div. (Fibreboard Corp.) 475 Brannan St., San Francisco, CA 94119
Globe Industries, Inc., 2638 E. 126th St., Chicago, IL 60633
Goodrich (B. F.) Co., Building Prods. Dept., 500 S. Main St., Akron, OH
Miracle Adhesives Corp., 250 Pettit Ave., Bellmore, LI, NY
Sisalkraft Div., St. Regis Paper Co., 55 Starkey Ave., Attleboro, MA

SANDERS
AEG Tool Div., (Ferrostaal Overseas

Decorative moldings are manufactured in wood, metal, plastic. You can buy cove, inside and outside corner trim, base shoe, picture molding, window and door trim, etc. Different patterns also are available in finished and unfinished strips

Corp.), 37–26 13th St., Long Island City, NY 11101
Black & Decker Mfg. Co., Joppa Rd., Towson, MD 21204
Millers Falls Co., 57 Wells St., Greenfield, MA
Milwaukee Electric Tool Corp., 13135 W. Lisbon Rd., Brookfield, WI 53005

SAWS
Boice Crane Div. of Wilton Tool Mfg. Co., Inc., 9525 Irving Park Rd., Schiller Park, IL 60176
Millers Falls Co., 57 Wells St., Greenfield, MA
Nicholson File Co., 676 Waterman Ave., E., Providence, RI 02914
Roberts Consolidated Industries, 600 N. Baldwin Park Blvd., City of Industry, CA 91747
Rockwell Mfg. Co. (Power Tool Div.) 676 N. Lexington Ave., Pittsburgh, PA 15208
Simonds Saw & Steel Div., Wallace-Murray Corp., Intervale Rd., Fitchburg, MA 01420
Yates-American Machine Co., Roscoe, IL
Black & Decker Mfg. Co., Joppa Rd., Towson, MD

Skil Corp., 5033 N. Elston Ave., Chicago, IL 60630

SCREENING
Chicopee Mfg. Co., Buford, GA 30518
Owens-Corning Fiberglas Corp., P.O. Box 901, Toledo, OH 43601
Plastic Woven Products Co., 51 Camden St., Paterson, NJ
Weather-Tite/Aristocraft Divs., Pacific Coast Co., 7103 Krick Rd., Cleveland, OH 44146
Kaiser Aluminum & Chemical Sales, 300 Lakeside Dr., Oakland, CA 94604
Macklanburg-Duncan Co., 4041 N. Santa Fe Ave., Oklahoma City, OK 73125
Phifer Wire Prods., P.O. Box 1700, Tuscaloosa, AL

SCREENS, DOOR AND WINDOW
Acorn Products Co., 12620 Westwood Ave., Detroit, MI 48223
Ador-Hilite (Sub. Rusco Industries, Inc.) 2401 W. Commonwealth Ave., Fullerton, CA 92634
Feather-Lite Mfg. Co., 21000 Hubbell Ave., Detroit, MI 48237
Homeshield Industries, Inc., Chatsworth, IL

454

Marvel Wood Corp., 110 E. Industry Ct., Deer Park, LI, NY 11729

Marvin Windows, Warroad, MN 56763

Rusco Industries, Inc., 1100 Glendon Ave., Los Angeles, CA 90024

SCREWS, WOOD

Aluminum Co. of America, 1501 Alcoa Bldg., Pittsburgh, PA 15219

Armco Steel Corp., 7000 Roberts St., Kansas City, MO 64125

Liberty Hardware Mfg. Corp., 44-39 Purvis St., Long Island City, NY 11101

National Lock Co., 1902 7th St., Rockford, IL

Reed & Prince Mfg. Co., Inc., Duncan Ave., Worcester, MA 01601

SEALERS, ASPHALT

Al-Chroma Paint Co., 2701 Chamber St., Stevens Point, WI 54481

Cabot (Samuel), Inc., 246 Summer St., Boston, MA

GAF Corporation, Building Products Div., 140 W. 51st St., New York, NY 10020

Norton Co., Coated Abrasive & Tape Divs., Dept. 6865, Troy, NY 12181

Sakrete, Inc., Fischer & B & O RR, Cincinnati, OH

United Gilsonite Laboratories, 1396 Jefferson Ave., Scranton, PA 18501

SEALERS, CONCRETE

American Sta-Dri Co., 4019 38th St., Brentwood, MD

Cabot (Samuel), Inc., 246 Summer St., Boston, MA

Chicago Adhesive Prods. Co., 4658 W. 60th St., Chicago, IL

Enterprise Paint Mfg. Co., 2841 S. Ashland Ave., Chicago, IL 60608

Hanna Paint Mfg. Co., 1313 Windsor St., Columbus, OH

O'Brien Corp., 2001 W. Washington St., South Bend, IN 46621

Rutland Products, 96 Curtis Ave., Rutland, VT 05702

3M Co., 3M Center, St. Paul, MN 55101

Watco-Dennis Corp., 1756 22nd St., Santa Monica, CA

SEALERS, CRACK/TUB

Anti-Hydro Waterproofing Co., 265 Badger Ave., Newark, NJ 07108

Consumers Glue Co., Inc., 1515 Hadley, St. Louis, MO 63106

Dow-Corning Corp., Consumer Products Division, P.O. Box 592, Midland, MI 48641

Macklanburg-Duncan Co., 4041 N. Santa Fe Ave., Oklahoma City, OK 73125

Miracle Adhesives Corp., 250 Pettit Ave., Bellmore, LI, NY

Savogran Co., P.O. Box 130, Norwood, MA 02062

Steelcote Mfg. Co., 3148 Gratiot St., St. Louis, MO 63103

United States Ceramic Tile Co., 1375 Raff Rd., S.W., Canton, OH 44710

Wilhold Glues, Inc., 8707 Millergrove Dr., Santa Fe Springs, CA 90670

SEALERS, WOOD

Allen Products Corp., 9214 Livernois, Detroit, MI

Cabot (Samuel), Inc., 246 Summer St., Boston, MA

Clarke Floor Machine Div., Studebaker Corp., 366 E. Clay Ave., Muskegon, MI 49443

Deft, Inc., 612 Maple Ave., Torrance, CA 90503

Elliott Paint & Varnish Co., 4525 W. Fifth Ave., Chicago, IL 60624

Jewel Paint & Varnish Co., 345 N. Western Ave., Chicago, IL 60612

Magic American Chemical Corp., 14215 Caine Ave., Cleveland, OH 44128

National Mfg. Corp., P.O. Box 189, Tonawanda, NY

O'Brien Corp., 2001 W. Washington St., South Bend, IN

Rez Co. (The), P.O. Box 142, Springdale, PA

Spe-De-Way Products Co., 8000 N.E. 14th Pl., Portland, OR

Wilhold Glues, Inc., 8707 Millergrove Dr., Santa Fe Springs, CA 90670

Wilson-Imperial Co., 115 Chestnut St., Newark, NJ

SEATS, TOILET

Aetna Plumbing Industries, Inc., 4701 W. Augusta Blvd., Chicago, IL 60651

American Plastic Products Co., 8745 Conant Ave., Hamtramck, MI

Crane Co., 4100 S. Kedzie Ave., Chicago, IL 60632

SHAKES

Canadian Forests Prods. Ltd., Hunting-Merritt Shingle Div., 9110 Milton St., Vancouver, BC, Canada

Evans Prods. Co., Building Prods. Group, P.O. Box 880, Corona, CA 91720

Georgia-Pacific Corp., P.O. Box 311, Portland, OR

Hines (Edward) Lumber Co., 200 S. Michigan Ave., Chicago, IL 60604

Long-Bell Div. (International Paper Co.) Box 479, Longview, WA 98632

Mauk (C. A.) Lumber Co., 1100 Elm St., Toledo, OH

Red Cedar Shingle & Handsplit Shake Bureau, 5510 White Bldg., Seattle, WA 98101

Shakertown Corp., 4416 Lee Rd., Cleveland, OH 44128

Weyerhaeuser Co., (Wood Prods. Group) Tacoma Bldg., Tacoma, WA 98401

SHEATHING

Celotex Corp., 1500 N. Dale Mabry, Tampa, FL 33607

Conwed Corp., 332 Minnesota St., St. Paul, MN 55101

Dierks Div.-Weyerhaeuser Co., 810 Whittington St., Hot Springs, AR 71901

National Gypsum Co., 325 Delaware St., Buffalo, NY

U.S. Gypsum Co., 101 S. Wacker Dr., Chicago, IL

SHEETS, ALUMINUM

Aluminum Co. of America, 1501 Alcoa Bldg., Pittsburgh, PA 15219

Hastings Aluminum Products, 429 S. Michigan St., Hastings, MI 49058

Howmet Corp. (Building Products Div.), Box 1167C, Lancaster, PA 17604

Kaiser Aluminum & Chemical Sales, 300 Lakeside Dr., Oakland, CA 94604

Revere Copper & Brass, Inc., 230 Park Ave., New York, NY

Reynolds Metals Co., Building Products & Supply Div., 325 W. Touhy Ave., Park Ridge, IL

Wolverine Aluminum Corp., 1650 Howard, Lincoln Park, MI

Premixed and prefabricated materials are boon to homeowner; both are designed to save time and mistakes. Cost may be slightly more; convenience may be worth it

SHELVES, CABINET

Ajax Hardware Corp., 825 S. Ajax Ave., City of Industry, CA 91747
Lazy Sather Hardware, Box 91, Ontario, CA
Stonier (Russ), Inc., 1375 Mercandise Mart, Chicago, IL 60654
Triangle Mfg. Co., 388 Division St., Oshkosh, WI
Washington Div. Ekco Building Products Co., 1250 Bedford Ave., S.W., Canton, OH 44701

SHELVING, PLASTIC

Clopay Corp., Clopay Square, Cincinnati, OH 45214
DuPont (E. I.) de Nemours & Co., Product Info. Section, Wilmington, DE 19898
Laminated Plastics, Inc., 1610 S. Buder Industrial Drive, St. Louis, MO 63144
Reiss Associates, Inc., Reiss Ave., Lowell, MA

SHELVING, STEEL

Add Sales Co., Inc., 403 N. 9th St., Manitowoc, WI
Cincinnati Sheet Metal & Roofing Co., 1725 Eastern Ave., Cincinnati, OH 45202
Dexion, Inc., 39-27 59th St., Woodside, LI, NY
Float-Away Door Co., 1173 Zonolite Rd., N.E., Atlanta, GA 30306
Hirsh Co. (The), 8051 Central Park, Skokie, IL
Metaline Products, Inc., 2625 Middlebury St., Elkhart, IN 46514
Redi-Bolt, Inc., 5334 Indianapolis Blvd., East Chicago, IN

SHINGLES, COMPOSITION

Bird & Son, Inc., Washington St., East Walpole, MA
Carey (Philip) Corp., 320 S. Wayne Ave., Cincinnati, OH
Celotex Corp., 1500 N. Dale Mabry, Tampa, FL 33607
Certain-Teed Products Corp., 120 E. Lancaster St., Ardmore, PA 19003
Flintkote Co., 400 Westchester Ave., White Plains, NY
Fry (Lloyd A.) Roofing Co., 5818 Archer Rd., Summit, IL
Johns-Manville Corp., 22 E. 40th St., New York, NY
Keystone Roofing Mfg. Co., Box 1549, York (Windsor Park), PA 17405

SHINGLES, WOOD

Evans Prods. Co., Building Prods. Group, P.O. Box 880, Corona, CA 91720
Georgia-Pacific Corp., P.O. Box 311, Portland, OR
Red Cedar Shingle & Handsplit Shake Bureau, 5510 White Bldg., Seattle, WA 98101

SHUTTERS

Addison Products Co., 10 Railroad St., Addison, MI
Hastings Aluminum Products, 429 S. Michigan St., Hastings, MI 49058

U.S. Aluminum & Chemical Corp., 11440 W. Addison St., Franklin Park, IL 60131
Woodcraft Millwork, P.O. Box 231, Moonachie, NJ

SIDING, ALUMINUM

Alcan Aluminum Corp., Building Products Division, Jacobus Ave., South Kearny, NJ 07032
Alsco, Inc., 225 S. Forge St., Akron, OH 44308
Aluminum Association (The), 420 Lexington Ave., New York, NY 10017
Nichols-Homeshield, Inc., 15 Spinning Wheel Rd., Hinsdale, IL 60521
Security Aluminum Co., 385 Midland St., Detroit, MI

SIDING, ASPHALT

Celotex Corp., 1500 N. Dale Mabry, Tampa, FL 33607
Flintkote Co., 400 Westchester Ave., White Plains, NY
GAF Corporation, Building Products Div., 140 W. 51st St., New York, NY 10020
Johns-Manville Corp., 22 E. 40th St., New York, NY
U.S. Gypsum Co., 101 S. Wacker Dr., Chicago, IL

SIDING, HARDBOARD

Abitibi Corp., 1400 N. Woodward Ave., Birmingham, MI
Evans Products Co., Building Products Group, P.O. Box 880, Corona, CA 91720
Georgia-Pacific Corp., P.O. Box 311, Portland, OR
Masonite Corp., 29 N. Wacker Dr., Chicago, IL
Flintkote Co., 400 Westchester Ave., White Plains, NY
National Gypsum Co., 325 Delaware St., Buffalo, NY
U.S. Gypsum Co., 101 S. Wacker Dr., Chicago, IL

SIDING, PLASTIC

Alsar, Inc., 21121 Telegraph Road, Southfield, MI
Bird & Son, Inc., Washington St., East Walpole, MA
Carey (Philip) Corp., 320 S. Wayne Ave., Cincinnati, OH
Mastic Corp., 131 S. Taylor St., South Bend, IN
Thermoplastics Corp., P.O. Box 15694, Charlotte, NC

SIDING, PLYWOOD

American Plywood Association, 1119 A St., Tacoma, WA 98401
Boise-Cascade Corp., P.O. Box 923, Boise, ID
Evans Products Co., Building Products Group, P.O. Box 880, Corona, CA 91720
Long-Bell Div. (International Paper Co.) Box 379, Longview, WA 98632
Weyerhaeuser Co. (Wood Prods. Group) Tacoma Bldg., Tacoma, WA 98401

SINKS, KITCHEN

Aetna Plumbing Industries, Inc., 4701 W. Augusta Blvd., Chicago, IL 60651
American Standard, 40 W. 40th St., New York, NY
Borg-Warner Corp., Plumbing Products Div., 207 E. 5th, Mansfield, OH
Elkay Mfg. Co., 2700 17th Ave., Broadview, IL
Kohler Co., Kohler, WI 50344
Modern Maid, Inc., Main & Holtzclaw Sts., Chattanooga, TN 37401
Youngstown Kitchens Div., Mullins Mfg. Corp., 605 S. Ellsworth Ave., Salem, OH 44460

SKYLIGHTS, PLASTIC

Afco Products, Inc. 44 Park St., Somerville, MA
Filon Div., Vistron Corp., 12333 S. Van Ness Ave., Hawthorne, CA 90250
Kemlite Corp., 101 N. Republic Ave., Joliet, IL
Plasteco, Inc., P.O. Box 9485, Houston, TX
Ventarama Skylight Corp., 174 Main St., Port Washington, NY
Wasco Prods., Inc. 595 North Ave., Wakefield, MA

SOFFITT SYSTEMS

Bird & Son, Inc., Washington St., East Walpole, MA
Carey (Philip) Corp., 320 S. Wayne Ave., Cincinnati, OH
Conwed Corp., 332 Minnesota St., St. Paul, MN 55101
Eastern Metal Mouldings, Inc., 5937 Concord Ave., Detroit, MI 48211
Harris, Inc., 200 E. Long St., Columbus, OH 43215
Homasote Co., Lower Ferry Rd., Trenton, NJ 08603
Masonite Corp., 29 N. Wacker Dr., Chicago, IL
National Aluminum Prods. Co., McFann Rd. at Route 8, Valencia, PA 16059
Schumacher (F. E.) Co., 200 Mill St., Hartville, OH 44632

STAIN, CONCRETE

Cabot (Samuel), Inc., 246 Summer St., Boston, MA
DuPont (E. I.) de Nemours & Co., Product Info. Section, Wilmington, DE 19898
Olympic Stained Products Co., 1118 Leary Way, N.W., Seattle, WA 98107
Rez Co. (The), P.O. Box 142, Springdale, PA

STAIN, WOOD

Cabot (Samuel), Inc., 246 Summer St., Boston, MA
Cook Paint & Varnish Co., 1412 Knox, North Kansas City, MO 64116
DuPont (E. I.) de Nemours & Co., Product Info. Section, Wilmington, DE 19898
O'Brien Corp., 2001 W. Washington St., South Bend, IN 46621
Sherwin-Williams Co., 101 Prospect Ave., N.W., Cleveland, OH 44101

STAIR, CONSTRUCTION KITS

Build-A-Stair Co., 550 W. Merrick Rd., Valley Stream, NY
Morgan Co., 601 Oregon St., Oshkosh, WI 54901
Woodcraft Millwork, P.O. Box 231, Moonachie, NJ

STAIRCASE, SPIRAL

American Panel Products, 1735 Holmes Rd., Ypsilanti, MI 48197
Metal Crafters, Box 577, Cedar Rapids, IA 52406

STONE, SYNTHETIC

Alsar, Inc. 21121 Telegraph Road, Southfield, MI
Bolen International, Inc., 7800 N. Milwaukee Ave., Niles, IL 60648
Decro-Wall Corp., 375 Executive Blvd., Elmsford, NY
Tapco Prods. Co., Inc., 9240 Hubbell, Detroit, MI

STUCCO, FACTORY MIXED

California Products Corp., 169 Waverly St., Cambridge, MA 02139
Dow Chemical Co., P.O. Box 426, Midland, MI 48640
Dunn (W. E.) Mfg. Co., 413 W. 24th St., Holland, MI 49423
Penn Crete Prods. Co., Inc. 2745 N. Amber St., Philadelphia, PA 19134
U.S. Gypsum Co., 101 S. Wacker Dr., Chicago, IL

TANKS, SEPTIC

Can-Tex Industries (Div. of Harsco Corp.) P.O. Box 340, Mineral Wells, TX 76067
Evans Brick & Pipe Co., Inc., Uhrichsville, OH 44683
Lehigh Sewer Pipe & Tile Co., Box 728, Fort Dodge, IA

Logan Clay Products Co., P.O. Box 698, Logan OH
Superior Clay Corp., P.O. Box 352, Uhrichsville, OH
Vega Industries, Inc., 402 E. Brighton Ave., Syracuse, NY

TAPE

Johns-Manville Corp., 22 E. 40th St., New York, NY
Metallic Plastics Corp., 300 Madison Ave., New York, NY 10017
3M Company, 3M Center, St. Paul, MN 55101

TAR

Cabot (Samuel), Inc., 246 Summer St., Boston, MA
Kol-Tar, Inc., 699 Adams St., N., Abington, MA
Miller Purcell Co., 244 W. 3rd Ave., New Lenox, IL

THRESHOLDS

Alsco, Inc., 225 S. Forge St., Akron, OH 44308
Aluminum Association (The), 420 Lexington Ave., New York, NY 10017
Feather-Lite Mfg. Co., 21000 Hubbell Ave., Detroit, MI
King Aluminum Corp., 1010 N. Fourth St., Miamisburg, OH
Macklanburg-Duncan Co., 4041 N. Santa Fe, Oklahoma City, OK 73125
Reynolds Metals Co., Building Products & Supply Div., 325 W. Touhy Ave., Park Ridge, IL
Sentry Stop-A-Draft Co., 715 St. Clair Ave., N.W., Cleveland, OH
Wooster Products, 901 Spruce, Wooster, OH 44691

TILE, CARPET

Armstrong Cork Co., 6402 Roosevelt,

Lancaster, PA
Mactac Consumer Prods. Div., Morgan Adhesives Co., 4560 Darrow Rd., Stow, OH 44224
Ozite Corp., 7-120 Merchandise Mart, Chicago, IL
Selck (Walter E.) & Co., 7125 W. Gunnison, Chicago, IL 60656
Tile Co. of America, Inc., P.O. Box 1709, Dalton, GA 30720

TILE, CERAMIC

Amsterdam Corp., 41 East 42nd St., New York, NY
Bruce (E. L.) Co., Box 397, Memphis, TN 38101
Mosaic Tile Co., P.O. Box 999, Florence, AL 35630
United States Ceramic Tile Co., 1375 Raff Rd., S.W., Canton, OH 44710

TILE, DRAIN

Amvit, 24480 Lakeland Blvd., Euclid, OH 44132
Frederic Brick & Tile Co., 4280 Natural Bridge Blvd., St. Louis, MO 63115
Krick-Tyndall Co., P.O. Box 268, Decatur, IN
Robinson Clay Product Co., 65 W. State St., Akron, OH

TILE, FLOOR

American Biltrite Rubber Co., Perrine Ave., Trenton, NJ
Armstrong Cork Co., 6402 Roosevelt, Lancaster, PA
Azrock Floor Products, Box 531, San Antonio, TX
Flintkote Co., 400 Westchester Ave., White Plains, NY
GAF Corporation, Building Products Div., 140 W. 51st St., New York, NY 10020
United States Ceramic Tile Co., 1375 Raff Rd., S.W., Canton, Ohio 44710

TILE, METAL

Crown Tile Corp., 125 Walnut Rd., S.E. Massillon, OH
Selck (Walter E.) & Co., 7125 W. Gunnison, Chicago, IL
Vikon Tile Corp., 130 N. Taylor St., Washington, NJ

TILE, PLASTIC WALL

Barclay Industries, Inc., 65 Industrial Rd., Lodi, NJ 07644
Congoleum-Nairn, Inc., 195 Belgrove Dr., Kearny, NJ
Mactac Consumer Prods. Div., Morgan Adhesives Co., 4560 Darrow Rd., Stow, Ohio 44224

TOOLS

Black & Decker Mfg. Co., Joppa Rd., Towson, MD
Crescent Tool Co., 200 Harrison St., Jamestown, NY
Estwing Mfg. Co., 2647 8th St., Rockford, IL 61101
Fuller Tool Co., 152-35 10th Ave., Whitestone, NY

Fence posts should be sunk into the ground about a third of their length, so buy them long enough. Most posts have been treated with preservatives. Always check local building ordinances before you build a fence; some codes limit height and position

Goldblatt Tool Co., 503A Osage St., Kansas City, KS

Millers Falls Co., 57 Wells St., Greenfield, MA

Nicholson File Co., 676 Waterman Ave., E., Providence, RI 02914

Plumb (Fayette R.), Inc., 4837 James St., Philadelphia, PA

Rockwell Mfg. Co. (Power Tooi Div.) 676 N. Lexington Ave., Pittsburgh, PA 15208

Sandvik Steel, Inc., Finished Prods. Div., 1701 Nevins Blvd., Fairlawn, NJ 07710

Simonds Saw & Steel Div., Wallace-Murray Corp., Intervale Rd., Fitchburg, MA 01420

Stanley Tools Div., The Stanley Works, 600 Myrtle St., New Britain, CT 06050

True Temper Corp., 1623 Euclid Ave., Cleveland, OH

Milwaukee Electric Tool Corp., 13135 W. Lisbon Rd., Brookfield, WI 53005

TRIM, WOOD

Arcata Redwood Co., P.O. Box 218, Arcata, CA 95521

Bendix Mouldings, Inc., 1112 E. Tremont Ave., Bronx, NY 10460

Georgia-Pacific Corp., P.O. Box 311, Portland, OR

Kimberly-Clark Corp., Forest Products Div., P.O. Box 697, Anderson, CA

Woodcraft Millwork, P.O. Box 231, Moonachie, NJ

VAPOR BARRIERS

Alton Building Products Div. (Textile Paper Prods., Inc.) Box 47, Cedartown, GA 30125

Aluminum Co. of America, 1501 Alcoa Bldg., Pittsburgh, PA 15219

DuPont (E. I.) de Nemours, Film Dept., Nemours Bldg., Wilmington, DE 19898

GAF Corporation, Building Products Div., 140 W. 51st St., New York, NY 10020

Warp Bros., 1100 N. Cicero Ave., Chicago, IL 60651

VENEER, FLEXIBLE

Forrest Industries, Inc., P.O. Box 178, Dillard, OR

Parkwood Laminates, 134 Water St., Wakefield, MA

U. S. Plywood Div. of U. S. Plywood-Champion Papers, Inc., 777 Third Ave., New York, NY 10036

Woodtape, Inc., 3911 Airport Way, S., Seattle, WA

VENTILATORS

Allen Ventilating Division, 704 Woodward Ave., Rochester, MI 48063

Emerson Electric Co., 1800 W. Florissant St., St. Louis, MO 63136

Hastings Aluminum Products, 429 S. Michigan St., Hastings, MI 49058

Macklanburg-Duncan Co., 4041 N. Santa Fe, Oklahoma City, OK 73125

Starline, Inc., 300 W. Front St., Harvard, IL 60033

WALLBOARD, ASBESTOS CEMENT

Carey (Philip) Corp., 320 S. Wayne Ave., Cincinnati, OH

Flintkote Co., 400 Westchester Ave., White Plains, NY

Johns-Manville Corp., 22 E. 40th St., New York, NY

Nicolet Industries, Inc., Wissahickon Ave., Ambler, PA 19002

WALLBOARD, GYPSUM

Barclay Industries, Inc., 65 Industrial Rd., Lodi, NJ 07644

Celotex Corp., 1500 N. Dale Mabry, Tampa, FL 33607

GAF Corporation, Building Products Div., 140 W. 51st St., New York, NY 10020

National Gypsum Co., 325 Delaware St., Buffalo, NY

U.S. Gypsum Co., 101 S. Wacker Dr., Chicago, IL

WALL COVERINGS

Barclay Industries, Inc., 65 Industrial Rd., Lodi, NJ 07644

Devoe Paint Div. (Celanese Coatings Co.) 224 E. Broadway, Louisville, KY 40202

Nationa! Gypsum Co., 325 Delaware St., Buffalo, NY

Textone, Inc., 6533 Bandini Blvd., Los Angeles, CA

U. S. Plywood Div. of U. S. Plywood-Champion Papers, Inc., 777 Third Ave., New York, NY 10036

WALLPAPER

Birge Co., 390 Niagara St., Buffalo, NY 14240

Cook Paint & Varnish Co., 1412 Knox, North Kansas City, MO 64116

Devoe Paint Div. (Celanese Coatings Co.) 224 E. Broadway, Louisville, KY 40202

Imperial Wallpaper Mill, Inc., 3645 Warrensville Center Rd., Cleveland, OH

Klee Chemical Coatings, 4011 Red Bank Rd., Cincinnati, OH 45227

Valspar Corp., 200 Sayre, Rockford, IL 61101

WATERPROOFING

Afco Products, Inc., 44 Park St., Somerville, MA

Dow Chemical Co., P.O. Box 426, Midland, MI 48640

DuPont (E. I.) de Nemours & Co., Product Info. Section, Wilmington, DE 19898

Flintkote Co., 400 Westchester Ave., White Plains, NY

Goodrich (B. F.) Co., Building Prods. Dept., 500 S. Main St., Akron, OH

Grace (W. R.) & Co. (Construction Products Div.) 62 Whittemore Ave., Cambridge, MA 02140

Tuff-Kote Co., 214 Seminary Ave., Woodstock, IL

Union Carbide Corp., Plastics Prods. Div., 270 Park Ave., New York, NY 10017

Warp Bros., 1100 N. Cicero Ave., Chicago, IL 60651

WEATHERSTRIP

Afco Corp., P.O. Box 5085, Alexandria, LA 71303

Ames Metal Moulding Co., Inc., 350 N. Midland Ave., Saddle Brook, NJ 07662

Dennis (W. J.) & Co., 9148 King St., Franklin Park, IL

Ever-Roll Mfg. Corp., 2104 W. Dorothy Lane, Dayton, OH

Macklanburg-Duncan Co., 4041 N. Santa Fe., Oklahoma City, OK 73125

Miller & Co., P.O. Box 779, Selma, AL

R O W Window Sales Co., 1365 Academy St., Ferndale, MI 48220

Schlegel Mfg. Co., 1555 Jefferson Rd., Rochester, NY

Sentry Stop-A-Draft Co., 715 St. Clair Ave., N.W., Cleveland, OH

3M Company, 3M Center, St. Paul, MN 55101

Zegers, Inc., 8090 South Chicago Ave., Chicago, IL

WINDOWS

Acorn Products Co., 12620 Westwood Ave., Detroit, MI

Amco Aluminum Corp., 8501 Hegerman St., Philadelphia, PA

Andersen Corp., Bayport, MN 55003

Architectural Aluminum Mfrs. Assn., One E. Wacker Dr., Chicago, IL 60601

Dorway Mfg. Co., 4515 Prentice St., Dallas, TX

Kawneer Co., 1105 N. Front St., Niles, MI 49120

Keystone Building Products, Box 1449, Harrisburg, PA 17105

Look Products Div. of Rusco Industries, Inc., Millen Industrial Park, Millen, GA 30442

Reynolds Metals Co., Building Products & Supply Div., 325 W. Touhy Ave., Park Ridge, IL

Rusco Industries, Inc., 1100 Glendon Ave., Los Angeles, CA 90024

Stanley-Artex Windows (Div. of The Stanley Works) 1890 N.E. 146th St., North Miami, FL 33161

Weather-Tite/Aristocrat Divs., Pacific Coast Co., 7103 Krick Rd., Cleveland, OH 44146

Wepco Div., Weatherproof Co., P.O. Box 45, Litchfield, IL

Western Wood Prods. Assn., 710 Yeon Bldg., Portland, OR 97204

WIRING AND LIGHTING

Circle F Industries, Box 591, Trenton, NJ 08604

General Electric Wiring Device, Dept. 95, Hathaway St., Providence, RI 02907

Sylvania Elec. Prod., Inc., 730 Third Ave., New York, NY

Thomas Industries, Inc., 207 E. Broadway, Louisville, KY

Westinghouse Electric Corp., P.O. Box 2278, Pittsburgh, PA 15230

brand names: know what to buy

AA-LOK (transfer tie for masonry walls) AA Wire Products Co., 6100 S. New England Ave., Chicago IL 60638

ABITIBI (building board, ceiling tile, insulation, sheathing) Abitibi Corp. 1400 N. Woodward, Birmingham, MI 48011

ACORN (cabinet, builders' hardware) Acorn Manufacturing Co., 68 Spring St., Mansfield, MA

ADAMATEAN (floor filler) O'Brien Corp. 2001 W. Washington, South Bend, IN

ADJUSTA (leveler guides) Adjustable Caster Co., 1411 Walnut St., Philadelphia, PA 19102

ADJUSTA-COLUMN (basement columns) Adjusta-Post Manufacturing Co., 605 W. Bowery, Akron, OH

ADLAKE (metal windows, doors, entrances) Adams & Westlake Co., Michigan St., Elkhart, IN

ADOR (aluminum sliding doors) Ador/Hilite, Rusco Industries, 2401 W. Commonwealth Ave., Fullerton, CA 92634

AIR KING (exhaust fans) Berns Air King Corp., 3050 N. Rockwell St., Chicago, IL 60018

AJAX (cabinet hardware) Ajax Hardware Corp., 825 S. Ajax Ave., City of Industry, CA

AJUST-A-RAIL (iron railings, columns) Locke Mfg. Co., 300 Ohio Street, Lodi, OA

ALLWEATHER (ventilators) Rudeen (N.H.) Co., 3356 Gorham Ave., S. Minneapolis, MN 55426

ALL-WEATHER (aluminum combination, jalousie, screen and patio doors) Moloney Co., 210 "A" St., Albia, IA

ALSIDE (aluminum building products) Alside, Inc., 3773 Akron-Cleveland Rd., Akron, OH 44309

AMCO (aluminum double-hung, sliding, awning and prime windows) Amco Aluminum Corp., 8501 Hegerman St., Philadelphia, PA

AMEROCK (cabinet hardware) Amerock Corp., 4000 Auburn, Rockford, IL 61101

AMROX (fiberglass masonry panels) Bolen International, Inc., 7800 N. Milwaukee Ave., Niles, IL

ANACONDA (copper flashing, gutters, roofing sheets) American Brass Co., 414 Meadow, Waterbury, CT

ANDERSEN (basement, casement, awning, double-hung, hopper, gliding wood windows and wall components) Andersen Corp., Bayport, MN

ANTI-HYDRO (Concrete hardeners, curing compounds, floor repair, antifreeze compounds; dampproofing compounds; concrete, brick and stucco paints; integral and surface-type waterproofing) Anti-Hydro Waterproofing Co., 265 Badger Ave., Newark, NJ

ARMSTRONG (resilient floors, building materials, adhesives, insulation, countertop & wall surfacing) Armstrong Cork Co., Lancaster, PA

AZROCK (asphalt floor tile) Azrock Floor Products, Box 531, San Antonio, TX 78206

AZTEC (ceramic free-standing fireplace) Condon-King Co., 5611 208th Ave., S.W., Lynnwood, WA

B

BALSAM-WOOL (blanket insulation) Conwed Corp., 332 Minnesota St., St. Paul, MN 55101

BARCLAY PLANK (melamine coated t&g panels) Barclay Industries, Inc., 65 Industrial Rd., Lodi, NJ

BEAR (abrasive paper, insulating and masking tape; abrasive discs and sheets) Norton Co., Coated Abrasive & Tape Divisions, Dept. 6865, Troy, NY

BERNZOMATIC (propane torches, lawn sprinklers and accessories) BernzOmatic Corp., 740 Driving Park Ave., Rochester, NY

BERRY (one-piece, steel sectional and fiberglass sectional garage doors) Berry Doors Div. of The Stanley Works, 2400 E. Lincoln Rd., Birmingham, MI

BESTWALL (gypsum wallboard; gypsum lath and plaster) Bestwall Gypsum Div. Georgia-Pacific Corp., P.O. Box 311, Portland, OR 97207

BESTWOOD (contact cement) Bestwood Corp., 51A Empire St., Newark, NJ

BETTER-BILT (sectional overhead garage doors and electric operators) Better-Bilt Door Co., White Horse Pike, Egg Harbor, NJ

BILCO (steel basement, floor and sidewalk doors; stair stringers) Bilco Co., New Haven, CT

BLACK & DECKER (portable electric tools) Black & Decker Mfg. Co., 600 E. Joppa Rd., Towson, MD

BLACK JACK (asphalt roof coating and cement) Gibson-Homans Co., 2366 Woodhill Rd., Cleveland, OH

BLUE STREAK (paint remover) Klean Strip Co., 2340 S. Lauderdale St., Memphis, TN 38106

BONDEX (cement & floor paint; waterproofing; cement patch) Reardon Co., 3616 Scarlet Oak Blvd., St. Louis, MO 63122

BONDWELL (concrete adhesive) Franklin Glue Co., 2020 Bruck St., Columbus, OH 43207

BOSTITCH (stapling hammers, pliers, tackers) Bostitch Div. of Textron, Inc., 842 Briggs Dr., East Greenwich, RI 02818

BRIGGS BEAUTYWARE (plumbing fixtures) Briggs Mfg. Co., 6600 E. 15-Mile Rd., Warren, MI 48092

BROAN (exhaust fans, range hoods, electric heaters) Broan Mfg. Co., P.O. Box 140, Hartford, WI

BRUCE (hardwood flooring) Bruce (E. L.) Co., Box 397, Memphis, TN

BRUSHES BY BAKER (paint brushes) Baker Brush Co., 83 Grand, New York, NY

BULLDOG (shovels) True Temper Corp., 1623 Euclid Ave., Cleveland, OH

BUZZMASTER (circular saws, blades, accessories) Buzzmaster, Inc., 606 Hartrey St., Evanston, IL

C

CABINET JEWELRY (cabinet hardware) Ajax Hardware Corp., 825 S. Ajax Ave., City of Industry, CA

CABINETPAK (panel system to renovate kitchen cabinets) Homewood Industries, 17641 S. Ashland Ave., Homewood, IL 60430

CALK-SCREW (screw shank nails) Maze Nails Div. of Maze (W. H.) Co., 400 Church, Peru, IL 61354

CAMPCRETE (emulsified asphalt binder) Camp Co., 9300 S. Sangamon, Chicago, IL

CANNONBALL (sliding door track and hangers) Starline, Inc., 300 W. Front, Harvard, IL

CANNON CRAFT (wood louver and screen doors; wood louvers and shutters; wood outside blinds) Cannon Craft Co., Sulphur Springs, TX

CASTILIAN (cushioned vinyl flooring) Armstrong Cork Co., 6402 Roosevelt St., Lancaster, PA 17604

CASTLE STONE (precast ledge rock) Tapco Products Co., 9240 Hubbell, Detroit, MI 48228

CEDAR-SAWN (cedar siding) Evans Products Co., Building Products Group, P.O. Box 880, Corona, CA

459

CEDAR WEAVE (prefabricated woven cedar fence) Early American Fence Co., Wells Rd., Escanaba, MI

CELEBRITY (stainless steel sinks) Elkay Mfg. Co., 2700 S. 17th Ave., Broadview, IL

CELLU-TONE SATIN (semi-gloss finish) Pratt & Lambert, 75 Tonawanda, Buffalo, NY

CHALLENGER (locks, door closers, overhead door holders) Challenger Lock Co., Div. of Eaton Yale & Towne, 2349 W. La Palma Ave., Anaheim, CA 92803

CHAMBRON (aluminum siding and accessories, shutters, aluminum doors and windows, garage doors, awnings and canopies) Chamberlain Mfg. Corp., 845 Larch Ave., Elmhurst, IL 60126

CHANNELLOCK (pliers and hammers) Channellock, Inc., S. Main St., Meadville, PA

CHIMNEY SWEEP (chemical soot destroyer) Miracle Adhesives Corp., 250 Pettit Ave., Bellmore, LI, NY

CHIP-STONE (texture vinyl flooring) Goodyear Tire & Rubber Co., Flooring Dept., Akron, OH

CLASSIC (vinyl asbestos floor tile) Flintkote Co., 400 Westchester Ave., White Plains, NY 10604

CLINCHER (wood and rubber felt weatherstrip) Dennis (W. J.) & Co., 9148 King, Franklin Park, IL

COLONEL LOGAN (ornamental iron) Logan Co., 201 Cabel, Louisville, KY 40206

COLOR-BLEND (wallboard nails in colors) Maze Nails Div. of W. H. Maze Co., 400 Church St., Peru, IL

COLOTRYM (shelf hardware, metal moulding, thresholds) Colotrym Div. of Futura Industries Corp., 35 S. Hanford St., Seattle, WA 98134

COM-A-DOR (door closers) Norton Door Closer Co., Div. Eaton Yale & Towne, Inc., 372 Meyer Rd., Bensenville, IL 60106

COMET (lock sets) Arrow Lock Corp., 4900 Glenwood Rd., Brooklyn, NY 11234

CONCORD (aluminum storm-screen window) Alsco, Inc., 225 S. Forge St., Akron, OH 44308

CONGOLEUM (enamel surfaced floor covering) Congoleum-Nairn, 195 Belgrove, Kearny, NJ

CONSOWELD (laminated plastic) Consoweld Corp., 700 Hooker, Wisconsin Rapids, WI

CONSUMERS (patching plaster, crack filler, spackling compound; asphalt and rubber tile cement) Consumers Glue Co., 1515 Hadley, St. Louis, MO

CON-TACT (self-adhesive vinyl wall tile) Comark Plastics Div., United Merchants, Inc., 1407 Broadway, New York, NY 10018

CONWED (suspended ceiling systems, ceiling tile and panels, hardboard, shutters, siding) Conwed Corp., 332 Minnesota St., St. Paul, MN 55101

COP-R-GUARD (flashing material) Weatherguard Service, 2339 Chatterton Ave., New York, NY

CORKTONE (asphalt and vinyl-asbestos tile) Kentile Floors, Inc., 58 Second St., Brooklyn, NY

CORRULUX (glass fiber-reinforced plastic panels) Johns-Manville, 22 E. 40th St., New York, NY

CRAK-STOP (crack sealer) Camp Co., 9300 S. Sangamon, Chicago, IL

CRESTLINE (wood windows and doors) Crestline, Inc., 100 Thomas St., Wausau, WI 54402

CURE-HARD (concrete curing and hardening compound) Meadows (W. R.), Inc., 22 Kimball, Elgin, IL

CUSHIONTONE (wood fiber acoustical ceiling tile) Armstrong Cork Co., Lancaster, PA 19604

CUSH-N-CLIP (resilient metal clip for wallboard ceiling construction) National Gypsum Co., 325 Delaware Ave., Buffalo, NY 14225

D

DAP (caulking, glazing and spackling compounds; putty) DAP, Inc., 5300 Huberville Rd., Dayton, OH

DECOBEAM (polyurethane beams) Reichhold Chemicals, Inc. (Reinforced Plastics Div.) 20545 Center Ridge Rd., Cleveland, OH 44116

DECORATOR (door and cabinet hardware) National Lock Co., 1902 7th St., Rockford, IL 61101

DECRA GUARD (printed woodgrain on flakeboard) Simpson Timber Co., 2000 Washington Bldg., Seattle, WA

DECRA-MOLD (wood mouldings for door faces) Decra-Mold Div., Agee Products Co., P.O. Box 75248, Oklahoma City, OK 73107

DEL MAR (bathroom accessories) Del Mar Mfg. Co., 12901 S. Western Ave., Gardena, CA 90249

DEVOE (brushes, enamels, exterior and interior paints and varnishes) Devoe Paint Div., Celanese Coating Co., Federal Land Bank Bldg., Louisville, KY

DEWALT (radial arm saws and accessories) Black & Decker Mfg. Co., 600 E. Joppa Rd., Towson, MD

DEXTER (builders' hardware) Dexter Lock Div., Kysor Industrial Corp., 1601 Madison, S.E., Grand Rapids, MI 49502

DIPNFLOW (paint brushes) Muralo Co., Inc., E. 5th and Hobart Ave., Bayonne, NJ 07002

DORWAL (aluminum sliding glass door) Acorn Products Co., 12620 Westwood Ave., Detroit, MI 48223

DRAFSTOP (weatherstrip-threshold) Duraflex Co., 3310 N.W. 30th, Miami, FL 33142

DRYLOK (dampproofing and waterproofing compound) United Gilsonite Laboratories, 1396 Jefferson Ave., Scranton, PA 18501

DUALINE (sliding door hardware)

Acme General Corp., 200 E. Railroad Ave., Monrovia, CA 91016

DUO-DOR (self-storing combination doors and windows) Wepco Div., Weatherproof Co., P.O. Box 45, Litchfield, IL

DURA-CRETE (acrylic patch) Penn Crete Products Co., Inc., 2745 N. Amber St., Philadelphia, PA

DURAFLAKE (smooth-surface particleboard) Duraflake Div. Williamette Industries, Inc., Albany, OR

DURA-SEAL (weatherstrip-sash balance) Zegers, Inc., 8090 S. Chicago Ave., Chicago, IL

DURHAM'S ROCK HARD (water putty) Durham (Donald) Co., Box 804N, Des Moines, IA

DUR-O-WAL (masonry wall reinforcement) Dur-O-waL National, Inc., 650 12th Ave., S.W., Cedar Rapids, IA 52404

DUTCH BOY (paints) National Lead Co., 111 Broadway, New York, NY

DYNA-BEAM (commercial ribbed aluminum siding) Lifeguard Industries, Inc., 4460 W. Mitchell Ave., Cincinnati, OH 45232

E

EAGLE (electric light fixtures and bulbs) Eagle Electric Mfg. Co., 23-10 Bridge Plaza, S, Long Island City, NY 11101

EASI-BILD (patterns, wood trim, picture frames) Easi-Bild Prods., Inc., 31 Saw Mill River Rd., Briarcliff Manor, NY 10510

EFFECTO (enamel) Pratt & Lambert, 75 Tonawanda, Buffalo, NY

ENAMELCLAD (roof coating system) Carey (Philip) Corp., 320 S. Wayne Ave., Cincinnati, OH 45214

ESTWING (hammers, carpenters' and lath hatchets, rock pics and sportsmen's axes) Estwing Mfg. Co., 2647 Eighth Ave., Rockford, IL

EVER-GRIP (floor tile adhesive) Ever-Tex, Inc., Mill St., Cranston, RI 02905

EXCELON (vinyl-asbestos flooring tile) Armstrong Cork Co., Lancaster, PA

EXPANDO (aluminum storm sash) Duo-Temp Corp., 786 Terrace Blvd., Depew, NY

E-Z GLAZE (glazing compound) Calbar, Inc., 2612-26 N. Martha, Philadelphia, PA

EZ-WAY (disappearing stairway) Ez-Way Sales, Box 300-65, St. Paul Park, MN

F

FABRIC X (paint roller covers) Wooster Brush Co., 604 Madison, Wooster, OH

FAMOWOOD (wood filler and putty) Beverly Mfg. Co., 9118 S. Main, Los Angeles, CA

FASHION-A-FENCE (pre-cut, packaged fencing) Potlatch Forests, Inc., P.O. Box 3591, San Francisco, CA

FEATHER-LIFT (weatherstrip-balance for double-hung wood windows) A R B Corp., 19433 John R. St., Detroit, MI 48203

FEATHER-LITE (aluminum combination and pre-hung doors) Feather-Lite Mfg. Co., 21000 Hubbell, Detroit, MI

FIBERGLAS (glass fibered batt or blanket insulation) Owens-Corning Fiberglas Corp., National Bank Bldg., Toledo, OH

FIBRETONE (acoustical fiberboard ceiling units) Johns-Manville, 22 E. 40th St., New York, NY

FILON (fiberglass-nylon reinforced plastic panels) Filon Div., Vistron Corp., 12333 S. Van Ness Ave., Hawthorne, CA 90250

FIRZITE (penetrating wod sealer-finish) U. S. Plywood Corp., 777 Third Ave., New York, NY

FLEXJOINT (caulking compounds) Pennsalt Chemicals Corp., 3 Penn Center, Philadelphia, PA 19102

FLEX-O-GLASS (plastic wndow material) Warp Brothers, 1100 N. Cicero Ave., Chicago, IL

FLINTKOTE (buildng products; flooring; adhesives) Flintkote Co., 400 Westchester Ave., White Plains, NY 10604

FLOAT-AWAY (bi-fold metal closet doors) Float-Away Door Co., 1173 Zonolite Rd., N.E., Atlanta, GA

FORESTONE (textured woodfiber acoustical ceiling tile) Simpson Timber Co., 2000 Washington Bldg., Seattle, WA

FRANTZ (garage doors, garage hardware) Frantz Mfg. Co., 301 W. 3rd, Sterling, IL

FRITZTILE (resin matrix terrazzo tile) Fritz Chemical Co., P.O. Box 17087, Dallas, TX

G

GAP'N LAP (pre-cut fencing) Potlatch Forests, Inc., P.O. Box 3591, San Francisco, CA 94119

GLAMOR-BOARD (plastic-surfaced hardboard) Pioneer Plastics Corp., Pionite Rd., Auburn, ME

GOLD SEAL (power tools) Dalton Mfg. Co., 20 S. Central, St. Louis, MO

GOLDEN JET (flexible plastic pipe) Celanese Plastics Co., 4550 Cemetery Rd., Hilliard, OH 43026

GREEN THUMB (garden gloves) Edmont-Wilson, 1282 Walnut St., Coshocton, OH 43812

GYPSOLITE (aggregate plaster) National Gypsum Co., 325 Delaware Ave., Buffalo, NY

H

HALLMARK (roofing shingles) Certain-Teed Products Corp., 120 E. Lancaster Ave., Ardmore, PA 19003

HANDI-CALK (caulking cartridges and bulk caulk) Gibson-Homans Co., 2366 Woodhill, Cleveland, OH

HANDI-GLAZE (glazing compound) Gibson-Homans Co., 2366 Woodhill, Cleveland, OH

HANDY-HOOKS (perforated hardboard, fixtures) Knape & Vogt Mfg. Co., 2700 Oak Industrial Dr., Grand Rapids, MI 49505

HANDYMAN (hand tools) Stanley Tools Div. of The Stanley Works, 600 Myrtle St., New Britain, CT

HARD TIP (circular saw blades) Heinemann Saw Corp., 2017 Navarre Rd., S.W., Canton, OH

HERITAGE (ornamental iron railings and columns) Gilpin Ornamental Iron, Box 226, Decatur, IN

H-GUN (airless paint spray gun) Spee-Flo Co., 4631 Winfield St., Houston, TX 77039

HI (plastic screw anchors; slotted tapping screws; toggle and expansion bolts; star drills; wire connectors) Holub Industries, Sycamore, IL

HI-LO (adjustable and straight steel basement columns; telescopic jack posts) Wolfe Steel Products Corp., P.O. Box 20065, Cleveland, OH

HOMASOTE (precision-built house components) Homasote Co., Lower Ferry Rd., Trenton, NJ

HOMEGUARD (cellulose loose fill insulation) Pal-O-Pak Insulation Co., Hartland, WI

HOMESHIELD (screened patio, porch and pool enclosures) Homeshield Industries, Inc., Chatsworth, IL

HUSKY (heavy-duty paint rollers) Rubberset Co., Crisfield, MD 21817

HYDRO-PLUG (fast-setting waterproof plug) Camp Co., 9300 S. Sangamon, Chicago, IL 60620

HY-TENSIL (aluminum nails; roofing and siding sheet) Nichols-Homeshield, Inc., 15 Spinning Wheel Rd., Hinsdale, IL 60521

I

IDEAL (window and floor squeegees) Dennis (W. J.) & Co., 9148 King, Franklin Park, IL

IDEAL (millwork, wood cabinets, windows and doors) Ideal Co., Box 889, Waco, TX

ILCO (padlocks; night latches; deadlocks; builders' hardware; door closers) Independent Lock Co., Fitchburg, MA

IMPERIAL (ornamental iron columns) Tennessee Fabricating Co., 1490 Grimes, Memphis, TN

INSELWOOD (asphalt-shake shingle design) Mastic Corp., 131 S. Taylor, South Bend, IN

INSULROCK (structural roof deck) Flintkote Co., 400 Westchester Ave., White Plains, NY 10604

J

JACK NUTS (hollow wall fasteners) USM Corp., Consumer Products Center, 221 Oley St., Reading, PA

JAMB-UP (aluminum and vinyl door weather strip) Macklanburg-Duncan Co., 4041 N. Santa Fe, Oklahoma City, OK

JIFFY-COVER (plastic drop cloth) Warp Bros., 1100 N. Cicero, Chicago, IL

JOBMASTER (powder-actuated tools) Ramset Fastening Systems, Winchester Group Olin 289 Winchester Ave., New Haven, CT 06504

JORGENSEN (steel bar and "C" clamps, handscrews) Adjustable Clamp Co., 409 N. Ashland Ave., Chicago, IL

K

KEM-GLO (interior enamel) Sherwin-Williams Co., 101 Prospect, N.W., Cleveland, OH

KENNATRACK (gliding door hardware) Kennatrack Div. of Ekco Products Co., 1250 Bedford Ave., S.W., Canton, OH 44701

KENTILE (asphalt, vinyl asbestos, solid vinyl, rubber and cork tile floor coverings; floor tile adhesives) Kentile Floors, Inc., 58 Second St., Brooklyn, NY

KLEAN CRETE (concrete and masonry etch and cleaner) Klean Strip Co., 2340 S. Lauderdale St., Memphis, TN 38106

KLEAN STRIP (paint remover) Klean Strip Co., 2340 S. Lauderdale St., Memphis, TN 38106

K-LUX (packaged luminous ceilings) K-Lux Products Div., KSH Plastics, Inc., 10091 Manchester Rd., St. Louis, MO 63122

KWIK (paint and varnish remover) Chemical Products Co., P.O. Box 400, Aberdeen, MD

KWIKEEZE (brush cleaner) Savogran Co., P.O. Box 130, Norwood, MA 02062

KWIK-SEAL (caulking compound) DAP, Inc., 5300 Huberville Rd., Dayton, OH 45401

KWIKSET (door locks; builders' hardware; locksets; installation jigs) Kwikset Sales & Service Co., Subsidiary of Emhart Corp., 516 Santa Ana St., Anaheim, CA 92803

L

LANGDON-ACME (mitre boxes) Millers Falls Co., Greenfield, MA

LARSON (saw horse and folding table-leg brackets; eye bolts; turnbuckles; wire hardware) Larson (Chas. O.) Co., P.O. Box E, Sterling, IL

LATEX CONCRETE (compound for sealing rough or spalled concrete) Camp Co., 9300 S. Sangamon, Chicago, IL

LAY-RITE (linoleum paste) Standard Paste & Glue Co., 3620 W. 38th, Chicago, IL

LAZY SATHER (cabinet hardware) Lazy Sather Hardware Co., P.O. Box 91, Ontario, CA

461

Dimension lumber ranges from 2 in. thick up to, but not including, 5 in. thick, and 2 or more in. wide. It includes rafters, studs, small planks. Dressed lumber is usually ⅜-in. smaller per dimension than the rough size

LEAD-EZE (lead anchors) Jordan Industries, Inc., 3030 N.W. 75th St., Miami, FL 33147

LEAD-SEAL (lead head nails) Deniston, Co., 3655 W. 127th St., Chicago, IL 60658

LEVEL-BEST (spackling compound) Savogran Co., P.O. Box 130, Norwood, MA 02062

LIFEGUARD (aluminum interlocking siding and roof shingles; aluminum gutters and downspouts; aluminum insulation foil; backer board) Lifeguard Industries, Inc., 4460 W. Mitchell Ave., Cincinnati, OH

LIGHTNIN FAST (vinyl latex primer) Masury Paint Co., Div. of ConChem Co., Inc., Bayard & Severn St., Baltimore, MD 21230

LIQUID RAW-HIDE (stains and clear finishes) Behr Process Corp., 1603 W. Alton St., Santa Ana, CA

LIQUID VELVET (wall paint) O'Brien Corp., 2001 W. Washington, South Bend, IN

LIQUID WRENCH (penetrant solvent for loosening rusted parts) Radiator Specialty Co., Charlotte, NC

LITE-BEAMS (plastic woodgrain finish beams) Lite Beam Div. of Am-Finn Sauna, Inc., Haddon Ave. & Line St., Camden, NJ 08103

LOCK-DECK (Douglas Fir, Idaho white, Southern pine and red cedar decking) Potlatch Forests, Inc., P.O. Box 3591, San Francisco, CA 94119

L-O-F (window glass) Libbey-Owens-Ford Co., 811 Madison St., Toledo, OH 43624

LONG-BELL (wood doors; kitchen cabinets; plywood; lumber) Long-Bell Div., International Paper Co., Box 579, Longview, WA 98632

LONG JOHN (paint roller) Bestt Rollr, Inc., 160 S. Brooke St., Fond du Lac, WI 54935

LUMINALL (paints, varnishes, enamels) National Chemical & Mfg. Co., 3618 S. May, Chicago, IL

LUSTRE LINE (thresholds, weather-strip, hardware and building specialties) Lustre Line Products Co., Richmond & Norris St., Philadelphia, PA 19125

M

MACCO (ceramic tile adhesives; cement mortars; cement grouts; cleaners; caulks, adhesives and sealers) Macco Adhesives Co., 30404 Lakeland Ave., Wickliffe, OH

MAGIC (epoxy glue, wood plastic, plastic aluminum, tub sealer, pipe joint compound) Magic American Chemical Corp., 14215 Caine Ave., Cleveland, OH

MAGNALOCK (locksets & latchsets) Sargent & Co., New Haven, CT

MAJESTIC (circulating fireplaces, dampers, grilles, incinerators, barbecue units) Majestic Co., Inc., 516 Erie, Huntington, IN

MARLITE (plastic-finished hardboard wall and ceiling paneling and accessories) Marlite Division of Masonite Corp., Dover, OH 44622

MASTER-CAULK (caulking compound) Calbar, Inc., 2612-26 N. Martha, Philadelphia, PA

MATCHMATES (drapery hardware line) Stanley-Judd Div. of The Stanley Works, Wallingford, CT 06492

MIAMI-CAREY (bathroom cabinets and accessories, ventilating fans, access doors) Miami-Carey Div., Philip Carey Corp., 320 S. Wayne Ave., Cincinnati, OH 45215

MIAMI STONE (concrete veneering stone) Miami Brick & Stone Co., P.O. Box 879, Miami, OK 74354

MIGHTY-MITE (magnetic catch) Ives (H. B.) Co., 50 Green St., New Haven, CT

MIGHTY-MITE (lightweight stud driver) Remington Arms Co., 25000 S. Western Ave., Park Forest, IL

MODERNWOOD (laminated block flooring) Modernwood Co. Div. of Standard Plywoods, Inc., P.O. Box 360, Clinton, SC 29325

MODULUX (lighted ceilings with plastic panels) Diffusa-Lite Co., 1 Forrest St., Conshohocken, PA

MOE LIGHT (residential lighting fixtures) Thomas Industries, Inc., 207 E. Broadway, Louisville, KY

MONSANTO (vinyl siding, gutters and downspouts) Monsanto Co., 200 N. 7th St., Kenilworth, NJ 07033

MUNFORD (asphalt and vinyl asbestos tile; adhesives) Holiday Ceramic Tile Co., 961 Confederate Ave., S.W., Atlanta, GA

MUTSCHLER (residential and institutional built-in components; hardwood kitchens) Mutschler Bros. Co., 302 S. Madison St., Nappanee, IN

N

NAFCOVE (rubber cove base) National Floor Products Co., Inc., Box 354, Florence, AL

NAILMASTER (hammers) Stanley Tools Div. of The Stanley Works, 111 Elm St., New Britain, CT

NEVAMAR (plastic laminates) Enjay Fibers & Laminates Co., Odenton, MD 21113

NICHOLSON (hacksaw blades and frames; files; hand saws; power saw blades) Nicholson File Co., 676 Waterman Ave., East Providence, RI 02914

NOAH'S PITCH (roofing cement) Carey (Philip) Corp., 320 S. Wayne Ave., Cincinnati, OH 45215

NOSCRUB (vinyl flooring) Goodyear Tire & Rubber Co., Akron, OH

NOVOPLY (all-wood sandwich panel of resin-impregnated chips & flakes) U. S. Plywood Corp., 777 Third Ave., New York, NY

NU-JAMB (double-acting spring hinges) Milwaukee Stamping Co., 803 S. 72nd, Milwaukee, WI

NUTONE (bathroom and wall heaters, range hoods, intercom systems, exhaust fans) NuTone Div. Scovill Mfg. Co., Madison & Red Bank Rd., Cincinnati, OH 45227

NU-WOOD (insulation board products) Conwed Corp., 332 Minnesota St., St. Paul, MN 55101

O

OLD CRAFTSMAN (pine paneling) U. S. Plywood Corp., 777 Third Ave., New York, NY

OLD ENGLISH (prefinished random-width plank) Bruce (E. L.) Co., Box 397, Memphis, TN 38101

ORANGE LABEL SISALKRAFT (reinforced waterproof building paper) Sisalkraft Div. of St. Regis Paper Co., 55 Starkey Ave., Attleboro, MA

ORTHO (insecticides) California Chemical Co., Ortho Div., Lucas and Ortho Way, Richmond, CA

OSMOSE STAINS (preservative penetrating stains) Osmose Wood Preserving Co. of America, 980 Ellicott St., Buffalo, NY 14209

P

PACEMAKER (door locks and latches) Harloc Products Corp., 680 Campbell St., West Haven, CT

PACESETTER (bi-fold hardware) Johnson (L. E.) Products, Inc., P.O. Box 114, Elkhart, IN

PACESETTER (locksets) National Hardware Co., 101-57 100th St., Ozone Park, NY 11416

PAINE (anchor nails, bolts, fasteners, pipe straps, etc.) Paine Co., 20 Westgate Rd., Addison, IL

PAINTSTIK (paint in stick form) Markal Co., 250 N. Washtenaw Ave., Chicago, IL 60612

PALCO (redwood lumber, siding, Fir flooring, panels) Pacific Lumber Co., 1111 Columbus Ave., San Francisco, CA 94133

PANEL CARE (wood refresher and polish) Benson Chemical Products, N 90 W14700 Commerce, Menomonee Falls, WI 53051

PANEL CLIP (clips for plywood roof sheathing) Panel Clip Co., 22506 Orchard Lake Rd., Farmington, MI

PANELFOLD (wood folding doors) Panelford Doors, 1090 E. 17th, Hialeah, FL

PANLUX (decorative plastic laminate) Polyplastex United, Inc., 870 Springfield Rd., Union, NJ

PARKWOOD (decorative plastic laminates) Parkwood Laminates, Inc., Wakefield, MA

PEBBLETONE (ceiling tile and drop-in panel) Flintkote Co., 400 Westchester Ave., White Plains, NY

PELLA ROLSCREEN (rolling insect screen) Rolscreen Co., Pella, IA

PENN-DIXIE (portland cement; high early strength and air-entraining portland cement; mortar cement) Penn-Dixie Cement Corp., 60 E. 42nd St., New York, NY

PERMABOARD (asbestos flat sheets) National Gypsum Co., 325 Delaware Ave., Buffalo, NY

PERMAGARD (plastic-resin surfaced plywood, doors, partitions) U.S. Plywood Corp., 777 Third Ave., New York, NY

PERMALIFE (vinyl flooring) American Biltrite Rubber Co., Trenton, NJ

PERMA-WHITE (aluminum storm and screen doors) Feather-Lite Mfg. Co., 21000 Hubbell Ave., Detroit, MI 48237

PERMITE (aluminum paint) Aluminum Industries, 3670 Werk Rd., Dayton, OH

PHOENIX (sash cord) Samson Cordage Works, 470 Atlantic Ave., Boston, MA

PITTSBURGH (interior and exterior paints; brushes) PPG Industries, 632 Fort Duquesne Blvd., Pittsburgh, PA 15222

PLASTIC STEEL (epoxy repair mate-

rial) Devcon Corp., 88 Endicott St., Danvers, MA 01923

PLASTIGARD (plastic-coated tile and lay-in panels) Celotex Corp., 1500 N. Dale Mabry, Tampa, FL 33607

PLATEBOARD (hardboard) Abitibi Corp., 1400 N. Woodward, Birmingham, MI 48011

PLUTO (drills, files, rasps, cutting pliers, hacksaw and sabre saw blades) Pluto Tool Co., 68 N. Central St., Valley Stream, NY 11580

PLY-VENEER (paper overlaid veneer) Weyerhaeuser Co., Wood Products Group, Tacoma Bldg., Tacoma, WA

POLYFILM (polyethylene film) Dow Chemical Co., Midland, MI

POWERGLIDE (door closer) Sargent & Co., 45 Water St., New Haven, CT

PREMIUM 30 (aluminum siding surfaced with DuPont Tedlar PVF film) Alsco, Inc., 225 S. Forge St., Akron, OH

PERMOULDED MEMBRANE (vapor seal) Meadows (W. R.), Inc., 22 Kimball St., Elgin, IL

PRESSURESEAL (sealing tape compound) Presstite Div., Interchemical Corp., 3762 Chouteau, St. Louis, MO

PRESTO SET (adhesive) U.S. Plywood Corp., 777 Third Ave., New York, NY

PRISMALITE (polystyrene plastic) Panelboard Mfg. Co., 100 James St., Somerville, NJ 08876

Q

Q-CALK (caulking cartridges) Gibson-Homans Co., 2366 Woodhill, Cleveland, OH

QUAMAGRA (crystal glaze mosaic tile) Quality Marble & Granite Co., 11961 Vose St., North Hollywood, CA

QUICK-FITS (cedar shake panels) Olympic Stained Products Co., 1118 Leary Way, Seattle, WA

QUICK PLUG (fast-setting cement to stop water leaks) Reardon Co., 3616 Scarlet Oak Blvd., St. Louis, MO

QUIKRETE (packaged concrete and mortar) Quikrete Co., 6225 Huntley Rd., Columbus, OH 43224

R

RAIN JET (underground lawn sprinklers; ornamental fountains; plastic pipe) Rain Jet Corp., 307 S. Flower St., Burbank, CA 91500

RANCH PLANK (plank-type hardwood floor) Bruce (E. L.) Co., P.O. Box 397, Memphis, TN

RANCH ROOF (asphalt shingles) Bird & Son, Inc., East Walpole, MA

RAPID CONTROL JOINT (masonry wall rubber control joints) Dur-O-waL National, Inc., 650 12th Ave., S.W., Cedar Rapids, IA 52404

RAWLPLUG (masonry fasteners) Rawlplug Co., 200 Petersville Rd., New Rochelle, NY

RAYLON (fiberglass panel garage doors) Raynor Mfg. Co., River Rd., Dixon, IL

RED DEVIL (glaziers' and painters' tools; floor polishers) Red Devil, Inc., 2400 Vauxhall Rd., Union, NJ

REGENT (aluminum storm sash) Duo-Temp Corp., 876 Terrace Blvd., Depew, NY

RESINITE (PVC film) Borden Co., Chemical Div., 350 Madison Ave., New York, NY 10017

RHINO (adhesives, mastics, caulkings) Pecora Chemical Corp., 300-400 W. Sedgley, Philadelphia, PA

RIB-DRAIN (colored building panels for walls and roofs) Ceco Corp., 5601 W. 26th St., Chicago, IL

ROTA-CLOSER (screen and storm door closer) Ridge Products, Inc., 2601 Industrial Pkwy., Elkhart, IN

RO-WAY (overhead garage doors and electric door operators) Rowe Mfg. Co., 614 W. 3rd, Galesburg, IL

R O W INSUL-DOOR (rolling glass patio door) R O W Window Sales Co., 1365 Academy St., Ferndale, MI

ROYAL AIRE (prefabricated chimneys) Malm Fireplaces, Inc., 368 Yolanda Ave., Santa Rosa, CA

ROYAL FILON (translucent fiberglass panels with lifetime guarantee) Filon Div., Vistron Corp., 12333 S. Van Ness Ave., Hawthorne, CA 90250

RUF SAWN (plywood) Simpson Timber Co., 2000 Washington Bldg., Seattle, WA 98101

S

SABER-TOOTH (self-drilling anchor) Rawplug Co., 200 Petersville Rd., New Rochelle, NY 10802

SAFE-T-VENT (roof ventilators) Starline, Inc., 300 W. Front, Harvard, IL

SAKRETE (bagged concrete and mortar mixes) Sakrete, Inc., P.O. Box 1, St. Bernard (Cincinnati), OH

SAW TOOTH (self-drilling masonry anchors) Paine Co., 501 Westgate Rd., Addison, IL 60101

SCHLAGE (door locks and hardware) Schlage Lock Co., 2201 Bayshore Blvd., San Francisco, CA

SCOTCH-BRITE (nylon clean-up pads) 3M Company, 3M Center, St. Paul, MN 55101

SEAL-O-MATIC (asphalt shingles) Johns-Manville, 22 E. 40th St., New York, NY 10016

SEAL-O-MATIC (door bottoms) Macklanburg-Duncan Co., 4041 N. Santa Fe, Oklahoma City, OK 73125

SED-N-COTE (cement paint) Seddon Co., P.O. Box 36, Springfield, MO

SHERWIN-WILLIAMS (housepaints) Sherwin-Williams Co., 101 Prospect, N.W., Cleveland, OH

SHOPMASTER (power tools) Shopmaster Div. Energy Mfg. Co., 6600 S. County Rd. 18, Minneapolis, MN

SHOPMATE (portable electric power tools) Portable Electric Tools Div., G. W. Murphy Industries, 1220 E. State St., Geneva, IL 60134

SHOPSMITH (multi-purpose woodworking tools) Magna American Corp., Raymond, MS

SKILSAW (power saws) Skil Corp., 5033 Elston Ave., Chicago, IL 60630

SNAP-A-BRUSH (disposable foam blade brush) Protection Products Div., U.S. Plywood-Champion Papers, 2305 Superior St., Kalamazoo, MI 49001

SOLITAIRE (cabinet hardware) Washington Div., Ekco Building Products Co., 1250 Bedford Ave., S.W., Canton, OH 44701

SPACKLE (spackling compound) Muralo Co., Inc., E. 5th and Hobart Ave., Bayonne, NJ 07002

SPANGLAS (fiberglass acoustical ceiling panel) Johns-Manville Corp., 22 E. 40th, New York, NY

SPEEDMATIC (tackers) Swingline, Inc., 32-00 Skillman Ave., Long Island City, NY

SPEEDSAW (portable jig and circular saws) Speedway Div., Thor Power Tool Co., 1421 Barnsdale Rd., La-Grange Park, IL

SPINDLE FLEX (large wood turnings) Stonier (Russ), Inc., 1375 Merchandise Mart, Chicago, IL 60654

SPINTEX (mineral wool insulation) Johns-Manville, 22 E. 40th St., New York, NY 10016

STA-DRI (waterproof masonry paint) American Sta-Dri Co., 4019 38th St., Brentwood, MD 20722

STANLEY (portable electric tools) Stanley Power Tools Div. of The Stanley Works, New Britain, CT

STANLEY (hand tools) Stanley Tools Div. of The Stanley Works, New Britain, CT

STRONG-WALL (insulating sheathing) Celotex Corp., 1500 N. Dale Mabry, Tampa, FL 33607

STYROFOAM (wall and ceiling insulation) Dow Chemical Co., Midland, MI

T

TAC-KIT (double-side adhesive for carpet tile) Mactac Consumer Products Div., Morgan Adhesives Co., 4560 Darrow Rd., Stow, OH 44224

TANGLEWOOD (vinyl-asbestos tile) Kentile Floors, Inc., 58 Second St., Brooklyn, NY 11215

TAPITS (self-drilling screws) Parker Kalon, Clifton, NJ

TAP-N-HOLD (shelf supports) Timber Engineering Co., 1619 Massachusetts Ave., N.W., Washington, DC

TEMLOK (sheathing & other fiberboard building materials) Armstrong Cork Co., Lancaster, PA

TEXOLITE (paint products) U.S. Gypsum Co., 101 S. Wacker Dr., Chicago, IL 60606

TEXTOLITE (decorative high pressure laminate) General Electric Co., Laminated Products Dept., Coshocton, OH

THERMOPANE (insulating glass) Libbey-Owens-Ford Co., 811 Madison Ave., Toledo, OH 43624

THOMAS (paint rollers; door chimes, intercom systems, central vacuuming systems) Thomas Industries, Inc., 207 E. Broadway, Louisville, KY

THOROSEAL (cement-base waterproofing) Standard Dry Wall Products, Inc., 7800 N.W. 38th St., Miami, FL

TILEMASTER (plastic wall tile; ceramic floor and wall tile) Tilemaster Corp., 4400 N. Harlem, Chicago, IL 60656

T-LOK (solid vinyl siding) Mastic Corp., 131 S. Taylor St., South Bend, IN 46624

TOOLKRAFT (portable electric tools) Toolkraft Corp., 700 Plainfield St., Chicopee, MA 01013

TOUCH-A-MATIC (electric switches) Eagle Electric Mfg. Co., 23-10 Bridge Plaza, S., Long Island City, NY 11101

TRINITY WHITE (plain & waterproofed white portland cement) Trinity White Div. of General Portland Cement Co., Box 324, Dallas, TX 75221

TUB-MASTER (sliding-folding tub shower door) Tub-Master Corp., 409 Virginia Drive, Orlando, FL

TWINSULATION (glass fibre blankets) National Gypsum Co., 325 Delaware Ave., Buffalo, NY

U

UNI-BOLT (self-anchoring masonry fasteners) Paine Co., 501 Westgate Rd., Addison, IL 60101

UPSON (screwdrivers, scratch awls) Upson Tools, Inc., P.O. Box 4750, Rochester, NY 14612

USS (galvanized roofing and siding) American Steel & Wire Div., U.S. Steel Corp., Rockefeller Bldg., Cleveland, OH

V

VAL-OIL (rust preventive, primer and colors) Valspar Corp., 200 Sayre St., Rockford, IL

VAN-COR (plastic pipe and fittings) Colonial Plastics Mfg. Co., 8107 Grand Ave., Cleveland, OH

VANGUARD (locksets) Weslock Co., 13344 S. Main St., Los Angeles, CA

VARI-PITCH (ventilating louvers) Louver Mfg. & Supply Co., 5605 Wooddale Ave., Minneapolis, MN

VENTWOOD (ornamental wood fencing) Howard Mfg. Co., Kent, WA 98031

VERSABORD (Douglas Fir wood shavings particle board) Weyerhaeuser Co., Wood Products Group, Tacoma Bldg., Tacoma, WA 98401

VERSA-TILT (self-storing storm-screen window) Wepco Div., Weatherproof Co., P.O. Box 45, Litchfield, IL

VISQUEEN (polyvinylchloride (PVC) pipe and vapor barrier.) Ethyl Corp., Visqueen Div., P.O. Box 2422, Baton Rouge, LA 79821

VULCO (component parts for alumi-

num screen doors, combination windows and doors) Vulcan Metal Products, 2801 6th Ave., S., Birmingham, AL

W

WAL-BOARD (wallboard installation and measuring tools) Wallboard Tool Co., 1708 Seabright, Long Beach, CA 90813

WALLMASTER (aluminum siding, shutters, soffits, accessories) Alcan Aluminum Corp., Building Products Div., Jacobus Ave., South Kearny, NJ 07032

WALL-TEX (wall coverings) Borden Co., Chemical Div., 350 Madison Ave., New York, NY 10017

WEATHERBEST (Red Cedar shakes and shingles; insulation board products; backer board) Creo-Dipt Co., 985 Oliver, North Tonawanda, NY

WEATHER-TITE/ARISTOCRAT (aluminum doors, windows, siding, rain carrying equipment, screening, jalousies, roofing and allied hardware) Weather-Tite/Aristocrat Div., Pacific Coast Co., 7103 Krick Rd., Cleveland, OH 44146

WEPCO (aluminum combination doors and windows) Weatherproof Co., Litchfield, IL

X

X-IT (paint remover) Schalk Chemical Co., 351 E. 2nd, Los Angeles, CA

X-90 SIDINGS (exterior hardboard sidings offering maximum resistance to weather) Masonite Corp., 29 N. Wacker Dr., Chicago, IL 60606

X-PANDA SHELF (prefinished steel adjustable closet shelves) Home Comfort Products Co., P.O. Box 68, Princeville, IL

Y

YACHTSMAN (paint brushes) Wooster Brush Co., 604 Madison, Wooster, OH

YANKEE (hand tools) Stanley Tools Div. of The Stanley Works, New Britain, CT 06050

Z

ZANZITE (interior wall finish) McDougall-Butler Div. of Bisonite Corp., 2250 Military Rd., Tonawanda, NY 14150

ZAR (crystallite coating for wood floors) United Gilsonite Laboratories, 1396 Jefferson Ave., Scranton, PA 18501

ZERO (weatherstripping, door saddles) Zero Weather Stripping Co., 415 Concord Ave., Bronx, NY

ZONOLITE (vermiculite insulating fill, plaster and concrete aggregates; masonry fill insulation) Construction Products Div., W. R. Grace & Co., 62 Whittemore Ave., Cambridge, MA 02140

AIRWAY—Space for air movement between insulation and roof sheathing.

ALLIGATORING—New paint coating that slips over old coating resulting in a coarse checking pattern. Old finish can be seen through fissures.

ANCHOR—Fastener used to secure timbers or masonry.

APRON—Member of inside window trim located against the wall beneath the stool of the window.

ATTIC VENTILATORS—Special openings in gables and roofs. See louver classification.

BACKFILL—Earth used to fill around or against foundation wall.

BACKING—A bevel on the top edge of a hip rafter, which lets roofing boards fit the top of the rafter without a triangular space between it and the bottom of the roof covering.

BASEBOARD—Board placed against wall around room next to floor, which forms a finish between the floor and wall.

BASE MOULDING—Moulding used to trim upper edge of interior baseboard.

BASE SHOE—Moulding used next to floor on interior baseboard. Carpet strip.

BATTEN—Narrow strips of wood used to cover joints, usually vertical joints.

BATTER BOARD—Temporary framework for locating corners when laying out foundation.

BEAD—Milled moulding or strip having a rounded surface.

BEARING WALL—Wall supporting any horizontal load in addition to its own weight.

BEDDING—Filling of mortar, putty or other component for firm bearing.

BED MOULDING—Moulding in the angle of a building and the side walls, i.e., between cornice and side walls.

BEVEL BOARD—Board used in framing a roof or stairway to lay out bevels, or angles.

BLIND NAILING—Nailing so that nailheads aren't visible on the face of the work.

BLIND STOP—A rectangular moulding, used in assembly of window frame; ¾ by 1⅜ in.

BOARD FOOT—Equivalent of a board 1 ft. square and 1 in. thick.

BOLSTER—Short horizontal timber placed on top of a column for support of beams or girders.

BOXING—Plank which boxes ends of joists.

BRACE—Diagonal support of framing lumber used to complete and support a triangle. Pieces fitted and fastened firmly to two others at any angle in order to strengthen the angle.

BRICK VENEER—Facing brick laid against a frame or sheathing in wall construction.

BUILDING PAPER—Asphalt or waterproofed paper used to help insulate before siding or roofing are applied.

BUILT-UP BEAM—A girder made of several heavy pieces of material to give the strength of one heavy beam.

BUILT-UP ROOF—Roofing composed of three to five layers of rag felt or jute saturated with coal tar, pitch, or asphalt. Top is finished with crushed slag or gravel. Generally used on flat or low-pitched roofs.

CANT STRIP—A wedge of lumber used at gable ends under shingles or at junction of the house and flat deck under roofing.

CAP—Upper member of a column, door cornice, moulding, etc. Also a plate across the top of a studding wall.

CASEMENT—A window in which the sash opens on hinges, swinging like a door.

CASING—Wide moulding used to trim door and window openings.

CHECKING—Fissures that appear with age in many exterior paint coatings, at first superficial, but soon may penetrate throughout the coating.

CHECKRAILS—Meeting rails sufficiently thicker than a window to fill the opening between the top and bottom sash made by the parting stop in the frame. They are usually beveled.

CLAPBOARD—Siding; a tapered board for siding or wainscoting.

COLLAR BEAM—A beam that connects opposite rafters above the attic floor; a tie between rafters on opposite sides for strength.

CONDENSATION—Beads or drops of water (and frequently frost and ice in extremely cold weather) that accumulate on the warm side of an exterior surface.

CONDUIT—A pipe, usually metal, in which electrical wire is installed.

CORBEL OUT—To project one or more courses of brick or stone from the face of a wall to support timbers.

CORNER BEAD—Strip of galvanized iron or wood, sometimes combined with a strip of metal lath, fastened at corners before plastering is applied.

CORNER BOARDS—Trim for the exterior corners of a house or other frame structure against which the ends of the siding butt.

CORNER BRACES—Diagonal braces cut into studs to reinforce the corners of wood framing.

CORNERITE—Metal-mesh lath cut into strips and bent to a right angle. Used for interior corners of walls and ceilings to deter cracks in plaster.

CORNICE—A projection that finishes the top of the wall of a building.

COURSE—A single layer of blocks or bricks.

COVE MOULDING—A three-sided moulding with a concave face.

CRAWL SPACE—A shallow space below a floor. It often is enclosed with skirting or a facing material.

CRICKET—A small water-diverting roof structure of single or double slope located at the junction of larger surfaces that meet at an angle.

CROSSBRIDGING—Diagonal braces that crisscross between the joists. Bridging can be wood or metal.

CROWN MOULDING—Moulding used on a cornice or where a large angle is to be covered.

DAMP-PROOFING—Any technique to keep water out of a building.

DECK PAINT—An enamel with resistance to mechanical wear; used on porch floors, stairsteps.

DIRECT NAILING—To nail into the initial surface or to nail to the junction of pieces joined. Also termed **face nailing.**

DOORJAMB—The surrounding case into which a door opens and closes. It has two upright pieces, called jambs, and a head, rabbeted and joined.

DRIER, PAINT—Lead, manganese, or cobalt which, in small proportions, help speed oxidation and hardening (drying) of oils in paints.

DRIP—A window sill or water table that allows water to drain clear of the side of the house below it. A groove in the underside of a sill that permits water to drop off on the outer edge, instead of running down the siding.

DRIP CAP—A moulding on the top exterior of a door or window to channel water away from the frame.

EAVES—The projecting lower edge of a roof.

ELBOW—An angle joint of pipe.

END MATCHED—Tongue-and-groove (t&g) edges of boards, usually flooring, or pine paneling.

EXPANSION JOINT—A bituminous fiber strip used to separate concrete or concrete blocks to prevent cracking due to expansion and contraction.

FASCIA—A flat board, band or face, used by itself or in combination with mouldings. It is located at the outer face of the cornice. Generally, that board of the cornice on which the gutter is installed.

FIBERBOARD—Large sheets of pressed wood or vegetable fiber made into building board for interior or exterior construction.

FILLER (WOOD)—A preparation used for filling and leveling pores in open-pored woods.

FIRE RESISTIVE—Materials for construction not combustible in the temperatures of ordinary fires; they also can withstand fires without serious damage for at least one hour.

FIRE STOP—A block fastened between the studs to stop drafts in event of fire.

FLASHING—Strips of roofing or metal used to waterproof roof valleys, around chimneys, gutters, etc.

FLAT PAINT—An interior or exterior paint that has a high proportion of pigment. It dries to a lusterless finish.

FOOTING—The spreading platform at the bottom of a foundation wall, pier, or column.

FOOTING COURSES—The bottom and heaviest courses of a piece of masonry.

FOUNDATION—The supporting portion of a building below first-floor construction, or below grade, including footings.

FRAMING—The rough lumber structure of a building. Includes interior and exterior wall, floor, roof and ceiling members.

FRAMING, BALLOON—A system of framing. All vertical structural elements of the bearing walls and partitions have single pieces jutting from the top of a plate to the roof plate; all floor joists are fastened to the roof plate.

FRAMING, PLATFORM—Floor joists of each story seat on a top plate of the story below or on the foundation sill for the first story. The bearing walls and partitions rest on the subfloor of each story.

FURRING—Strips to provide nailing surfaces for lath and space for insulation. Narrow strips of board nailed to walls and ceilings to form a straight surface for lath or other finish. Strips of wood or metal fastened to a surface to even it, form an air space or give it greater thickness.

GAMBREL—A symmetrical roof that has two different pitches or slopes on each side.

GIRDERS—A beam used to support wall beams or joists.

GIRT—(Ribband)—A horizontal member of walls of a full or combination frame house. It supports the floor joists, or it is flush with the top of the joists.

GLOSS ENAMEL—Paint made of varnish and sufficient pigments to provide opacity and color. Enamel forms a hard coating, has maximum smoothness, and a high degree of gloss.

GROUT—Mortar for joints and cavities of masonry work.

GYPSUM LATH—Wallboard applied to studs for a plaster base. The lath provides a chemical bond with the plaster.

GYPSUM PLASTER—Gypsum mixed with sand and water for base-coat plaster.

HARDWOOD—Lumber from broadleaved, deciduous trees.

HEARTWOOD—Wood extending from pith to the sapwood; the cells no longer participate in the life processes of the tree.

HEEL OF A RAFTER—The end or foot of the board that rests on the wall plate.

HIP ROOF—A roof that rises in planes from all four sides of a building.

I-BEAM—A steel beam with a cross section resembling the letter "I".

INSULATING BOARD OR FIBERBOARD—A low density board made of wood, sugarcane, cornstalks, or similar materials. It usually is pressed to thicknesses of ½ and 25/32 in.

JACKRAFTER—A short rafter between a wall plate and a hip rafter. Short rafters that form a gable or the start of a new roof.

JAMB—The side piece of an opening. The side post or lining of a doorway, window or other opening.

JOISTS—Wooden or metal material supporting the floor boards.

KERF—A cut made by a saw.

KILN DRIED—Lumber dried in an oven to shorten drying time.

LATH—Strip or sheets of wood, metal, gypsum, or insulating board fastened to the frame of a building for a plaster base.

LATTICE—Wood or metal strips, rods or bars.

LEDGER BOARD—A support for second-floor joists of a balloon-frame house.

LEDGER STRIP—Lumber nailed along the bottom of the side of a girder on which joists rest.

LIGHT—Space in a window sash for a single pane of glass. Also that pane of glass.

LINTEL—A horizontal member that supports a load over an opening such as a door or window. A header.

LOOKOUT—A short wood bracket or cantilever to support an overhanging portion of a roof.

LUMBER, BOARDS—Yard lumber less than 2 in. thick and 2 or more in. wide.

LUMBER, DIMENSION—Yard lumber from 2 in. to, but not including, 5 in. thick, and 2 or more in. wide. Includes joists, rafters, studding, planks and small timbers.

LUMBER, MATCHED—Lumber that is edge-dressed and shaped to make a close tongue-and-groove joint at edges or ends.

LUMBER, SHIPLAP—Lumber that is edge-dressed to make a close rabbeted or lapped joint.

LUMBER, TIMBERS—Yard lumber 5 or more in. in the least dimension. Includes beams, stringers, posts, caps, sills, girders and purlins.

MATCHING—Cutting edges of a board to make a tongue on one edge and a groove on the other; tongue-and-groove.

MEETING RAIL—The bottom rail of an upper sash; the top rail of a lower sash of a double-hung window. Sometimes called the check rail.

MILLWORK—Generally all building materials made of finished wood. Millwork includes inside and outside doors, window and door frames, blinds, porch work, mantels, panelwork, stairways, mouldings, interior trim. Does not include flooring, ceiling, or siding.

MORTISE—A slot cut into a board, plank, or timber, usually edgewise, to receive the tenon of another board, plank, or timber to form a joint.

MOULDING—Material, usually patterned strips, used to provide ornamental trim.

> **BASE**—A moulding on the bottom of a baseboard.
>
> **LIP**—A moulding with a tip which overlaps the piece against which the back of the molding rests.
>
> **RAKE**—The cornice on the gable edge of a pitch roof.
>
> **PICTURE**—A moulding shaped to form a support for picture hooks.

MULLION—The material between the openings of a window frame.

MUNTIN—The members dividing the glass or opening of sash, doors, etc.

NOSING—The front edge of a stair tread which projects over the riser; a rounded edge of a board.

O. C. (ON CENTER)—The measurement of spacing for studs, rafters, joists. The dis-

tance between the center of one member to the center of the next member.

O. G. (OGEE)—A moulding with a profile in the form of a letter S.

PAPER, SHEATHING—A building material, generally paper or felt, used in wall and roof construction to block air and moisture.

PARTING STOP OR STRIP—Wood used in the side and head jambs of double-hung windows to separate the upper and lower sash.

PENNY—As applied to nails, it originally indicated the price per hundred nails. The term now designates the length of a nail. It is symbolized by the letter "d".

PIER—A column of masonry used to support other structural members.

PILES—Long posts driven into the ground upon which a footing of masonry or other timbers is laid.

PITCH—The incline or rise of a roof. Pitch is expressed in inches of rise per foot of run. Also expressed by the ratio of the rise to the span.

PLATE—The top horizontal piece of the wall of a frame building upon which the roof rests. A horizontal structural member supported on posts or studs. A shoe or base member.

PLATE CUT—The cut in a rafter which rests on the plate.

PLUMB—Exactly perpendicular; vertical.

PLUMB BOB—A weight on a string to aid in obtaining an absolutely vertical line.

PLUMBING WALL—A wide partition, usually 2 x 6 studs, for enclosing plumbing pipes.

PRIMER—The first coat of paint in a paint job that has two or more coats.

PULLEY STILE—The member of a window frame which contains pulleys.

PURLIN—A timber supporting several rafters or the roof sheathing directly.

QUARTER ROUND—A moulding with a quarter-circle cross section.

RABBET—A rectangular corner cut out of an edge.

RAFTER—A structural member of a roof to support roof loads. Rafters of a flat roof are called roof joists.

COMMON—Rafters which run square with the plate and extend to the ridge.

CRIPPLE—Rafters which go between joists and hip rafters.

HIP—Rafters extending from the outside angle of the plates toward the apex of the roof.

JACKS—Rafters square with the plate and intersecting the hip rafter.

VALLEY—Rafters extending from an inside angle of the plates toward the ridge of the house.

RAIL—The horizontal members extending from one post or support to another.

REFLECTIVE INSULATION—Sheet material with one or both surfaces of comparatively low heat transmission.

REINFORCING—Steel rods or metal fabric placed in concrete slabs, beams, or columns to increase strength.

RESIN-EMULSION PAINT—Paint, the vehicle (liquid part) of which consists of resin or varnish dispersed in fine droplets in water; analogous to cream (which is butterfat dispersed in water).

RIBBAND (LEDGERBOARD)—A horizontal strip notched into the studs to support joists.

RIBBON—A narrow board let into the studs to add support to joists.

RIDGE BOARD—The board placed on edge at the ridge of the roof to support the upper ends of rafters.

RIDGE POLE—A horizontal board on which the top ends of the rafters rest.

RISE—The vertical distance through which anything rises, as the rise of a roof or stair.

RISER—Each of the vertical boards between treads of a stairway. The upright part of a step.

ROLL ROOFING—Roofing material, composed of fiber and saturated with asphalt, that is supplied in rolls.

ROOF SHEATHING—Boards or sheet material fastened to the roof rafters over which shingles or other roof covering is laid.

ROUGH OPENING—Space left in studding for windows and doors.

RUBBER EMULSION PAINT—Paint, the vehicle of which consists of rubber or synthetic rubber dispersed in fine droplets in water.

SADDLE—Another name for a finished door sill.

SAPWOOD—The outer zone of wood, next to the bark.

SATURATED FELT—Felt impregnated with tar or asphalt.

SCRATCH COAT—The first coat of plaster, which is scratched to form a bond for a second coat of plaster.

SCOTIA—A hollow moulding used as a part of a cornice; a moulding under the nosing of a stair tread.

SCRIBING—Fitting woodwork to an irregular surface.

SEALER—A finishing material, either clear or pigmented, usually applied directly over uncoated wood.

SEAT CUT or PLATE CUT—The cut at the bottom end of a rafter to allow it to fit on a plate.

SEPTIC TANK—A concrete or metal tank for waste drainage.

SHAKE—A handsplit shingle, usually edge grained.

SHEATHING—Wallboards and roofing boards generally applied to rafters and studs.

SHEATHING PAPER—The paper used under siding or shingles for insulation.

SHINGLES, SIDING—Various kinds of shingles, some specially designed, that can be used as the exterior wall covering of a structure.

SHIPLAP—Finished lumber with joints rabbeted or lapped.

SIDING, BEVEL (LAP SIDING)—Used as the finish siding on the exterior of a house or other structure. It is usually manufactured by resawing dry square-surfaced boards diagonally to produce a wedge-shape.

SIDING, DROP—Usually ¾ in. thick and 6 in. wide, machined into various patterns. Drop siding has tongue-and-groove joints.

SLEEPER—Wood or metal pieces laid on concrete for a nailing surface for flooring.

Material laid on the ground to support floor joists.

SOFTWOOD—Any lumber from a tree bearing needles and cones.

SOIL COVER (GROUND COVER)—A light roll roofing or plastic used on the ground in crawl spaces to minimize moisture permeation.

SOIL PIPE—Metal or composition pipe placed underground as part of a plumbing job.

SOIL STACK—A general term for the vertical main of a system of soil, waste, or vent piping.

SOLE—A 2 x 4 in. piece of lumber used as a base for stud walls. Also called SOLE-PLATE.

SPECIFICATIONS—Written or printed directions stating details of the construction of a building.

STAIN, SHINGLE—A form of oil paint, very thin in consistency, used on shingles.

STAIR CARRIAGE—A stringer for steps.

STAIR RISE—The vertical distance from the top of one stair tread to the top of the next one above.

STANCHIONS—Posts, usually 4 in. metal pipe, used to support girders.

STIRRUP—A metal device on which to hang joists from a supporting member.

STOOL—A flat, narrow shelf forming the top member of interior trim at the bottom of a window.

STRING, STRINGER—A timber or other support for cross members.

STUCCO—A fine plaster used for interior decoration and fine work; also for rough outside wall coverings. Portland cement is its base.

STUDDING—The framework of a partition or the wall of a house; usually 2 x 4s.

SUBFLOOR—Boards or sheet material laid over joists, over which a finish floor is laid.

TERMITE SHIELD—A sheet of metal on top of a concrete foundation and beneath a sill to block termites.

THRESHOLD—The beveled piece of material over which the door swings.

TIE—Metal tabs nailed on sheathing and embedded in masonry to tie the two together with an air space between.

TIE BEAM (COLLAR BEAM)—A beam to tie principal rafters of a roof together.

TIMBER—Lumber with cross section over 4 x 6 in. such as posts, sills and girders.

TOENAILING—A nail driven at a slant.

UNDERCOAT—A coating applied before the finish coat of a paint job. It may be the first of two or the second of three coats.

VALLEY—The internal angle formed by two slopes of a roof.

VAPOR BARRIER—Material used to block the flow of vapor or moisture into walls and thus prevent condensation within them. There are two types of vapor barriers: a membrane that comes in rolls, and the paint type, which is applied with a brush. A vapor barrier must be part of the warm side of a wall.

VENEER—Thin sheets of wood. Or a facing of brick, stone, or composition applied as a finish to an outside wall.

VENT—A mechanical device installed to provide a flow of air.

VERGE BOARDS—Boards that finish eaves on a gable end of a building.

VERMICULITE—A mineral closely related to mica; it expands on heating to form lightweight material with insulation quality. Used as bulk insulation, as aggregate in insulating and acoustical plaster, and in insulating concrete floors.

VERTICAL SIDING—Boards applied vertically on the outside of a house.

WAINSCOTING—Matched boarding or panel work covering the lower part of a wall.

WASH—The slant on a sill, cap-ring, etc., to allow the water to run off easily.

WOODEN BRICK—Piece of seasoned wood, made the size of a brick, and laid where it is necessary to provide nailing space in masonry walls.

470

The page number refers to the first page on which specific information can be found.

index